D1106172

LAST TRAIN TO
AUSCHWITZ

LAST TRAIN TO AUSCHWITZ

*The French National Railways and the
Journey to Accountability*

Sarah Federman

THE UNIVERSITY OF WISCONSIN PRESS

The University of Wisconsin Press
728 State Street, Suite 443
Madison, Wisconsin 53706
uwpress.wisc.edu

Gray's Inn House, 127 Clerkenwell Road
London ECIR 5DB, United Kingdom
eurospanbookstore.com

Printed in the United States of America
This book may be available in a digital edition.

Library of Congress Cataloging-in-Publication Data

Names: Federman, Sarah, author.
Title: Last train to Auschwitz : the French National Railways and the journey to
accountability / Sarah Federman.
Description: Madison, Wisconsin : The University of Wisconsin Press, [2021] |
Includes bibliographical references and index.
Identifiers: LCCN 2020035409 | ISBN 9780299331702 (cloth)
Subjects: LCSH: Société nationale des chemins de fer français—History. |
Railroads—France—History—20th century. | World War, 1939-1945—
Deportations from France. | World War, 1939-1945—Transportation—France. |
Holocaust, Jewish (1939-1945)—France. | Jews—Persecutions—France—
History—20th century. | France—History—German occupation, 1940-1945.
Classification: LCC HE3070.S65 F43 2021 | DDC 940.53/1813—dc23
LC record available at https://lccn.loc.gov/2020035409

publication supported by a grant from
JEWISH FEDERATION OF GREATER HARTFORD

This book is dedicated to

Sarah Federman

Born October 21, 1926
Deported from France, August 19, 1942
Murdered at Auschwitz at age 15

Contents

Illustrations

Tables

Preface

Before I started the research for this book, the Holocaust never captured much of my attention. Thinking back, I'm surprised it didn't, given that I grew up amid stories about my Jewish grandfather, Jacob, who escaped from Poland with his brother in 1917, well before Hitler came to power. They escaped under a fence, fleeing to avoid being pulled into the Russian Cossack army, which had declared war on the Bolsheviks. The boys traveled to Palestine, where Zionists slapped identifying armbands on them. They learned English while building roads and becoming *Halutzim* (pioneers), Jewish people who immigrated to Israel to develop the land. The Zionists helped them make their way to New York City, where in 1919 they eventually reunited with an older brother, Morris, and moved to the Lower East Side. German, Polish, Yiddish, and Hebrew—languages now associated with the persecutor and the persecuted— went dormant in my family. Papa Jack, as we called him, had never spoken about World War II until I asked to interview him for a class assignment. It was 1998. He was then in his nineties. Before I even pressed "record," he said, "I just saw on the news that they finally caught one of the Nazis. I just can't understand what took them so long!"

I expected family stories from the interview, but until that moment I had no idea that behind our fragmented family history stood something deeper, a sense of justice delayed, unfulfilled. His outrage planted something deep in me that I could not consciously process. At the time, I thought that authorities simply needed time to find the responsible individuals; I didn't realize that sometimes no one wanted to. Long after he passed, I learned that the US intelligence service had even recruited some Nazis.[1]

At the time, I just listened to Papa Jack tell his personal story, moving as quickly as possible through the murder of his siblings who stayed behind. Grief constricted his throat as he uttered their names for the first time since the 1940s. Try as I might, I still cannot decipher their names when I hear the recording.[2]

Life rolled along. I fell into the family advertising business on Madison Avenue. After I spent a few years in corporate life in Manhattan, the company transferred me to Paris to help with the transition of a recently acquired company. As I packed up for what would become a three-year assignment, a former history professor with whom I had become friends made an unusual request.

"Find out if those French train drivers kept their jobs after the war!"

He was referring to the conductors of the deportation trains that traveled from France toward the death camps in the east. I promised to do so but forgot his request for about three years. I occasionally awoke from the reverie of Parisian life when seeing dried flowers affixed to buildings honoring the young men shot at those very spots during the liberation of Paris. And I could not ignore the plaques in front of so many schools commemorating the Jewish children rounded up and deported. Almost all were murdered. In Paris, one encounters World War II almost by accident as one ambles about in the midst of the prewar architecture.

World War II became all the more visceral when, in March 2009, work brought me to our Warsaw office in Poland. What had been a whisper of the war in Paris was a full roar in Warsaw. The city's lack of prewar architecture reminds visitors that the war utterly demolished the city. When I told a colleague, Marek, about my grandfather's successful flight from Poland and the murder of his siblings, he we wanted to take me to visit Treblinka, one of the most murderous death camps. After a week of lackluster responses to our sales presentations, neither of us wanted to spend a Saturday at a death camp. But we persisted and arrived at Treblinka on a frigid, snowy morning. As we pulled up, a small group of young people—waving an Israeli flag—piled into a van. The camp was now empty except for us. The stillness of death, amplified by the Polish winter, left us quiet for quite some time. We crunched silently through the snow until Marek found his voice and began to explain where the old railway station had been.

"You see, right there?" He pointed. "They built a facade with a fake clock so that deportees would believe they had entered a town, not a death camp. This kept people calm, allowing the Nazis to lead them directly into gas chambers." I later learned that the Nazis had also posted fake rail schedules, signs with arrows pointing to different cities, and even a ticket window. On that day, only rusty rail tracks, mostly hidden by the snow, remained.[3]

When I returned to my daily life in Paris, I found myself staring fixedly at the tracks whenever I waited for the metro. Rail tracks eventually became so haunting that I began taking the bus to my boyfriend's apartment in St. Michel.

One day, I decided to tell him the reason for my strange new aversion to trains. To which he replied, "That was a long time ago. You need to get over it." His response especially surprised me in view of his own Jewish ancestry.

In time, I would lose the boyfriend and keep the trains.

Turning my full attention to the question of French trains during the war took time, however. The signs in Paris nudged me first, then the trip to Poland, and then one life-changing Sunday when I stopped by the Mémorial de la Shoah, Paris's Holocaust museum. To enter, I passed two armed guards and double security doors. I then wandered around the outside courtyard looking at the names of the deportees from France. I wondered if there had been any "Federmans"—and there it was. Trembling, I ran my fingers across the engraved letters of my own name. Except for the birth date, my name appeared just as it did in the foyer in my apartment building in the eighth arrondissement.

It could have been me. It could have been my family. The gravity of the thought collapsed time. The victim register on the computer in the museum's lobby could reveal only a date of birth (October 10, 1926), nationality (Polish), and date of deportation from France to Auschwitz (August 19, 1942), on Convoy 21. At fifteen, Sarah Federman was the oldest of the fifty children on the convoy, one of whom was her twelve-year-old sister, Jacqueline, who would not live to see her thirteenth birthday, which would arrive just days after she died in the gas chambers.[4] Seeing my own name, I recalled my friend's question: "*Did* the French drivers of the deportation trains keep their jobs after the war?" I now wanted to know the answer for myself. This question proved to be the initial driving force behind this book. The research felt like the fulfillment of a karmic contract, something I had promised to do long ago and had just now remembered.

Shortly after I saw my name on the memorial wall, my friend Gina forwarded to me a *New York Times* article about legislation in Florida and California aimed at blocking the Société Nationale des Chemins de Fer Français (SNCF, French National Railways) from bidding for high-speed rail contracts until the company made amends for its role in the Holocaust.[5] At the time, I knew nothing of the contemporary debates. This compelling justice battle ignited my research, turning the project into a study about the present as well as the past. In between digging through various archives, friends and colleagues helped me secure meetings with SNCF executives, historians, and French Jewish leaders. I moved to Washington, DC, to continue this research as a doctoral student. The university's location now put me in proximity to US ambassadors, lawyers, legislators, lobbyists, and other Jewish leaders working on the conflict. I attended legislative hearings and other related events. I soon found myself working pro bono with the US State Department and the House of Representatives on the conflict. Thanks to the help of the United States Holocaust Memorial Museum, I reached out to more than one hundred Holocaust survivors in France and the United States who had escaped persecution in France. I spoke with ninety of them, many in person, about their feelings toward the SNCF conflict.

Rather than using formulaic interview methods that guide people through a static set of questions, I interviewed people conversationally and whenever possible spent unstructured hours with them, especially with survivors who had the time. We walked through the Versailles gardens and along the Normandy beaches, visiting Holocaust museums and deportation sites, attending funerals, and drinking countless cups of tea in their homes and espressos at local cafés. I attended commemorative events in France and the US and participated in survivor group potlucks. As a result, I soon met many people's families and learned about their lives beyond the Holocaust. Survivors talked about their struggles with their grown children and their own declining health. Between listening to old records and spending hours thumbing through photo albums, I discovered the depth of their losses and the myriad ways they found meaning in the aftermath of the Holocaust. For some, restitution made a difference. Many attended ceremonies or volunteered to chat with school children or joined lawsuits. Jacqueline, like some survivors, read avidly about the Holocaust. I now have an entire bookshelf filled with her books, bequeathed to me after her death. Hundreds of hours listening to tragic stories sometimes overwhelmed me. After I expressed bewilderment at all he had suffered, one survivor said, "Well, you picked a melancholy subject, Sarah. But as bad as you think it was, it was really worse."[6]

I sometimes felt ashamed when the emotional impact of their stories made me want to stop returning the messages that filled up my voicemail and inbox. But I felt more compelled to keep going, to continue these relationships, and as a result I can now add rarely heard perspectives to the conversations about the trains. One scholar expressed astonishment at my findings: "I know survivors, and they don't say things like this." But, in fact, they *did* say these things, often more than once. With so much written and produced about the Holocaust, many scholars and journalists and their audiences have unconsciously made up their minds about how survivors think. So, they either fail to seek out different perspectives or, when they hear them, simply discount them as outliers. The Holocaust testimonies collected through the Survivors of the Shoah Visual History Foundation (now the USC Shoah Foundation) and other well-intentioned organizations helped create these norms.[7] Understandably, journalists reporting on the conflict often seek out the most vocal, colorful survivors; they also cannot engage in the multiyear research needed to situate these conflicts historically and socially. Survivors said many things during our time together; sometimes they spoke for and sometimes against the railroad. Sometimes they saw the SNCF debates as being irrelevant to their lives. They had other concerns. A number said that their overall experiences had taught them about the dangers of hate and the importance of forgiveness. Yet others expressed racist views and remain consumed with resentment. Genocide does not always produce the kinds of victim narratives that publics favor. I believe that removing these sometimes-complex perspectives ultimately becomes another form of erasure.

When I shared my preliminary findings, scholars had a lot of opinions about how I should pursue my research and frame my findings. Some urged me to focus on the legal history, arguing that survivors already take up too much space in contemporary debates. "Their stories get in the way," someone once told me. "Survivors had their say a while ago."

I disagree. The French historian Jean-Marc Dreyfus points out that for more than seventy-five years, Holocaust accountability debates have occurred in the absence of survivors.[8] Legalism prefers neat victim–perpetrator binaries, and survivors show us that these categories consistently prove far too simplistic. This study of the SNCF conflict, while offering a detailed historical look at the trains' role and the legal debates, keeps those most affected by the atrocities in the center. Otherwise, legal debates too easily distort the past and thwart our understanding of how these atrocities occur and the best way to respond. Furthermore, when we remove the voices of those most affected by mass violence, we run the risk of making justice decisions on the basis of a dangerous imaginary, one that, as Karl Jaspers and Hannah Arendt warn, can lead us right back into totalitarianism.

Trains often played complex roles in survivors' lives. Trains were sites of interrogation and deportation but also places where couples fell in love or hid during risky escape attempts. Sarah Federman's first intercity SNCF ride carried her and her family to Normandy, where they spent their only family vacation. Along the way, the three children, Sarah, Jacqueline, and Raymond, stuck their faces to the windows, giggling at their first sight of grazing cows.[9] Sarah later traveled on the SNCF between Paris and the Pithiviers internment camp, where the family waited a few weeks in detention. SNCF trains then carried her parents, Margarite and Simon, first to Drancy and then on to Auschwitz on August 2, 1942, while the girls spent another two weeks in Pithiviers. On August 19, Sarah's last SNCF train departed from Drancy and, after a three-day journey, rolled up on one of Auschwitz's forty-two parallel tracks.[10] She was gassed upon arrival.

Interspersed with these kinds of horrific stories, survivors also described the SNCF as a victim of the occupation and a hero in the Resistance. These three intersecting roles—victim, perpetrator, and hero—make the train company's "true" identity hard to nail down, rendering a response seventy years after the fact all the more complicated. This book examines the SNCF's roles during the war and the vitriolic debates about the company's responsibility to make amends in the aftermath of the war. I intend for this book to help us understand the past and enrich conversations about corporate accountability today.

Acknowledgments

My first debt of gratitude is to the survivors who shared with me their stories along with their often-complicated feelings about the past. For some, I was the first person they had spoken to about the war. The contemporary conflict had become so contentious that some interviewees met with me secretly, wishing to remain anonymous. Numerous professionals made themselves available to help me understand the story behind the public discourse. For example, the French ambassador for human rights, Patrizianna Sparacino-Thiellay, left her door open to me, as did a number of SNCF executives. Together, these meetings, combined with archival research, enabled me to outline this conflict so that readers can explore the full contours of the contemporary debates and come to their own conclusions about what ought to be done.

Thank you to the United States Holocaust Memorial Museum, Stanford University's Hoover Institution, the Harvard Law Library and the Harvard Business School Library, the Library of Congress, and Maryland State Archives for their assistance. Thank you also to the French National Archives, the Mémorial de la Shoah archives, the SNCF archives, and the archives of the Association pour l'Histoire des Chemins de Fer en France (AHICF) for their assistance in France. The following professionals, academics, family, and friends helped me produce this book and carry its emotional weight. I love the acknowledgments list presented here because it includes people who often disagreed. Seeing their names together reminds me that questions of corporate accountability and about how to respond in the aftermath of violence belong to us all.

Diane Afoumado, Jennifer Allison, Kevin Avruch, Ivan Babanovski, Rabbi Andrew Baker, Leora Bilsky, Philippe Boukara, Leo Bretholz, Ludivine Broch, Jonathan Bush, Albert and Marianne Calo, Jon Cardin, Sara Cobb, Michael Cosgrove, Vivian Grosswald Curran, Michael Curtis, John Dale, Dana Dolan,

Ambassador Douglas Davidson, Ann Ditmeyer, Steve Ditmeyer, Jean-Marc Dreyfus, Leslie Dwyer, Stuart Eizenstat, Bernard Emsellem, Paul and Betsy Eschholz, Jeri Famighetti, (Papa) Jack Federman, Simone Federman, Ben Ferencz, Klara Firestone, Eric Freedman, Michael Gelb, Sophie Giloppe, Martin Goldman, Rosette Goldstein, Mark Goodale, Derek Gottlieb, Tobias Greiff, Aaron Greenfield, Marc Gurwith, Corinne Hershkovitch, Donna Hicks, Susan Hirsch, Chip Hauss, Douglas S. Irvin-Erikson, Deborah A. James, Rositta Kenigsberg, Henry Kerner, Serge Klarsfeld, Alan Kors, Lindsay Sarah Krasnoff, Alain Leray, Alain Lipietz, Nathan MacBrien, Magnus Manhart, Jennifer Margulies, Michael Marrus, David Matchen, Patrica Maulden, Sarah McLewin, Sheila McMahon, Elizabeth A. Nakian, Burt Neuborne, Ronald Niezen, Michael Olester, the Ota family, Robert Paxton, Guillaume Pepy, Susan Perry, Don Philipps, Marie-Noëlle Polino, Richard Prasquier, Raphael Prober, Mindy Reinstein, Kirill Reznik, Philippe Rochefort, Brenda Romero, Remi Roquette, Sandy Rosenberg, Mark Rothman, Henry Rousso, David Ruzie, Susan Sandler, Carlos Sluzki, Sam Solvit, Jessica M. Smith, Colleen Speers, Ambassador Patrizianna Sparacino-Thiellay, Susan Steckler, Ajantha Subramanian, Hannah Taieb, Harriet Tamen, Helen Tomalin-Costes, Charles Tenenbaum, Dominique Trimbur, Ashley Valanzola, Richard Weisberg, Harriet Welty, Hannah Yagil, Ambassador François Zimeray, and Catherine Znamirowski. A special thank you to Ronald Niezen, who came into my life at just the right time, for many reasons. His decades of publishing experience, knowledge of scholarship, and compassion carried me through the various challenges that occurred toward the final stages of this project.

The Witnesses
(excepting those who requested anonymity)

Renee R. Alexander, Arlene Aronowitz, Robert Berger, Jacqueline Birn, Pierre Blum, Robert Boruchowitz, Esther Caspi, Edith Cord, Anny (Buchstab) Coury, Pierre Degenszajn, Yvette-Levy Dreyfuss, Arnold Einhorn, Judith Epstein, Raphaël Esrail, Renée Fauguet-Zejgman, Stanley Federman, Suzanne Federman, Peter Feingold, Claude and Joisane Friedman, Charlotte Gal, Albert Garish, Albert Glicenzstejn, Martin, Goldman, Rosette Goldstein, C. Peter R. Gossels, Marc Gurwith, Aaron, Greenfield, Lou Helwaser, Lillian Horowitz, Marcus Horowtiz, Deborah A. James, Simon Jeruchim, Dan Jordan, Simon Kahn, Stanley Kalmanovitz, Alice Kaplan, Rositta Kenigsberg, Myriam Kern, Freddie Knoller, Pieter Kohnstam, Fred Lefkovic, Samuel Levi, Stephan Lewy, Hannh and Max Liebbmann, Lea and Paul Lieberman, Michel Margosis, Harry Markowicz, Liliane Marton, Margit Meissner, Giacomo and Perla Nunez, Jeanette Olson, Mina Parson, Samuel Putterman, Walter W. Reed, Micheline

Rotblut, John and Renee Rothschild, David Ruzié, Alexandre Saulinier, Joseph Sulc, Margaret Shultz, James Smallhout, Susan Soynika, Charles Srebnik, Faye Stern, Helga Stern, Claude and Elaine Ungar, Daniel Urbjetel, Leon Vermont, Freda Wineman, Manfred Wolf, Raymond Zaks, Adolphe Zdroui.

LIBRARIES AND ARCHIVES

Association pour l'Histoire des Chemins de Fer en France (AHICF); Fondation pour la Mémoire de la Shoah (FMS); National Archives, Paris; Baker Library, Harvard Business School; Harvard Law School Library; Hoover Institution, Stanford University; Maryland State Archives; Mémorial de la Shoah; Nahum Gelber Law Library, McGill University; Science Po Library, Paris; SNCF archives; United States Holocaust Memorial Museum; University of Baltimore Law Library and Robert L. Bogomolny Library.

FUNDING AND SUPPORT

Anonymous donation from a survivor interviewee; Carey Institute for Global Good, Writing Residency; Fondation pour la Mémoire de la Shoah; George Mason University, Presidential Scholarship; Institute for Humane Studies; Kathryn Davis Fellowship for Peace, Middlebury College; Minvera Institute, Tel Aviv University; University of Baltimore; Writer's Residency Program, Amtrak.

Abbreviations

ADL   Anti-Defamation League

AHICF   Association pour l'Histoire des Chemins de Fer en France
           (Association of French Railroad History)

AJC   American Jewish Committee

ATS   Alien Tort Statute (1789); also known as the Alien Tort Claims
           Act (ATCA)

BART   Bay Area Rapid Transit

BRICS   Brazil, Russia, India, China and South Africa

CDC   Caisse des Dépôts et Consignations (Deposits and
           Consignments Fund)

CDJC   Centre de Documentation Juive Contemporaine (Contemporary
           Jewish Documentation Center)

CGQJ   Commissariat Général aux Questions Juives (Commissariat-
           General for Jewish Affairs)

CGT   Confédération Générale du Travail (General Confederation of
           Labor)

CIVS   Commission pour l'Indemnisation des Victimes de Spoliations
           (Commission for the Compensation of Victims of Spoliation)

CNRS   Centre National de la Recherche Scientifique (National Center
           for Scientific Research)

CRIF   Conseil Représentatif des Institutions Juives de France
           (Representative Council of French Jewish Institutions)

CSR   Corporate Social Responsibility

CSX	Chessie Seaboard
EPIC	Établissement Public à Caractère Industriel et Commercial (Public Establishment of an Industrial and Commercial Nature)
FMD	Fondation pour la Mémoire de la Déportation (Foundation for the Memory of the Deportation)
FMS	Fondation pour la Mémoire de la Shoah (Foundation for the Memory of the Shoah)
FSIA	Foreign Sovereign Immunities Act (1976)
GFP	Geheime Feldpolizei (German Secret Police)
HVD	Haupt Verkehrsdirektion (German Head of Transport Management)
IAPT	Israelites, Allemand, Polonais, Tchèque (Israelites, Germans, Poles, Czechs)
ICC	International Criminal Court
IHR	Institute for Historical Review
IHTP	Institut d'Histoire du Temps Présent (Institute for the History of Present Time)
ISR	Israel Railways Ltd.
MARC	Maryland Area Regional Commuter
MBTA	Massachusetts Bay Transportation Authority
NS	Nederlandse Spoorwegen (Dutch National Railways)
OHCHR	Office of the High Commissioner for Human Rights
OSE	Oeuvre de Secours aux Enfants (Society for Assistance to Children)
PBS	Public Broadcasting Service
PICS	postincarceration syndrome
POW	Prisoner of War
RSHA	Reichssicherheitshauptamt (Reich Main Security Office)
RTLM	Radio Télévision Libre des Mille Collines (Thousand Hills Free Television Radio)
SCAP	Service de Contrôle des Administrateurs Provisoires (Control Service for Provisional Administrators)
SNCF	Société Nationale des Chemins de Fer Français (French National Railways)

STO	Service du Travail Obligatoire (forced labor service)
UGIF	Union Générale des Israelites de France (General Union of the Israelites of France)
UN	United Nations
UNGPs	United Nations Guiding Principles on Business and Human Rights
USC	University of Southern California Foundation
USHMM	United States Holocaust Memorial Museum
VRE	Virginia Railways Express
WVD	Wehrmacht Verkehrsdirektion (German Railways Armed Forces Traffic Directorate)
ZNO	Zone non-occupé (French unoccupied zone)

LAST TRAIN TO
AUSCHWITZ

Introduction

The Making of a Conflict

As I write this, the individuals who planned and carried out the Nazi agenda during World War II are almost all dead. Occasionally, a story surfaces about how to handle an elderly concentration camp prison guard or bookkeeper who had long escaped accountability. Soon these stories will die away. With so few original actors remaining, survivors and descendants who are still seeking justice must swat at phantoms.

Or must they? Even with individuals gone, states and corporate entities provide another locus for justice pursuits and atonement. In 2019, for example, the German Reimann family announced its plans to donate roughly €10 million to help atone for their ancestors' use of slave labor during the war and for their support (political and financial) of Adolf Hitler and his antisemitic policies.[1] While the Reimann family and JAB Holdings, worth $19 billion, might not be household names, many of their brands are: Dr. Pepper, Krispy Kreme Donuts, Panera Bread, Peets Coffee, Keurig, Au Bon Pain, Pret à Manger, Einstein's Bagels, Jimmy Choo, and Coty.[2]

In August 2020, Continental—a German company known today for its tires, brakes, and sensors used to advance autonomous driving—released an eight-hundred-page study of the company's activities during the war as well as the activities of its subsidiaries. The company commissioned historian Paul Erker to conduct this research. Using company archives, Erker discovered that in order to produce the tires needed to support the German military war effort, Continental used slave labor from concentration camps, abusing many to the point of death. No executives were held accountable after the war.[3]

In recent years, the French, Dutch, and Hungarian national railway companies have found themselves called upon to atone for their participation in the Holocaust. The French railway company, the subject of this book, was embroiled in conflict for more than a decade but found some respite after reaching a

$60 million settlement in 2014. In June 2019, the Nederlandse Spoorwegen (NS, Dutch National Railways), allocated roughly the same sum to compensate deported victims and their direct descendants.[4] Atonement discussions extend beyond Europe. In October 2019, a South Korean court asked Nippon Steel and Sumitomo Metal to pay damages for slave labor used during the war.[5]

Some companies, which ostensibly atoned for their role in the war long ago, are being called to answer for new crimes; Volkswagen, recently implicated in a colossal emissions fraud, finds itself examined yet again, along with Holocaust-complicit Siemens, for activities involving China's detention camps in Xinjiang province.[6] There are new crimes identified from new actors as well. In February 2019, Dutch courts convicted two executives for sending 168 chemicals (likely used to make chemical weapons) to Syria.[7] In August 2019, an Oklahoma court ordered the Johnson & Johnson Company to pay $527 million because, the court found, the company knew the dangers of potent new opioids and oversold the benefits. Two thousand other opioid-related lawsuits await hearing.[8] A drug distributor, McKesson, and two producers, Purdue and the Sackler family, are also being held accountable for their role in the opioid crisis. Corporate criminal accountability for mass crime is gaining increasing attention. And with this attention comes a reexamination of World War II and a rethinking of the ethical obligations of corporations. With so many businesses engaged in so many activities over time, deciding where to focus becomes the first challenge.

The French National Railways and the Holocaust

In 1976 the preeminent Holocaust scholar Raul Hilberg chastised social scientists for overlooking the importance of the railroads in the Holocaust. He observed scholars treating railroads as a fringe operation of the Holocaust rather than, as he put it, "indispensable at its core."[9] Today, railroads are no longer overlooked. In fact, in contemporary Holocaust accountability, debates concerning trains often take center stage. In spite of Hilberg's efforts to attract the interest of fellow academics, it was ultimately survivors and their advocates, not social scientists, who raised public awareness. And while the Deutsche Reichsbahn, the German railway system, played the most significant role in the Holocaust, survivors fighting for amends from the Société Nationale des Chemins de Fer Français (SNCF, French National Railways) can be largely credited with this turn.

During the German occupation of France (1940–44), France was initially divided into an occupied zone and a free zone, operating under the direction of the Vichy government but working closely with the Germans. Under the direction of both the German military and the Vichy governments, the state-owned SNCF played a role in transporting approximately seventy-six thousand

Jewish deportees to death camps in seventy-nine convoys in conditions that for some made the journey as horrific as the destination.[10] In 1978 Serge Klarsfeld became the first to compile a list of all the French victims. We know that these convoys traveled multiple days with little food, water, breathable air, sanitation, or space to sit down. Only an estimated 3,500 people, or roughly 4.6 percent, of the deportees returned.[11] Today "deportations" have become synonymous with the extermination of the Jews, but this was not always the case. In fact, for the first thirty years after the war, the word "deportation" in France evoked the image of the French resistant who was transported and killed for standing up to the occupier.[12] But because many contemporary debates about the SNCF's role in the war in the United States focused primarily on the treatment of the Jewish deportees, this book does so as well.

During the past three decades, survivors, first in France and then in the United States, have challenged the company to make amends for deporting Jews to the death camps. While they met a dead end in courts in both countries, their persistent advocacy successfully encumbered the company with boycotts and bad press in some US states where the company sought rail contracts.[13] Separated by more than seventy years and 3,800 miles from the events in question, both survivors and the company executives found themselves continually interrupted and immobilized by the past.

How did these debates find their way to the United States? They followed the railroad. Since the war, the SNCF has become a world leader in all aspects of rail transport with worldwide revenue of roughly $44 billion.[14] The company has won commuter and high-speed rail contracts in countries such as the United States, Israel, India, Saudi Arabia, Morocco, and the United Arab Emirates. In the United States—through its subsidiary Keolis, of which the SNCF holds a 70 percent share—the SNCF successfully secured the Virginia Railways Express (VRE) contract and the Massachusetts Bay Transportation Authority (MBTA) contract, the latter being the largest contract in the history of Massachusetts.

Those challenging the company, most forcefully in Florida, Maryland, Virginia, and California, argued that the company willingly collaborated with the Nazis, determined the conditions of the transports, and profited from the deportations. Before allowing the SNCF to pursue any more contracts in the United States, this group demanded that the company compensate victims, apologize, and offer greater transparency about its wartime activities. In 2001, when the challengers launched their first lawsuit and successfully lobbied state legislators, news outlets grabbed hold of the story.[15]

The SNCF responded to these public attacks by saying that the company was state-owned and therefore operated under constraint during the war.

In September 1939, France declared war on Germany (in response to Germany's invasion of Poland). The Third Reich launched its offensive against France in May 1940.[16] France quickly fell and signed an armistice agreement on June 22, 1940. Article XIII of this agreement placed the SNCF under the direction of the Third Reich and required France to make all trains available to the Germans in the occupied territory. The agreement took effect on June 25, 1940, placing the SNCF under the German thumb for the duration of the war. Compensation claims, the SNCF said, must therefore be directed to the French government, which owned the majority of the railway company and signed this armistice. Present-day SNCF executives also reminded those attacking the company that the SNCF suffered many material and personnel losses: a number of *cheminots* (railway workers) were killed for their participation in the Resistance.

More surprisingly, perhaps, some survivors also defend the company. Pierre Blum, for example, whose father, Henry, was deported on Convoy 77, said, "As a machine [factory], the SNCF was obligated [to participate in the deportations]. This conflict is not on the right side. . . . It's the Americans who did this, I think."[17] His comment also points to the tensions between survivors still in France and those who have moved abroad. This variety of opinion will return as a central theme in the pages that follow.

Legal Liability

In both countries, the SNCF skirted liability through legal technicalities. In France, for example, the SNCF first protected itself by pointing out that the company operated under *private* law during the war and could not be tried in a civil or criminal court. In the United States, on the other hand, the SNCF needed only to mention its *public* ownership to receive the protection of the US Foreign Sovereign Immunities Act (FSIA), which protects countries from lawsuits by individuals. As a mixed public-private entity, the company could play different hands without changing the facts. And while the SNCF is partially state-owned, it operates independently as a business both nationally and internationally. This makes the conflict a salient site of study for corporate accountability. The SNCF's participation in nonjudicial measures to respond to its legacy of mass violence also makes this a relevant study for postconflict and transitional justice scholars. The field of transitional justice, while beginning largely with the Nuremberg trials, shifted toward nation building during the Cold War, and since the turn of the millennium the field has expanded to include a larger human rights agenda.[18] Transitional justice mechanisms now include transparency, apologies, compensation, commemoration (memorials), and trauma services.[19]

Even though the SNCF maintains legal impunity and has never paid survivors directly, the company has not ignored its role in the Holocaust. Since the 1990s, it has opened its archives and commissioned an independent report on its wartime activities, made apologies, and contributed to Holocaust commemoration. The SNCF's amends-making activities help us explore little-examined questions such as: What happens when corporations apologize and create memorials? Are these efforts sincere or simply an attempt to skirt financial accountability? One thing is clear: corporate actors have been long overlooked as key contributors to postconflict healing.

The path forward is fraught. Susan Ariel Aaronson and Ian Higham's words ring true: the wounds created by mass crime cannot be easily healed by "apologies, time, or new management."[20] While the SNCF eventually won over much of the French Jewish leadership, the company struggled to satisfy survivors within France and abroad. But it was not so easy. Lou Helwaser, whose mother was deported, hired the Paris-based lawyer Corinne Hershkovitch to help her take on the SNCF in France. Lou also joined the US-based class action lawsuit. Over some coffee and sweets on her patio, Helwaser told me that she remains furious that the company has not paid survivors directly, even though she was glad to learn that the SNCF made some other efforts to atone.

THE SETTLEMENT

In spite of maintaining legal impunity, the pressure from those still seeking justice led to a negotiated settlement between the French and US governments. This is not unusual; gaping holes in law make settlements by far the more common outcome of litigation against corporations.[21] The SNCF debates unearthed a group of about one hundred survivors who had not been covered by any compensation program. Negotiations began between the governments over how to compensate these individuals and, it was hoped, through this settlement end this battle over the SNCF's accountability. The resulting negotiations between the US and France led to a much-publicized $60 million settlement, signed on December 8, 2014, at the US Department of State.[22] The settlement signing, as I experienced it, illustrates some of the rocky terrain of this conflict and the challenges of being an academic observer of a fraught legal contest.

The day of the event, I grabbed my passport and headed to the US Department of State. On the way, I called a survivor friend, Jacqueline, who had also planned to attend. We met at the door, handed over our IDs, and were issued security badges. Together, Jacqueline and I watched the lobby fill with the myriad characters involved in the conflict. One very elderly survivor, now mostly deaf, told us that she had lost everyone except her grandmother. A middle-aged woman told us that she was there on behalf of her now deceased mother, who had survived the Holocaust. Then the legal teams, most of whom I had previously interviewed, arrived, including the lobbyist Aaron Greenfield, Maryland delegate Kirill Reznik, and lawyers Harriet Tamen and Raphael Proper and members of their legal team who helped challenge the SNCF. Soon the French Holocaust activist Serge Klarsfeld and his son, Arno, arrived. Serge, a survivor himself, and his wife, Beate, had spent decades pursuing German Nazis and French Vichy collaborators, including Kurt Lishka, Paul Touvier, Maurice Papon, Jean Leguay, René Bousquet, and Klaus Barbie, "the Butcher of Lyon," whose participation in the deportations figured prominently in the lives of survivors.[23]

The attendance of the Klarsfelds underscored the significance of the event. Klarsfeld had long shared his opinions about the SNCF conflict with the public and once with me in his apartment while he scurried around photocopying documents, his dog following him back and forth from the copier to the table. He handed me the original police round-up orders—the ones that authorized the deportation of Sarah Federman and thousands of others. My heart pounded as the past became real.

His son Arno also attended. Arno, named after his deported grandfather, had served as the SNCF's defense lawyer, as had Serge Klarsfeld. How had France's lead Holocaust activist and his son come to defend the SNCF? This had not always been the case. Serge Klarsfeld had reproached the SNCF in the early 2000s for its role in the Holocaust.[24] A handful of activists in the French Holocaust commemorative community told me that he started defending the SNCF after the company made a significant contribution to his compensation program for orphans. Others simply believed that he thought the company had done enough to make amends. When I called to ask him about his change of position on the matter, he said that he had discovered new information suggesting that the SNCF had not received payment for the deportations.[25] French lawyer Corinne Hershkovitch, who helped clients retrieve stolen artifacts as well as take on the SNCF, interpreted Klarsfeld's position as an expression of his distaste for any effort that felt like Jews trying to get rich off the Holocaust.[26] Serge Klarsfeld's change of heart was one of the many important turns in a conflict that has lasted far longer than the war and that could outlive all those directly touched by the deportations.

Staffers escorted us upstairs to the anteroom of the Treaty Signing Room. We surrendered our phones to a security guard standing under a large portrait of Michelle Obama. The Treaty Room itself looked like a perfect hybrid of Versailles and the Oval Office; the curved walls and embedded columns interspersed among classic portraits gave the room a presidential feel, while a glistening chandelier hanging over an intricately laid wood floor was reminiscent of the French palace—a fitting setting for this historic French–American agreement.

No SNCF executives were present because both governments and the SNCF wished to keep the company out of these negotiations. As a state-owned company, the SNCF had always said the French State would compensate survivors on its behalf. Today, France would demonstrate its willingness to do so. All the same, almost everyone present understood the connection of this settlement to the debates over the company's responsibility for deportations during the Holocaust. Both the Department of State and the SNCF expected this $60 million settlement to end the stateside boycotts and lawsuits against the company.[27] But if the governments and the SNCF wanted peace, they would need to satisfy the lead lawyer for the survivors, Harriet Tamen, who had worked pro bono on this case for almost two decades.[28] Appeasing her would be difficult.

Tamen stood in the center of the room surrounded by her team. True to form, she declared to her team and the surrounding legislators that this whole settlement was a waste because it would not apply to those who had lost both parents on the trains. She asserted that Stuart Eizenstat, on behalf of the US government, should not sign the agreement. Her office had criticized Eizenstat for completing the negotiations as quickly as possible to stop state-level legislation from obstructing the SNCF's bid for contracts in the United States.

But not all of Tamen's team shared her opinion. One lawyer who worked with Tamen said she believed good work had been done and that it was important to get the agreement out and move forward. Other members of her team also thought that this settlement would be enough. Tamen ignored these dissenting views and turned to Congresswoman Carolyn Maloney (D-NY), saying again that the agreement was no good and that as soon as the event was over, they needed to move into action.

Staffers asked us to take our seats. Though they had roughly twenty chairs reserved for the survivors, fewer than ten attended. The lead negotiators, Stuart Eizentstat and the French Ambassador at Large for Human Rights, Patrizianna Sparacino-Thiellay, entered. Eizenstat spoke first. He outlined the agreement, describing how the settlement would cover victims not included in other compensation programs and allow people to resubmit claims if their first one had been rejected. Eizenstat closed his statement by saying how much he had enjoyed working with the French ambassador. Sparacino-Thiellay then rose and took her turn to speak. She emphasized the tremendous gravity of the Holocaust and trembled as she shared words that mourned this period of human history and the treatment of victims in the aftermath. At the end of her speech, there was a champagne toast, and she hugged Eizenstat—she and some of the audience were moved to tears.

The staff then ushered us back into the anteroom to share in the champagne.

A few days passed before the settlement details circulated. The Department of State estimated that around 2,000 applicants (about 100 direct survivors and 1,900 descendants) could benefit. The settlement applied to three main groups and their beneficiaries. The first group, who would receive at least $100,000 each, included deportees from France who were citizens of any country except France (who had been covered under a 1946 pension program) and those in countries that already had compensation agreements: Belgium, Poland, the former Czechoslovakia, and the United Kingdom.[29] The United States, Israel, and all other countries had no agreements. Ambassador Douglas Davidson said no one at the US Department of State knew why the United States had not created and signed a similar agreement.[30] The settlement might give one the impression that France had shirked its responsibility to compensate deportees, but, in fact, other countries, including the United States and Israel, had *also* failed by not pursuing agreements earlier.

The second category of people covered by the agreement was spouses of the deportees. Payments would vary for these individuals. The third group was individuals standing for survivors or their spouses who had died after World War II. Payments to these beneficiaries would also vary at the discretion of the US Department of State.[31] While the French government alone would cover the $60 million for restitution, there was a separate clause in the agreement that required the SNCF to contribute $4 million to Holocaust commemoration and education. Because of the survivors' advanced age, the US Department of State, whose legal department would manage the distribution of the funds, promised a quick turnaround and relatively lenient requirements for claimants to qualify for compensation. (Unfortunately, few survivors could meet the original deadline, and 50 percent of the claims were originally rejected. Eventually the department extended the timeline and monies were distributed to the few who qualified.)

Upon hearing that some beneficiaries could receive more than $100,000, survivors living in France were aghast. This seemed like an enormous sum and was larger than the payments they had received. The amounts seemed greater because they would arrive as a lump sum and compensate for all the years recipients should have been receiving payments but did not. In other words, the agreement offered compensation retroactively.[32] The amount of the restitution, however, was only one of the factors that bothered a number of Jews and non-Jews back in France. The French Parliament generally just disliked the agreement. "They think it is 'bad at its core' but will have to pass it," said Alain Lipietz, a Paris-based descendant and former litigant against the SNCF, when we met at Berthillon, a well-loved little ice cream shop on a picturesque island in the Seine. Then he laughed and added, "The agreement has all the things [French] Parliament hates addressing: business, Americans, Jews, and compensation for the Second World War."[33] French citizens, including himself, would likely be paying for these survivors through their taxes, he added.

The French government eventually ratified the agreement; claimants started sending applications to the Department of State on November 2, 2015, and continued doing so through January 20, 2017, the last day of the Obama administration.

Those who received the money were not unequivocally pleased. Stanley Kalmanovitz received $204,000. His father was gassed at Auschwitz after arriving on convoy 67 from France. Both Stanley and his sister survived their deportation to Auschwitz on convoy 71. His sister, who had become a French citizen, never received any compensation. About the settlement, he said, "The money came at a good time in my life. Having not expected to live this long, I was close to running out of money. Of course, I am grateful, BUT this is not a settlement of conscience, this is a commercial 'gamble' settlement. The opportunity to be awarded large construction contracts was the guideline, not anything else."[34]

Kalmanovitz's concern that France settled only to support the SNCF's business interests points to a significant conundrum at the intersection of transitional justice and corporate accountability and at the heart of this book. When companies compensate victims, make apologies, and so on, do they do so out of genuine concern for victims or for business interests? This mattered to many survivors whom I interviewed for this research. Many pointed to the difference between simply receiving a check and receiving an acknowledgment of the suffering they had endured. Caring mattered. They wanted their loss to be both visible and legitimized. There is a lesson in this for corporate amends making: business owners need to think about how to demonstrate sincerity. This sincerity also helps reassure us all that their crimes and moral compromises will not be repeated.

THE LAST TRAIN TO AUSCHWITZ

Before advancing any further, I believe that the highly politicized subject matter of this book warrants some clarifications about terms. First, I use the definition of "survivor" employed by the United States Holocaust Memorial Museum (USHMM), which "honors as survivors any persons, Jewish or non-Jewish, who were displaced, persecuted, or discriminated against due to the

racial, religious, ethnic, social, and political policies of the Nazis and their collaborators between 1933 and 1945. In addition to former inmates of the concentration camps, ghettos, and prisons, this definition includes, among others,
people who were refugees or were in hiding."[35] In France, the term "survivor"
traditionally only applied to those who had survived death and concentration
camps. Only later did hidden children and others begin adopting the term,
but in France the broadened definition is still contested. This book uses the
definition employed by the USHMM because it dominated the US debates
and includes the widely varying groups directly touched by the deportations.
I refer to "compensation" demands, rather than "restitution" or "reparations,"
because this was the word most often used by those fighting the SNCF in the
United States and because they have different meanings in French.[36]

Finally, a few words about what the book includes and what it does not.
Last Train to Auschwitz discusses how the conflict unfolded in France and the
United States, with a slightly greater emphasis on the United States. Even though
much of my research occurred in France, I accessed and participated in more
of the US events as they unfolded. I also place somewhat more emphasis on
the US context because more has been written about the French side of this
conflict by French scholars and conflict participants.[37]

Because the public debates in the United States demonstrated so little understanding of France during and after the war, I dedicate the first three chapters
to wartime France. These historical chapters aim not to provide a definitive
history but to introduce readers to the complexity of the times by presenting
the SNCF as a victim of the occupation, a perpetrator of the Holocaust, and
a hero in the Resistance. Highlighting these multiple wartime roles serves not
to absolve the SNCF of its responsibility but to help us understand how participation, especially corporate participation, in mass atrocity actually occurs.

Historical accuracy is critical, but this is not solely a history book. Nor is it
solely a legal study. Readers interested in the legal contours of these debates
can find the lawsuits and full legal citations in the notes and in the appendix. I hope this will assist lawyers and legal scholars who can use this book
to support their work on related cases. In the text, however, I present the lawsuits and related legislation as it relates to the lived experience of victims, advocates, and professionals. Scholars interested in the intersection of transitional
justice and corporate accountability largely look at them from a legal perspective.[38] The predominance of legalism in the field of transitional justice shapes
the understanding and pursuit of justice.[39] A strictly legal history, therefore,
would both perpetuate legalism's hold on the field and constrain my ability to
share the restorative justice lens that guided my research and is expressed in
my findings.

Now for what this book *is*: it is a study of corporate accountability that explores whether accountability occurs and the consequences of impunity for the victims as well as our broader sense of morality. Many actors continue in their positions of power with impunity, so how did the SNCF remain ensnared for so long? The cumulative effect of advocacy on both sides of the Atlantic helped advance notions of corporate accountability beyond French trains, helping related cases in Hungary and the Netherlands. Advocacy also advanced notions of corporate accountability beyond the Holocaust. In a broad sense, the voices advocated for compensation destabilized corporate power and exposed the many remaining legal loopholes that prevent corporations from being called to account for actions and policies that cause mass harm. For these and other reasons, Holocaust survivors play a central role in this book.

In the past seventy-five years, issues of Holocaust restitution have often been debated in the absence of survivors.[40] Any shifts toward survivor inclusion have occurred slowly and with much hesitation, especially in France. The French historian Annette Wieviorka credits the Eichmann trial specifically with catalyzing the shift toward survivor testimony as the preferred discursive style of post-atrocity narration.[41] Yet she felt that, while survivor sentiments deserved respect, the historian ought to distance herself from these emotions in order to construct a proper telling of history. As time moves on, however, we are learning that sometimes their disjointed, seemingly fanciful stories can prove more accurate than archival records.[42]

Increasingly, Holocaust scholars add survivor voices to their historical works. Saul Friedlander's celebrated *Nazi Germany and the Jews* includes victim stories more or less unequivocally, claiming that they make a vital contribution to our understanding of history as well as of victimhood and perpetration.[43] Friedlander argues that only the emotions of compassion and caring can ignite and sustain the energy needed to respond to loss and to prevent future occurrences of such atrocities. Other respected Holocaust scholars and those focusing on wartime France now similarly include survivor testimony.[44]

This book includes survivors' voices not so much to offer a more accurate telling of the Holocaust—a worthy project in itself—but rather to ensure that their varied opinions regarding harm and restitution remain part of the macro-level justice debates. Discarding some perspectives as "incorrect or irrational and therefore irrelevant" takes away their right to narrate their own experience.[45] To help keep victims' voices central, I include them at the end of each chapter in sections I call "Voices from the Last Trains" and also interweave their stories throughout the book—not just as survivors but as witnesses. When Giorgio Agamben mapped the etymology of the word "witness," he found two origins: *Tetis*, a person between two rival teams, and *Superstites*, a person who has lived through an experience from beginning to end and therefore has authority to speak on the subject.[46] I, as a scholar and author, serve as witness in the *Tetis* sense, whereas the survivors are witnesses in the *Superstites* sense—they have lived through the experience and are therefore authorities. Centralizing victims also speaks to the critique of the early Nuremberg trials, during which victims were largely excluded.[47] Furthermore, little time remains for survivors to speak for themselves. This book provides a platform for some of their personal stories as well as their opinions regarding justice matters.

Though the testimony genre has recently gained in credibility, some remain skeptical. There are those who still consider survivor views irrelevant or somehow less important than a document drawn from the depths of an archive or the opinion of a lawyer. In addition to a dignity violation, this also shows a misunderstanding of how law and society intersect in a democratic society. Treating survivors only as victims, permitted to share only their personal stories but not their views on what should happen next, asserts a hegemonic control over the aftermath of the violence. I often watched survivors being left behind during debates, treated almost like children. This book responds to this exclusion by including their perspectives—even when they do not sit comfortably with facile assumptions about how survivors should be—and by treating their perspectives as intrinsically valuable, as a form of expertise.

As experts, they taught me to think about the issues more broadly. While I discussed the SNCF at length with survivor interviewees, we also spent hours talking about their lives before and after the war and their opinions about justice in general. Limiting their voices to the SNCF debates both distorts the effect of the Holocaust on their lives and reduces them to "Holocaust survivors" rather than seeing them as otherwise ordinary people who were trapped in a terrible war and who happened to be targeted and slated for elimination. The inclusion of their wider stories helps counterbalance what can become (and in fact became) a very arcane discussion. Expanded survivor stories help us remember why these debates matters at all.[48]

A Battle of Narratives

The contemporary SNCF debates can be understood as a battle of narratives. Various groups vied for control over which of the SNCF's wartime roles would dominate and hence determine the company's actions. To capture the conflict dynamics, in addition to following the various news stories, I interviewed participants and traveled anywhere people were talking about the SNCF conflict. Then, I mapped the various viewpoints, conducting a narrative analysis of the discursive landscape.[49] Ninety interviews with survivors who had escaped persecution in France added important—and variegated—voices. I also met with leading Vichy historians, including Michael Marrus, Robert Paxton, and Henry Rousso.[50] Understanding the contemporary contentions in both France and the US required multiple meetings with senior SNCF executives, French Jewish leaders, and the diplomats working on the conflict. Stateside, I met with the senior legal teams and ambassadors working on the conflict. To better understand the historical context, I conducted my own archival research. I accessed the French National Archives, the SNCF archives, the Fondation pour la Mémoire de la Shoah (FMS) archives, the Hoover Institution and the archives of the Association pour l'Histoire des Chemins de Fer en France (AHICF) while contributing informally to the research efforts of the US House of Representatives, the US Department of State, and the *Washington Post*. Attending legislative events also provided me with a front-row seat to the conflict as it unfolded.

While the book includes a variety of victim perspectives, I focus particularly on five individuals and their families: Daniel, Samuel, Abram, Henri, and Estéra, all of whom were transported on the last trains from France to Auschwitz. Convoy 77 was the last train from Paris to Auschwitz, and Convoy 78, departing from Lyon, was the last train from France to Auschwitz.[51] While "last trains" left from other parts of Europe bound for Auschwitz—Anne Frank was on what would become the last train from the Netherlands to Auschwitz—I invite readers to imagine being on *this* last train, a train bound for this same death camp over a month *after* the Allies arrived in great force a mere 125 miles away in Normandy.

This temporal proximity of these departures to D-Day underscores the SNCF's complicated identity during the war. During and just after D-Day, SNCF trains ran in two directions, both furthering and undermining the Nazi agenda. Some SNCF workers heroically sabotaged trains of German soldiers and armaments going west to fend off the allies, while other cheminots coordinated and drove trains crammed with deportees to the town Novéant-sur-Moselle near the German border, where they would be taken over by German personnel to continue the journey to a death camp.[52] Telling the stories of those aboard these trains while recounting acts of heroism amplifies the multiple activities of the rail company and its workers.

There is a schizophrenia to this history. When the French government signed away the railways to the Germans in the 1940 Armistice, the SNCF found itself a "victim" of the occupation; and those SNCF workers who had been murdered for their brave acts of resistance helped classify the company as heroic. But when the SNCF transported the deportees, it acted as a perpetrator. The first three chapters address the validity of each identity. The answer to the question of whether a corporation is complicit may depend on what part of the corporation you consider.

Transitional justice scholars increasingly urge us to become more comfortable with overlapping identities.[53] Some survivors agreed, feeling quite comfortable with the notion that a person or group played multiple roles in the war. Others saw players in more binary terms and critiqued those who saw what Primo Levi called "grey zones."[54] Peter experiences this critique, he says, when he talks about both his parents' murder at Auschwitz and the appeal to him (at the time) of Nazi symbols and identity. Before coming to France, Peter had spent time in Berlin, where he read books about Jews being the "poison mushrooms" of Europe. The books described how Jews lied, cheated, stole, and hung Jesus on the Cross. As a first grader, he said it sounded true to him. "I never associated with being Jewish," he told me. Only at nine years old, when he asked his parents for permission to join the Hitler Youth, did he learn of his Jewish identity. He was very upset when his parents told him he could not join because members of the Hitler Youth were given a shiny dagger and a uniform. "What nine-year-old doesn't dream of such a thing?" he asked. For this reason, Peter said, he understood those who joined the Nazi movement, and this understanding often upsets his Jewish friends. "They think I'm a Nazi," he said.[55]

André spoke to me about his own appreciation of complexity when we met at his home in Palaiseau, France. André escaped the Nazis several times, including once at a metro station when a guard saw his yellow star and had him wait against a wall while he went off to collect others. André ran. The building concierge saved his family during the Vel d'Hiv roundup in Paris by lying, at risk of his life, about their whereabouts. Ultimately, his father was deported from the Drancy internment camp and then murdered at Auschwitz. His mother barely survived the war and spent much of her postwar life so ill that André had to return to an orphanage.[56] Regarding restitution, André said, "You cannot want everything . . . you have to understand the time period . . . people were selling people all the time: Jews, communists, Resistants, others. People had very little money. It was a complicated time, but there were a lot of *Justes* [good people]." He provided this example of a *Juste*: the woman in charge of a children's hospital who saved his life, at risk of her own, by hiding him. When the Nazis asked whether the hospital had any Jews, she replied, "We have no Jews here, only sick kids." Roughly 80 percent of the French survivors residing in France whom I interviewed shared similarly complex perspectives about the war years.

Meanwhile, in legislative chambers and legal offices and in news stories, the binaries predominated. One spoke either for or against the SNCF. Middle positions were seen as naive, weak, or, at worst, apologist. In emphasizing the multiple roles of the SNCF, this book responds to the distortions of this binary environment and attempts to make space for deeper public reflection and engagement.

Corporate Accountability for
Massive Human Rights Violations

For too long and still in many places, post-atrocity accountability discussions neglect corporations. Addressing corporate accountability allows for a more holistic accounting of atrocity and its social and legal aftermath. Including businesses in this discussion will become increasingly important as these entities, especially transnational corporations, have greatly increased in power and scope. If we measure the size of entities by comparing their GDP and revenue, we find that 51 percent of the world's largest entities are corporations; 49 percent are countries. Walmart is now larger than 170 of the world's 195 countries.[57] And while some economists and others may contest whether these are appropriate metrics to compare, the data points provide a sense of the comparative size of corporations to states. International corporations will continue to dwarf many of the countries in which they operate. This also means that any region with an outbreak of violence likely has business entities participating in and/or suffering from it. From the start, corporations developed in ways that were meant to protect the owners and shareholders from personal liability. Accountability was supposed to be diffused.

Postconflict mechanisms that ignore these actors and focus on state-centric programs are not adapted to our current era. The SNCF conflict demonstrates the transnationality of the debates surrounding corporate responsibility for human rights and postconflict restitution, especially when the diaspora is involved. Ultimately, genocide studies, transitional justice, and conflict resolution sideline the role of businesses at their own peril—and at the peril of victims. Corporations are important agents of both violence and peace.

Postconflict studies, genocide studies, and transitional justice have each long marginalized the role of corporate players.[58] This was not always the case; between 1946 and 1949, the Nuremberg Military Tribunals held roughly a dozen corporate directors accountable for their companies' wartime activities.[59] These "industrialist cases," which took place in Germany and the United Kingdom, are often referred to as the birthplace of corporate accountability for human rights abuses.[60] They did not focus on crimes against Jews specifically but established—at least in rudimentary terms—that entrepreneurs, even if not instigators of these abuses, could be held accountable for facilitating and/or profiting from them. Beyond complicity, the tribunals also established that companies could play a central role in fulfilling the aims of a totalitarian state and that they could have "criminal aims."[61] The tribunals left much unanswered about how to handle corporate entities, but they at least began grappling with what has become a central question of our times.

After this initial postwar burst of interest in corporate complicity matters, little advanced for the next few decades. The International Criminal Court, established in 1993, could try only *natural persons*, rather than *legal persons* (entities such as companies). Even if the International Criminal Court and other criminal courts could try legal persons, the prosecution would face the difficult task of proving that the accused entity possessed both *mens rea* (a guilty mind) and *actus reus* (a guilty act). The SNCF's *actus reus*, its participation in moving the deportation trains, is undisputed. The company, however, did not necessarily want to participate in these human rights violations. We are also unsure of how much the drivers and executives knew about the destination. Proving *mens rea* is challenging because confusion remains about the location of a corporation's "mind." The question of whether the corporate consciousness, or intending mind, resides solely within the company's agents or exists as something greater than the whole has vexed scholars for years.[62]

Survivor advocates found other ways to hold corporations legally liable. Transnational Holocaust litigation in the 1990s involving banks and other enterprises (including the SNCF) raised the matter again. Beginning in the 1990s, international trials growing out of the genocide in Rwanda also raised the question of business participation. Attention to corporate players received yet another push in 2008, when the International Commission of Jurists published a report, "Corporate Complicity and Legal Accountability."[63] Without leading to many convictions, this report buoyed the corporate accountability discourse more generally. It argued that enabling mass crimes in any manner could be considered complicity and could potentially lead to legal liability.[64] Liability, it claimed, required knowledge of the abuses and proximity to the crime and perpetrator.[65] Leigh Payne et al. identified 349 cases of corporations held liable for crimes against humanity since the close of World War II but still consider these efforts "ephemeral" because they failed to set any agreed-upon global standards or result in many significant convictions.[66]

Corporations' growing size and their increasingly evident role in global affairs make questions of corporate accountability for complicity harder to ignore. It is fortunate that transitional justice and other fields increasingly consider the intersection of business and postconflict work.[67] But the turn has been slow and not universal. Why? Corporations serve more often as enablers or beneficiaries rather than as direct perpetrators of violations. Hence, their participation can be overlooked or sidelined.[68] The privileging of short-term projects in postconflict work, the prevalence of structural violence, and the resources of political elites have all contributed to masking corporate culpability and continue to do so.[69] Lawyers interested in holding corporations accountable have mostly relied on "soft law," such as the United Nations Guiding Principles on Business and Human Rights, because international criminal law remains "a problematic site for addressing corporate responsibility to involvement in mass atrocities."[70] The conception of companies as stabilizing agents in post-conflict contexts weakens support for accountability measures for corporate crimes.[71]

Because of these trends and legal loopholes, corporations find themselves with more exculpatory rights than positive obligations in protecting human rights. True, corporations can at times face liability, reputational damage, and loss of investor confidence, but more often than not, they walk away unscathed or with a proportionally small price to pay—often significantly less than the profits built upon mass harm.[72] There are no international institutions able to enforce obligations. As a result, the *Harvard Law Review* observes, "corporations . . . remain immune to liability, and victims remain without redress."[73] With no means of addressing the human rights obligations of corporations, the fields of genocide studies and transitional justice turn back to the more accepted individual and state perpetrators, thereby distorting the landscape of complicity.

Holocaust scholars have not entirely ignored corporate participation; a number of academic and trade books consider complicit businesses—*Industry and Ideology*; *Less than Slaves*; *Business and Industry in Nazi Germany*; and *IBM and the Holocaust*.[74] These works, however, tend to focus on the war years and on the trials that took place immediately in the aftermath. In this book, by contrast, I go beyond the immediate postwar era to consider the long-term consequences of mass atrocity. I also engage with extralegal concerns such as these: Beyond financial compensation, how can corporations best respond in the aftermath of mass crime? How do the transitional mechanisms of transparency, commemoration, compensation, and apology function when a corporate actor participates in mass crime? Who decides when the corporation's debt to individuals and society has been paid, and according to what criteria?

Neutrality on a Moving Train

Just as the literary theorist Northrup Frye asked scholars to "stand under" a text, I stood under the narratives circulating about the SNCF, trying not to take sides.[75] My own opinions remained in a state of flux. I began my research in France enraged at the SNCF for its participation in the Holocaust. Then, after time spent with the French Jewish leadership and SNCF officials, I was heartened to learn how much the company *had* done to make amends. When I returned to the United States, I soon found myself sympathizing with those still fighting. Maybe the company *should* pay directly and not hide behind the government. Some of these litigants claimed, in ways that drew me to agree, that apologies without compensation can feel insincere. That said, many survivors emphasized how much they appreciated the apology offered in 1995 by Jacques Chirac, then the president of France, for the country's complicity in the Holocaust. Many of these individuals also received some compensation. Others who received both apologies and compensation felt glad to have both. Many often added that, of course, they could never make up for the losses. My sympathies and convictions were pulled in response to each of these reasonable points.

As the historian Howard Zinn aptly pointed out, "One cannot be neutral on a moving train."[76] The neutrality with which I hoped to be perceived proved impossible to attain. Within the first five years of research, I found myself part of the story and part of people's lives, at one point even helping reunite brothers who had been largely estranged since Auschwitz. Because of the strong victim–perpetrator binaries circulating during this conflict, I also found myself navigating some very uncomfortable political terrain. A survivor named Leon Vermont warned me about this. Leon had lost much of his family in the deportations, escaping France to the United States only to be drafted into the US army to fight in the Battle of the Bulge. He helped liberate the death camps under the command of General Patton and then interrogated Nazis captured during the liberation. When I explained my research topic, he said, "You are well aware, Sarah, I am sure, that the subject is *très délicat, la SNCF, c'est la France!*" (the SNCF *is* France).[77]

By this Leon meant that the SNCF is a well-loved symbol of France, so any perceived attack on the company could be perceived as attacking the country's honor. In Paris today, one sees almost as many SNCF logos as French flags. In fact, they resemble each other, sharing the same colors and feel. The SNCF maintains a special place in French society; the French are simultaneously proud of and frustrated by their trains (the latter especially during strikes), but if you mention the war, they often defend the company. Hundreds of informal conversations with French coworkers, friends, and strangers helped me better understand the SNCF's unique place in French society and the questions we are still not supposed to ask.

Americans have no easy equivalent. While it may be ubiquitous and long part of the American psyche, no one would likely say that Coca-Cola *is* the United States. Add to this the tremendous place the Vichy period still holds in French memory. It soon became clear to me that the war years hang over France in a way that most Americans cannot understand.[78] With so many violent conflicts in the second half of the twentieth century, World War II may seem like a distant, even if significant, memory. But even today, if you were to try going to a social gathering in Paris and ask what people's parents and grandparents did during the war, you might not be invited back.

This research also at times ensnared me in the political or legal quests of others. When I was invited to the House of Representatives to help educate the team working on the conflict, I found that some—especially the younger staffers—were not especially interested in learning anything new. They had heard that the SNCF once had a role in the deportations and wanted to punish them—discussion closed. The lawyers, on the other hand, exerted pressure. When I was midway through my research, a lawyer working pro bono on the case pressured me to hand over all my research materials. He said that if I wanted to help ensure that history was written correctly, I would give his team everything I had found. I found his request disquieting; lawyers working on active cases have strategic interests in particular versions of past events. Colleagues cautioned me to avoid legal entanglements and to keep clear of such confrontations. The French historian Henry Rousso, for example, refused to testify on the Holocaust restitution cases in France, believing that the system of history and justice ought not to be intertwined in this way. Conversations I had separately with the historians Michael Marrus and Robert Paxton confirmed their preference to avoid legal proceedings and political debates as well. Regarding the SNCF conflict, Marrus expressed concern about how the legal structure disfigured both history *and* justice. He warned that legal battles "draw too tight a circle of legal accounting around an event, thereby distorting not only the memory and historical representation of one part of the Holocaust but losing sight of the wider quest for historical justice."[79]

Legal proceedings are not the place to write histories. During the Eichmann trial, Hannah Arendt also pushed back on using court cases as opportunities to produce histories.[80] They have different aims, different methods, she argued. Richard Wilson similarly notes, "Courts often endorse one version above all others, whereas historians may integrate elements of competing accounts."[81] Even truth commissions, created to help mitigate adversarial legal frameworks and create space for testimony, act, as Ronald Niezen says, as "bad historians."[82] These spaces do have important aims and make significant contributions, but largely not historical ones. French lawyer Corinne Hershkovitch, who represented 250 litigants against the SNCF in France, provides an important caveat. She finds her efforts thwarted by historians who she says insisted that the SNCF had no choice but to participate in the deportations and would not consider other perspectives.[83] In France, she says, the historians completely controlled the story of the past, making it hard for survivors or others to challenge the dominant accounts. Without any attempt to produce such a final account, this book offers a historical appraisal to help readers make sense of the past and think through what, if anything, ought to be done today. Amends-making efforts have the greatest resonance when treated as part of an ongoing effort rather than as culminating events. As Diane Enns observed, "death is irreversible; after genocide and war, the scales of justice cannot be balanced."[84] Bounded approaches push for silence and, in doing so, can entrench power structures and further agendas with a vested interest in certain outcomes or versions of history.

To say that *Last Train to Auschwitz* takes an open-ended approach to justice is not to avoid moral judgments or to promote amnesia. An open-ended approach means acknowledging that the answer to the question "Has justice been served?" will always depend on who, when, and where you ask. An open-ended approach also underscores the inevitability of what Stuart Eizenstat calls "imperfect justice." Those who survived often lost their identities as well as their families and homes. Many lives have been completely defined by a genocide in which the SNCF played an indispensable role.

VOICES FROM THE LAST TRAINS

I first met Daniel at the Mémorial de la Shoah in Paris, where we were both attending the seventieth anniversary ceremony for Convoy 77. Of the nearly eighty convoys that departed from France for the death camps during World War II, Convoy 77 was the last deportation train from Paris to Auschwitz. Daniel found himself aboard this train, which left on July 31, 1944—a month and a half after D-Day. The convoy carried roughly 1,300 people, including 300 children.[85] The deported individuals hailed from thirty-seven countries. While the majority were from Eastern European countries, a few were from Egypt, Palestine, Algeria, Greece, Morocco, or Turkey.

Survivors, descendants, and others participating in the ceremony read the names of the victims of Convoy 77. One very elderly man came up to the podium and stood there for several moments, trying to regain his composure. When it became clear that he would not be able to utter the name of his deported son, a woman retrieved him and helped him sit down. Another person stood up and offered to read his son's name. After the ceremony, George Mayer, one of the event's organizers, invited anyone who had been aboard that last convoy or who had any information about the victims to a meeting in the third-floor conference room. Mayer explained that because the Germans kept poor records after D-Day, we would have to piece together the story of those 1,300 individuals. A website would be created with a page dedicated to each person.[86]

Fifty people crammed into the poorly ventilated room to hear how they could help construct this history. Mayer opened the meeting by sharing the story of his own father, who was a passenger on Convoy 77. His father, thirty-five years old at the time of his deportation, spent nine months at Auschwitz before the liberation. When found, he weighed barely seventy pounds.

I listened from the back row in order to leave room for the survivors. Daniel, even though somewhat hard of hearing, also sat in the back. He was deported on that same convoy at age thirteen along with his brother, then age fifteen. We introduced ourselves and started chatting. I asked him if he knew the woman sitting in the front who had also been on Convoy 77 as a young girl.

"She won't talk to me," he says.

"Why not?" I asked.

"I don't know. She has become more closed in her old age."

They had never formally met.

After the meeting, Daniel scribbled his phone number on a piece of paper, encouraging me to call him if I had any questions. On the way out, I passed his parents' names on the memorial wall among those of the approximately seventy-six thousand other French citizens who were deported to Nazi camps. I called him the next day and made the first of what would be many appointments.

Daniel lives outside Paris in nearby Versailles, the former home of kings and queens. I hopped on a train from the St. Lazare station and arrived thirty minutes later at Versailles Rive Droite. Daniel met me with a welcoming smile. I proudly recounted to him my memory of coming to this very train station one chilly September day, having finished a challenging sixteen-kilometer race from Paris to Versailles. He told me that was pretty impressive, but I felt sheepish two hours later when he told me about his two-week-long death march in January 1945, a roughly six-hundred-kilometer journey from Auschwitz in Poland to the Mauthausen concentration camp in Austria, where his spent his fourteenth birthday.

As we strolled toward his home, just a few blocks from the rail station, he asked about my research. I explained that I study the role of the SNCF in the deportations of Jews during World War II, the company's postwar efforts to make amends, and the ongoing conflict in the United States over whether the company had done enough to entitle it to do business there. He did not know anything about the class action lawsuits and legislation in the United States—he had never sought compensation from the company.

We arrived at his home, and he unlocked the door to the apartment where he had lived for forty-eight years. Because of the dark entryway, my eyes needed a few seconds to adjust. The first object to come into focus was a long, antique wood dining room table that extended the whole length of one wall. Daniel and his wife had fed seven children at this table. The apartment felt stately, self-respecting, well settled, and empty.

The home was very still. Daniel's wife had died ten years earlier—he still wore his wedding ring. He led me into the living room, which had a dark leather couch and a few elegant chairs. The room had the uncomfortable stillness of a space that had once been filled with the gaiety and chaos of a large family but was now quieted with loss and dispersal. The living room looked out over a grassy area with trees and a couple of rose bushes. The opposite wall was covered with photos of his many children, his wife, and an impressive array of grandchildren.

In the coming years, Daniel would speak more about his estrangement from his brother than about any kind of retribution or compensation for his suffering. So it was fitting that he began our first meeting by saying he was both excited and surprised that I was already communicating with his brother, Samuel. He wanted to know how I had found him. I explained that Samuel had responded to my email sent through the United States Holocaust Memorial Museum's third-party contact service.

Daniel said, "We are very different, my brother and I. He is not very communicative. He never told me about your email. He never wanted to provide his testimony and never wanted to have kids. . . . I had seven! . . . My brother and sister thought I was crazy [for having so many children]. After the war, I had nothing. I wanted roots, and I wanted descendants. Also, I did not want the Nazis to win!! So, I had many children." He paused. "I also think my conversion to Catholicism bothered him." Daniel explained that he had always felt Catholic, having grown up in a Catholic country. Many Jewish immigrants in France whose parents were not religious had similar experiences, though few converted. Born French to parents who had received citizenship in 1938, he discovered he was Jewish only when the police came and took away his parents.

He and his brother spoke once a week but had very little to say to each other, which Daniel attributed to their vastly different lives. Samuel and his wife, Elise, live a very quiet life in Alsace. Aging has made their world even smaller. Elise can no longer ride her bike with Samuel, and the stairs up to their apartment are difficult for her. Samuel runs errands, but other than this he rarely leaves their apartment. Daniel, however, lives an active life even as he approaches his nineties. Sometimes during my future visits to France, Daniel and I struggled to find time to meet because of his volunteering, meetings with refugees or students, and the time he spends with his children or visiting aging friends in the hospital. In 2015 Daniel won France's highest medal of honor (L'ordre national de la Légion d'honneur) for the work he did during his retirement on behalf of France's persons with disabilities. Having raised a son with Down syndrome, he wanted to help others. He proudly showed me his medal, the photos, and the speech he gave at the ceremony at Versailles. I would later find that this difference in how the brothers lived their lives was not unusual: among those who survived the death camps, some tried to become invisible, like Samuel and Elise, whereas others responded by living prolifically, like Daniel.

When I first asked Daniel his thoughts on the ongoing conflict involving the French National Railways, he was not sure how to respond. He listened when I summarized the contemporary conflict, first in France and then in the United States, over the SNCF's role in the Holocaust. He paused and said, "I do not see that we can reproach the SNCF in particular or the drivers of the trains. . . . I think the SNCF was simply under constraint, just as I [at Auschwitz] also worked under constraint, though of course under different conditions."[87]

To be angry at the SNCF, he said, would mean he would also have to be angry at the people who turned in his parents, those driving the cars that picked up his parents, the bus drivers who drove them all to the Bobigny (deportation) train station, the train conductors who took them to Auschwitz, and the Church, which had not been particularly helpful. He would also have to be angry at the neighbors who took their furniture. He would go crazy, he said, being mad at all these people.

This is not to say that he was satisfied with the compensation France provided. After the war, he and his siblings had only their lives—no home, no parents, no food, and no clothes. Separated by the war, they did not even have one another. Only in the 1990s did the family receive some financial compensation. Daniel thought the fund could have been administered better because the state made no distinction between losing one parent and losing both. He said there is a real difference when both are murdered: "You have no one," he explained.

Before heading out to lunch, Daniel and I called Samuel. Over the phone, Samuel inquired about the lawsuit against the SNCF and the battle raging in the United States.

When I finished explaining the conflict, he asked, "Why are you polarizing the case in this way?"

"Samuel, I'm not polarizing it," I replied. "I'm just telling you how the conflict is playing out."

He laughed, seemingly enjoying my pushback. He told me that he did not agree with the lawsuits and then encouraged me to call back if I had any questions. He quickly hung up, and Daniel and I went to lunch. Daniel talked about his career as the head of human resources for a large company with more than a thousand employees. He wondered if maybe observing so much suffering during the war had made him want to help other people with their conflicts.

Today, what causes Daniel real distress is not the Holocaust but watching the news about events happening in the Middle East and the refugee crisis in Europe. "I know that look in their eyes. I had it too. They have no idea what is going on." Tearing up, he confessed, "I feel so powerless."

Daniel does his best to contribute. He meets with the refugees in France, supporting them during their difficult transition. He showed me a book filled with their signatures and words of appreciation for his time.

At the end of our first visit, Daniel walked me back to the train station. I asked him if he felt he had cheated death by surviving the Holocaust.

"I did until my wife died of cancer," he said.

He told me his friends are in their nineties, and many are sick. Now he must watch them die. Death is everywhere—again.

"This is why it is good to have young friends, too!" I offered.

"Yes, indeed!"

At the train station we hugged and said our good-byes, both already looking forward to our next visit. I ran my pass through the ticket machine and walked through the turnstile. Daniel followed.

When I noticed that he too had passed through the turnstile, I said, "Wait, did you just pay to take me to the platform?"

"Don't worry," he said nonchalantly. "It costs me almost nothing."

"Why not?"

"I have a pass because I was deported!"

Then he chuckled, saying, "Maybe that's why I'm not mad at the SNCF."

"How much of a discount do you get?" I asked.

"Seventy-five percent," he replied.[88]

"Why not 100 percent? They might as well just give you the full discount."

He paused, smiled wryly, and said, "I guess because I got the first trip for free!"

PART I

The War Years

CHAPTER ONE

The German Occupation

The SNCF as Victim

There was a saying during the war, the wheels have to roll for the war, which means the trains have to keep on going.

—RUTH "MARGOT" DEWILDE, Auschwitz survivor

WHEN CRIMINOLOGIST Nils Christie introduced his concept of the "ideal victim," he placed in our minds the image of a little old lady mugged in broad daylight on her way home from seeing her sick sister.[1] She is "ideal" because her innocence is unquestioned. Her vulnerability makes her worthy of social protection. Transitional justice scholars have also gone on to discuss the dynamics of pure innocence. In both contexts, ideal or "true" victimhood demands total innocence.[2] Diane Enns defines purity as being incapable of causing suffering to others.[3] Seeing children, little old ladies, and innocent families rounded up evokes images of pure innocence.

But what about a train company? Can a corporation ever be a victim? The SNCF could hardly position itself as an ideal or pure victim, but executives did their best to assert claims of victimization when facing accusations in the United States about its Holocaust-complicit past. Speaking in 2011 to critiques of the company's wartime role, former SNCF America president Dennis Douté said, "Assets were plundered and destroyed, its employees and their families threatened, and hundreds of them executed."[4] These words, while factually accurate, did not disclose the more comprehensive truth; instead, it offered a justification and did little to appease those who were still distraught about the company's past. Suggesting any equivalency between lost material assets and hundreds of lives during wartime to participation in the systematic killing of approximately seventy-six thousand individuals does not sit well with many.

This chapter reflects on how the SNCF was able to see itself as a victim of the German occupation. The purpose of this exercise is not to expunge the

SNCF's record or to justify or apologize for the company's actions. Exploring the SNCF's claim to victimhood helps us understand the context in which the SNCF operated. The fields of genocide and postconflict studies have become more comfortable with the overlapping positions many inhabit during mass violence.[5] We cannot know the contours of war and violence if we deny any party its full, complex story. Identifying one group or person as embodying the essence of the crime may satisfy a need to have a readily identifiable perpetrator to hold accountable, but it does not help us understand how the average person or the average company can end up participating in inexpressibly abhorrent acts.

THE SNCF AT THE DAWN OF WAR

In August 1937, when Sarah Federman was eleven years old, the Popular Front voted to nationalize the country's railway network. Léon Blum, the first Jew and the first socialist to serve as prime minister, knew the timing was right to create a singular, coherent railway network throughout France.[6] Private owners of the individual rail companies were on the verge of bankruptcy. The largest, the Chemins de Fer du Nord, belonged to the Rothschild family, which was frustrated by the state-capped ticket prices. Railway construction and maintenance demanded enormous investment, and the price caps made recouping this investment all but impossible. The Rothschilds and other railway owners would be relieved to be able to divest themselves of their losing enterprises and receive lavish compensation for their railway companies.[7]

On January 1, 1938, the state officially created the SNCF (Société Nationale des Chemins de Fer Français) as a conglomerate of five major private rail companies, making the SNCF the largest French company. Robert Henri Le Besnerais, the last general director of the independent Compagnie du Nord line, became the first general director of the SNCF, a position he maintained during the war. The SNCF's ownership was split between the previous owners, who retained a 49 percent share, and the state, which acquired the remaining 51 percent, promising to buy out the private owners over a forty-five-year period. Upon the SNCF's creation, the state controlled the budgets, policies, and appointments to the board. Private owners had no role in the operation of the company.[8] While slightly weighted toward state ownership, however, the SNCF managed its own affairs and billed the state for various activities. In this way, the railways acted like a corporation left to fend for itself during the war. Later, through its subsidiaries, such as Keolis, that bid for contracts internationally, the SNCF also became an international business. Economists might term it a "multinational enterprise," whereas in United Nations parlance the company can be considered a transnational corporation.[9]

In 1938 the national railway employed roughly 500,000 workers, which is more employees than today's United Airlines, American Airlines, Southwest Airlines, and Delta Airlines combined.[10] As of 2021, Amtrak has 17,000 employees. Uniting private individual railroad companies into a single enterprise and coordinating activities without email or even fax machines required tremendous coordination.

From September 1939 to April 1940, France and Germany were engaged in what became known as the Phony War (*drôle de guerre*).[11] During the German invasion of France, the SNCF transported two million French soldiers to stave off the Germans, saw one-fifth of its railway workers drafted, and repaired twenty-two stations hit by German bombs. In panic, SNCF executives moved the Paris-based headquarters to Lamotte-Beuvron in the Sologne region, approximately 150 kilometers southwest of Paris. The rails struggled to transport the two million fleeing French citizens, many from Paris. Unable to meet the demand, the SNCF left many would-be passengers stranded.[12]

Sarah Federman witnessed this exodus at the Gare Montparnasse. Her brother Raymond writes, "There was a mad crowd at the station. People were boarding just any train without even checking where it was going. People were arguing, pushing. It was a real panic."[13] As their mother forced their way into a railcar, "my father behind us was holding onto the hands of Sarah and Jacqueline. It was the first time I had seen my father's love for his daughters. He looked desperate."[14] While not as bad as the deportation trains to come, people had to stand, inhaling the smoke of the engine. People coughed, children cried, "people kept asking where the train was going but no one knew."[15] For the foreign-born Jews, this chaos presaged what was to come. But for now, the Jews found themselves no more or less protected than any other French citizen.

Within a month, France had fallen.

Thirty-five thousand SNCF workers were taken prisoner, more than a thousand were killed, and many others fled.[16] The SNCF's estimated 515,000 employees at the start of 1938 had been reduced to 400,000 cheminots by May 1940.

In September 1940 the government appointed Pierre Eugène Fournier as SNCF president, a position he held through July 1946. Fournier was a technocrat, not a railway man. For three years prior to running the SNCF, he had served as governor of the Bank of France. His background made him an apparently solid choice for this hybrid corporate-government position. Jean Berthelot, an SNCF technician, became the minister of transport under the Vichy regime. Robert Le Besnerais remained director general. In their complementary roles, these three acted, for the most part, as an extension of the state under conditions of war and occupation.

The SNCF under the Occupation

Loss of Control: Rolling Stock

The French government signed an armistice with Germany on June 22, 1940, in Compiègne, the very site where Germany had signed its surrender in 1918.[17] To relieve Germany of the burden of governing all of France, Germany allowed a French puppet government to administer the *zone libre* (the "free zone" in the south of France) and to operate in the occupied zone under German direction. The newly formed Vichy government, named after the spa town where its capital was located, would be instated to manage the free zone in France. At the very least the German occupation needed an impotent France, so it disarmed the French military and corralled the French soldiers into prisoner of war camps.

The SNCF became one of the few French entities permitted to pass between the occupied and unoccupied zones; yet it lacked the freedom this might suggest. Article 13 of the Convention Franco-Allemande d'Armistice requisitioned the French railways and required that the French government preserve and maintain the railways, roads, canals, and costal transportation services. Most important for the SNCF, Article 13 stated, "The French Government will see to it that in the occupied region necessary technical personnel and rolling stock of the railways and other transportation equipment, to a degree normal in peacetime, be retained in service."[18]

The Germans prohibited railway sabotage and required all broken rails to be fixed immediately. After signing the armistice, SNCF director Robert Le Besnerais said the company intended "to obey the letter of the law, in the strict limit of the inevitable."[19] In July, however, a month after the armistice signing, the SNCF directed questions about the terms of the agreement to the Armistice Commission at Wiesbaden and to the German authorities. Its questions concerned its ability to maintain commercial activities after satisfying German demands and the commitment of the French state to pay for the German transports.[20] Early on in the occupation we see the SNCF's pushback against working for free and a fierce protection of its own commercial activities. It soon would feel the weight of the occupation.

At the start of 1940, prior to the armistice, the company's inventory included 60,000 steam locomotives, 450,000 ordinary wagons, and 1,500 passenger cars.[21] By August, the Germans had requisitioned 80,000 of the SNCF's 450,000 wagons and 1,000 locomotives.[22] By December 1940, more than 182,692 SNCF wagons traveled on German rail lines outside France. The SNCF, at this point, had been fully taken over, but, like France more generally, it was allowed to run itself without interference so long as German needs were met first. In other words, during the occupation, the SNCF had a new boss, one that could make any demand, at any time, at any price. As in a typical hostile corporate take-over, executives, not wanting to lose their jobs, may have officially expressed their willingness to accept the new realities, but few, if any, celebrated.

In September 1941, a little more than a year after the armistice, SNCF president Pierre Eugène Fournier reaffirmed, without great enthusiasm, the company's commitment to satisfying German demands: "France, while nonetheless maintaining its reservations, is disposed, in the context of political collaboration, to find a practical solution that allows the SNCF to help Germany so long as the vital needs of France are assured."[23] A bureaucrat by training, Fournier sought a practical way to move forward.

By March 1942, even though the Germans had requisitioned nearly half of the SNCF inventory, the company churned along transporting paying passengers, German soldiers, livestock, war materials, and raw materials (e.g., coal).[24] Workers, who for decades had felt underpaid for such dangerous work (working on coal-fueled railways was especially dangerous), found themselves under even greater burdens, now with a supervising authority that had no interest in their grievances. The Germans suspended the unions, including the railway unions that had long served as a voice for workers.

Even without their unions, SNCF workers had more protection than most. However, these protections and any independence afforded to the company soon weakened and then effectively disappeared after November 1942.[25] The December 7, 1941, bombing of Pearl Harbor made the war a *world* war, and the SNCF felt the reverberations of this shift. The relative freedom experienced by the SNCF enterprise in 1941, diminishing in 1942, plummeted after 1943, when roughly five thousand more German cheminot supervisors arrived.[26] This roughly doubled the railway supervision. Moreover, instead of continuing to be supervised by the Wehrmacht Verkehrsdirektion (WVD, German Railways Armed Forces Traffic Directorate), the Haupt Verkehrsdirektion (HVD, German Head of Transport Management) now supervised the company. The atmosphere changed, and the Germans now controlled more than 50 percent of the organization. SNCF morale collapsed.

The US–British invasion of French North Africa in November 1942 prompted Germany to occupy the formerly "free zone" in southern France. In fully occupied France, the SNCF retained control over only daily management, not executive planning.[27] The Reichsbahn, the German National Railways, began drafting SNCF workers. The early protections of SNCF workers disappeared, and many were arrested, imprisoned, held hostage, or murdered. When Germans began to reassign the SNCF staff, the executives resisted. SNCF managing director Robert Le Besnerais told the Germans that if they wanted more workers, they ought to free the eighteen thousand SNCF prisoners held captive.[28] This was to be one of the last gestures of dissent before the company found itself more fully under Nazi authority. The rolling stock and the company's operators seemed equally valuable to the executive team when the occupying forces moved into the previously designated free zone in the south of France. By 1944, the Wehrmacht Verkehrsdirektion, the department responsible for the transport of German troops, directed the entire railroad.

Various SNCF departments pushed back on German demands, at least initially. On December 29, 1942, for example, Münzer, the German official responsible for French rail activity, wrote a letter to the SNCF, saying, "The spirit of collaboration within the SNCF leaves something to be desired."[29] The French, it appeared, were not happy about their loss of autonomy.

Loss of Control: Billing

The SNCF did not "profit" during the war like some companies did. German companies, such as Hugo Boss, flourished during the war. Hugo Boss's profits soared as his company fulfilled increasing demands with the help of slave labor.[30] For the SNCF, however, the German occupation became an emotional and financial burden, not an opportunity for financial gain. Some cheminots used the occupation to advance their careers, but many simply suffered. By the summer of 1944, the SNCF faced an enormous financial crisis, operating with a deficit of six million francs.[31]

The SNCF did not work for free but had little control over receivables. It billed for all its transports, both to keep the rails running and to demonstrate independence from the Germans. Initially, state-ordered transports would be paid for by the French state, the Vichy government. The SNCF also received payment from German military divisions for transports of coal, munitions, German soldiers, livestock, food, and other resources used to support the war. Although the SNCF billed, the Germans rarely paid the full monies invoiced; in many cases, the SNCF received roughly half of the invoiced amount.[32] This incensed the SNCF executives, who tussled over sums due.

The SNCF, the French (Vichy) government, and the Germans often debated the question of payment.[33] In a letter dated November 8, 1940, for example, the SNCF requested payment for transporting German soldiers. It invoiced the French state, which, it claimed, in July 1940 had agreed to pay on behalf of the Germans. The SNCF and the French state organized a meeting to deliberate the issue. In September, the French minister of the interior, the secretary of finance, and the secretary of communications announced that the Germans would pay directly for the transport of their soldiers. SNCF officials asked which German department they ought to bill. The French state replied that they should bill General Huntziger of the Armistice Commission. When the SNCF invoiced Huntziger's office, however, the Armistice Commission told them that the Germans had never agreed to pay the SNCF for this transport. Huntziger's office wrote, "The SNCF must take on without the right of remuneration all of the constraints resulting from the transports for the German army."[34] Impotent in the face of such bureaucratic maneuvers, the company found that the costs of war weighed heavily. As the war progressed, the demands on the SNCF more than quintupled. The Germans pushed the company to its limits, and the SNCF found its proverbial hands bound—lacking control over its rates and rolling stock as well as its personnel.

Loss of Control: Personnel

The Germans understood that the SNCF could operate at a financial loss but could not operate without its cheminots. Therefore, immediately after the June 22, 1940, armistice, the Germans liberated hundreds of SNCF workers who had been arrested for participating in suspected acts of sabotage, missing identity papers, passing the demarcation line, undertaking communist activities, and engaging in altercations with German soldiers. The Germans decided that releasing these "criminals" would be worth the risk if in exchange they could count on timely deliveries. They calculated correctly; most cheminots caused little trouble—at first.

By 1943 the Germans needed even more resources to support their campaign throughout Europe; they started sending SNCF workers to help meet this demand. In March 1943, the German delegate of the minister of communications wrote to the French minister of the interior and to the secretary of industrial production and communication requesting that the SNCF provide ten thousand workers to support German railroads.[35] This included five thousand train conductors and about the same number of workshop workers. Of these, 2,700 refused or left the company. To stop this loss of his cheminots, SNCF president Fournier had the SNCF train unemployed men who volunteered to go to Germany.[36] First informally through what was called a relève ("relief" workers) and then later through a program titled Service du Travail Obligatoire (STO, forced labor service), the Germans drafted roughly between eighteen thousand and twenty-four thousand SNCF workers.[37]

In exchange for their displacement, the cheminots initially received some physical protection. In November 1943, German authorities reconfirmed their commitment to protect the railway workers by promising not to take SNCF workers hostage. By 1944, however, when German defeat seemed likely and railway sabotage increased, this protection of SNCF workers diminished. On April 2, 1944, for example, German soldiers assassinated twenty-two SNCF agents and their families in response to acts of sabotage. Two days after the incident, the French ambassador from the occupied zone issued a formal protest to General Feldmarschall Karl Rudolf Gerd von Rundstedt recounting the events: "At 22h45 [10:45 p.m.] military transport train 9872 going from Baisieux-Tit to Amiens was derailed because of a rupture in the railway caused by an explosion at KM 7,500."[38] No one on the train was hurt, and none of the military supplies were stolen. "At 11p.m., in ASCQ where they had stopped, the head of the station, Monsieur Carre, called his night agents to stop the train traffic on track 2. A German officer from the derailed train, and several other German soldiers, walked into Carre's office and shot three station agents, gravely injuring Monsieur Carre and two others. The soldiers then went into the village, woke up 22 other SNCF workers in their homes and killed them."[39]

The event shocked the company and the French government because the SNCF had, until then, been largely protected from such butchery. The French ambassador wrote, "It is the first time since the occupation of France by German troops that such things have occurred."[40] He declared that these unjustified deaths would result in grave consequences, including the withdrawal of support for the German effort. The SNCF directors tried to save those cheminots condemned to death for participation in the sabotage. The rift between the SNCF and the Germans increased, and relations worsened. The war demanded more of everything, both from the company and from the railway workers, who found themselves increasingly under German control. To say that the SNCF operated independently during the war would be untrue. SNCF workers ultimately served as indentured servants to the German occupier, at first protected only for their instrumental worth and later discarded when seen as too troublesome. The company operated at a loss, rarely recuperating costs, and often found its rolling stock taken away. By the war's end, for example, of the 172,438 covered railcars maintained by SNCF before the war, 6,125 had been destroyed and 116,381 had been removed by the occupying forces. Of the SNCF's 17,058 prewar steam engines, by the war's end 250 had been destroyed and 3,288 had been requisitioned by the German occupying forces.[41]

For a company, these conditions were clearly unsustainable. But to suggest that this company suffered as a *victim* during the war can sound like an attempt to draw a moral equivalence to the suffering of individuals. A company cannot "suffer" or be a "victim," especially when its losses are measured against the murder and torture of individuals. Those working on other cases at the intersection of corporate accountability and postconflict studies may see similar tensions. Contemporary debates demonstrate how bestowing *personhood* on a corporation invites such moral equivalences: the loss of profits to the loss of lives. Some people in France and the United States ardently resisted such equivalences when the company sought sympathy for its wartime losses.

The SNCF's victim status starts wobbling even more when we examine the deportations. The following section describes how the Nazi agenda to exterminate the Jews and other undesirables infiltrated France and eventually the SNCF. Understanding the SNCF's role in the deportations requires first understanding the state of Jews in France at the dawn of World War II.

FRANCE AND JEWS

During World War I, France saw a generation nearly decimated. France needed young families to sustain and rebuild the country. To build this workforce, France invited industrious Eastern Europeans, many of whom were ethnically but not religiously Jewish, to immigrate. Eastern Europeans fleeing poverty and persecution in their home countries responded eagerly to this invitation.

The promise of financial opportunity and liberty proved short-lived for these new arrivals. The economic downturn in the 1930s incited France to turn on its recent immigrants—who now made up 70 percent of the Jewish population—and close the door to new ones.[42] To preserve the few existing jobs for French citizens, the country severely restricted immigration and made acquiring (and, soon, maintaining) nationality nearly impossible. By the time the Germans arrived, France had already begun making itself inhospitable to foreigners, both Jewish and non-Jewish.[43]

In the summer of 1940, the French government began writing and implementing antisemitic legislation. Marrus and Paxton identified 143 antisemitic French laws generated by the Vichy government.[44] Much has been written about the isolation of Jews from French society; they were barred from swimming pools, parks, libraries, restaurants, cultural activities, and movie theaters and allowed to shop or use phone booths only at certain times. Jews also had a permanent curfew. On July 22, 1940, Vichy created a commission charged with revoking naturalizations issued since 1927; fifteen thousand French citizens and six thousand Jews lost their citizenship.[45] This meant that many immigrant families that had been granted nationality would lose this status and the rights that went with it. Soon, Jews in the occupied territories had to wear the yellow Star of David whenever they were outside their homes.[46]

To restrict the rights of people, one first had to know who they were. Today, visitors to the Mémorial de la Shoah in Paris can see the thousands of French police file cards, stacked neatly in wooden boxes, used to identify and count France's Jews. The first census of the Jews in France began in June and July of 1941. French citizens helped; the government received more than three million letters from lay people denouncing their neighbors, coworkers, and "friends" as Jewish. Given that the Jewish population of wartime France was not even half a million people, these three million denunciation letters from the public demonstrate the eagerness with which much of the public participated in the removal of the Jews.

SNCF's Protection of Jewish Cheminots

In the summer of 1940, the Germans began applying their antisemitic policies to the SNCF. On July 24, 1940, a Mr. Goeritz from the WVD wrote to Le Bernerais, the director general of the SNCF, telling him "to abstain in the future from delegating people of Jewish race or origin to attend negotiations or conferences with himself or other officers or functionaries of the WVD." Five days later, Le Bernerais responded, without protest, saying that he had passed along this "useful" information to all SNCF departments and regions. Legal adviser Eric Freedman, who found these documents in the SNCF archives, pointed out the total lack of pushback from the SNCF.[47] He says the company could have simply stated that it had no way of knowing who among its employees was Jewish. Perhaps it already kept such records, he surmised, even before the Germans required a list of Jewish employees.[48]

Three months after that correspondence, a law enacted on October 3, 1940, prevented Jews from serving in all public functions or as heads of public companies. SNCF president Fournier suggested that indispensable engineers, such as the well-known Henri Lang, who was head electrician for the Paris-Lyon line, be transferred to subordinate positions.[49] In spite of this and the strong *esprit de famille* within the SNCF, on July 20, 1941, the personnel director of the SNCF reported the existence of the 121 Jewish workers to the Germans.[50] According to Ludivine Broch, "by mid-August 1941, eighty-two Jews working in the SNCF were to be fired." This left another twelve awaiting their fate.[51] Some, like Pierre Levy, were forced into early retirement. Other cheminots reported as "Jewish" requested that the SNCF remove the designation. In rare cases, the Germans "forgave" the Jewishness of an SNCF worker, likely because they needed his expertise. On July 6, 1942, for example, Germans liberated SNCF employee Julien Lemme, arrested earlier for not wearing his yellow star.[52] In at least one case, SNCF managing director Robert Le Besnerais spoke on behalf of an employee; he saved cheminot Paul Ehrmann by arguing that he was not Jewish.[53] Such interference on behalf of Jewish employees was inconsistent. SNCF's president, Pierre Eugène Fournier, refused to assign a cheminot named Robert Lévi to a post in the free zone, allowing him only to go on leave without pay. Lévi lived off his retirement package, resentful of Fournier's failure to protect him.[54]

While advocating for Jewish employees did not seem to put SNCF executives in any personal danger, the bureaucratic process required to save a life was long and uncertain. The minister of transport, Jean Berthelot, attempted to save Henri Lang, one of the company's most respected directors. On August 16, 1941, the SNCF pleaded before the Commissariat Général aux Questions Juives (CGQJ, Commissariat-General for Jewish Affairs), the division handling Jewish issues, not to deport engineer Henri Lang. It argued that Lang, a World War I veteran, provided exceptional scientific services. The Commissariat declined the request. Friends pleaded with Lang to make his way to the free zone, but out of a sense and pride and duty he refused to leave his post.[55] He was arrested in December 1941 in his home in front of his wife and two girls and then deported on the *first* train to Auschwitz, on March 27, 1942.[56] Lang died six weeks after arriving at Auschwitz. The SNCF sent his daughter Catherine to the free zone and tended to her in numerous ways, including inviting her to lavish dinners and helping her get into school in Lyon.[57] In 2001 Catherine Béchillon argued that the company could have simply transferred Jewish employees to the free zone, saving many lives, including that of her father.[58] This would have kept them safe for at least a little while longer; when Germany eventually took control of all of France, nowhere would be safe. The lack of strategic maneuvering makes the SNCF seem acquiescent to the antisemitism, only interfering on behalf of a favored colleague.

German Demands to Remove Undesirables

In 1942 the SNCF had to transport more than paying passengers, livestock, fuel, soldiers, and armaments in support of the Germans' war effort. It was now called upon to remove undesirables from France and to take them to one or another of the German extermination or concentration camps. The Vichy government, on behalf of the Germans, soon directed the SNCF to begin transporting political prisoners, Jews, and others.[59] The SNCF transported an estimated 86,827 of these individuals to Germany during the war. A majority eventually died of overwork, torture, or execution. The SNCF did not celebrate these transports—they were both tragic and costly. The armistice agreement required the SNCF to organize and operate these trains, so any resistance would have put the company at war with the occupier—a dangerous prospect.

The order for the removal of Jews from France came from Germany via Heinrich Himmler's Reichssicherheitshauptamt (RSHA, Reich Main Security Office) in Berlin. Adolf Eichmann then organized the deportation of the Jews through the RSHA's Bureau of Jewish Affairs.[60] The Germans determined that deportations from France—totaling 100,000 Jewish adults, or roughly one-third of France's Jewish population—would begin in 1942.[61] Theodor Dannecker, the SS officer responsible for organizing and supervising the French roundups, estimated that this would require the transportation of fifteen thousand Jews per month until completed.[62]

THE SNCF's CLAIM OF VICTIMHOOD

The SNCF clearly did not initiate the deportations or the antisemitic policies. Ultimately, the SNCF agreed to fulfill the German demands as required by the armistice, although the leadership demonstrated no special enthusiasm for fulfilling these demands. Letters back and forth arguing over payments made clear that the SNCF would not work for the Germans free of charge. The SNCF ended the war operating under a huge deficit and with destroyed assets. Roughly two thousand SNCF workers had been killed for acts of subversion, and thousands had been displaced abroad. Some SNCF employees leveraged the professional opportunities presented by the war, but most simply struggled under its demands and risks. They survived with little food and under constant threat—a harrowing existence. In this way, they were much like the average French person: tired, afraid, and for the most part more concerned with their own survival than with the concerns of their neighbors. Yet the weariness, fear, or lack of interest among SNCF workers regarding the deportations had very grave consequences for Daniel, Samuel, Estéra, and thousands of others, even if France's Jews overall had a greater chance of survival than those in other countries.

Roughly 90 percent of French-born Jews survived the Holocaust. France deported roughly 25 percent of all its Jews, a comparatively small number when considering that Hungary and the Netherlands almost completely exterminated their Jewish populations. What explains this relatively high survival rate? Though Philippe Pétain stood as the chief of state during the occupation, by April 1942 Pierre Laval, a French politician and cabinet member of the Vichy regime, acted as the head of government.[63] Laval was no friend of the Jew or those fighting for a free France; in 1943 he became the head of the Milice, the Vichy police force created to combat the Resistance. He firmly supported the German occupation and agenda and hoped to satisfy the Germans by deporting the stateless foreign-born Jews.[64] At the same time, Laval wanted to "protect" French-born Jews because he feared losing overall French support, especially if he deported war veterans. This hesitancy to commit to the eradication of all Jews threw off Germany's schedule and roundup plans.[65]

Eichmann, as head of the Bureau of Jewish Affairs, for example, threatened to exclude France from the roundups because of a debacle over schedules.[66] His threat came after a disorganized deportation train departure on July 15, 1942. Correspondence between Eichmann and Heinz Röthke, the SS officer working with Dannecker, showed that, "when a deportation train missed its scheduled departure from Bordeaux July 15, 1942, Eichmann was furious. He telephoned the *Judenreferat* in Paris to deliver a blast that must have withered Heinz Röthke, the new man in charge."[67] Eichmann called the affair "disgraceful" and said to Röthke something to the effect of "Well, if you cannot do it, maybe we should scratch France off the list of countries capable of removing its Jews." Röthke apparently dissuaded him.[68] The trains ran smoothly after this. Had the French government pushed back just a little more, perhaps thousands of lives could have been saved and, for the living, decades of postwar suffering avoided.

On the other hand, Eichmann's threat to exclude France from the deportations may have been empty words, because the Germans had made clear that eventually they planned to take all of France's Jews—except those under sixteen. Laval possibly offered to add the Jewish children of immigrant families to make up for the loss in numbers.[69] He also may have done so to avoid the administrative hassle of caring for all these newly created orphans.[70] Laval's eagerness to include those under sixteen apparently unsettled even the Germans. Laval responded by saying only that he had given the Allies a chance to take in these troublesome Jews and they had refused; he also wrote to foreign newspapers explaining that sending the children with their parents was a matter of "national health and hygiene" and would free French soil of this overpopulation of immigrants.[71] The Vichy government did not want to deal with the young children in the camps and on the trains because little children are harder to manage. Eichmann eventually acquiesced, accepting Laval's suggestion to take the children. As a result, in 1942 French police—often harshly—rounded up 6,000 children, of whom 1,032 were under the age of six, and the SNCF helped ship them to Auschwitz. The six- to twelve-years-olds accounted for 2,557 of this group of deportees, and the oldest, between thirteen and seventeen, totaled 2,464.[72] In total, between March 27, 1942, and August 18, 1944, the French—via the SNCF—facilitated the transport of approximately 76,000 deportees (from France), including a total of 11,400 children on an estimated seventy-nine convoys.[73]

Sarah, eleven just before the war, was now sixteen. She and her sister were counted among these children. Forced into Convoy 21, they began their one-way trip on August 19, 1942. The inclusion of French immigrant children enabled Dannecker to almost reach his goal of 100,000 Jewish deportees from France.

VOICES FROM THE LAST TRAINS

In 1942, knowing she had to flee Paris, Estéra moved her two daughters and her son from their home, 14 rue des Écouffes in the Marais, and placed them in a home for Jewish children in the eighteenth arrondissement of Paris. Born French, her children would have some special privileges, such as being able to go out and receive visits from their parents.

The Gestapo and the French police, however, started using these "visiting days" to round up the remaining adults. During one raid, Estéra Zyto hid in the armoire in her daughters' room. An officer entered and, seeing just two girls crying, walked out. Estéra knew she could not visit again. Believing her children were protected, Estéra immediately left for the free zone to reunite with her husband. Her children, however, were far from safe; the Vichy government would soon come for them.

Estéra never made it to the free zone; neither did her husband, Lazare Skornik. Lazare had his one-way trip to Auschwitz from France, via Drancy, on Convoy 70, on March 27, 1944. Knowing he was dead, Estéra nonetheless left her children at the Jewish home and followed her husband's instructions to bring whatever gold or valuables she had and exchange them for money at a location he had noted in Lyon. There, French police met Estéra at the door having already discovered Jews using this site to convert possessions into cash.

Estéra found herself in Lyon at a most treacherous moment. SS Captain and Gestapo member Klaus Barbie, "the Butcher of Lyon," wanted to finish the job of deporting the Jews. So he prevented German soldiers from using trains to retreat during the D-Day onslaught and demanded that the Gestapo and French police cram roughly 650 people (438 men, 12 children, and 200 women), including Estéra, onto a deportation train.[74] Without allowing a word of good-bye to her children, the French police placed her on what would become the last convoy from France—number 78—traveling from Lyon directly to Auschwitz. Her train departed August 11, 1944, two months after D-Day and two weeks before the liberation of Paris.

On July 31, 1944, two weeks prior to Estéra's departure, the last convoy from Paris to Auschwitz—Convoy 77—had left the Drancy internment camp. Two young brothers, Daniel and Samuel, found themselves aboard this train. They both had grown up seeing themselves as French. "The word 'synagogue' wasn't even in my vocabulary," Daniel once explained to me. They and their younger sister, Sophie, were all born in France and spoke French even to their Yiddish-speaking parents. Their parents had moved from Poland in the 1920s when France welcomed immigrants to supplement the post–World War I labor shortage. To provide for the family, their father found a job working seven days a week at a metal company. This left him little time or energy to spend with the children, but his work allowed the children to want for nothing and to enjoy (at least temporarily) the freedom of living in France. Prior to the occupation, the company transferred the family to a worksite in what would become the free zone

Lou's brother, Marcel; her sister, Clara; their mother, Estéra; and Lou. Photo taken in June 1945, a year after Estéra returned from Bergen-Belsen. (Courtesy of Lucienne Helwaser)

during the occupation. When the Germans invaded France, the family, unfortunately, moved back to Paris for "safety."

In Paris, on Thursday, February 19, 1943, Daniel spent his twelfth birthday at home celebrating with his family; the children had no school on Thursdays. The police interrupted their celebration, however, knocking on the door and asking his parents to get into the car so that they could be taken to the Prefecture to check their identification papers. One of Daniel's schoolmates had likely denounced the family, his sister later said, but they probably had no idea of the consequences. Daniel recalls their departure: "Without violence and with no more than a casual 'au revoir,' my parents got into the car."

With the parents gone, Daniel stayed home with five-year-old Sophie after fourteen-year-old Samuel hopped in the car to help his parents with translations. Their parents and Samuel waited for hours in the Prefecture. Whether his parents knew what awaited them, Samuel did not know. At the time, he believed that they might be called to engage in forced labor. During the interminable wait, Samuel said he felt empowered when a disgruntled policeman was forced to accompany him to the bathroom. The sense of power proved ephemeral. The day ended with police escorting his parents out one door and sending Samuel home alone to his siblings. No explanations. No promises.

Not long after, another car stopped in front of their home, this time taking the children. Daniel, realizing his parents would not be returning, went into a state of shock that would last more than two years. Understanding nothing about the events unfolding before her eyes, young Sophie did not shed a tear. The police delivered the children to a Union Générale des Israelites de France (UGIF, General Union of the Israelites of France) building; while this organization had many purposes, Daniel said it was used to separate foreign-born from French-born Jews. "There, within a few hours and without violence, a family was torn apart," recalls Daniel.

Sophie, too young for school, was placed with a French Christian foster family in Houdan; Daniel went to an orphanage, and Samuel was sent to a children's home managed by the UGIF. During holidays, Daniel mostly stayed at his school while others went home on weekends to see their parents. He felt stabs of pain when they returned with gifts and food—items that showed they had parents and parental love. Daniel could not yet think of himself as an orphan.

As the children tried to make sense of their surroundings, SS Brunner, operating from the Drancy internment camp, was informed that the Allies had landed at Normandy. He wanted to fill his convoys as quickly as possible. He ordered the police and the Gestapo to round up the remaining Jewish children. Even though the Allies had landed in full force in Normandy in June 1944, France remained under German control for some time. The Allies advanced east to attack the strategic targets necessary to win the war rather than south toward Paris, which would not be liberated until August. Convoys would continue out of France until the end, contributing to the murder of thousands more.

During July 1944, between D-Day and the liberation of Paris, Daniel's school was let out for summer vacation. "It was the shortest vacation I ever had," Daniel recalls. With nowhere else to go, he and Samuel went to UGIF's Lamarck Center in Paris. Within days of his arrival, between July 23 and July 24, buses lined up in front of the twelve different student houses and transported all three hundred children to the Drancy internment camp. The boys had no idea they had begun the very same journey taken by their parents a year and a half earlier. Nor did they know how their sister was faring. Only years later would they learn of the abuse she had endured during this period.

Even though the Allies had arrived to liberate France, the boys were taken to the fully functioning Drancy internment camp. French police and the Gestapo "checked in" their belongings upon arrival and sent them to dorm rooms.

"Except for having to live in close proximity, I have very few memories of the camp," says Daniel. "Perhaps because we stayed for such a short time or perhaps because what happened afterwards was so much worse; it suppressed everything that happened before."

On July 31, 1944, French buses and bus drivers carried Daniel and Samuel to the Bobigny train station just outside Paris. SNCF workers operated in the background, preparing the trains for departure. Without violence, the French police, supervised by armed German soldiers, pushed adults, including the elderly, and children into the merchandise wagons. With such little legs, the children needed help climbing in. The wagons had two cisterns, one with potable water and another for waste.

"We soon realized there would not be room for us all to sit down at the same time," Daniel recalls. The small opening for air had been mostly covered over, making it hard to breathe in the hot August temperatures. Once the doors were locked from the outside, they found themselves in the dark, packed together like produce.

No one knew they were aboard the last train from Paris to Auschwitz.

CHAPTER TWO

The Deportations

The SNCF as Perpetrator

The Nazis may have killed everyone, but the SNCF wrapped them up and delivered them.

—HARRIET TAMEN, lawyer

IMMEDIATELY AFTER THE WAR, most French people could strongly empathize with the SNCF's representation of itself as a victim of the occupation; they too had suffered personally and materially under German and Vichy rule. But by the turn of the millennium, the SNCF would more often find itself seen not as a victim but as a perpetrator—especially in the United States. On July 30, 2013, almost sixty-nine years to the day after Convoy 77 departed Paris for Auschwitz, New York senator Charles Schumer proposed the Holocaust Rail Justice Act to the US Senate.[1] Litigants (survivors and descendants) and their lawyers who had found no recourse in French or American courts supported the act, which would authorize district courts to pursue lawsuits against the railroad division of the French government. With this bill, they could sidestep the Foreign Sovereign Immunities Act (FSIA), which prevented US district courts from seeking damages from the SNCF directly.[2]

Even though the bill's introductory text suggests that all railways complicit in the Holocaust could be held accountable, the congressional findings speak only of the SNCF. The act states (among other things) that the French National Railways during World War II:

(1) operated independently,
(2) collaborated willingly,
(3) determined the conditions, cleaned the transports, and
(4) conducted the trains that carried deportees and more than seventy-five thousand others for a profit.[3]

Even though the bill did not pass, its existence and related media announce-ments promoted an image of the SNCF as an extension of the Nazi regime. This chapter considers these accusations, among others, with the goal of en-riching simplified public debates.

THE QUESTION OF INDEPENDENCE AND WILLING COLLABORATION

The Holocaust Rail Justice Act's first claim was that the SNCF maintained autonomy during the occupation. Georges Ribeill and Michel Margairaz inter-preted the Franco-German Armistice as forcing the SNCF to operate exclu-sively under the authority of Germany and the French government.[4] The HVD managed all operations of the trains. Wieviorka points out that while the Ger-mans oversaw the scheduling, the SNCF retained ownership of its materials (e.g., trains, wagons).[5] Retaining any ownership created a certain amount of jealousy within the Vichy regime. Other French government agencies per-ceived the SNCF as having a bit more independence than they did.[6] Marie-Noëlle Polino, formerly with the Association pour l'Histoire des Chemins de Fer en France (AHICF, Association of French Railroad History), and now an employee of the SNCF, explained to me that "after the armistice treaty, SNCF was allowed to operate trains for the French economy only when all demands of the German armies and authorities had been satisfied. In this sense, they did [everything] the Germans ordered to get the freedom to have their own transport schedules; for instance, trains for French civilians."[7]

The SNCF maintained as much independence as possible, showing no interest in German interference in their affairs, and, accordingly, the Germans at first demonstrated little interest in overinvolving themselves in the affairs of the company. By occupying rather than conquering France, the Germans saved resources. According to Broch, "Germans wanted to control the SNCF but only from afar, enough to ensure that they could make the most of the French economy without wasting men and materials on setting up an intense supervisory system."[8] In short, "German control, French execution."[9] In 1940, after the armistice, the Nazis briefly set up a transportation division in Paris but within a month returned all control, except for coastal operations, to the French. As a result, from 1940 to 1941, the SNCF fulfilled (and billed for) all German requests while retaining majority control over its operations. The SNCF often consulted the Vichy government, rather than the Germans, regard-ing its activities. During these years, the Germans rarely issued orders, but when they did, the SNCF did not welcome German involvement in its affairs.

While occasionally sending disgruntled responses to German demands (as noted in chapter 1), the SNCF cooperated more than it resisted, fulfilling most

German orders on time and with relatively little supervision. This worked out well for the Germans, who had few resources to invest in France. When the occupation began, a mere sixty thousand German soldiers arrived in France to oversee forty million people. Only six thousand Germans monitored the roughly 515,000 SNCF workers that the company employed at the beginning of the war, in 1939.[10] By the end of 1943, the number of German monitors would increase to thirty-four thousand.[11]

At the start of the occupation, running such a complex operation with so few German overseers required complicity on many levels, including a variety of insiders who became necessary accomplices.[12] The German railway engineers, many of whom had retired shortly before the war, found themselves, at least initially, getting along surprisingly well with some of the French engineers.[13] Because many SNCF workers were cheminots first and French patriots second, an easy, simpatico relationship developed between some railway men from the two countries. At times, German engineers protected the SNCF workers in the face of the Gestapo, and some cheminots even tried to persuade the Germans to join the Resistance.[14] However, as the war advanced and tensions increased, such geniality subsided. In particular, the SNCF workers did not appreciate the increased control over their operations that occurred from 1942 on.

A question posed by those determining present-day accountability is how this shifting autonomy affected the deportations. Many deportation trains left during the period of relative independence. The first departed France on March 26, 1942, four months before the Vichy government and the Nazis increased their surveillance of the SNCF. Forty-four deportation convoys left France in 1942, most leaving *before* November, when restrictions increased in response to the Allied landing in Morocco.

Organizing Deportations

The bill also accused the SNCF of organizing the deportations. The Germans ordered and then supervised the SNCF cheminots who arranged, managed, and drove the deportee transports as far as a town called Novéant, on the German border.[15] After studying the SNCF archives, Christian Bachelier concluded that, "apart from the timetables, the SNCF's Central Movement Services did not decide very much. The planning of the convoys—number of cars, hay, pitchers, toilet buckets—all came from the Ministry of Interior."[16]

In 1942 Eichmann brought to the RSHA the individuals in charge of organizing the deportations in France, the Netherlands, and Belgium. At this meeting, organizers decided that 100,000 French Jews would be deported from both the occupied and unoccupied zones.[17] When SS Captain Theodor Dannecker (representing Adolf Eichmann in the RSHA in charge of Jewish matters) returned to Paris on June 15, 1942, he communicated the deportation plan to the French authorities, reducing the number by more than half, to forty thousand.[18] Dannecker maintained regular contact with the HVD in Paris, the German division overseeing the SNCF.[19]

Few archival documents remain that detail the SNCF's participation in the Jewish deportations. One report summarizes a series of meetings between July 15, 1942, and August 4, 1942, with Vichy, the Occupier, police, and the SNCF's Head of Technical Delegation convened to discuss the deportations. The SNCF technician (whose name remains unknown) expressed a desire for discretion in the way the trains were named and concern regarding the less than precise programming the Germans had in mind. This SNCF technician allegedly selected the French term used for the deportation trains, Transports IAPT (Israelites, Allemand, Polonais, Tchèque; Transport of Israelites, Germans, Polish, Czechs; in German, *Sonderzüge* [special trains]).[20] The convoy was organized to transport 1,000 deportees and 150 guards. SNCF workers corresponded with the local French prefectures about these "special" trains.[21] Recognizing that the sight of these wagons would horrify observers, the delegation decided to use smaller, less visible rail stations. This suggests that they knew the nature of their crimes.

Foreign-born Jews arrive at the gare d'Austerlitz station during a deportation action from Paris, 1941. (Copyright United States Holocaust Memorial Museum, courtesy of Serge Klarsfeld, Beate Klarsfeld Foundation)

The Vichy government and the SNCF's senior executives became increasingly involved in the deportations. By the summer of 1942, Vichy organized the wagons while the local prefectures managed the transports as well as the refueling.[22] On September 30, 1942, SNCF president Pierre Eugène Fournier presided over a meeting of his Conseil d'Administration. A carbon copy of the meeting's minutes mentions four trains of "Israelites" departing from Beaune-la-Rolande, Oleron, Pithiviers, and Portet-St-Simon to the east and from Bourget, near the Drancy internment camp, from which most detainees departed for Auschwitz.[23]

Who exactly had responsibility for these trains? Toward the end of the war, we see German officers presiding, with the SNCF enacting their plans. Looking specifically at Convoy 77, the officers listed as responsible included the German officers Adolf Otto Eichmann, Alois Brunner, Heinz Röethke, Helmut Knochen, and Ernst Brüeckler. Vichy officials also participated in the organization of Convoy 77: Louis Pellepoix de Darquier, commissioner of Jewish affairs, and Jean Leguay, a senior police official.[24] SNCF officials clearly had a chain of command above them. They did not operate independently.

Conditions of Travel

The Holocaust Rail Justice Act states that the SNCF determined the horrific conditions in which Daniel, Samuel, and approximately seventy-six thousand others traveled. Samuel said the voyage to Auschwitz was "not so bad." They had some straw on the floor of the wagon and room to sit down. They even had some food and water. His brother, Daniel, says, "Oh, Samuel always makes it sound like we were on a vacation!" Daniel remembers the voyage differently. He recalls the discomfort of having to stand, the indignity of having to defecate in front of others, and the cries of babies and small children. But on some things the brothers agreed. Both sadly recalled the baby born at the Drancy internment camp, who then traveled in the railcar with them. Like many convoys, Convoy 77 traveled for four days and three nights with the one air hole boarded up. The August heat became unbearable. Deportation trains rarely had priority on the tracks, often stopping for hours to allow freight, military, or passenger transports to pass; sometimes they were brought to a halt because someone had sabotaged the rails.

This section considers the SNCF's ability to determine these conditions, which varied from convoy to convoy. First, a note about the kinds of railcars used. *Within* France, the SNCF transported deportees from roundup locations to various internment camps mostly via third-class passenger cars. The first convoy that left France for Auschwitz in 1942 was also a third-class passenger train, as was the last train to depart from Lyon (Convoy 78), which carried

Estéra.[25] When he became responsible for the Final Solution in France, SS Captain Theodor Dannecker issued orders that the deportees travel in what we now call cattle cars.

Third-class passenger trains eventually proved too small and expensive. In addition, the Germans found the many doors and windows in passenger cars harder to guard; passenger trains required two hundred guards. As a result, the second convoy, which departed on June 5, 1942, and subsequent convoys carried deportees in cattle cars that required far less supervision and were far harder to escape from.[26] These convoys had been used to transport men in the Franco-Prussian war and during World War I, and many of these same cars transported French soldiers to fight Germany. Some wagons still had painted on their exteriors (and still bear today) the maximum number of horses or soldiers the car could carry, often forty men or eight horses. During the Holocaust deportations, these cars were crammed with upward of one hundred individuals.

Some may notice the anachronistic use of the term "cattle cars," which emerged mostly after the war. British English refers to them as wagons, and in American English they may be called freight cars. In French they are sometimes referred to as merchandise cars (*les wagons de merchandise*). Many of today's American-based survivors often use the term "cattle car," and similar terms were used during the war. In a note that she threw from her deportation train, however, Madeline Herscu used the phrase *à bestiaux*, animal wagon, to describe the mode in which she found herself traveling.[27] Simone Veil, a survivor of the Auschwitz-Birkenau concentration camp and former president of the European Parliament and member of the Constitutional Council of France, similarly described them as *wagons à bestiaux*.[28]

Victims traveled in these underequipped convoys all over Europe, suggesting that the SNCF did not establish the poor conditions—but neither did the company seem to resist them. Prior to Dannecker's takeover of the deportations from France, the SNCF may have had more freedom in determining conditions.[29] With Dannecker in charge, however, the SNCF either received commands directly from the Germans or had them handed down via the French government. The information was then communicated through the French police and eventually to the SNCF.

A telegram from the Interior of the Second Police Office to the Prefecture in Toulouse dated July 30, 1942, stated, "The train will be composed of two third class animal wagons containing 30 passengers and two guards. Arrange with straw. . . . Assure the installation in each wagon of drinkable water and sanitation pails."[30] Correspondence within the SNCF discussed the straw for the wagons, the slop buckets, and how refueling would take place.[31] Discussions also occurred between French police. A telegram between French police divisions discussed the conditions similarly: "Arrange the wagons with straw, Vichy's office of nourishment authorizes direct debit for the minimum amount necessary. Assure the installation of each convoy, a pitcher of drinkable water, a sanitary pail. This can be bought or furnished from your department—This material will be delivered from a train at the Tournus train station and recuperated by those in my charge."[32]

The phrase *bureau des fourrages* in the telegram referred to the office that managed the nourishment, and the message used the word for animal feed, not human food, suggesting yet another step in the process of dehumanization. On July 4, 1942, when the French government executed Dannecker's deportations orders in Bordeaux, an official told M. Charron, the provisions intendant, that in four days his office should have fourteen days of provisions ready for five hundred people, to include:

- enough soldier biscuits for seven days
- 1,000 kg of green beans
- 1,000 kg of flour
- 50 kg of coffee
- 65 kg of margarine
- cheese and salted meat if possible.[33]

Rarely if ever did deportees receive this full amount. The provisions they received often proved barely edible for man or beast; rotten tomatoes and fruit often made them sick. With water scarce, one Jewish deportee said, the sardines and dried sausage were too salty to risk eating.[34] Other survivors recalled receiving little food, if any, while on the trains. The SNCF did not seem to be included in these conversations about the quality or quantity of food provided to the deportees.

Witnesses

People nearby began to notice and comment on the conditions among the deportees that they witnessed. In a letter dated August 28, 1942, a manager in Tarn-et-Garonne (the southwest region of France) wrote to that department's prefecture expressing concern about the conditions: "I have the honor of informing you that the departure of 84 foreign Israelite workers has left Septfonds this morning from the Caussade station. It is unfortunate that the organization of this convoy had been very poorly done to the point where 84 men were confined in one wagon while three other wagons served for baggage. It seems that it would make more sense and it would be more humane to put

21 men in each wagon with their baggage, which would permit normal hygienic conditions."[35]

Many others were likely also confused about why people could not remain with their belongings, allowing them to have more space in the wagon. A French military policeman who managed the convoy that left from the French internment camp at Gurs on September 1, 1942, also expressed dismay at the conditions: "In truth, the special train of September 1 was transporting a mixed group of men, of women, of elderly, of sick and wounded who were left to their fate once the train had departed. With the exception of those traveling in the two passenger cars, the group was parked on straw, humid with urine. The women were desperate, without hope, to satisfy their natural needs out of the sight of strangers. The sight of this train left a powerful impression on the non-Jewish French population who saw it."[36]

The sight may have left an impression of disgust and indignation, but not enough to rouse much action. Perhaps witnesses were too weary or too afraid to complain; though some clearly spoke up, the deportation trains would roll on, mostly unimpeded, for two more years.

By 1944 the number of deportees crammed into the cars had often doubled and in some cases even quadrupled.[37] Increasingly during these voyages, some deportees had "soft" deaths, caused by asphyxiation, hypothermia, or thirst. Survivors often said the panic of thirst and the swelling of their tongues proved far more terrifying than the anticipated destination.[38] Others simply sweltered in the summer and froze in the winter in these wooden boxes. Air openings, when present, were often small and well above eye level. For most, the ride was dark and tumultuous. Without shock absorption, the wagons threw the adults, children, babies, elderly, and the handicapped from side to side, occasionally breaking bones.

SNCF's Attitude toward the Transports

Those reviewing these past events today often want to know what the workers *felt* about being involved in the deportations. Of course, a company does not have emotions, but people do. Unfortunately, these people are all dead. So, what can we surmise about how workers felt about being part of these deportations? According to Ribeill, "The SNCF did not worry about what it was transporting. There was an administrative culture of public service which was 'odorless and colorless' and a list of tasks to respect. Whether it be first class passengers traveling or deportees, the transporter did not see what was inside the wagons, there was a cold attitude."[39] Leo Bretholz, who escaped his deportation convoy, saw more fatigue than antipathy even in the French citizens: "Convoys such as ours were simply another little splinter of the war, of which they had grown weary, from which they turned to take care of their own lives."[40]

If bystanders saw the horrific conditions in the railcars, so too did the SNCF workers tasked with the transports; no one near those trains could have been blind or deaf to the atrocities before them. Yet protests from SNCF workers, if they existed, did not find their way into archives or oral history. In sum, the SNCF may not have *established* the travel conditions, but neither did it seem to *oppose* them. Archives show that SNCF executives pushed back when Germans demanded heavy shipments at implausible speeds for a fraction of their cost, but not on behalf of the deportees. The SNCF also demanded full payments when the Germans delayed or refused to pay in full. Why not, then, resist the conditions? Were workers afraid of being deported themselves? We can only guess. Perhaps, had the SNCF incurred the costs for the third-class passengers or provided additional railcars to improve the conditions, the Germans might have acquiesced. There is no evidence suggesting that the SNCF ever considered or made such suggestions.

Stealing from the Deportees

Just four months after the French and US governments signed a $60 million settlement in 2014, hoping to put this conflict to bed, a group of litigants launched a class action lawsuit out of Chicago. These litigants, whose lawyers wanted to make use of the Alien Tort Statute, accused SNCF workers of stealing from the deportees while they waited in the internment camps and as they boarded the trains. I want to briefly address this accusation. The cheminots had little access to people's belongings, especially at Drancy, because the German guards and the French police collected personal items as soon as deportees arrived at the internment camp.

Stanley Kalmanovitz, recalling his own deportation to me, responded upon hearing the accusation of theft, "Nonsense. No such thing. Number one, we had very little exposure to railway workers. There were some civilians working there, right-wing, fascists, Germans, French police. They didn't steal anything. The same suitcase I packed and the suitcase I took to Auschwitz was the same."[41] Of course, each deportation site may have been different. Perhaps someone had access and stole something; this would be hard to prove in court with all the perpetrators and most of the witnesses dead.

Eric Freedman, a scholar and a representative of the Simon Wiesenthal Foundation who served as a legal advocate for those seeking restitution from the Commission pour l'Indemnisation des Victimes de Spoliations (CIVS, Commission for the Compensation of Victims of Spoliation), says the real theft would have taken place at the Austerlitz station, where Jewish belongings were housed while being sorted.[42] The SNCF wagons were then used to transport stolen Jewish items back to Germany.

Little direct evidence suggests theft by cheminots. However, railway workers had long had a reputation for stealing—and this may help explain the stickiness of the accusation. In the early nineteenth century, railway workers were notorious for taking portions of coal, wheat, wood, and wine shipments. Many considered this a make-good for their paltry salaries and the dangers of their work.[43] A man could lose an arm or a life in a split second if he stopped paying attention. Many did suffer accidents because coal-fueled trains exposed them to extreme temperatures and fumes. Broch says this common and well-known theft also emerged out of boredom.[44] During the war, the Vichy regime did report increased rates of theft, either because of more rigorous reporting or because theft had actually increased. The cheminots lost all mechanisms through which to air their grievances when the Confédération Générale du Travail (CGT, General Confederation of Labor), founded in 1895 and the main union representing the cheminots, folded during the war and became a Resistance organization.[45] Theft might have been a means of expressing dismay or the result of increased worker desperation or simply greater access to more goods.[46] In sum, it would not have been out of character to steal from the Jewish deportees, although railway workers likely did not have access to these goods at the deportation sites.

THE ROLLING STOCK

The Holocaust Rail Justice Act accused the SNCF of providing the rolling stock for the deportations. The Franco-German Armistice requisitioned the company's entire rolling stock. So, shouldn't the company be held accountable for how it was used during the war? If Germans had used their own wagons, the modern-day SNCF could be more easily exonerated. Use of German wagons would suggest separate agendas. Janine Boulou recalls her fellow cheminots being very upset when the Germans came and took the company's wagons.[47]

When I raised the issue with several survivors during interviews, some were almost disgusted with such an irrelevant point. I asked a woman who found herself on a deportation convoy at age eight if she remembered whether the train was French: "How am I supposed to know whose train car it was? I was being separated from my mother, that's all I knew."[48] For those deported, such questions can seem entirely beside the point—and who can blame them for their reaction?

Today's SNCF executives, however, cannot dismiss the question of railcar ownership so easily. They must explain how railcars emblazoned with the company name circulated around Europe filled with innocent, suffocating people of all ages. We now know that SNCF locomotives carted the majority of convoys departing from France. Once at the border, non-SNCF drivers carried the deportees on to various death camps.[49]

In some cases, German railcars arrived in France to transport the deportees.[50] A letter dated July 28, 1942, from Heinz Röthke, the SS lieutenant in charge of Jewish affairs from 1942 to 1944, discusses these German cars. Röthke wrote, "Starting in August 1942 there will be 13 convoys of Jews. As the Wehrmacht Verkehrsdirektion transportation leadership confirmed yesterday, rolling equipment is available and ready to go for all trains for the month of August. The evacuation will continue to be carried out *by German freight cars as has been done up to this point*. It is necessary to change the trains of the Jews within the ZNO [unoccupied zone] because the *Jews must leave Drancy in the German merchandise trains* prepared under the direction of Wehrmacht."[51]

No documents yet found indicate that the Germans requested that the SNCF use empty passenger trains or merchandise trains for use in the deportations.[52] Other sources also point to German control. Raoul Merlin, an SNCF employee at the Compiègne station, from which many convoys departed, described how Germans commanded the gathering and preparation of the wagons at this station.[53] Days before the departure, the station received a group of covered wagons (French or German) that had been ordered by the Germans. The German railway workers told SNCF employees to choose those acceptable for transport, eliminating those with missing or loose floorboards. Some railcars would carry officers and soldiers, others would transport weapons, and still others would carry deportees. Merlin reports that the military authorities conducted very thorough final examinations, replacing a couple of vehicles they deemed not secure enough to prevent escape.[54]

Shaking the perpetrator label has become very difficult for the SNCF today because not only were their railcars used to transport French deportees, but the Germans often used the same SNCF railcars to deport others throughout Europe to extermination camps. Photographs show SNCF railcars being used for this grim purpose, especially in Eastern European countries. The Germans saw the SNCF's railcars as theirs to use as they pleased. A train departing Hungary on a Tuesday could arrive Poland in a few days and then head back to France to pick up more deportees. The trains used outside France operated with no participation from SNCF workers or drivers. The SNCF executives and cheminots had contact only with their trains in France. The SNCF's brand name sits almost as a silent witness, watching innocent individuals crammed into and extracted out of its cavity.

Jewish roundup in Marseille, January 1943. The SNCF's name is visible on the train car on the right. (Mémorial de la Shoah/coll. Bundesarchiv)

Who Drove the Trains?

A simple question about whether the train drivers kept their jobs after the war prompted the research for this book. Answering this question required first determining who drove the trains. French train drivers and French police took the deportees to Novéant-sur-Moselle, near the German frontier, roughly 300 kilometers from Paris. The RSHA, the Reich Main Security Office in Berlin, handled the logistical operations related to the deportations. German drivers took over the trains at the border, carrying them from there to the death camps.[55]

Survivor Bernard Le Chatelier recalls this transfer of authority: "In the middle of the night, during a stop, the wagon doors opened. We thought we had arrived. No, we were only at the frontier and were now being taken by a SS team. Armed with batons . . . they would get into the wagons and, hitting us, would move us into half of the wagon, where they could count us again."[56] The SS team and non-French drivers delivered the deportees in the last leg of their journey toward execution.

Cleaning the Transports

The Holocaust Rail Justice Act alleges that "the . . . SNCF cleaned the trains after each trip, removing the corpses of persons who perished during transit due to the execrable conditions of the train cars."[57] The convoys arrived at the camps covered with at least three days of excrement, vomit—and, often, corpses. One convoy, later named Le Train de la Mort (the train of death), departed from Compiègne and arrived at Auschwitz with five hundred dead. Who tended to the gruesome task of removing the bodies and mopping up the human excrement? Not the SNCF. Even those cars that had been stopped and cleaned midjourney appear not to have been cleaned by SNCF workers. This was primarily because the SNCF workers did not travel with the trains to their destination. Francis Rohmer, head of clinical neurology at Strasbourg's School of Medicine, survived a brutal voyage from Compiègne on July 2, 1944, to the Dachau concentration camp. Rohmer recalls the train stopping just beyond the northeast French town of Revigny-sur-Ornain. The doors opened, and those in charge yelled, "*Raus, Schnell!* [Get out, quickly!]" The living descended. Then, he says, "They put in our car the dead from the neighboring wagons. . . . Once the transfer of the dead was completed, they had us get into another wagon that was bigger."[58] Even when this horrific task was performed midtrip, the SNCF workers do not seem to have been involved. Dannecker's directive suggests that, in at least some cases, *deportees* cleaned the arriving railcars: "One Jew shall be designated, with the responsibility of maintaining orders during the trip and of cleaning the car at the end of the trip. That Jew shall also bring along sanitary equipment. Since freight cars are used for such convoys, at least one slop pail shall be provided for each car."[59] Research easily dismisses the claim that SNCF workers cleaned the cars upon arrival, but once publics imagine the SNCF removing corpses and fecal matter, such an image becomes difficult to dislodge.

Did the SNCF Know the Destinations?

The Holocaust Rail Justice Act and related litigation suggest that the SNCF officials knew the destinations of these convoys. What exactly did they know? The executives likely knew more than the workers, simply because few cheminots worked near the deportation trains that departed from a handful of the hundreds of SNCF stations.[60] Trains tended to leave from the smaller stations to avoid attracting attention. Those workers who saw those trains can never forget what they witnessed that day. Cheminote Janine Boulou worked in Pantin (located between Paris and Drancy). Just twenty years old, she noted in her diary what she saw of the deportations. She said, "everyone was traumatized" by the sight of people packed "like sardines," their hands plastered against the openings and that the workers spontaneously came out and gave them a little snack or whatever they had. While they might not have known the destination, she said the workers knew the people would never come back.[61] She recalls seeing the RATP buses arrive in front of her office. Further-more, destinations like "Auschwitz" had no meaning at the time. Information about the camps did not circulate easily in France, even as late as 1944. During the war, deportees waiting at the Drancy internment camp outside Paris would say they were off to *Pitchipoi*—a Yiddish word meaning some unknown desti-nation. Who could have imagined such a terminus?

Nevertheless, word spread about the camps. *J'Accuse*, an underground French newspaper that circulated in the Drancy internment camp, informed internees about their most likely future. As early as 1942, the paper reported that torturers "are burning and asphyxiating thousands of men, women and children deported from France."[62] Once deportees knew, it is likely that the SNCF senior execu-tives, as well as the railway workers whose underground press discussed the persecution of the Jews, also had a fairly good understanding of the Nazi plan to exterminate them.[63]

Those few cheminots who were working in these stations and were close enough to see the transports and those who drove the trains would clearly have observed the atrocity before them. Even without knowing the destination, they must have wondered how such an unhappy voyage could lead to a happy destination. Bystanders like Édith Thomas described the sight: "I saw a train pass by; at the head of the train, a wagon containing the French military police and the German soldiers. Then, came the cattle cars, packed. The skinny arms of children clinging to the bars. A hand outside flapping like a leaf in a storm. When the train stopped, voices cried, 'Momma!'"[64] What more did people need to know?

THE QUESTION OF PROFIT

The Holocaust Rail Justice Act asserts that the "SNCF allegedly charged an ordinary passenger coach fare for the deportations, calculated per person and per kilometer, and considered these trains as ordinary commercial activities."[65] Responding to this claim requires that we address two questions. First, did the SNCF profit from the German occupation? Jonathan Bush notes that those who benefited from an "economic windfall" catalyzed by the Holocaust included—more often—the Nazi state, its party members, and the Germans themselves.[66] Research now shows that companies like Hugo Boss, which pro-vided Nazi uniforms, did see significant profits.[67] The SNCF, however, did not experience such financial gains. The company lost money during the war.

The question people really want answered, however, is whether the SNCF charged the Germans, the French government, or the passengers for the depor-tations. Payment for the deportations varied by country. In some countries, Jewish deportees paid for their own deportation, through either taxes or forced ticket purchases. Dutch Jews had to pay five guilders for their trip, and if they were unable or unwilling to pay, the Dutch National Railways (NS) billed the Germans.[68] The NS ultimately billed the Germans roughly $2.6 million (in today's currency) for the transport of Jewish deportees from the Netherlands.[69] Croatia, by contrast, *paid* Germany to remove its Jews. On October 9, 1942, the Croatian finance minister Vladimir Košak agreed to pay Germany 30 Reichsmarks for each Jew removed.

Raul Hilberg found that in France, "the SS secured the agreement of the German military commander that transportation costs attributable to travel on French soil up to the German border were to be covered from the military occupation budget."[70] In some cases, the RSHA paid the invoices for the deportations.[71] Ultimately, though, taxpayers likely paid for the transports via German-imposed taxes.[72] In correspondence between the German police budget specialists and the German minister of finance, Germans announced a rate of 76,000 Reichsmarks for eighteen trains headed to Auschwitz from France and stopping at the German border. The voyage from the border to Auschwitz cost 439,000 Reichsmarks, and the RSHA covered this cost.[73] What remains unclear, however, is *who* received the Reichsmarks for the journeys to the camps—the SNCF, France, or a German travel agency? Hilberg found that generally, "whenever one or more currency zones were crossed by trains the entire bill was payable to the railroad that was in charge of the first segment of the trip."[74] This suggests that the SNCF likely received payment.

Bachelier concluded that the SNCF billed Germany and received payment for all its services. The only unremunerated work he found was the SNCF's offer to carry prisoner of war (POW) Christmas parcels.[75] A memo dated 1940 between French departments stated that the company would be reimbursed for the transport of deportees and their escorts. Provisions would be paid for by another department.[76] Often the French Ministry of the Interior or the camps appear to have paid for internal SNCF transports carrying deportees, whereas the Germans appear to have paid for the trains heading to the east.

The SNCF issued a number of these invoices for internal transports after D-Day. On December 22, 1944, the Prefecture of Haute-Garonne forwarded an invoice from the SNCF for 210,385 francs issued for the transport of "detailed and evicted" persons from his department, likely to Drancy. He sent the invoice to an accounting office in Paris.

In one letter, the secretary general of the police informs the prefect of Haute-Garonne that the internment camps and the SS ought to pay the SNCF invoices, not the state.[77] However, debates over payment continued well after the liberation of Paris, between August 19 and August 25, 1944. As late as May 29, 1945, French government offices debated how to handle the SNCF invoices. The

SOCIÉTÉ NATIONALE DES CHEMINS DE FER FRANÇAIS

SUBDIVISION DU CONTROLE
des
RECETTES VOYAGEURS

212, rue de Bercy
PARIS (12e)

SERVICES FINANCIERS

COMPTABILITÉ ET CONTROLE
DES RECETTES

Transports du Ministère de l'INTÉRIEUR

FACTURE N° 45.373

des transports exécutés pendant le ......Ier trimestre...................... 19 44,

le compte de ...la Préfecture de la Haute-Garonne.........et dont les dé

sont portés dans les relevés annexés à la présente facture, appuyés des pièces justificati
C.F.F. - G.G. 1069→   XX/IV 40754 — Bernard Frères, Paris (?-43)

DÉSIGNATION DES RELEVÉS	SOMMES
Montant des transports figurant sur le relevé ci-joint (Camp d'internement, Centres de séjour surveillé, Internés, Expulsés etc..)	210.385
SERVICE FINANCIER 24 OCTO 1944 2519	
TOTAL......	210.385

Dressée par le Chef de Bureau,
soussigné,

Certifié exact
Roc, le 30.
Le Chef du Camp

Certifié la présente facture s'élevant à la som
de Deux cent dix mille trois ce
quatre vingt cinq francs neuf
décimes.

Paris, le 12 AOU 1944 19

LE CHEF DE LA SUBDIVISION
DU CONTROLE DES RECETTES VOYAGEURS,

SNCF invoice for internal transport of internees and other evicted persons, dated
August 12, 1944, two months after D-Day. (Courtesy of Serge Klarsfeld)

minister of the interior wrote to the minister of finance requesting that the 166,618 francs demanded by the SNCF for transports to the Drancy internment camp in August 1942 be paid out of a "special treasury fund" used to pay for German demands.[78]

Payments for Trains to Death Camps

Only two known documents exist regarding payments for the transport of Jewish deportees from the French border to Auschwitz. A letter dated September 15, 1942, sent from the SNCF to the Loiret prefect refers to "four special trains" that departed France for Novéant.[79] The SNCF's Commercial Service asks the prefect whether they should send the invoice to them or to the minister of the interior. We can assume that eventually actual invoices were sent. The fact that no one has found them simply suggests that they were destroyed.

One invoice, shared with me by Serge Klarsfeld, passed between two German agencies: the Gestapo and a German travel agency. The invoice was issued by an office called the Middle European Regional Travel Office, created as a subdivision of the Deutsche Reichsbahn (German National Railways). This office sent the invoice to the Commanding Officer Ministry (the Gestapo) for the movement of this "Special Jewish Train," noting that this train would not operate on a normal schedule. This invoice billed for the transport of 1,500 Jews from Bobigny to Auschwitz and calculated the rate using the metric per person, per kilometer. It seems to suggest that payment for at least some of these transports occurred between German divisions and did not include the SNCF.[80]

Those challenging the SNCF through lawsuits and legislation often underscored that the company billed per head, per kilometer for the transport of the deportees. The gruesome metric, echoed in many public debates and newspaper articles, aimed to prove the sinister intent of the SNCF. However, this metric must be placed in historical context. In the 1940s and earlier, trains used the metric of "per head, per kilometer" to determine the rate for all paying passengers, German soldiers, and livestock. Anything or anyone with a head was calculated this way. To a train company, German soldiers, cows, Jews, chickens, and passengers were all calculated as "things" to be transported. This dehumanizing metric may highlight the deeper problem of how industrialization and capitalism often devalue life. The per head, per kilometer metric speaks more to the contribution of industrialization to the Holocaust than to the SNCF's dehumanization of Jews or other deportees.[81]

Better to Work for Free?

Bachelier, commissioned to compile a wartime history based on the SNCF archives, took issue with debates over invoicing.[82] For him, the question of

Invoice between two German agencies for a "Special Jewish Train" of 1,500 Jews from Bobigny (France) to Auschwitz, February 10, 1944. (Courtesy of Serge Klarsfeld) financing was beside the point: He considered *any* participation a moral wrong. Would transporting the deportees for free have been a higher moral choice? Would not free shipments have further supported the German war effort? Marie-Noëlle Polino, during her tenure as a senior staff member of the AHICF, argued that by charging the Germans for every transport of soldiers, armaments, and so on, the SNCF asserted independence and communicated to the Germans their dissatisfaction with the occupation.[83] Current debates may raise similar conundrums—when it comes to business, nothing serves a company more than free services. The question really ought not have been whether the SNCF made a profit but whether the company, as Bachelier pointed out, should have participated at all—if, in fact, there was a choice.

To date, no one has found invoices issued by the SNCF for deportation trains heading out of France. Likely the SNCF charged someone; the company rarely worked for free. Bernard Emsellem, SNCF's head of corporate social responsibility, suspects that the relevant documents were destroyed right after the war.[84] At the moment, we have invoices for transports only *within* France, a number of which were issued after D-Day. Regarding the accusation that the SNCF profited financially from the German occupation, this seems unlikely. The archives show that the Germans paid only a fraction of what the SNCF billed. As the war advanced, the demands grew, and the payments decreased. The SNCF survived the war but did not profit from it. Whether the SNCF ought to have accepted payments for the deportation trains or simply refused to drive the trains remains for readers and future generations to deliberate. One fact remains undebatable, however, one that casts the SNCF's chairman in a more sinister light: the priority he gave to a state-assigned project of "Aryanization."

The SNCF President Helps France Aryanize

Even before the deportations began, the president of the SNCF played a significant role in squeezing Jews out of French society. Fournier's former position as governor of the Bank of France made him a good candidate when Vichy needed an administrator to "Aryanize" Jewish businesses. Aryanization was aimed at removing all Jewish influence over society. This included the seizure of businesses as well as of valuable assets such as art collections. Vichy's Ministry of Finance and Industrial Production initiated the Aryanization of Jewish businesses to head off Germany's ability to acquire Jewish assets and use them for their own ends.[85] They were as concerned with the Germanization of their economy as they were eager to remove the Jewish presence. Fournier's job was effectively to "de-Jew" the economy, while keeping the money within and for France. In 1940–41, while serving as SNCF president, he did just that.[86]

The Vichy government officials appointed Fournier as the first director of the Service de Contrôle des Administrateurs Provisoires (SCAP, Control Service for Provisional Administrators).[87] This government office, created by Vichy, was tasked with eliminating all Jewish influence from the economic life of occupied France and, unlike the police, made no distinction between foreign-born Jews and longtime French citizens.[88] The Vichy regime initially chose Fournier for his financial knowledge and because he was a professional technocrat with a reputation for being honest, straightforward, and rigid, as well as a patriot.[89] Aryanization of Jewish businesses meant that a Jewish merchant or artisan would be forced to sell his or her business to an Aryan neighbor or a competitor. In a few rare cases, a kindly employee or partner would buy the company and preserve it for the original Jewish owner. Most Jews, however, lost their businesses and with them the means to support their families. Fournier, while not initially thrilled with the appointment, accepted.[90] He announced to the other administrators of SCAP, "This is a public service mission. . . . It demands tact on your part, you will often find yourself in the presence of difficult situations; you will need to avoid brutality and upsets that distract from the larger mission that you have received."[91]

Fournier also encouraged those under him, when identifying Jewish businesses, to do more than target religious Jews. He encouraged identification of those who were "racially" Jewish, warning them not to be confused by those who claimed to have been baptized.[92]

The French police oversaw the dispossession of Jewish property and businesses.[93] France did not want the Germans to appropriate this financial bounty. Over time, German authorities would become more involved, but they had to rely on French assistance.[94] Fournier, compensated for his work within SCAP, proved highly effective in his role. During his tenure, SCAP evolved from just monitoring Jewish businesses to selling or closing them.[95]

At the beginning of Fournier's term, Paris had roughly 11,000 Jewish businesses (7,737 held in private ownership and 3,455 held as incorporated businesses).[96] Fournier proudly announced that the organization had successfully Aryanized more than 4,500 Jewish businesses in order to meet the German deadline of December 26, 1940.[97] While in 1940 the Germans directed SCAP to give the Jewish business owners the money from the sales, eventually Jewish owners received no reimbursement. Money was even taken from the Rothschild family, which still had a financial stake in the SNCF. SCAP's work resulted in the acquisition of over five billion francs.[98]

Fournier resigned from the position, not on moral grounds but because he despised having German authorities meddle with his work. In the end, he appeared not so much pro-Vichy as anti-German. He supported Philippe

Pétain, chief of state during the Vichy regime, as a means of asserting French independence. On June 6, 1944 (D-Day), the Germans arrested Fournier for being troublesome and held him for a week before releasing him.[99]

No evidence suggests that Fournier resisted his role in SCAP or in the deportations. Do Fournier's actions or inactions characterize the SNCF as a perpetrator? What about the executive team's minimal efforts to protect its Jewish cheminots? Does this characterize the SNCF as antisemitic? Because the company clearly did not initiate the deportations, some wonder whether it can be held accountable today for not having stopped them. Fournier saw himself as a victim of the occupation and found German meddling in his affairs—and French affairs more generally—intolerable. The SNCF's institutional history labels him neither a hero nor a perpetrator. In fact, few histories of the SNCF offer more than passing acknowledgment of Fournier. He was a mere technocrat who did his job, most say. In this way, he and the executives represent the very sort of mechanization that facilitated the Holocaust and the very sort of pragmatism that leads many companies into human rights violations. Fournier also represents the commitment to the company's mission before all else. He kept the trains rolling, while seemingly indifferent to the repugnant nature of the transports.

The SNCF as Perpetrator

As for the Holocaust Rail Justice Act and the claims of the Chicago-based lawsuit against the SNCF, the company did not appear to collaborate willingly with the Germans. It did not seem to have had a say over the use of its convoys, nor did it establish the conditions of travel—but nor for that matter did it seem to protest. The SNCF workers likely never cleaned out the convoys upon their arrival to the camps, and they would have had little opportunity to steal deportee possessions. As for profit, the company charged for transports within France, but no invoices remain to definitively prove that the SNCF received payment for deportation transports to the German border. Such documents, if they existed, were likely destroyed.

The SNCF participated in the Holocaust—this we know. And, if degrees of complicity exist, the SNCF emerges as less villainous than the German Reichsbahn, the German National Railways, which Alfred Mierzejewski claims "made its peace with the Nazi party during 1934 and participated fully and knowingly in the implementation of the Holocaust."[100] The SNCF leadership and personnel demonstrated indifference toward the fate of the Jews, focusing instead on their own affairs, and likely knew little about the killing centers.[101]

The Holocaust Rail Justice Act allegations wobble under close scrutiny, but they also highlight some crucial questions about accountability. Company leadership showed no signs of resisting the deportations or even opposing the travel conditions. The company also had less control over its affairs than the contemporary claims suggest. We know that everyone who contributes to harm acts within particular sociopolitical contexts. Does this mean we are never responsible for our actions? The existence of heroes and wayward individuals in almost every context of mass violence suggests that individuals retain some amount of agency and can respond to moral wrongs in a variety of ways.

The crucial role of the SNCF in the deportations makes the company a salient focal point for this discussion. Does the crucial nature of the SNCF's participation make the company more accountable or simply more visible than other companies? As with many corporate accountability conflicts, by the time the failure becomes clear, those who should be held accountable are hard to find. In other cases, the legal lacunae and the tremendous work required for settlements mean that companies rarely pay for their crimes or deeply atone for them. Fewer still publicly demonstrate and reflect about their direct participation. As I show in later chapters, the SNCF remains one of the rare companies to engage in this morally reflective process, even if this engagement required much external pressure. But for the first fifty years after the war, the company found itself celebrated for its heroism because of its role in the Resistance. In the next chapter, I focus on how the SNCF received such honors and maintained its legendary status for so many decades.

VOICES FROM THE LAST TRAINS

Estéra arrived at Auschwitz from Lyon in a third-class passenger car. Because this train did not pass through the sorrowful Drancy internment camp, passengers knew less about the hell awaiting them than some other arrivals. Upon arrival at the camp, Estéra escaped immediate gassing only because the Nazis had temporarily run out of Zyklon B. This bought her some time. During the admissions process, she claimed to be an Aryan married to a Jew. Germans tattooed a number on her arm to reflect this designation. They eventually discovered her Jewishness and crossed out the first tattoo and issued another number across her forearm. She told the female Kapo (a prisoner in a supervisory role appointed by SS guards) that if she was murdered, her husband, Lazare, a well-known member of a clandestine group of resistants and other nonconformists known for their violent acts, would come to kill her. She knew Lazare was dead but hoped the threat would frighten the woman. It worked. Out of fear, the Kapo assigned her to cleaning the latrines, saving her—again—from the gas chamber.[102] She survived through a combination of luck, audacity, and tenacity.

Successful escapes were rare. Leo Bretholz and his friend Manfred Silberwasser never saw Auschwitz because they used shirts soaked in urine to pry open the bars of a small opening in their Convoy 42. When the train slowed around a turn, the boys squeezed themselves out of the tiny opening. There were roughly 1,000 people on that transport, of whom 773 were gassed immediately upon arrival.[103] Of those selected for forced labor, all but two would be killed at Auschwitz by exhaustion, sickness, beatings, or eventual gassing.[104]

Daniel and Samuel did not escape. Upon their arrival at Auschwitz, they were overwhelmed by the strange sights and sounds. Daniel recalled emerging from the railcar and sucking in his first breath of fresh air in days. Even in the August heat, the air felt good in his lungs and provided some reprieve from the sickening odors of the railcar created by four days of defecation, urine, vomit, and sweat. Samuel, a little older, immediately understood that they had traveled beyond civilization. He pulled out the 1,000 francs his father had given to him and ripped them up. He knew they would be of no use here. Having studied German in school, he deciphered the commands, which, while comprehensible to him, were physically hard to follow. The three days spent crammed together provided little opportunity for the deportees to stretch their muscles. As much as they all wanted to respond to the orders shouted at them and to quickly get away from the stench of the railcar, their bodies moved unsteadily. The elderly could barely descend. The baby born in Drancy was left lying on the straw.

The SS lined them up as they approached and separated those fit for hard labor from the children, women, elderly, and those who had been caught trying to escape. Daniel waited behind Samuel for his designation. Guards selected fourteen-year-old Samuel for hard labor. Then Daniel stepped up.

The SS officer hesitated.

Even though Daniel was not yet a teenager, for some reason the guard included him in the group of adults right behind Samuel. Daniel turned to his brother and said, "They made a mistake. I am supposed to be with the children!"

Samuel told him to be quiet and not mention it again. Samuel understood that anything other than manhood meant immediate death. Of the 1,300 people on the convoy, including 328 children, 726 were sent immediately to the gas chamber.

"I was almost 727!" Daniel said.

Over the next ten months, 365 of those who survived the journey on Convoy 77 and the selection process died of fatigue, starvation, or disease (most commonly typhus or dysentery); 209, of whom 18 were minors, would survive. Daniel and Samuel were two of these eighteen. Daniel said some came to refer to him as the youngest known French person to survive the death camps.

Today, Daniel becomes incensed when people call Auschwitz a "work camp." The living conditions, labor demands, and malnourishment were designed to kill, he explains. Death just occurred a bit more slowly for those who were not immediately gassed. After they were selected for hard labor, the Nazis sent the boys through a series of administrative steps to process them as prisoners in the camps. First, the boys had to get undressed in front of each other and the guards. Everyone was embarrassed because the journey had put them in an awful state. Guards (likely prisoners themselves) coarsely shaved Daniel and Samuel from head to toe, often nicking them and causing them to bleed. Then they sprayed them against infection and tattooed their arms with an identification number. The most painful, Daniel says, was the tattoo: "Not because the tattoo hurt, but because the SS had stripped me of my personhood." Because the brothers had consecutive numbers, they were never separated during their imprisonment at Auschwitz. At the end of the intake process, they each received an ill-fitting uniform, a bowl, and a pair of wooden shoes.

When they saw each other again, Daniel said, they laughed: "We looked like we were in a disguise. . . . We looked like clowns." They had never seen each other without hair, wearing wooden shoes, and in such ill-fitting clothing. "It was the only time we laughed," recalls Daniel.

Time, the last vestige of civilization, disappeared soon after Samuel and Daniel found their names replaced by the freshly tattooed numbers on their arms. A loudspeaker roused the boys each morning, demanding that they, along with sixty thousand other prisoners, stand and be counted. They had no time to even use the bathroom. Guards first did a head count, then a roll call by number, along with a search of the barracks for the dead or nearly dead. Everyone had to be accounted for before the roll call ended. So as not to lose work time, the Germans moved relatively swiftly in the morning. They then led prisoners to a worksite where they toiled until sunset, digging a ditch. "We never learned the purpose of this project," says Daniel. Every day was the same; changing seasons offered only variety in the nature of suffering. Winter days promised fewer hours of hard labor, for example, but, since the prisoners lacked gloves and proper clothing, much harsher conditions. Every day ended with an excruciating evening roll call. The enslaved men, exhausted and weakened from a day of labor, stood for hours while Germans counted the day's survivors. The roll call would be prolonged by the hanging of anyone who had tried to escape that day. Because the men weighed so little, those hanged did not die immediately. The prisoners were forced to remain standing and watch the slow death of those who had tried to save themselves.

Those who survived ended the day famished. The boys received two servings of "nourishment" to sustain them. At midday, they drank weak soup while standing. The camp staff mockingly scooped up more and would not give it to them. Daniel explained, "If you asked for more or even looked them in the eye, they would beat you or kill you. A slave doesn't look at his master!" In the evening, they received a small piece of bread and either cheese or meat. They slept in wooden barracks on some straw.

Daniel said to Samuel, "If we survive, there is a good God."

Samuel said, "Well, not everyone gets a good God," referring to all those who continued to perish before their eyes.

In April 2016, when Samuel shared this memory with Daniel, Daniel said, "I remember clearly that it was you who said that, not me." They cannot be sure. Perhaps their souls had become so intertwined by this point that what one of them experienced was also experienced by the other. They had few other conversations in the camp. Daniel repeatedly complained to his brother about his fatigue and hunger. Samuel, anguished by his inability to help his brother, told Daniel to stop asking questions.

"We need to save our energy," he said.

Daniel really did need to conserve his strength. At twelve years old, he could not keep up with the labor designed for grown men. He thinks a Kapo (prisoner supervisor) took pity on him, assigning him the task of using the wheelbarrow to move cadavers, rather than continue with the hard labor of digging.

"Wasn't transporting the day's dead horrific?" I asked.

"Death was normal for us. It was everywhere. It wasn't anything shocking anymore."

He attributes his survival to such acts of pity; another guard on the worksite allowed him to work in the German kitchen, where he had access to some nourishing soup. "I don't know if I would have survived without that extra food," he said. "I was already at the limit. . . . I felt terrible that I could not bring any back for Samuel, but it was soup; I had no way to carry it."

"Some people find it hard when I tell that story," he says. "They cannot accept that a German took pity on me and showed some kindness. Maybe I reminded [the guard] of his own son. I don't know."

Daniel survived, but each day he slipped further from his prewar self. His brother had stopped speaking to him both to save their energy and because he lacked answers. In this silence, furthered by the presence of few other French-speaking prisoners, "I became more and more like an animal, allowing my survival instinct to take over."

Daniel recalls only one day when both time and speech returned: Christmas 1944. The prisoners did not work on Christmas day: "We remembered there was such a thing as months, weeks, and days. The presence of time liberated us for an instant." The brothers spent the day creating in their minds huge sandwiches with everything on them—they would create them again and again. Daniel felt his hunger increase, which he considered a good sign: "It meant I was alive!" The next day, time disappeared again, placing them back in a liminal state until July 1945 when the sound of bombs in the distance inspired hopes of liberation.

They learned that Auschwitz would close because of the Russian advance, not the victory of the Allies. The remaining prisoners began what historians now call "death marches": walking all day and sometimes all night from Poland to Austria on a journey that took roughly seventeen days. They learned to sleep while walking.

"We just could never really learn to sleep in the rain, though," Daniel says.

The precious blankets protecting them from the cold as they marched became unbearably heavy whenever snow turned to rain. After a roughly two-week journey that killed hundreds, the boys arrived at Mauthausen, a concentration camp in Austria. Daniel turned fourteen here. Even with 150 annexes, Mauthausen was smaller than Auschwitz. They were marched roughly 80 kilometers to sequentially more ill-equipped camps, the first made of brick, the second made of wood, and the final camp—likely Gunskirchen—made of only tarps. Months had passed since they left Auschwitz. Winter descended upon Austria. By this point it had been almost forty weeks since the day of their deportation—a period that Daniel later equated with the forty years the Jews roamed the desert in exile.

CHAPTER THREE

The Resistance

The SNCF as Hero

Stopping a train is not simple, Mademoiselle.

You can get killed stopping a train, especially if you are French and the train is German.

—The Train, 1964

I COME NOW to the question of the SNCF's heroism. Times of crisis and their aftermath bring out several kinds of heroes, each with different roles and resources. I found three types of heroes: daily heroes, superheroes, and postwar justice heroes. *Daily heroes* (1) were not personally targeted by the regime, (2) had everything to lose, and (3) used tools available to many people. The ordinariness of their social position and resources serves as a reminder that everyone can be extraordinary, but most choose not to be.

In contrast, *superheroes* have access to special resources giving them extraordinary power. Raoul Gustaf Wallenberg exemplifies such a person. He saved thousands of Jews using the power he had to issue protective passports while serving as a Swedish envoy in Budapest. Oskar Schindler hid more than a thousand Jews in his munitions factories in occupied Poland. Those with access to and knowledge of the railways had the potential to become superheroes in a similar way. The Dutch Railway workers, for example, helped catalyze the German collapse by engaging in an eight-month strike at the end of the war, ordered by the government in exile. Some SNCF workers also leveraged their access to the rails to help others. Unfortunately, in both rail companies the most dramatic efforts occurred only after most of the deportations had already occurred. Among the SNCF's wartime executive leadership (as opposed to the workers), we find even fewer acts of heroism, even broadly defined.

The last category of hero is the *justice hero*. Justice heroes emerge in the aftermath of war as the activists (often survivors or descendants) and legal professionals who advocate for victims. These legal advocates frame the public discourse surrounding what justice means. Justice heroes also do the behind-the-scenes work needed to create the conditions of due process.

Before turning to SNCF heroism, I want to distinguish *acts* of resistance from actually being *in* the Resistance—with a capital "R." In France, formal members of the Resistance acted as both superheroes and daily heroes by engaging in a multitude of coordinated activities. Through complex networks of communication, they produced underground newspapers, created false identities, organized the protection of Allied troops, and assisted in various escape attempts. From these activities came the myriad heroic postwar stories that continue to capture attention through movies, popular fiction, and nonfiction. Today, a popular joke in France is that everyone had an uncle in the Resistance. If one tallied all these "uncles," they would outnumber the occupying Germans. Of the roughly 400,000 SNCF employees, 2,229 lost their lives as a result of the German occupation and 443 died in combat during the liberation of France.[1] This loss of life totals less than 1 percent of the company's employees.

This show of resistance was higher than the comparable figures for Germany, where Raul Hilberg noted that among the railway workers, "no one resigned, no one protested, and hardly anyone asked for a transfer."[2] But are the SNCF numbers sufficient to bestow the title of hero or victim on the SNCF? Contemporary business owners often assume that at least 1 percent of employees are actively stealing or subverting the company's mission in some way at any given time. Those activities rarely translate into corporate reputations for subversion, especially when the acts are committed by company agents and not the executives.

In the SNCF, as in France, most acts of resistance challenged the German occupation rather than Jewish ostracism and subsequent deportations. To save themselves, Jews formed their own organizations. Once he leaped out of his train headed for Auschwitz, for example, Leo Bretholz was saved by a Jewish Resistance group that provided him with a new name and the false papers necessary to secure his safe movement around France. Yet Bretholz soon found himself under arrest again and spent more time in prison. In October 1943, he escaped another French train headed from Toulouse to the Atlantic coast, where the Germans wanted prisoners to build fortifications. After this escape, Bretholz formally joined the Jewish Resistance group known as La Sixième (The Sixth). He worked with the Resistance for barely six months before he collapsed with a hernia in Limoges. In May 1944, a month before D-Day, someone found him lying on a bench and sent him to a hospital. He would soon rejoin the Resistance, remaining hidden until the end of the war.[3] Bretholz's story shows how the protection these groups could offer was limited; for those with few choices, membership was worth the risk. Many were saved. Some individuals, acting as daily heroes, gambled their lives when they hid Resistance fighters or Jews in their homes, falsified identity papers, or engaged in similar activities.

People living in occupied France more often expressed their resistance in small, symbolic ways. Not long after French police took his parents, Samuel recalls his small moment of resistance prior to his own deportation. He had stepped out to purchase some bread on rue des Rosiers in the Marais, the Jewish district of Paris. While he had enough money for the bread, the storekeeper explained that purchases now required a ration card. A German soldier, sympathetic to Samuel's predicament, handed him the necessary card. But Samuel refused to take anything offered by a German official, he said, even when resistance meant hunger.

Some joined the Resistance at a young age because their families joined. Other children did so of their own volition. One survivor, also named Samuel, ran away and joined the Resistance at the age of six. He threw grenades at German soldiers and transported secret documents in the wool of the sheep he shepherded. After he was stabbed by a German soldier, the Resistance sent him to Denmark for safety. He proudly rolled up his pant leg to show me his scar.[4] In the postwar period, French Jews arrested for their participation in the Resistance eagerly attached themselves to the hero label. This helped them be seen—and to see themselves—as more than victims.[5] The SNCF would do the same.

The SNCF and Resistance

For years, a wall-size bronze mural of a group of cheminots sabotaging the rails was proudly displayed on the first floor of the SNCF's headquarters when it was located at Montparnasse in Paris. The mural celebrates the moment when the Allies landed at the Normandy beaches and some SNCF workers, in conjunction with Resistance organizations, sabotaged their own trains filled with German armaments to thwart the German response to the Allied invasion. The 1947 popular film *La Bataille du rail*, which claims to use actual footage of these derailments, immortalized the saboteurs and cemented the image of the SNCF Resistance fighter into French consciousness. Like the film, the nationalist leaflet *La Guerre du rail* (1948) served as emotionally powerful propaganda. The galvanizing text recounts the critical days of sabotage: "The instant of the final strike has come. One must react, all together at once, and definitively paralyze the enemy."[6] The leaflet speaks of resistants' bravery as well as their sacrifice, comparing the destruction of their precious machines to a kind of personal amputation. The trains were their subsistence and pride and, for some, even extensions of their bodies. The story closes by highlighting again "the value of these artisans of the track who have sacrificed everything, bread, family and existence in order that France can live."[7] Though no one challenges the veracity of this event, Marrus and Paxton question whether the SNCF's sabotaging of the German trains—sent in response to D-Day—was less about the liberation of France and more about the mere fatigue of being dominated.[8] The resentment of domination surfaced again when a number of cheminots led a strike on August 10, 1944, to help liberate Paris.[9] Even in this most heroic of times, however, nothing was done to stop the convoys headed east to the death camps.[10] The last trains to Auschwitz arrived unobstructed.

This chapter now considers where acts of resistance occurred and where they did not within the SNCF. The company had its own deeply ingrained esprit de corps that helped operate this complex operation with roughly half a million employees and the need for relentless precision. This esprit was ingrained in railway workers—first trains, then country.

As I have already noted, SNCF executives did not welcome German interference in their affairs, and most cheminots shared this sentiment, but whether this lack of enthusiasm made the SNCF a heroic entity is another question. To deter acts of subversion, the Vichy government referred to resistants as "terrorists." Following their promise to fulfill German commands, the SNCF executives reported those among its ranks who were suspected of engaging in terrorist activities. For a railway worker, to resist was to be labeled an enemy of one's company as well as the state.

This returns us to a broader question about corporate identity. Where does it reside? In the hearts and minds of a company's insubordinate agents? If so, how many need to resist before the organization becomes identified by these acts? Even if the SNCF had two thousand heroes, that figure would constitute less than 1 percent of the total employees. This reflects a similar proportion of Resistance fighters to the overall French population (who made up less than 1 percent of the total populace)—hardly enough to categorize the group as a whole. If we decide that a company's identity resides in the actions of its executives, then the SNCF emerges from the war as just another disgruntled French agency acting under duress during the occupation. Heroism recognizes outstanding achievement, achievements that defy the norm. Being disgruntled during an occupation is hardly a heroic response.

SNCF Executives and the Resistance

Clearly, when discussing acts of resistance as well as the official Resistance and the SNCF, we need to distinguish between the SNCF as an organization, its executives, and its cheminots. When I asked SNCF America CEO Alain Leray about the claim of organizational "heroism," he wanted me to remind contemporary students of the war that the SNCF could not hang a sign out and advertise its membership in the Resistance.[11] In a strict sense, he is right. The company could not officially join as an entity without creating tremendous problems for itself; if the Germans had discovered any official participation, they would have increased surveillance and punishments of high-ranking officials. The company acted as an extension of the occupied French state—and therefore of the German state.

Careful surveillance and reporting by SNCF executives of all resistance activities, however, suggests an unwillingness to turn a blind eye to even to the small acts that posed no threat to the operation of the railways. The company carefully recorded acts of subversion by employees or anyone else who interfered with the proper functioning of the railways. The company reported only sporadic acts of resistance between 1940 and 1941, but such acts increased in 1943 and then became quite frequent and well organized by 1944.[12] As acts of resistance increased, so too did company repression. To this end, the minister of transport, Jean Berthelot, dedicated himself fully to destroying communism (and its associated acts of protest) in France, starting with the SNCF. He identified 100,000 SNCF workers as communists, but because that figure constituted 20 percent of the company, he asked Fournier to create a list of the most dangerous individuals.[13] The executives maintained a file on the political affiliations and values of each worker.[14] In 1941 Robert Le Besnerais, the director general of the SNCF, created a file for "suspected agents" and authorized his subordinates to use any means necessary to locate and immediately suspend all those railwaymen who did not operate in a spirit of collaboration.[15] His list of 1,290 suspects led to many arrests and some deportations to concentration camps and death camps.[16]

In sum, the Vichy government, in concert with SNCF leadership, banned political participation, rail sabotage, and the use of the SNCF trains to pass clandestine messages between the occupied and unoccupied zones—actions that could cost a worker his job and, possibly, his life. Some of these messages were communications between members of the Resistance, while others were simply notes passed between family members searching for one another. Le Besnerais wrote to SNCF personnel on January 14, 1941, stating, "By the order of August 18, 1940, I remind personnel of the obligation imposed on SNCF agents to observe the occupier in the strictest sense. Agents of all levels must by THE ABSOLUTE NECESSITY rigorously observe these prescriptions. I remind you specifically that it is formally forbidden to carry or let others carry documents that could injure Germany, the German army or its managers . . . Those agents found guilty . . . will experience the most severe administrative sanctions that can lead to dismissal."[17] Le Besnerais concludes by demanding that agents turn over all anti-German propaganda.

In 1941, members of the SNCF executive team met regularly with the Vichy minister of the interior (who oversaw the division that managed the French police), promising to help any way they could. In August 1941, Le Besnerais wrote, "We must not miss any indicator, any information that can help the police find the guilty parties and those committing acts of sabotage."[18] Le Besnerais reported proudly that six hundred SNCF agents in the occupied zone had been "eliminated" for subversion. The circulation of underground communist papers and other propaganda slowed dramatically. The executives felt relieved because they feared communist influences and other liberation movements would pull apart their tightly knit organization. SNCF executives continued pressuring employees to comply. In December 1941, Le Besnerais issued a new statement to his staff saying that anyone transporting any mail or aiding any French prisoner would be immediately sanctioned.[19] Though this declaration, SNCF executives deterred resistance activity and thwarted communication between separated loved ones.

While mail exchange did not damage SNCF rolling stock, some acts of sabotage did. These acts became an additional cost of war, upsetting company executives who already felt the burden of increasing wartime demands and insufficient payment. At the beginning of the occupation, the French state headquartered at Vichy told the SNCF that the government would not cover war-related expenses caused by sabotage. The SNCF would have to absorb the cost, they said. Executives used the company circular to reach the corporation's nearly half-million employees, imploring them to protect the machines and, in doing so, to protect the lives of their fellow countrymen. The SNCF had become so effective at eliminating sabotage early in the occupation that it became an example for other government divisions: Berthelot, the head of SNCF transport, advised the postal system how to be similarly effective at squashing defiant acts.

The company complied with commands from higher-ups, but as the demands of war increased, so too did the tensions between SNCF executives and the occupier. In vain, the SNCF executives advocated for the freedom to operate more independently. In 1943 German officials placed additional pressure on the company to protect its railways from sabotage. The SNCF responded to the Germans by saying it would report acts of sabotage only to the military and police authorities, claiming that SNCF staff were neither equipped nor trained to actively or effectively fight these acts.[20]

The executives fought for company independence whenever possible but overall seemed uncommitted to the causes of the resistance. Where resistance

SNCF discouraging rail sabotage via its company newspaper, circa summer 1944. Translation: Sabotaging the Machines? Sabotage of Provisions! Who can protect the machines and the life of your comrades? YOU, RAILWAY MAN. (Le Centre des Archives Historiques de la SNCF)

existed in the company, it could be found lower in the ranks—far from the politically compliant management.

SNCF Railway Workers and the Resistance

The SNCF workers had no official resistance organization of their own. Instead, many belonged to outside groups such as Combat or Ceux de la Libération.[21] Because workers knew how transportation operated and the timing of its activities, many Resistance organizations recruited SNCF workers. The cheminots' responses to this recruitment were mixed. Broch notes, "Cheminots were uncomfortable with violent resistance and industrial sabotage since the late nineteenth century."[22] Political moderates committed to their trains, they were not historically inclined to destroy their precious machines or involve themselves in political disputes.

Yet, among individual SNCF workers, some acts of resistance occurred. Mostly they facilitated the well-organized plans of other groups rather than hatching and executing plans of their own or engaged in symbolic acts such as making jokes about the German occupiers or painting a V for *victoire* or other symbols used by Gaullist or Bolshevik supporters.[23] Jeanne Legrain Bedos, a cheminote during the war, recalls her fellow railway workers adding something to a German wine shipment to turn the wine to vinegar by the time it reached its intended destination. She noted that many observed *la loi de silence* (the law of silence). The risk of even talking about such actions could get one killed because one never knew who one could trust.[24] Some people simply refused to make eye contact with the Germans. Other acts had more tangible results; these included slowing trains or altering signs to send trains filled with German soldiers to the wrong location. Because authorities rarely knew to whom to assign responsibility, the slowing of trains (*ralentissage*) had been popular for years prior to World War II as a means of expressing personal or political grievances.[25]

The *esprit de famille* (or esprit de corps) within the company, which espoused values of duty and loyalty, kept the workers united in their task of maintaining a functioning railroad and, at the same time, deterred many from participating in acts of subversion.[26] The pride of being a railway worker cannot be understated. Janine Boulou, a cheminote and the daughter of a cheminot, said that for her father, the SNCF was sacred. She experienced the company as *une famille solidaire*, a supportive family.[27] SNCF employees were linked like railcars, united by loyalty and carried forward by the sheer momentum of their endeavor to deliver goods, people, and livestock throughout France. Everyone contributed to moving the trains forward. Everyone in France relied upon them doing so. The SNCF family came first, perhaps even before country, and surely before non-Christian deportees who had immigrated from the east and spoke unfamiliar languages.

Broch points out that the definition of *cheminot*, in the dictionary *Petit Larousse*, emphasized rigor, obedience, punctuality, patriotism, and quasi-militaristic values.[28] The company relied on love of profession and the reinforcing power of conformity to maintain the complex network of rail shipments. Operating such an enormous amount of rolling stock, schedules, and staff demanded precision and consistency, not creativity and/or individuality. Revolutionary, disobedient behavior was physically dangerous and not encouraged. Promotions were earned by diligent enactment of policy rather than by divergent thinking. The railway functioned as a traditional patriarchal hierarchy. Management operated top-down, and workers obeyed the order of command, much like in the military. Safety depended on precise communication between parts; the cheminots' lives—even in peacetime—were in one another's hands. As a result, workers focused primarily on their internal corporate hierarchy rather than on the national one.

Although the company was hierarchical in structure, this strong spirit of camaraderie made the SNCF a hospitable site for communist activity. In July 1941, a year after the Franco-German Armistice, a communist paper called *La Tribune des cheminots* (Railway workers' tribune) called for acts of sabotage: "One must sabotage the transports of armaments, supplies, and German troops. The trains must not leave. The trains must be made unusable, the wagons must burn with their war materials, the stops and signals must be blocked."[29] After this announcement and another posted in another communist paper, *l'Humanité*, the SNCF reported an increase in the number of acts of sabotage, including derailments and immobilized trains.[30]

Sabotage was not taken lightly anywhere within the SNCF. It would be dangerous for the cheminots in two ways: they could crush their fellow workers or trigger retribution. More often, they found other means of thwarting the German occupier, such as:

- Helping prisoners, members of the Resistance, and the persecuted move from the occupied zone to the free zone;
- Sharing information about the movements of German transports;
- Distributing underground newspapers;
- Offering technical knowledge about how to sabotage trains to members of the French Resistance;[31] and
- Sabotaging railroad tracks and railcars by cutting breaks or disrupting axles with sand or rocks.[32]

Consequences

SNCF executives and Germans authorities responded to a variety of acts of resistance performed by SNCF workers. Some of those responses were relatively benign. The November 11 Protest in 1943, for example, honored the anniversary of the World War I armistice signed with the then-defeated Germany. An SNCF *chauffeur de chaudière* (boiler operator) placed a French flag atop a chimney forty meters high. Word of mouth led to a gathering. By 10 a.m., all personnel working at that location stood before the flag with heads bare, singing "La Marseillaise," the French national anthem. After a discussion with the German soldiers, workers had a moment of silence and pulled the flag down.[33]

Some performed these acts with relatively few consequences, whereas others lost everything. Léon Bronchart, the most renowned resistant within the SNCF, transferred secret messages between regions, derailed his merchandise train, and used an acid mixture to set fire to his machine.[34] On October 31, 1942, he refused to drive a train filled with political prisoners and, later, one carrying German soldiers.[35] In response, the SNCF refused to pay his bonus, and on October 30, 1942, he lost his SNCF title. Crucially, Bronchart was not shot or deported for his refusal to drive the trains.[36] Even though he resisted with relatively minor consequences, no other railway workers seemed to follow his lead. There are no reports of anyone else refusing to drive any trains. Why not? Perhaps because they viewed others suffer consequences for subversion. The following railwaymen suffered greatly for disobedience.

- German officials condemned M. Berger, second in command at the Poitiers railway station, for trafficking war materials in an occupied zone. They listed his crime as acting *"contre l'Ordonnance du Führer"* (against Hitler's order). Imprisoned from July 29, 1940, through April 28, 1945, he spent four years and nine months in prison, including two years in an isolation cell.
- Dr. Lamper, caught in 1942 for acts of resistance in the Southeast Region, was killed in Camp Vaihingen, a labor camp in Germany known for working and starving its prisoners to death.
- K. Rozet, Inspection SES, Second VB Resistant, caught in March 1943, was deported to Auschwitz.[37]

Acts of sabotage could also place the lives of colleagues, family, neighbors, and friends at risk. On April 16, 1942, someone sabotaged a train on the Paris–Cherbourg line carrying German soldiers on leave.[38] The security police in Berlin reported that the derailment killed twenty-eight Germans and wounded thirty others. The Geheime Feldpolizei (GFP, German Secret Police), the judicial police, and the French military police, along with other offices responded by

- Searching the homes of communist suspects;
- Controlling the schedules of those living in towns near where the bombing occurred;
- Visiting 88 hotels, searching for suspects;
- Verifying the identities of 527 travelers;
- Arresting 700 individuals between April 16 and April 18;
- Finding 51 individuals who had been missing in town at the time of the attack;
- Closing all sporting and entertainment events;
- Enforcing a curfew between 7:30 p.m. and 6:00 a.m.;
- Arresting 4 people for being suspected Gaullists (supporters of Charles de Gaulle and a free France); and
- Killing 30 hostages, none of whom were deemed responsible for the derailment but who were considered part of terrorist groups that were directly or indirectly complicit.[39]

In total, thirty hostages were killed by French and German police forces in retribution for the roughly thirty Germans killed in the sabotage. All those near the site felt the horror of the retaliation.

Over time, more people understood that winning the war required stopping the trains. As such, those willing to actively work to liberate France increasingly looked to derailments. Initially, only the cheminots knew how to stop trains, but their knowledge would eventually be transferred to those who took it upon themselves to teach others.[40] Rail sabotage became emblematic of the French Resistance, which might explain how the SNCF came to be bestowed with the title of wartime hero; but it was not always the railway workers who led the charge.[41] For example, a matchbook was distributed that provided simple instructions for how to derail trains. Although the matchbooks were distributed in France, the U.S.-based Diamond Match Company produced them.[42] It was not uncommon for Jews and others who escaped to the United States to seek ways to support—by any means available—those they left behind.

Acts of Resistance on Behalf of the Deportees

Thus far, the discussion of SNCF resistance has focused on upending German domination rather than helping the deportees. The Vichy historian Henry Rousso, however, remarked that whatever margin of maneuver the SNCF workers had, they used it infrequently to assist the deportees.[43] Marrus and Paxton noted that "nothing interfered with the transports to Auschwitz . . . even in

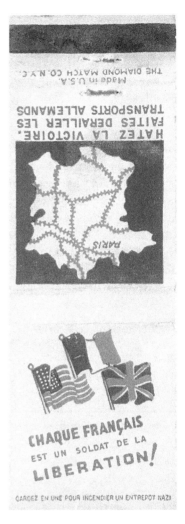

THE DIAMOND MATCH CO. N.Y.C.
Made in U.S.A.

HATEZ LA VICTOIRE.
FAITES DÉRAILLER LES
TRANSPORTS ALLEMANDS

PARIS

CHAQUE FRANÇAIS
EST UN SOLDAT DE LA
LIBERATION!

GARDEZ EN UNE POUR INCENDIER UN ENTREPÔT NAZI

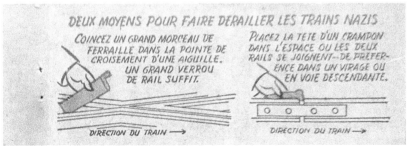

DEUX MOYENS POUR FAIRE DÉRAILLER LES TRAINS NAZIS

COINCEZ UN GRAND MORCEAU DE
FERRAILLE DANS LA POINTE DE
CROISEMENT D'UNE AIGUILLE.
UN GRAND VERROU
DE RAIL SUFFIT.

DIRECTION DU TRAIN →

PLACEZ LA TÊTE D'UN CRAMPON
DANS L'ESPACE OU LES DEUX
RAILS SE JOIGNENT—DE PRÉFÉR-
ENCE DANS UN VIRAGE OU
EN VOIE DESCENDANTE.

DIRECTION DU TRAIN →

A matchbook provides instructions to anyone in possession of it on two ways to derail trains, circa 1944. (Courtesy of Michael Samuels) the summer of 1944 when substantial derailments and sabotage affected other shipments."[44] Broch emphasizes that during the occupation, the average railway worker, like the average French person, did not understand Jewish persecution as separate from other forms of persecution, mostly political.[45] The Jewish deportation convoys made up just less than half of the deportation trains driven by the cheminots.[46]

What is strange, however, is the lack of executive protest regarding the execrable conditions on the trains. SNCF executives spoke up when German requests exceeded the company's capacity and when the company did not receive payment. Yet nothing has been found among the SNCF executive correspondences to show that anyone protested the deportation convoys or their prevailing conditions.[47] From the German perspective, except for the occasional late train, all went smoothly.

The cheminots, at least in some ways, expressed their dismay. Broch points to vehement passages in cheminot publications suggesting some desire to refuse to drive deportation trains carrying people to forced labor.[48] For the most part, however, the company men followed orders. Sometimes those orders helped people; the SNCF drove special trains to allow Jewish children to visit families in the free zone.[49] These trains also carried many of these same children to their deaths. Is the company to be celebrated for these family reunion transports or condemned for the deportations?

Even when it came to deportation convoys, on-time trains remained the priority for both SNCF employees and executives. Louis Cambournac, SNCF regional director, wrote to his superior at SNCF, Robert Le Besnerais, distraught over the tardy departure of a last-minute train of deportees headed to the Sobibór concentration camp. Cambournac wrote that incidents that delay the timely departure of deportation trains worsen relations with the occupier; the trains must leave on time.[50] The archive in the central office of German security that recorded all details of the deportations and every associated action has no record of any major problems in France.

The Vichy historians Michael Marrus and Robert Paxton saw the lack of SNCF resistance on behalf of the Jewish deportees as "a curious blind spot affected [by] the French railway system, which managed widespread, organised resistance to all kinds of German demands—except deportations to the east."[51] Derailments or destruction of the tracks, some argue, would have been futile and put too many people in danger.[52] Rarely could a train be derailed without crushing its contents; and even if deportees did escape, who could guarantee that they could be hidden after the derailment?[53] Had SNCF workers and Resistance members known more about the destination, perhaps they might have taken the risk.

This is not to suggest that SNCF workers *never* assisted. Acts of resistance on behalf of the deportees performed by individual cheminots include providing hiding places in the deportation wagons, loaning SNCF uniforms for acts of deception and escape, and slowing trains to allow passengers to jump off.[54] The following sections describe some other ways cheminots assisted the deportees.

Offering Water

The Germans determined that the deportees should have some drinkable water in their convoy, but not all deportees received water; some traveled for days with nothing to drink. Those who suffered thirst said the horror of this desperate feeling remained with them throughout their lives. Occasionally, Red Cross workers, Quakers, civilians, and some SNCF workers attempted to provide water to deportees trapped in convoys awaiting departure or stopped for hours in atrocious heat or unbearable cold. One survivor, Francois Rohmer, recalls his experience on his four-day transfer from Compiègne to Dachau. The train would occasionally stop, and "during these stops, surveillance was less strict. [French] Railway workers could pass us water, renewing our courage."[55] Access to the convoys varied throughout the war. One SNCF employee, Raoul Merlin, who worked at a station from which the deportation trains departed, said that early in the war, staff could pass people food and water through the holes in the wagons. In the months leading up to the liberation, however, the Germans forced them to remain at least 100 meters away. Merlin remarked that even "certain German soldiers were themselves appalled" at their superiors for refusing the victims this simple kindness.[56]

Some SNCF workers also refused this kindness. One telegram issued from the Vichy government to the SNCF asks the railway company to provide water because apparently the SNCF had not been doing so. However, SNCF station managers sometimes blocked the distribution of water. In 1942, when the Red Cross and Quakers from the United States and Britain tried to help the deportees by offering them food and water, SNCF executives complained that these efforts prevented the trains from leaving on time.[57] This shameful moment underscores the fact that while some tried to help, others refused.

Mailing Letters

Water and provisions being difficult to deliver, caring cheminots found other small ways to aid the deportees without disrupting the timeliness and functioning of their machines or risking their lives. When possible, deportees threw scraps of paper carrying messages—often last words—and mailing addresses out of any openings they could find in the railcar. In some cases, deportees scribbled numerous addresses hoping to ensure that at least one message would arrive. Some cheminots collected these scraps after the trains departed, then placed them in envelopes and mailed them to their intended recipients—some of whom might already have been dead or on their way to the camps. When received, the notes often became family treasures.

Collecting and mailing these letters became increasingly difficult as the war progressed. During the last months of the occupation, German officers searched for jettisoned notes more thoroughly, and SNCF workers could send only letters that the Germans had overlooked. Some cheminots whispered to people to throw the letters out only once the train moved 200 or 300 meters away from the station because the Germans swept them up after the departure.[58]

Charlotte Delbo, who was on a convoy train in January 1943, discusses these letters: "We took from our bags paper and pencils and wrote notes: 'that the person who finds this would please have the kindness to let X know that her daughter . . . his wife . . . Christiane, or Suzanne, or Marcelle—has been deported to Germany. We are in good spirits. See you soon.' Each ending with 'I'll come back.'"[59]

Madelaine Herscu wrote to her parents:

From I don't know where
Sunday July 19, 1943
My dear parents,

Maybe this is a last letter to tell you that I am leaving in a livestock train of 1,600 people, 50 per wagon. Don't worry on my behalf. I am with comrades and my fiancé Roger Rybacq. We leave for Poland but I will see you after the war in our house.

Do not cry for my fate. I have what I need; I am Jewish and must suffer. Until now we were with the French police and we were fine. But for the past three weeks we had the Germans and it was terrible. Stopping mail was not sufficient, they hit us with batons daily—they wanted to know the addresses of our parents or families to stop them. . . . The person who finds this letter will have a good heart and put it in the mailbox to reassure my parents whose two daughters were stopped and of whom they have had no news.

Madelaine Herscu
Convoy 57[60]

Another letter, this one from the deportee Eva Golgevit, has a different tone:

Drancy July 30, 1943
My dear friend,

Fate would have it that you would become a godmother to my child faster than you would have wanted it. I did not have a chance to speak to you before I left. I do not know where to find my son, where I must go to find him, when one day he will come back to life. However, I leave courageously with the firm conviction that my son will not be abandoned. That you, I dare say, "my dear friend," stay to look after him after I am gone.

I am no more than a number in a wagon crammed in . . . but do not worry about me. I am in good spirits and I am counting on returning quickly. I send you a huge hug with all my love and maternal love, if cruelly proven. A kiss for my Jeannot. Hello to my family. In three hours we leave at dawn. I send you kisses, more kisses and cry to you with all my strength "Goodbye."

Your Eva

Eva Golgevit
Convoy 58

Pierre Blum told me that his parents, Henri and Simone Blum, slipped a note out of Convoy 77. Henri had been stopped by the Gestapo on June 14, 1944, just eight days after D-Day, after his employer's family denounced him. A few days later, his wife and sister-in-law went to a grain factory to get a package to Henri in the internment camp. The Gestapo was waiting for them. The two women were transported to Drancy, where they joined Henri. From the railcar in which they were deported, the Blums were able to write the following and add an address: "We hope the children are okay. We hope they are in good hands." They successfully pushed the note through an opening in the railcar, and a railway worker found it and sent it to its destination. Pierre spoke wistfully about this brief note, which found its way to the children. At the time of the interview, while in his late eighties, Pierre was greatly distressed that he and his sister had not been able to locate the slip of paper with his parents' last words.[61]

Escapes

Mailing letters and serving water demonstrated that some cheminots cared, and these acts did ease some suffering. Of course, what people most needed was help escaping. Escapes were difficult and dangerous, yet in rare cases some SNCF workers orchestrated successful getaways.[62] Maurice Lemaire, regional president of SNCF's northern division, noted this danger. He described how watchmen guarded the trains closely, shooting all prisoners who managed to escape from the wagons. Lemaire wrote in a letter, "The soldiers responsible for the trains were armed with submachine guns and would have used them without hesitation at the slightest provocation. At night, there were floodlights on the trains."[63] When the SNCF workers could no longer approach the convoys without the risk of being shot, they could offer only moral support, Lemaire said. This support was not trivial to those who received it. Charlotte Delbo recalls that during her journey in January 1943, a railway worker whispered, "They are beaten. They lost Stalingrad. You will return soon. Have courage, little ones!"[64]

In some cases, SNCF workers could get close enough to assist with escape attempts and did so by hiding tools such as clamps, chisels, hammers, and hacksaws underneath the hay in the rail cars.[65] Such instruments even helped SNCF secretary Raloux, who found himself deported on September 17, 1943, along with 139 others. Only 23 arrived in Weimar (the train's destination) thanks to the hidden tools that allowed the other deportees to cut through the walls.

Most assistance occurred before deportees reached the convoy trains. Freddie Knoller recalls the afternoon of August 26, 1942, when his sister and nieces had gone out and he stayed at home with his mother.[66] A railway worker in the Resistance brought the two of them to the train station, hiding them in a piece of furniture with two doors; an exterior door faced the railway station, and the other faced the platform where the train would arrive. Emile, the head of the railway station, informed them that the Milice (which Paxton describes as the infamous parapolice force) surveilled the front of the station and the train platform.[67] The SNCF workers smuggled Knoller's mother into a hidden train compartment that closed with a key while he stayed hidden in the furniture. With his mother hidden, they traveled safely just 300 kilometers south of Paris, just beyond the line of demarcation and therefore inside the free zone. Their lives had been saved thanks to these SNCF workers.

Raymond Zaks told me how an SNCF cheminot helped save his family: "My life is indebted to the railway workers and the Resistance!" At their first station, a railway worker told them to board after the whistle blew. This helped them board for free. As the family settled into their seats, they felt the train moving forward and then rolling back. The train had been pulled back to the station so that officials could search for escaping Jews. Raymond was sitting with his friend Benjamin. The controller asked for everyone's papers, and when he came to Raymond, he leaned in within two centimeters of Raymond's face. Raymond suspects that because of his blue eyes, the controller never asked for his papers. He had asked everyone else, and four people were taken from that train that day, all likely headed toward deportation.[68]

Another railway worker later helped them again. The *chef de gare* (station manager) at Chantenay-Villedieu told his family that after the whistle blew, the five of them could jump on the train unnoticed. He pointed to an unused train wagon sitting on the tracks. After roughly an hour of waiting in the wagon, the locomotive was attached. The train carried them to the station at Moulins, in the occupied zone. The wagon stopped in the middle of the tracks before the entrance to the station, allowing them to hop off without being seen. They were thus able to avoid the police checkpoint.[69]

Jacqueline Birn, a hidden child during the war, shared with me her story of how a railway worker saved her family. Five carloads of Gestapo officers rolled up to the house where she and her family were hidden. The Gestapo had come to demand a secret code used by the Resistance and known by the SNCF cheminot who lived with his family on the main floor. What the Gestapo did not know is that the cheminot also knew about the Jewish family hidden in the house on the second floor. The man neither released the code nor denounced Jacqueline's family. The Gestapo arrested, tortured, and imprisoned him in Limoges, returning him home after three weeks. Jacqueline attributes her fond feelings for the cheminots to this incident.[70]

The Largest SNCF Rescue

The largest coordination of SNCF efforts on behalf of the deportees was referenced briefly by Marrus and Paxton: "railwaymen apparently helped about fifty Jewish children escape from one convoy in September 1942 and may also have smuggled some tools into baggage cars to help prisoners to break through the floorboards."[71] An independent historian, Grégory Célerse, recently discovered more about this rescue.[72] Célerse discovered a number of people from Lille, a city north of Paris, who claimed that the SNCF workers had helped save them. During our day together in Lille, Célerse told me about his careful work identifying the thirty-six people who were rescued on September 11, 1942, the day of the Jewish New Year. Of those, twenty-two were under the age of eighteen.[73] SNCF workers had witnessed the increasing number of arrests of Jewish people in town, which intensified after the Germans required that Jews wear the Star of David. On the day of the roundup, a woman beseeched a worker to save the children, including her own. He did. Of the six hundred Jews who found themselves on the deportation platform at Fives station, the SNCF workers could save just a few dozen, which they did by hiding them in an old dormitory, passing babies through parked train windows. Once the deportation train departed, the SNCF workers, among them the station manager, worked to raise funds for the refugees. The police never discovered the activities of the estimated twenty-three SNCF workers. In 1954 those SNCF workers involved in the rescue received either letters of congratulations or medals from the government for their acts of courage and dedication.[74]

Another commemoration of heroism took place more recently. On September 11, 2016, the city government of Lille hosted a commemorative ceremony.

Six survivors attended the ceremony, as did the SNCF's Alain Leray and Bernard Emsellem, Grégory Célerse, and two hundred members of the community. The city unveiled a plaque at the old Gare Saint Sauveur, a converted merchandise railway station. The rescues in Lille came from the spontaneous engagement of several SNCF workers, not the executive team. This successful effort occurred early in the war, in 1942. Most acts of resistance occurred in 1944, when the Allies had gained momentum and German defeat seemed more likely.

In August 1944, two months after D-Day, SNCF staff prevented SS Captain Aloïs Brunner from sending one of the last convoys from an internment camp (the article does not specify which camp).[75] Another report describes an incident in which SNCF employees informed the Maquis (French guerrilla Resistance fighters) about a loaded deportation train, which the workers rehitched to send it somewhere other than its intended destination. The Maquis then carried out the actual rescue.[76] The SNCF report described the incident as follows:

> August 4, 1944, an SNCF employee discovered that at the Peyraud station, the Germans guarded a wagon of 70 deportees. The employee hopped on his bike and rode to the station to inform the Maquis. At 1 a.m., the train staff rehitched the wagons, sending the train to Annonay (near Lyon), instead of Compiègne via St. Rambert, its intended destination. When the train arrived at Annonay, the convoy stopped in front of the station. A German got out, thinking he was at St. Rambert. The Maquis began firing; gunfire continued throughout the night. The Germans put up a white flag of surrender but fighting soon recommenced. Eventually, the Germans put the deportees in front to protect themselves from the shooting; three deportees were killed. This act of resistance resulted in the liberation of 67 deportees.[77]

These sixty-seven deportees owed their lives to the SNCF workers and their collaboration with the Resistance.

While resistance efforts thwarted the departure of that train, Brunner, just prior to fleeing France, succeeded in directing one more train out to Buchenwald from Drancy. This time the bus drivers refused Brunner's order to transport the deportees to the train station. This refusal, while symbolically important, did not stop the trains. The roughly fifty individuals were forced to walk the short thirty-minute trip to the rail station on August 17, 1944, and joined the last convoy leaving France to Buchenwald.[78]

During the war, many people found themselves forced to choose between horrible options—and often more than once. SNCF workers were no different. The majority of SNCF employees, like the majority of the French people, took on many postures—passive collaborator, victim, opportunist, diligent employee, loyalist, antisemite, resistant, and, at rare moments, Jewish protector. (The popular French television program *Un Village Français*, first released in 2009, compellingly depicts these changing roles.)

As Broch points out, most cheminots were "ordinary workers," neither great champions of the Jews nor great cowards.[79] The SNCF railway workers clearly did not initiate the deportations, but neither did many appear to do much to stop them. Not all survivors with whom I spoke faulted the company for this inaction. Stanley Kalmanovitz, deported on convoy 71 with his sister and his family's only survivor, asked me, "What was the French railroad supposed to do? Someone has the gun at your head, what do you do? You take the bullet? Then, if everyone takes a bullet, who's left?"[80] He went on to point out how often we (Jews) wanted others to take a bullet for us, but we would not take one for ourselves. He had no special animosity toward the company, even though he thinks their amends-making efforts are motivated entirely by business interests.

In this chapter I have reviewed some brave actions and kind words, but likely many other actions occurred; not everything was recorded. Hundreds of small towns in France had railway stations and housed SNCF employees. Each of these villages had its own networks and tendencies toward collaboration and/or resistance, and each existed as its own little microcosm of the war.

The SNCF as Hero?

Clearly some individuals engaged in heroic acts, but was the SNCF as a corporate entity a hero? This question leads to us to the conundrum of corporate personhood. Where does the company's soul lie? Is it with the executives who reported sabotage, did little to save their own Jewish workers, and pushed water barrels away from packed convoys so that the trains could depart on time? Or with the few courageous souls who assisted individuals?

When under attack, contemporary company executives sometimes say that "the SNCF served as a cog in the Nazi machinery," or words to that effect. The Germans used their trains to achieve their agenda, they say. While the SNCF was clearly no fan of the occupation, the use of the term "cog" obscures 400,000 thinking individuals. A "cog" cannot make choices; those who organize and drive trains can. Individuals made difficult choices, under terrible constraints, but made them nonetheless. During the Vichy period, any choice other than total submission often carried great risk. But to construct the SNCF as only a composite of machines exonerates not just those individuals who assisted but— perhaps far more dangerous—all of us. We too participate in large and small ways in the suffering of others, often under no orders at all. Our purchases, investments, votes, and careers affect lives. Under far less constraint, we all contribute to but remain removed—as were many of the SNCF workers—from the profound despair caused by our merely following along. Is a desire to expunge the SNCF connected to a desire to expunge ourselves?

There were long-term consequences of SNCF collaboration, not just for those murdered but for those who survived. Seen during the war as enemies of humanity, who were they now? Did they matter at all? In the immediate aftermath of the Holocaust, survivors focused on physical and economic survival and finding loved ones, leaving them little energy to think about their societal identity in postwar France. The government and the SNCF, in contrast, committed money to postwar identity construction. With the help of the French government, the SNCF emerged from ashes as a publicly celebrated hero. This singular story of heroism would endure unchallenged for nearly fifty years.

Given the more than three thousand skeletal-looking Jews who returned from the camps, it is astonishing that the company retained its singular identity of glory for so long. The next chapter, which begins part II, also shows how cries for "accountability" began to fracture the company's legendary image. These cries eventually shifted the SNCF's narrative about itself and made room for survivors' stories and claims for restitution. The tales of heroism sit awkwardly next to survivor narratives like the one that ends this chapter. For most, there were no heroes of any kind.

VOICES FROM THE LAST TRAINS

Daniel and Samuel recall awakening in Austria one day to find that they had not been liberated so much as abandoned. German authorities had fled the Mauthausen camp and its annexes, taking with them any remaining provisions. Noting the absence of guards, about two thousand people, including the brothers, had the strength to stumble away. In their search for food and help, the boys found a garden cabin with an open door. Samuel thinks the owner, fearing these teetering cadavers coming out of the woods, simply left the door open and ran away.

"We did not open a cupboard or touch a thing," Samuel recalls proudly. "We just found a place to sleep."

A short time later, two American soldiers discovered the boys.

Daniel, then fourteen years old, weighed roughly fifty-five pounds. "I was about the weight of my skeleton," he estimated. Concerned the boys had typhus—a contagious disease that killed many in the camps and during the liberation—an American soldier quickly placed them in a truck with other former prisoners gathered from around the camp. The truck drove them to a school courtyard. Samuel found some water and tried to serve it to Daniel. The liquid just dribbled down his chin.

"Can you imagine? My brother was too weak to even swallow!" recalls Samuel.

More than seventy years later, when telling the story, he leans over and grips his eyes to block the tears.

"That was the worst moment of the whole thing," he says. Would his brother die now, in the moment of their liberation?[81]

During a separate interview, Daniel retells the same moment when Samuel tried to pass him water. "I read in my brother's eyes that I was lost. . . . I had no strength for him or myself."

Samuel ran out and found an American with a Red Cross armband and said with his broken English, "My brother is dying. He is fourteen."

"Forty?"

"No, fourteen!"

The man ran to Daniel and picked him up.

"When I saw his clothes, I thought not even a scarecrow has such shredded clothing," Samuel recalled. Then he said, "The man did not encourage me to follow him. I don't know why, but I just stood there. I don't know why I did not run after him."

Daniel was carried away. Almost dead from starvation, typhus, scurvy, and dysentery, he fell into a coma.[82]

With Daniel gone and presumed dead, Samuel returned to the bunk beds in the school courtyard where the soldiers had originally placed them. He slept for days. The caregivers diagnosed Samuel with typhus and took him to a hospital in Vienna, Austria, where he stayed until the afternoon of June 26, 1945—more than a year after D-Day. On this day, doctors strapped Samuel to a stretcher and flew him back to Paris. His flight landed in the Paris–Le Bourget airport, from which he was taken to the Hôpital de la Salpêtrière. He arrived in Paris still clutching a German army jacket that at some point (he forgot exactly when and where) he had instinctively grabbed for warmth.

Aunt Hélène, their father's sister, located Samuel through contacts at the Hôtel Lutetia and visited him in the hospital every day. She also took Samuel's sister Sophie, who had spent the war hiding with a family and was now seven years old, to visit him. The young girl did not recognize her brother. They had been separated for more than two years, and Samuel had been dramatically changed by the camp. The doctors soon transferred him to the Hôpital Bichat in Paris. The family was in tatters.

Daniel's coma persisted. The family, unsure of his fate, spent six months mourning his death.

Daniel was somewhere between life and death during these months, "They would immerse me in water and sometimes I would have a flash of consciousness. But that's all, just a flash," Daniel explained. When he regained awareness, he found himself in a hospital in Dôle, France, near the Jura mountains. He had some faint memories of his time at Auschwitz, but he had no idea who he was. As he slowly recovered, he communicated enough fragments for the hospital administration to locate Aunt Hélène. She gave Samuel, who was now in Paris, the hospital address. In a letter dated September 8, 1945, Samuel wrote the following to Daniel:

My dear Daniel,

How happy I was to have received your news. I spent much time knowing nothing about what had happened to you. I was worried. Now, when you are back, you will see how much better it will be.

I also returned directly to Paris, in quite a state. But at present, I am in pretty good shape and can go out. Don't worry about anyone. I found Sophie looking superb. She is very close to Paris and thinks about you often. It was Aunt Hélène who told me about your return. She is also happy you are well. She is very happy you are being tended to and taken care of.

We will take care of you, soon. You don't need to worry about anything. As soon as you are near me, you will receive lots of visits from comrades who have not forgotten you—[they have] especially not forgotten two escapees from Auschwitz.

We would be so happy to hear some of your news. Hopefully we will see you soon.

I will write you again soon. I send best wishes from all of your friends and kisses from Sophie and your Aunt, plus thousands of mine.

Your brother, honored to see you soon.

Samuel

"When I saw his handwriting, I felt an electric shock through my body. I immediately remembered everything!" recalls Daniel.

He wrote back with surprisingly stable handwriting and understandably fragmented thoughts:

September 15, 1945
My dear Samuel,

I received your letter a few days ago and it had quite an effect on me, at first I didn't want to believe and even now it feels strange.

I am doing well in this rehabilitation center. However, there are times when I feel so depressed that I am not myself, especially when I think of Sophie . . . and then . . . I am surrounded by people taking good care of me. They make me laugh. I laugh and a few moments later, I cry.

These memories of Auschwitz, of Mauthausen, of our journey, of our trials, of our separation; then emptiness. I remember in flashes . . . dreams, delirium, visions. . . . Another big emptiness, I find myself somewhere else, then again somewhere else, and finally here, where I am better than where I have been. I am starting to understand; a great change is happening in me, but I don't know what, nor how. I have an inkling, if only to fool myself, but in images I perceive, I seem to understand after all.

A great voyage, a liberation, kinship; but the reality is mixed with my nightmares of the kind that . . .

I think however, of truth, but it is something that is unsettling . . . of the kind that, in reflecting, I forget everything.

But finally, I live; and you as well, and Sophie as well. What is done is done. I hope to see you soon, with Sophie, in good health both of you, and it is with this wish that I leave you not without an affectionate embrace that a brother has for his own.

Your brother who is doing better,
Daniel

Neither mentioned their parents. Both say they knew their parents were dead, but they never said it out loud. Violence creates silences even in the closest relationships. They wrote a few more letters planning their reunion in Paris. Once he had been nourished and with much of his memory restored, doctors decided that Daniel was too healthy to stay in the hospital. He was too young for a convalescent home, so doctors decided to transfer him in October 1945 to the Hôpital Bichat in Paris, where his brother was also recuperating. They celebrated their imminent reunion. Just as Daniel prepared for his transfer to Paris and reunion with his brother, a turn in Samuel's health would delay their visit for another year. Those caring for Samuel decided that a pulmonary issue he had developed would best be treated in Switzerland. So, Samuel and about twenty others boarded a train headed for the Swiss Alps just as Daniel was about to depart for Paris.[83]

"As we passed Dôle [in eastern France] in the middle of the night, I knew Daniel was not far away . . . I was sad," Samuel recalled.

With his brother ensconced in the mountains of Switzerland, Daniel remained in Paris alone, recovering in the same hospital where Samuel had been just weeks before. A number of patients in the hospital knew his brother; the emptiness consumed him.

"Imagine a boy of fourteen who comes back from hell! Who has no family, no social place, no roots. He floats. He is incapable of starting school normally again," Daniel said. Madame Lazare, a well-connected and wealthy woman, came upon Daniel in the hospital and eventually became the legal guardian of the brothers. She provided food, shelter, and eventually jobs. She moved Daniel to one of her properties in southern France near Aix-en-Provence. Daniel, tremendously grateful for the shelter, always felt like an outsider. This home provided for his physical needs, he said, but there was no warm family for him. Focusing on the future helped him avoid getting pulled back into a disastrous past. When he tried to pick up any fragments of his own past, he found only pain. For example, when he visited the bank to withdraw whatever little money his parents had saved, the bank teller told him the account had been closed due to "inactivity." Daniel said, "I understood the bank had their policies, but I was really hurt."

Companies could settle back into policies far more easily than people could settle back into their lives. Hiding behind bureaucracy and rules, large businesses and government agencies reformulated their priorities without having to justify themselves. Survivors had no recourse and would not for many years. The government efforts sought to revitalize the economy; France needed to rebuild more than it needed justice. But did France rebuild its railroads and strengthen its banks at the cost of leaving indelible marks on the hearts of children and many others? Did the postwar period in some ways inflict additional wounds? Daniel still remembers the pain of his visit to the bank where the teller told him he could not withdraw his parents' small savings because of account inactivity. Are victims supposed to forget the police, buses, and trains that helped rip their lives apart? Businesses and organizations clearly help restore order, but if they do so by slamming the door on the past, we risk inflicting additional harm. Silence ought not to be the price of recovery.

Over a year later, Samuel returned to Paris. During his convalescence in Switzerland, he had fallen in love with Elise, a young woman who had answered an advertisement in the paper seeking girls with good writing skills who were interested in helping the hospitalized patients. The payment would be a few pieces of chocolate. "Why not?" Elise thought. She received a photo of Samuel. She liked him and sent him a photo of herself. They became fast friends. Soon Samuel would be visiting her family.

"They welcomed me with a smile," recalls Samuel. "At that point, anyone who welcomed me with a smile was, well, family."

In 1945, too young to marry and with no ability to provide for Elise, Samuel traveled to Paris alone. He wanted to give Elise time to reflect on their union, given how little he had to offer. He stayed a few nights with Aunt Hélène in Paris before joining Daniel in Aix-en-Provence on Madame Lazare's property. Their long-awaited reunion occurred at the Marseille train station.

"At this point, we were like only children. We had had different experiences growing up," says Daniel. He meant to say that each felt like an only child, with experiences so different from those of the other. What they shared had all been destroyed.

The brothers spent just a short time together before their next separation. Samuel returned to Paris to continue his studies, and Daniel moved on with his life and studies in Aix-en-Provence. About returning to school, Daniel said, "This was one of the most isolating experiences because I had left as a child and returned a man. I felt so separate from the other students. They seemed so young. I felt more comfortable with the adults." Yet the adults in their life never stayed around long. Aunt Hélène, who had reunited the boys and provided them with the only picture they have of their parents, died within a few years of their return. In 1946 doctors made note of Daniel's healthy body weight and good coloring and declared him healed from the whole experience. Only in 1948 did the Association for Deportees encourage Daniel to find another doctor who could confirm that indeed the deportations had taken their physical toll, but the psychological impact was never investigated or even noted.

After completing his studies in Aix-en-Provence, Daniel returned to Paris to find that his brother had already moved in with Elise, his fiancée. The couple married in March 1951 and soon moved to Côte d'Ivoire and then went on to Cameroon, spending eight years in Africa. They were happy to disappear. "The French colonies were independent at this point and needed help building infrastructure," Samuel explained. Samuel and Elise decided not to have children.

"I felt too mixed up inside myself after the war."

During the eight years of separation, the emotional distance between Samuel and Daniel grew. During this time, Daniel converted to Catholicism. "We were not really raised in any religion. I always felt Catholic. I was raised French," he explained. He even attended a few months of seminary to become a priest.

When I shared this information, Samuel said, "Daniel never told me about that. He was afraid I would not approve, which I didn't."

But instead of becoming a priest, Daniel fell in love. He and a group of friends attended an orchestral rehearsal at the Théâtre de Châtelet in central Paris. The performance would be broadcast on the radio the following day, but the public could attend the live rehearsal for a nominal fee. Daniel's future wife, Collette, also attended the concert with a group of her friends. As the groups realized they had some friends in common, they started to merge. Daniel noticed her right away and began his attempts to attract her interest. "I became the clown that night," he said. "She thought I was too much." It took some time, but he eventually won her over. At twenty-two years of age, in 1954, Daniel married Collette and began his own family. He considers his marriage the determining element in his socialization back into the world. She nursed him through his nightmares, and, he says, in a way she raised him. "I was kind of a wild savage when she met me," Daniel said about their early days, reminding me that he was just a boy when his parents were taken and that he had spent his adolescence at internment and death camps.

The couple went on to have seven children.

Samuel, on the other hand, withdrew. "Once Daniel had converted to Catholicism and had a large family, I didn't think he needed me anymore," Samuel said.

Daniel's life was indeed full. He was a proud father, husband, and head of human resources for an insurance company with 2,500 employees. France honored him at Versailles with the Légion d'honneur for his work on behalf of the disabled. Yet he often mourned his separation from his brother.

When I asked them individually if I could write about their relationship and not just the war years, they each approved. Daniel wanted people to understand how violence shatters relationships, not just bodies. The wounds of the Holocaust never come close to disappearing. During one visit, we enjoyed a sunny walk around Versailles and a delicious lunch at his favorite restaurant and cheerfully chatted about love, family, work, and health. Back at his apartment, I prepared some tea, and we settled in the living room surrounded by dozens of family photos and other memorabilia to chat some more.

To my surprise, Daniel leaned his head back and, after a moment of silence, said, "I'm still not sure if it would have been better to have died than to live with the memories of Auschwitz."

PART II

Accountability

CHAPTER FOUR

Holding the SNCF Accountable

The government should establish justice before railroads.

—MAURICE ROLLAND, 1952

AFTER THE WAR, Maurice Rolland, a lawyer and member of the French Resistance, declared, "justice before railroads," but the French state disagreed, choosing to prioritize rebuilding France and to purge the country of its most notorious collaborators.[1] There were some immediate postwar attempts at justice in Germany during the Nuremberg trials. Some of these trials focused on corporate actors. The post-Nuremberg Military Tribunals conducted by the US military between 1946 and 1949 tried a dozen corporate board members for their companies' support of the Nazi war effort and various other crimes.[2] While executives from I. G. Farben, Flick, and Krupp, among others, faced jail time, none served more than eight years before heading off to run postwar Europe in various capacities. Not only did Alfried Krupp walk out of prison in 1951 (a decade before his initial full sentence would have been served) with his property restored, but a 1957 *Time* magazine cover story highlighted Krupp's contribution to postwar economic development. The article barely mentioned his close collaboration with the SS in establishing conditions of slave labor in his factories, which led to his conviction in 1947 for crimes against peace and crimes against humanity.[3]

Lack of political and social will thwarted judicial processes involving corporations in other ways. Early in her career (long before becoming a prominent legal anthropologist), Sally Falk Moore found herself responsible for gathering and reviewing archival documents for Nuremberg prosecutors investigating the chemical conglomerate I. G. Farben. The barriers she faced tell us much about the tenor of the times. I. G. Farben's chief archivist claimed to be unfamiliar with the organization of his neatly arranged files, which expanded over several floors. Moore sought assistance from an American army major in charge of the Farben complex, but he refused to assist her because he disagreed with the Nuremberg prosecutions and especially those involving the prosecution of the industrialists.[4] Countless moments like these culminated in the exculpation of the majority of guilty parties. Consistent with this trend, the rail company executives, vital to the extermination of the Jews as well as the Nazi expansion, were never held accountable.

France emerged from World War II like most of Europe—too cold, hungry, and perhaps too disoriented to do much justice seeking. Many French citizens were climbing over rubble hoping to locate loved ones, exhume bodies, recover objects of value (especially stolen gold in the form of jewelry, wedding rings, and teeth), and piece together any other remnants they could find of their lost world.[5] With national infrastructure in tatters, rehabilitating the railroads became a top priority for the government.[6] By the war's end, fewer than 50 percent of the SNCF's rail lines and 15 percent of the locomotives were operational.[7] Without railroads, no food could be brought to the starving French people or support the more than two million French prisoners of war, returning laborers, and deportees. The country had to rebuild 25 percent of its buildings and needed railroads to help do so.[8] Railroads meant life. Justice was a luxury good.

In this environment, the SNCF easily emerged as a national war hero for its ability both to rebuild France and to serve as a site of national pride. Chapman notes the postwar French government's preference for administrative and technocratic rule worked well for the hierarchical railway company, already run by technocrats.[9] For these reasons, the SNCF rose powerfully from the ashes of war.

For most who survived, the war shattered identities. Many child survivors found themselves without parents and homes. Some of these children completely lost track of who they were. At a train station café in Normandy, Josiane told me how her parents hid her in a convent in Belgium, where she had stayed for three years.[10] At age five, Josiane says she did not know she was Jewish or even that she had parents. Because the convent raised her as a Catholic orphan, she believed herself Catholic. When her parents came for her, she could not speak to them: they spoke only Yiddish, and she spoke French. Her story is not uncommon.

Parents who returned often did so as shells of their former selves. Some committed suicide; many others developed neurological or emotional disorders. Josiane's mother had lost several children in the Holocaust—siblings whom Josiane had never known. Her mother developed epilepsy, and as a child Josiane remembers often finding her on the floor in convulsions. Josiane eagerly married her current husband, Claude, at age seventeen, she says, in order to separate from her family's sadness. The couple moved to Morocco. This too was not uncommon. Those who survived often lost track of, ran from, or suffered within surviving family units. As a result, members of many Jewish families became strangers to one another. The story ended only for those who perished; the approximately three thousand survivors of the French Jewish deportations needed to reconstruct not just their lives but their own sense of humanity and dignity.[11]

After a short period of mourning and accountability, President Charles de Gaulle sought to restore France and its pride through what amounted to a deletion of the Vichy period.[12] While historians still debate the extent of this *refoulement*, or repression, the survivors with whom I spoke experienced the postwar period as one of erasure. Before the war became taboo, France did have a short period of *épuration* (purges) led by Charles de Gaulle's government, which opened more than 300,000 cases against alleged collaborators and began trials against the leaders of the Vichy government, starting with Philippe Pétain, who served as head of state in the Vichy government. On August 15, 1945, four days before the battle to liberate Paris began, judges stripped Pétain of his military honors and sentenced him to life imprisonment. He died six years later. Pierre Laval, who worked directly under Pétain during much of the occupation, also faced trial for high treason. He was held accountable as leader of the Vichy government and for ordering the French people *not* to assist the allies after they landed at Normandy.

Other collaborators, however, found themselves granted shocking levels of amnesty. Of the 300,000 cases, a little more than half were judged. The others were dismissed for various reasons.[13] In 1949, for example, the government acquitted René Bousquet, the secretary general of police under the Vichy regime, because of his supposed participation in the Resistance. In the 1990s, when the tenor of the times had shifted, he would stand trial for the arrest and deportation of Jews between April 1942 and November 1943.[14]

In the early days, trials did not focus on the Jewish roundups, seizure of property, or deportations, and Jews were rarely invited as witnesses.[15] The French people were told to wipe their tears and reunite by rebuilding rather than pursuing villains. Not everyone agreed; some engaged in what might best be called vigilante executions of alleged collaborators. Scholars debate the exact number of these civilian-initiated executions; some say there were ten thousand, whereas others cite figures as high as fifty thousand.[16] French courts supported de Gaulle's efforts to press forward by trying to seal the lid on the war. In 1946, for example, the Conseil d'État, the highest court for administrative cases, issued the Ganascia decision, a legal ruling that forbade victims to take legal action against the state.[17] This decision resulted in eighteen years of impunity for the French government and even longer for the SNCF.

The SNCF Purges Collaborators

The SNCF had its own period of purges before branding itself as a wartime hero. During this period of *épuration*, 467 SNCF staff were designated guilty of *indignité nationale* (national indignity) for acts of collaboration. But no one, not SNCF president Fournier, Besnerais, the other SNCF executives, or any of the railway workers, lost their job for participating in the deportations.[18] Fournier maintained his position in part because postwar France believed it needed railroads more than justice. Besnerais found himself targeted as a collaborator, but, rather than stand trial, he simply retired. Lawyers called Besnerais as a witness for Pétain's hearing; a video of his testimony shows him defending himself with the words "I am nothing but a technician and I was called upon by the government for a precise mission to restore communication, transport, and to put together a work program for those out of work." Before leaving the stand, he bowed to Pétain. Berthelot, the minister of transport, underwent his own trial. He also defended himself by claiming to be a technician and asserted that his actions were beyond reproach.[19] The question (mentioned in the preface) that originally prompted the research for this book—"Did the train drivers keep their jobs after the war?"—can now be answered: Yes, *all* the train drivers kept their jobs after the war.[20] No wartime employee or executive made amends publicly, and almost all were dead by the time of the more contemporary debates.

Several factors contributed to this lack of accountability within the SNCF. The company did not hold anyone accountable immediately after the war for participating in the Holocaust because Jewish persecution was not yet distinguished from other forms of persecution. Moreover, the French National Railways earned a reputation for protecting its staff from *any* postwar purges. A commissioner working under René Mayer, the minister of public works, who had responsibility for addressing collaborators within the transportation industry, noted how the strong bonds of loyalty among the railway workers protected most from the purges. He observed what he called a kind of conspiracy— friends saving friends—even though the collaborators clearly deserved to be removed: "There is a great malaise within the SNCF, and it appears that the identification of some of its directors as being collaborators, anti-social and lacking in the moral attributes of a chief, is taboo. There is a kind of conspiracy going on, and friendships appear such that the men in question are saved, even though we are fully aware that they no longer deserve their place within the company, considering the current circumstances."[21]

The SNCF, with its strong *esprit de famille*, protected its workers. By the mid-1950s, the term *déportés* still made no distinction between those deported for political reasons and those deported for race.[22] The Holocaust was yet not part of the French consciousness and, by extension, not part of the SNCF's story. This helped the company emerge from the war as a hero—an identity that stuck until the late 1980s.

THE SNCF BECOMES A HERO

So, how does a company that participated in the deportations and protected collaborators from postwar trials secure a position as a hero of the resistance for five decades? With the assistance of the French state, of course. The SNCF's participation in the sabotage of the railways during D-Day made the French National Railways a tangible site for national pride. The SNCF became (and remains) a *lieu de mémoire*, or memory site, for the Resistance.[23] On August 26, 1944, the same day that Charles de Gaulle—with German snipers still shooting at him—led a victory parade down the Champs Élysées in Paris, the Conseil National de la Résistance, a resistance organization that coordinated different wartime efforts, congratulated SNCF president Fournier for the company's acts of sabotage during the war. As early as 1945, a number of individual railway workers, such as Arthur Vallois, received the Médaille de la Résistance (Medal of Resistance) for their acts of bravery.[24] Though the convoys carried thousands to Auschwitz beyond D-Day, France was simply too ablaze in celebration to acknowledge the killing centers to which it sent many of its people.[25]

As noted in chapter 3, a film, *La Bataille du rail*, ultimately helped secure the SNCF's place in the national psyche as a wartime hero. In 1944 the SNCF planned to hold an open competition for filmmakers willing to create a film about the company's role in the Resistance. In the end, the SNCF funded the film and maintained control over the screenplay and the editing.[26] René Clément had already created a shorter film on the railroad's role in the Resistance, making him a good choice for the 1946 film.[27] A major morale booster for postwar France, the movie climaxes during the D-Day railway sabotages coordinated with the Maquis, the armed combat group of the French Resistance. Some cheminots worked with the Resistance to sabotage trains filled with German armaments headed west to combat the fast-approaching Allies. These acts of sabotage helped secure the Allies' successful landing; the Germans could not defend themselves from the Allied invasion without the tanks and other armaments that had been overturned en route. The film has all the excitement of an early war production; some even claim that some scenes include bits of original footage collected during the war.[28] Other than a few small allusions to the deportations—a couple of Jews being led without force out of a train station—the film neglects to mention the trains still heading east toward the death camps.

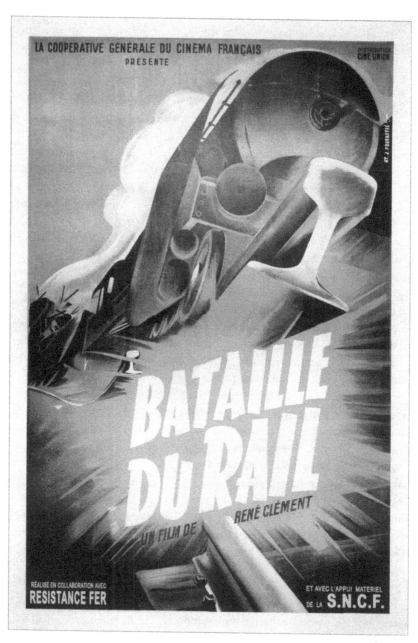

Poster for the 1946 film *La Bataille du rail*. (Courtesy of the Everett Collection)

During the 1950s, accolades continued for the SNCF. On May 10, 1951, the SNCF received the government's highest medal of honor—the Légion d'honneur—for acts of resistance.[29] The SNCF was the first company to receive the award.[30] To secure the SNCF's heroism in history, not just in the popular psyche, the government commissioned Paul Durand, a son and grandson of railway workers, to work as a committee correspondent of World War II. Durand's mission was to interview cheminots who had participated in or witnessed resistance within the SNCF. Durand's findings became a book titled *La SNCF dans la guerre: Sa résistance à l'occupant* (The SNCF during the War: Its resistance to the occupier). The title presents resistance within the company as a statement rather than a question. The deportations are mentioned sporadically.

There was some contestation within the SNCF during the postwar years over who deserved the recognition; Louis Armand, a railroad engineer and resistant who had supervised the Plan Vert, the sabotage during D-Day, along with SNCF executives, claimed heroism for the company, whereas the Communists and CGT train union members remember the heroism as being theirs.[31] Despite these competing claims, the preceding chapter shows that company leadership clearly opposed the sabotaging of the railways throughout the war. But at the time, France was heavily invested in amplifying myths about French resistance.[32] As part of this effort, the SNCF and the French government bestowed upon the company a singular wartime identity. For the time being, survivors, too consumed with survival and fearful of speaking up, did not challenge this narrative. Incomplete stories and the production of myths can have material consequences. Hilde Lindemann Nelson argues that community ethics are at stake when narratives cannot do their full moral work.[33] This is perhaps why Henry Rousso calls this time France's "unfinished mourning" period.[34] Cutting off public discourse after the short period of purges thwarted the deep reflexivity required for healing and dealt victims an additional blow. Their experience did not yet have public legitimacy.

SILENCES WITHIN SURVIVORS' HOMES AND WITHIN THE SNCF

Scholarly (and public) debate continues over how and whether the French spoke about the Holocaust in the decades immediately after the war. Words such as "repression," "silence," and "taboo" circulate in attempts describe postwar discourse related to Jewish persecution in France. François Azouvi challenges the notion of a period of "Grande Silence" after the war, saying that the genocide was never absent from French consciousness, whereas Annette Wieviorka, Beate and Serge Klarsfeld, and Henry Rousso and Arthur Goldhammer say this period of repression lasted until the 1970s.[35] Who is right?

These ongoing disagreements reflect, in part, different understandings of silence. For some people, silence simply suggests without voice or without public reception of voices. Silences do not exist simply as blank spaces but carry the unsayable, have genealogies, and reflect the uncomfortable fit between discourse and memory.[36] Silences are not uniform; silences have contours that point not just to an inability to speak but to the inability of certain stories to be heard and legitimized in critical public or domestic spheres. What memories ultimately upload into what Maurice Halbwachs calls "collective memory" is a pastiche of collective, individual, borrowed, and historical remembrance.[37] The resulting public memory is often used for strategic ends.[38] Azouvi argues that speech about the Holocaust existed in postwar France, just not in a way that registers to our modern ears.[39] Yet this lack of audibility tells us something. In contrast, our ears have no trouble hearing the echoes of Nuremberg or the heroic narratives of the SNCF.

How postwar silences operated (or did not) in every corner of French society from churches to political chambers is beyond the scope of this book. That said, I support those bravely grappling with the complexity of collective memory. During numerous interviews for this study, survivors expressed clear rules about what could and could not be discussed in their homes immediately after the war. Internal politics at the SNCF helped prevent any counterstory from tarnishing its identity as a wartime hero. Whether or not all homes or institutions had similar politics around speech is not the point; in the spaces of greatest interest to this study, certain topics remained off limits. Some claim that silences meant complicity, a precursor to resistance, a survival mechanism, or defiance.[40] Regardless of the intention of such silencing, the norms shaping what was sayable had material and emotional consequences.

Organizational and domestic silences often had different aims. Samuel refused to talk about his experiences at Auschwitz immediately after the war because he feared no one would believe him. Ester, living on the Upper West Side when we met, told me she feared losing friends and still does. "Who wants to hear about such horror?" she asked.[41] Numerous child survivors vividly remember being silenced at home when they asked about the war. The postwar decades became a period during which people reconstituted identities and assiduously went about rebuilding their lives. For those who did want to discuss what happened, few words existed to even articulate their experience; the words "genocide" and "Holocaust" had just emerged and the true meaning of Auschwitz, Treblinka, Sobibór, and Final Solution were yet to be understood. De Gaulle wanted to move forward. Few wanted to talk about the past.

The postwar silence, preferred by many adults, proved excruciating for children.

Manfred, whose family moved about occupied France during the war, told me about some fragments of his parents' postwar conversations. One day his father began talking about their struggles to survive during the war. His mother cut him off, saying, "Don't upset the children, Max.'"

His father continued: "If we hadn't fudged things, where would we be? We would be dead in Auschwitz!!"

To which his mother replied, "Yes, Max, you're right, but don't upset the children."[42]

Children had many questions about how their families survived, but few parents wanted to answer these questions, perhaps because of survivor guilt—guilt for having been unable to save other family members and friends—or because of the compromises they had made in order to survive.

Myriam Kern agreed about the difficult silence that descended. When she asked her parents where the money came from to pay people throughout their long, arduous escape, they either ignored her questions or said, "I don't know," "It was complicated," or "It's in the past." At age eleven, she had many questions about the murder of her aunt, uncle, cousins, and grandmother. When a friend encouraged her to write her story about the war, she filled pages detailing the family's escape and a memory of two men disguised as women who had their dresses ripped off by authorities and were then shot. No one believed her at the time. As of 2014, she remained haunted by the image: "I guess they will find the bodies someday."[43] She showed me her diary; I asked why the postwar pages were blank. The sentences trail off, she explained, because she still cannot find words to write about that period. The silence in the home transferred to silence on the page, a blank space that she still cannot fill in.

André Zdroui explained that, out of respect, children did not ask their parents questions. He knew his parents were consumed with the task of finding them an apartment, money, work, and food. He said parents often shushed children when they asked about the war. There was so much left unsaid in those years. André and his wife, Isabelle—also a child survivor—appreciated our time together because they wanted to talk about the difficult postwar period. They said they found few people interested in hearing much about it.[44]

After the war, Leo Bretholz had no immediate family in Paris and no one to ask what had happened to them. The Resistance helped Bretholz continue on to New York, where he arrived on January 19, 1947. He then headed south to join his aunt and uncle in Baltimore, Maryland. He worked for a few years in textiles and soon met Flo, whom he married in 1952. They had three children, Myron, Denise, and Edie. Only in 1962 did Bretholz discover that his mother and sisters had been murdered at Auschwitz in April 1942. Decades

Survivors Isabelle and André Zdroui holding cards issued by German authorities in 1944 announcing the deportation of their respective fathers. After five decades of marriage, the couple pulled out their World War II memorabilia and discovered that their fathers traveled on the same deportation train to Auschwitz. Photo taken in August 2014. (Author photo)

later, Bretholz would eventually take on the SNCF by gathering more than 160,000 signatures on a change.org petition. He spent the first few postwar decades, however, building a new life and a new identity. During this period, some restitution programs did take shape. In 1946 France established its first compensation program to provide pensions to French citizens who had suffered under the antisemitic policies of the Vichy regime.

The sections that follow demonstrate a shifting relationship with history. This is not unique to France or to the postwar period; each generation, and each group within that generation, narrates its past to fit into social norms, shifting contexts, and contemporary conundrums.[45] We have seen examples of this as recently as 2015, when Jean-Marie Le Pen, founder of the far-right Front National (and father of Marine Le Pen, now president of the National Rally, as the party has been called since 2018), told his supporters in an interview that the Holocaust was just a detail of the war. Taking a different tack in the direction of nationalism, former president of France Nicolas Sarkozy used stories of the Resistance to leverage political support.[46] Pursing a pure version of history is a fantastical task. There are too many voices for a unified story. An official history is always clouded by the spirit of its time and subject to political uses. We can, however, study the telling and reception of stories. The most audible versions of the past tell us who has the most relative sociopolitical power. Groups often assign the roles hero, victim, or perpetrator differently. Whether or not one group's version of the past has widespread social traction tells us about that group's social position. The following looks at how wartime stories shifted in relation to these changing power dynamics.

1960S–1980S: The Slow Move toward Accountability

Identities, once woven into the social fabric, do not unravel easily. Those deemed heroes do not easily relinquish their medals. At the same time, the singular stories of heroism, told and retold, began to sound stale and incomplete as the embers of war cooled. During this cooling, France experienced a renewed search for perpetrators, which began with individuals and eventually included companies like the SNCF.

1960s

In 1964 France incorporated "crimes against humanity" into law with no statute of limitations. This put war crimes back on the table.[47] Even with this shift, no collaborators would face trial for another fifteen years. Perhaps this was because digging up stories of collaboration was considered unpatriotic.

Historians, those permitted to gaze backward, first brought the issue to the forefront. In 1961 Raul Hilberg's epic, *The Destruction of the European Jews*, crashed into the world, detailing the mechanisms and machinations of the German bureaucracy.[48] In 1961 Adolf Eichmann went on trial in Jerusalem and Olga Wormser-Migot completed a much-respected dissertation discussing the German concentration camps.[49] Robert Paxton's *Parades and Politics at Vichy*, released in 1966, became the first of a number of his books to sketch in irrefutable detail the dark underbelly of wartime France.[50] Yet many French people, including Jews, were not quite ready to hear about collaboration and antisemitism. Marcel Ophüls's four-hour film *Le Chagrin et la Pitié* (The Sorrow and the Pity) accused the Vichy regime of having more collaborators than

members of the Resistance.[51] The 1960s release of the film in France was ironically thwarted by Auschwitz survivor (and, later, the first president of the European Parliament) Simone Veil, who delayed the film's showing, arguing that it
offered an overly simplistic view.[52] Curiously, stories of resistance were not yet
critiqued for *their* oversimplistic renditions.

1970s

In the 1970s, the voices calling for accountability were amplified. A country not
historically fond of American intervention could not deny the reverberations
of Paxton's findings. He led a kind of narrative liberation of France. People
would now be able to speak more openly about what they knew or suspected
to be true. Americans too were having an awakening. The 1978 NBC-TV
series *The Holocaust* brought the atrocities of World War II into the homes
of more than 100 million Americans.[53] This increased the global conversation
about the Holocaust. In spite of the expansion of the discursive space around
the Holocaust in the public sphere, within the homes of Jews and non-Jews,
silence mostly still reigned.[54] Daniel would not speak of Auschwitz for more
than thirty years. His brother, Samuel, spoke about it only a little to his wife.
Their sister, Sophie, refused to speak to anyone. Archives would remain closed
for years. New trials would begin, but survivors would not always be willing
or able to share their testimony.

1980s

Rousso considers the 1980s the "obsessive" period, when discussion of the war,
focused mostly around Jewish issues, seemed to continue endlessly.[55] This turn
was catalyzed by the publication in 1981 of Michael Marrus and Robert Paxton's book, *Vichy France and the Jews*, which used archival sources to outline
French antisemitic policies.[56] In 1987 the Public Broadcasting Service (PBS) in
the United States broadcast Claude Lanzmann's ten-hour documentary *Shoah*
over four nights.[57] Interviews with perpetrators, including train drivers, shocked
and horrified those who saw the film.

Also in 1987, Serge Klarsfeld and his wife, Beate, succeeded in bringing Klaus
Barbie, "the Butcher of Lyon," to trial.[58] Barbie earned his nickname from his
grotesque torture of Gestapo prisoners in Lyon. Barbie operated the Mont-
Luc prison where Abram—of Convoy 77—resided for fifteen days. The German authorities then sent him to Drancy and, eventually, Auschwitz. Abram,
murdered upon arrival at Auschwitz for trying to escape from Convoy 77, had
two daughters, Renée and Cecile, who followed the Barbie trial closely. Their
mother could have participated in the trial but adamantly refused to speak
about the war. In 1991 she died at age eighty-seven, having never said a word
on the subject. Her daughters cut out and saved every article they could find

about the trial. Decades later, Renée would hand down the entire collection of clippings to her own daughter. Families literally passed down stories and with them transgenerational trauma.[59]

Estéra also could have participated in the trial; her convoy, Convoy 78, left Lyon because Barbie insisted that the last trains be used for deportations, not for retreating German soldiers. But she too refused to speak about the war. Others did, however, and with the help of depositions from more than seven hundred resistants and Jews, on July 4, 1987, the judge sentenced Klaus Barbie to life imprisonment.[60] He died behind bars four years later. Whether these judicial efforts showed concern for the Jews or an attempt to locate and persecute fascists (and therefore fascism) remains contested.[61] But trials they were. Justice had become a renewed topic of conversation, even though many perpetrators and collaborators remained protected. French president François Mitterrand sheltered a number of friends and at the same time, for a while at least, considered Serge Klarsfeld his "Enemy #1" because of Klarsfeld's refusal to accept the veil placed over past misdeeds.[62]

The SNCF underwent its own identity shift during the 1980s. The year 1983 marked the end of the forty-five-year railroad buyout period for the SNCF. With the previous private owners having divested their share in the company, the SNCF was transformed into a different legal entity. The French government designated the SNCF an Établissement Public à Caractère Industriel et Commercial (EPIC, Public Establishment of an Industrial and Commercial Nature). The company remained state-owned but could engage in commercial activities prohibited to the state. Identities also shifted. By the end of the 1980s, the discursive landscape around collaboration and the Holocaust had been reconfigured, and the SNCF's postwar impunity would soon wear off. While perhaps this "obsessive" period, as Rousso called it, exhausted those who engaged in and moderated many of these seemingly interminable conversations, they collectively helped lay the groundwork for the unfinished business of the war. In the 1990s, courts would hold critical perpetrators accountable, challenging statutes of limitations and other legal loopholes in ways that would facilitate access to justice for Holocaust survivors as well as victims of other atrocities around the world.

1990S: THE HUNT FOR PERPETRATORS AND BUSINESSES UNDER SCRUTINY

After the Cold War, independent lawyers representing large numbers of litigants launched a variety of cases related to the Holocaust.[63] While some scholars, such as Wieviorka, attribute the shift in litigation related to the Holocaust to changes in public sensibility within France, the fall of the Berlin Wall also proved a crucial turning point for Holocaust litigation globally.[64]

To understand how notions of accountability emerge first discursively and then legally requires thinking systemically and therefore beyond one's own borders. The fall of the Berlin Wall and the subsequent end of the Cold War opened formerly off-limits archives and led to the discovery of documents formerly believed to have been destroyed. Germany was no longer divided; now restitution issues could be discussed with a single Germany.[65]

After Germany, Switzerland was the next country to be exposed. Burt Neuborne, a renowned civil liberties lawyer who played a leading role in Holocaust-related lawsuits, sees the liability of Swiss banks for their wartime activities as closely connected to the fall of the Berlin Wall: "As long as Soviet communism was perceived as an external threat to the United States and Europe, Switzerland would remain untouchable on Holocaust issues because we needed strong Swiss financial support to shore up the West. That's how Switzerland wriggled out of the post–World War II negotiations on making reparations for its assistance to Nazis. Once the Berlin Wall fell, Switzerland lost its shield. Now it was only a matter of time until Swiss bank secrecy could no longer serve as an impenetrable barrier to Holocaust reparations."[66] Until this time, most Nazi-complicit corporations—like the Swiss—had faced no legal accountability.[67] During the same post–Cold War period, many victims in Soviet-controlled regions received compensation as well.[68]

Only in the late 1990s would major German firms and the German government create a $5.1 billion compensation fund for victims.[69] US involvement in French settlement debates also began during this period. Cumulatively this barrage of Holocaust-related litigation would guide human rights lawyers for years, offering lessons about how to hold corporations accountable for a wide variety of violations.[70]

For France, the first major push involved the banks. In the 1990s, the French Mattéoli Commission conducted research on the efficacy of existing restitution programs and examined unclaimed bank accounts. The commission identified sixty-two thousand individuals who possessed roughly eighty thousand bank accounts.[71] US-based lawyers, representing thousands of claimants worldwide, considered the Drai Commission, which was tasked with distributing these funds, problematic. The list of accounts remained private, and the commission lacked the organization to handle so many claims with the backing of the law. The US lawyers feared that survivors might never receive the money. To right these wrongs, major US Jewish organizations such as the Simon Wiesenthal Center encouraged the efforts of the American lawyers Richard Weisberg, Stuart Eizenstat, Harriet Tamen, and Ken McCallion, who filed three class-action suits against the three major French banks. Their efforts led to a settlement involving eight banks.[72] Working with the Mattéoli Commission, the settlement established a $50 million fund to compensate those victimized by French banks during the war years. Tamen reluctantly signed off on the terms but later considered this decision "the biggest mistake" of her life.[73] She felt she could have done better for the survivors. In the coming years, she had the opportunity to do so, working tirelessly and pro bono to represent her litigants in the fight against the SNCF.

The settlement brought justice to some victims, but there still remained numerous living perpetrators at large. By the mid-1990s, only four leading collaborators had been convicted for the crimes they committed during the Vichy regime. The Klarsfelds worked to renew indictments against the previously exonerated René Bousquet and continued spotlighting all Frenchmen in high political positions who had advanced the anti-Jewish agenda under Marshal Pétain.[74] In 1994 Paul Claude Marie Touvier became the first French person condemned for crimes against humanity. He received life imprisonment for his massacre of Jews.[75] He died in prison two years later. In 1998 French courts also convicted Maurice Papon for his role in the Jewish deportations, ending the longest trial in French history. The court determined that the French state should be held responsible for Jewish persecutions. This established the legal culpability of the French government, changing the nature of the debate and the cases to come.[76] As an extension of the French state, the SNCF—the French *national* railroad—soon found itself the target of lawsuits.

The SNCF's Fall from Hero to Perpetrator

During the 1990s, litigants challenged, and eventually shattered, the SNCF's long-held singular identity as a wartime hero. The hero's armor, once tarnished publicly, could never return to its original splendor, but the juridical will within French courts proved a challenge. Wartime legal professionals and courts at all levels of the system passionately enforced the Vichy government's antisemitic legislation with little to no German supervision.[77] Kurt Schaechter, orphaned by the Holocaust, became the first to attempt to take on the railway giant in these same courts. The Schaechter family had fled persecution in Austria only to find itself persecuted in France.[78] In the early 1990s, Schaechter secretly copied twelve thousand documents from the Toulouse archives for the years 1938–49; he found the invoices the SNCF had issued to the French government (discussed in chapter 2). Schaechter announced his findings to the media and caused quite a stir.

When some historians critiqued Schaechter's important discoveries, he responded by saying his work was political, not historical or economic. He approached the public prosecutor of the Tribunal de Grande Instance de Paris (the high authority court in Paris), who responded by claiming that because French law created liability for legal persons (companies) only in 1992, one could not sue the company retrospectively. Therefore, the Tribunal would not pursue the case. Regarding his demands for transparency, the Tribunal encouraged Schaechter to contact the SNCF directly.[79]

In a letter dated September 9, 1999, Schaechter asked the attorney general (*le procurer de la République*) to charge the SNCF with high treason.[80] He focused on the trains that continued after D-Day, highlighting how the company repaired the rails damaged by the Allied bombings in order to ensure that the deportees arrived at their destination. Seeing the attorney general as his last hope, he threatened the French state with the consequences of not pursuing the suit: to reject this case in France would open the possibility of attacking the SNCF as a legal entity in European courts. He acknowledged further down in the letter his understanding that current international law provided no means for holding collective entities accountable for crimes against humanity. Even the Rome Statute, which had established the International Criminal Court (ICC), was oriented toward individual offenders and did not give the court jurisdiction over entities.[81] Within the ICC, this decision to exclude corporations was reached after much debate; ultimately the majority of countries believed in immunity for corporations, so no agreement could be achieved on this issue.[82] The International Court of Justice—the judicial arm of the United Nations—settles only disputes between states, not those between companies and states or companies and individuals.

To date, no international judicial body can try legal entities such as corporations.[83] The International Criminal Court has reconsidered this possibility at times but remains too overwhelmed by the demands of its current mandate.[84] At the moment, only individuals can be tried by the ICC. After the Rwandan genocide, for example, the International Criminal Tribunal for Rwanda convicted three leaders of Radio Télévision Libre des Mille Collines (RTLM, Thousand Hills Free Television Radio) of genocide, crimes against humanity, and incitement to genocide. A local *gacaca* court also sentenced a radio announcer to life imprisonment, but in neither case was the radio station itself on trial.[85] In international criminal law, corporations remain unreachable. Even when domestic courts are available, raising the profile of these cases often requires independent research and advocacy by the victims.

Seeking other sources of leverage against the SNCF, Schaechter threatened to produce a film revealing his archival findings; in fact, he said, he had provided his unedited findings to editors and producers abroad. Schaechter closed his letter reassuring the *procureur* that he could provide enough documentation to build the argument. He referred to witnesses (who wished to remain anonymous) who had provided him testimony indicating that the railway workers who drove the deportation trains were paid extra or volunteered.[86]

In 2003, when Schaechter had reached age eighty-two, a court heard his case.[87] Suing for one symbolic euro, his lawyer, Joseph Roubache, made several arguments. He argued that the SNCF had exceeded German orders and that the company's use of code names for the deportation trains indicates that officials knew the nefarious nature of these transports. Roubache also argued that SNCF workers closed and locked the convoy doors and also discouraged volunteers from giving food and water to the detainees. The court read its decision at the Palais de Justice. It dismissed the case on a technicality—because of a ten-year statute of limitations. Roubache responded, arguing that the ten-year statute of limitations clock should have started ticking only from the moment at which Schaechter acquired the documents. The court held firm. Schaechter appealed, and the case was turned down again in 2004.[88]

The public attention given to this case spawned a growing interest in the archives: the SNCF archive center in Le Mans reported an astonishing 120 visits and 600 requests for information in 2003 alone.[89]

Three years after he first launched the case, the eighty-five-year-old Schaechter received some acknowledgment. On March 31, 2006, at the long-closed train station that served Noé and Longages, a commemorative plaque was installed acknowledging the thirty railcars that had left the station, heading first to Drancy and then to Auschwitz-Birkenau. Schaechter made a ten-hour round-trip voyage from Paris, where he resided, to witness the installation at what he considered the most important deportation station in the southwest of France.[90] The mayor of the Longages region and the regional director of the SNCF also attended the 2006 ceremony. Eighteen standard bearers, two buglers, and a drummer commemorated the dead. The SNCF announced that the ceremony would last no more than one hundred minutes on account of the train schedule—another haunting reminder that having the trains run on time remained a priority. Schaechter was pleased about the ceremony but disappointed that the mayor of Noé refused to post a similar commemorative plaque at the site of the internment camp in the region. Schaechter died just two years later, in 2007, at age eighty-six.[91]

Even though his findings were seen as insufficient evidence for the courts, Schaechter hoped a professor would someday publish a book using his findings, which fill fifty-four archival boxes. Thanks to an Amtrak Writing Residency, which offers writers a chance to ride the railways while working on their books, I rode a symbolic train from Washington, DC, to California to visit Stanford University's Hoover Institution, where Schaechter's documents awaited. A retired musical instruments salesman, he had attached many of his notes, seemingly for stability, to the back pages of instrument catalogs—a touching reminder that at the end of the day, Schaechter was just a man who had lost his family and who spent the last years of his life trying to right the wrongs of the Holocaust.

The SNCF Continues Its Appearances before French Courts

Even though, as Georges Ribeill observed, the matter of deportation remained taboo within the SNCF by the end of the 1990s, Schaechter's work made other claims audible.[92] On the heels of Schaechter's struggle, Jean-Jacques Fraenkel, president of Offshore Coordination of Deported Children, filed a complaint against the SNCF for crimes against humanity.[93] His father, a famous dentist and former military officer, and his mother were both deported and murdered two years apart at Auschwitz. At the time that he launched the suit, Fraenkel was living in Victoria, British Columbia. He used the lawsuit to challenge the SNCF's positioning as a "hero" while still acknowledging that many individual SNCF workers were members of the Resistance. In the end, he claimed, the company did nothing to prevent the deportations. For this reason, he sought international recognition from the SNCF and from the French government for their crimes. He hoped this would help him to pay tribute to his murdered family and shift national memory.[94] In 1998 the court dismissed the case for insufficient evidence.

The lawsuits kept coming. The most prominent French case, that of the Lipietz family, almost succeeded. On November 14, 2001, Alain and Georges Lipietz (son and father, respectively) filed suit against the French state for the injuries suffered by Alain's mother, father, and stepfather.[95] Their lawyer, Rémi Rouquette, advised the plaintiffs to add the SNCF to their claim, arguing that the SNCF existed as a juridical entity separate from the state and was therefore suable.[96] Alain Lipietz conceded that his father had no particular grudge against the company. They filed their suit in the Administrative Court of Toulouse against both the French State *and* the SNCF.[97]

Arno Klarsfeld, son of the Holocaust activists Serge and Beate Klarsfeld, served as a lawyer for the SNCF and argued that the Gestapo organized the transport to the Drancy internment camp, not the SNCF. Furthermore, he claimed, Georges Lipietz never took the trip via the SNCF from France to Auschwitz. The SNCF transferred him only *within* France.[98] Arno Klarsfeld insisted that the SNCF had no control over the management of the voyage.

The case outlived the plaintiff.

On June 6, 2006, five years after the case was filed and three years after the death of Georges Lipietz, the court read its decision to a large room of jurists, journalists, and others.[99] Before the ruling, the prosecuting lawyer, Rémi Rouquette, summarized the plaintiffs' case: "The Lipietz family did not want to go to Drancy . . . they did not buy a ticket to Paris and were not, in effect, customers of the SNCF. So, the railway had no business having them on the train. . . . It never did anything, or tried to do anything, to slow down the rhythm of the convoys, even after the Allied landings."[100]

Rouquette also noted that while the SNCF often protested its own exploitation, it never seemed to protest on behalf of the deportees and the deplorable conditions in which they traveled. Moreover, it greedily charged third-class rates for delivering deportees who had been packaged like merchandise.[101] The plaintiffs also presented a telegram showing that the SNCF had refused water to deportees, which they submitted as proof of unnecessary cruelty.[102]

The SNCF's attorney responded that the company had no autonomy during the war. He then argued a legal technicality: at the time of these events, the company operated under private law; therefore, any cases against the SNCF for these offenses would need to take place in a civil or criminal court, not an administrative one. As noted previously, in France, the SNCF plays its hand as a *private* company; in the United States, it would find itself protected by its *public* status.

The French government's commissariat, Christophe Truilhé, responded with the court's ruling.[103] He did not accept the SNCF's attempt to move the case to a different court on account of its private status. Instead, he said the SNCF, in spite of its status as a mixed public and private company, was managed by the French state. The court said this explained why the company never issued official orders. France had no statute of limitations on crimes against humanity, but this applied only to charges brought in criminal court, not administrative courts such as the one hearing this case.[104] The SNCF, he said, acted on its own behalf and not on behalf of the occupying authorities. The court also claimed that the SNCF went beyond the demands of both Vichy and the Nazis.

According to the court, the SNCF's autonomy to pursue its financial interests during the war prevented the company from claiming that others determined the transportation conditions. Therefore, the Tribunal of Toulouse condemned the state and the SNCF. The beneficiaries received €62,000 from the French state—a symbolic win for many, but a financial gain only for the Lipietz family.

The SNCF appealed and won.

In March 2007, the Administrative Court of Bordeaux cited a Vichy decree issued on October 10, 1943, which transformed the SNCF into a limited liability company.[105] This limited liability status placed the SNCF legally—the court argued—back under the French government. The Lipietz family appealed the Bordeaux decision, this time before the Conseil d'État (the Supreme Court for administrative cases). The Conseil d'État also sided with the SNCF, this time arguing that the company could not be liable because it lacked the authority to deport people. While it ruled in the SNCF's favor, the court claimed that, even if the SNCF had to conduct these transports, it surely did not for a minute reflect upon the consequences.[106]

After the judgment, Lipietz said he and his family received numerous antisemitic letters.[107] By 2012, his uncle Guy refused to speak in public about the conflict, fearing antisemitism.[108] Those who sued the SNCF had to cover their own legal fees—which meant that only those with means could even begin the litigation process.

Historians began expressing concern about these legal proceedings for different reasons. Regarding the Toulouse decision, Henry Rousso said, "We have entered into a dangerous and unhealthy process." He feared that recrimination could go on indefinitely.[109] Marrus saw history and law working at cross purposes: historians analyze catastrophes and "courts render judgements according to the law."[110] Ribeill expressed his reservations in more direct terms, discrediting this campaign against the SNCF and considering the invoices produced by Schaechter and the Lipietz lawsuit as "harassment" of the national railway.[111] Ribeill accused French lawyers of fighting the SNCF with arguments based on scant historical evidence.[112] Yet one outcome of the litigation was clear: the SNCF's singular identity as hero had been irrevocably damaged.

A Chorus of Demand

Even though the French courts proved a dead end, the cases unleashed a chorus of demand for accountability. Some 1,800 people launched complaints against the SNCF after Lipietz had his initial (albeit later overturned) win against the SNCF in the Toulouse administrative court.[113] Then-SNCF president Anne-Marie Idrac personally received an estimated two hundred letters demanding compensation for survivors and their descendants around the world. One such letter came from Josiane Friedman, a survivor living in Paris, who requested compensation for the deportation of her two siblings and her husband, Claude. Josiane's brother had been deported on Convoy 42 along with Leo Bretholz. Josiane did not need the money, she said. Her request to the SNCF was largely symbolic. Back in 2006, just after the Toulouse decision on the Lipietz case, Josiane sent the following letter to the SNCF. The letter, written by the couple, threatened legal action if the company did not respond directly to their demand for financial compensation.

Madame Director of the SNCF
34, rue de Commandant René Mouchotte
75014 Paris

Madame Director,

I hereby request, through the heritage of succession, payment of damages to repair the prejudices caused by your public establishment, with the French state, for [my family's] arrest and transport by train in inhumane conditions.

The requested sum [is in the appendix]. The origins of this demand can be found in the attached appendix. The absence of a positive response within two months of this demand will lead to legal action. *The wagons were prepared by the SNCF and carried by the SNCF as merchandise wagons. They were practically rolling prisons.* It is therefore incontestable that the acts committed by your public establishment, like those committed by the state functionaries, constitute complicity in crimes against humanity, as established both through the work of historians and jurisprudence.

The finding is not as was found in the Lipietz case against the State and the SNCF.[114] The harm lies clearly in the deprivation of liberty in violation of the most basic principles of law, the appalling conditions of the transport and detention. All persons who have undergone this fate suffered throughout their lives from severe psychological disorders and the survivors suffer until they die.[115]

Josiane signed the letter and in the appendix detailed the deportations. She requested €400,000: roughly €130,000 each for herself and her two siblings, a bold request.

Arno Klarsfeld, who had represented the SNCF during the Lipietz case, responded to the couple's letter, explaining that the company had had no choice regarding its participation. He said the SNCF had been constrained and the workers would have been shot for disobeying. Deeply disheartened by the letter, Josiane and her husband, Claude, moved on with their lives.[116] The legal defense of the SNCF by both Serge Klarsfeld and Arno Klarsfeld emphasized, once again, the complicated, overlapping roles of the parties involved. The Klarsfelds, known as some of the most renowned Nazi hunters, defended the company against survivors' and families' lawsuits. In doing so, they found themselves in disputes with some of those whose family stories they had uncovered and whose families they had once helped compensate through an orphans program that Serge Klarsfeld had initiated and that the government had signed into law back in July 2000.[117] The Klarsfelds' defense of the SNCF did not convince everyone that the company had made sufficient amends, but legal justice became increasingly difficult to pursue in France.

Those in France who had any lingering hopes for justice after the Lipietz trial likely surrendered them when the Conseil d'État issued a decision in *Hoffman-Glemane v. France and SNCF* that closed all French administrative courts to Holocaust-related cases.[118] However, courts that hear criminal and civil cases (rather than administrative ones) remain an open possibility.[119] To date, no one has attempted this approach.

Reactions to the high court's decision varied. When I asked Serge Klarsfeld about this change of heart, he said he felt satisfied because the restitution programs established in the 1990s addressed his primary concerns. Hélene Lipietz, part of the Lipietz case and a former public law attorney, wrote that the decision "hurt her heart."[120] She believed that not enough had been done to support the needs of survivors, many of whom never received compensation for suffering or prejudice. In 2009 the European Court of Human Rights further absolved France, saying its efforts to remunerate the victims and commemorate the Holocaust "provided full and fair compensation, both morally and materially."[121]

The French public continued to wrestle with the SNCF's various wartime identities even if the courts refused to participate. A flurry of popular books and films kept the public thinking about the SNCF's role in the Holocaust discussion.[122] For some, as I now show, the debate over the SNCF's accountability spilled into the streets.

Voices from the Last Trains

Lucienne (Lou) sued the SNCF on behalf of her mother, Estéra, who was in Convoy 78, but lost. Because the French legal system prohibits class action lawsuits and contingency fees, she never recouped her legal costs. She remains bitter about this double financial loss.[123] Her battle was not only over money, she said. It was about recognition, which she still struggles to receive in France. In 2010, as a bus made its usual route through Paris, the driver announced that all riders must descend because a strike up ahead had blocked the street. Lou exited with the other passengers and began walking. When she turned the corner, she saw a parade of striking SNCF workers marching toward her carrying a sign that read "Cheminots de Lyon"—workers from the station from which her mother had been deported.

"It's not now that you ought to be going on strike, but during the war when my mother was taken!" she cried out.

A few of the men apologized, saying that they had not been there and they were very sorry for her loss. Not everyone expressed compassion.

A female SNCF worker said to her compatriots, "Why is she complaining? She didn't die."

Lou was horrified.

After recounting the story, Lou said, "There are two kinds of people in the world: those who can talk about the Holocaust and those who cannot. I just cannot deal with those who cannot."[124]

After the war, many could not talk about the Holocaust, and many still cannot. Many books about the Holocaust and Vichy France end at D-Day or thereabouts, contributing to silence about the postwar years, which many survivors said were the hardest of all. Those on the last trains to Auschwitz know that the war did not end at D-Day; neither did it end at the liberation of Paris. Those who survived stumbled out of horror into a world that had no words for what they had just experienced—and that did not particularly want them.

Lou still carries vivid memories of collecting her mother, Estéra, an experience for which she only later had words. Estéra had been deported from France with a group of women, all transported on tarp-covered rail platforms to Bergen-Belsen; 90 percent of those transported would die of typhus. The British eventually liberated Bergen-Belsen. A friend of Estéra's had to reassure the soldiers that even though she weighed only 30 kilograms (about 65 pounds) and looked dead, she was indeed still alive. Once their physical strength returned, the two women would see each other every day for the rest of their lives. But at first, Estéra was too weak to even be transported from Bergen-Belsen. To add to her wounds, an SS officer had cracked open her skull and knocked out her teeth. The beating temporarily blinded her. The British tended to her for a month until they could strap her to a stretcher and fly her to Paris to recover at the Hôpital de la Salpêtrière (the same hospital where Samuel had been taken). She arrived at the hospital not only with her injuries from the beating but with typhus and nearly dead from starvation. Liberating troops had learned that camp survivors were often too weak to be fed immediately.

During Estéra's deportation and recovery, the family that was assigned to care for her young daughters, Lou and Clara, had largely neglected the girls. Many children suffered in such makeshift homes. The couple could barely care for themselves; the husband drank and the wife was too sick to move. "We lived like pigs," Lou recalled. The girls were on the verge of starvation when they received a message to come to the hospital to claim their mother. Their aunt brought them to the Hôpital de la Salpêtrière, the most colossal hospital complex in Paris. One can imagine how the small girls made sense of this enormous structure. Louis XIV had commissioned the Hôpital de la Salpêtrière in 1565 to house fifty thousand homeless and other outcasts. In 1945, almost four hundred years later, the hospital still tended to the city's homeless outcasts, this time the deportees.

Hospital staff led the children to a room of about a hundred women who looked more like cadavers than human beings.

"You have to understand," says Lou. "I didn't even understand what the war was. I did not know what 'Jewish' meant or 'deportation' or even that I had parents. I thought I was a good Catholic."

The staff brought them to a woman whose skull stayed together only thanks to stitches and bandages. The children were terrified.

"It was worse than anything in a horror movie," Lou recalled.

Seven-year-old Clara clung to Lou's leg. They saw that the woman who the nurses said was their mother had two sets of numbers tattooed on her arm. (The first one had been crossed out when the guards discovered she had lied about being married to a Jew.) They did not recognize this skeletal creature. Lou's eyes were quickly drawn to the woman lying next to their mother. The skin around the woman's mouth had completely receded. Lou, who had not spoken a word during the three years of separation from her mother, finally spoke, "What happened to her face?"

"*Elle a eu faim* [she was hungry]," Estéra replied weakly from her bed, trying to help her daughters make sense of the horror they were witnessing for the first time.

Lou could not understand how hunger could make that woman's lips disappear. She turned and saw a flea crawl up her mother's nightshirt.

"You have to understand; no one knew about the camps at this time," Lou explained. "People had no idea what to make of these skeletons coming home."

Estéra's children (Lucienne, Marcel, and Clara) during their stay at the home for Jewish children, 1942. (Courtesy of Lucienne Helwaser)

Their mother, too sick to live with the children right away, lived separately for a time. By June 1945, Estéra could walk again. Her beautiful thick hair had returned and oral surgeons had replaced her teeth, but she remained severely visually impaired for the rest of her life. A few months after being reunited with her daughters, Estéra announced to the girls that they would soon pick up their brother, who had been hidden elsewhere, at the train station. Lou had forgotten she had a brother. When he arrived, the family would try to reconstruct itself as a unit without referring to the past.

"Our hair grew back, we removed the Jewish stars from our clothing, and we were told to move on to other things," Lou explained. Her mother would say nothing to her about the war for the rest of her life. Most of what Lou learned about her family's story came to her later, from the research of others.

Nothing was simple during the war, or after. In 2021, with her husband (also a survivor) recently deceased due to COVID-19, Lou spends much of her days sitting alone still trying to make sense of it all.

CHAPTER FIVE

The SNCF Struggles to Clear Its Name

Our company operated these trains up to the border. Under duress,
unquestionably, but it did so nonetheless.

—GUILLAUME PEPY, SNCF chairman

TRANSITIONAL JUSTICE SCHOLARS, focusing on the aftermath
of mass violence, now largely accept that freedom to talk about (and
interpret) the past is as important as atoning for it. For this reason,
transparency has become a mainstay of transitional justice and postconflict
processes more broadly.[1] Many believe that transparency and forums for discussion prove as vital for overcoming the durable effects of mass violence as
compensation. If we cannot speak openly, then how can we be sure the persecution is truly over? Violence blocks narration. Perpetuating these silences allows
some forms of violence to continue.[2] Trauma remains embodied and without
an outlet. While speaking alone rarely provides the catharsis many hope for,
trauma festers where speech is prohibited. In these contexts, communities and
individuals remain fragmented—sometimes for decades or whole generations.[3]
Dialogue, a means of retethering fragments, becomes thwarted when perpetrators are dead or inhuman. Sigfried Giedion argues that mechanization slowly
took command of human life through technological advances.[4] If he is correct,
we either must hold technology accountable or consider the ethical implica-
tions of our advances. This is increasingly a question for our times.

The SNCF conflict provides a rare example of what accountability looks
like when a company in command of powerful technologies participates in a
variety of transitional justice practices: commemoration, education, apology,
and transparency. While the SNCF engaged in these practices, the company
struggled to be simultaneously a source of technological innovation, a profit-
seeking company, and a *lieu de mémoire*.

The SNCF emerged from the 1990s with its heroic identity shattered. Richard Prasquier, the head of the Conseil Représentatif des Institutions Juives de
France (CRIF, Representative Council of French Jewish Institutions), France's
leading Jewish organization, said that the SNCF could only alter its now tainted

126

reputation by telling the truth.[5] He clarified this statement during our meeting in his office. He said that by the "truth" he meant "the SNCF must take responsibility for all aspects of its history, not just hold onto the noble tale of *The Battle of the Rail*."[6] A more complicated story needed to be told, he said, and the company's executives would have to tell it. Guillaume Pepy, the SNCF president; Bernard Emsellem, head of corporate accountability; and Dennis Douté and Alain Leray, the CEOs of SNCF America, would lead this work. These executives found themselves caught in a process that they did not create and for which they had no formal training. As SNCF America CEO Alain Leray so aptly put it during one of our meetings, "My training is in automotive mechanics. I am not a historian!"[7] Their experiences, told through this book, can now guide others. Of course, rarely do we receive formal training tailored to our biggest professional and personal challenges. The cheminots in wartime France never received training on how to respond when their company was requisitioned by Nazis. Furthermore, the *devoir de mémoire*, the moral obligation to remember a tragedy, has never been reserved solely for historians. The enormous pain created by violent human action throughout the ages is always left for the living to address.

Stepping down from its postwar hero pedestal was a delicate matter. Companies stand to lose their reputation and with it, profit. So, how did the SNCF manage this paradoxical challenge of improving its image by publicly acknowledging its role in the Holocaust? It was not easy; the more the company acknowledged its dark past, the more it became associated with this past. The SNCF first made efforts on its own but eventually teamed up with the Fondation pour la Mémoire de la Shoah (FMS, Foundation for the Memory of the Shoah), an organization that educates the French-speaking public about the Holocaust, assists survivors, and promotes Jewish culture while addressing contemporary antisemitism. The SNCF also teamed up with the Centre National de la Recherche Scientifique (CNRS, National Center for Scientific Research), France's leading independent research institution, to better understand its wartime history. These efforts led to what transitional justice scholars call transparency efforts.

TRANSPARENCY AND TRUTH-TELLING

Many consider truth-telling the requisite starting point in the wake of mass atrocity. André du Toit defines "truth" as an achievable and worthwhile detailed accounting of political atrocities that occurred.[8] Some claim that peace would not be possible without the quest for truth.[9] In postconflict contexts, many believe that social peace and the reestablishment of law rely on this quest.[10] Some challenge truth's attainability and desirability for individuals and society, although few would advocate for repression or denial.[11] Stanley Cohen's work distinguishes among various forms of denial used to cover up atrocities or protect various parties in their aftermath.[12] Cohen considers "official denial," conducted by governments or institutions, as one of the most extreme forms of coverup. The fifty-year silence maintained by a government-owned entity like the SNCF could be considered a form of official denial. Therefore, undoing the singular narrative required an official and public process.

By the turn of the millennium, those in the United States challenging the company repeatedly claimed that the SNCF continues to deny its history. This is simply untrue. The company shifted its narrative, slowly and cautiously, but it shifted nonetheless. In 1992 SNCF president Jacques Fournier signed a contract with the Institut d'Histoire du Temps Présent (IHTP, Institute for the History of Present Time), operating under the CNRS, to research its wartime history.[13] According to Henry Rousso, who oversaw the research, "the report was commissioned because there was a legal proceeding in France for crimes against humanity. . . . So, the initiative was an internal problem and not related to the wave of transparency at the very beginning, even if the discussions I had with the SNCF afterwards were very open minded. They never wanted to hide anything. They didn't even know what should be hidden."[14] (More than a decade later, I observed the same level of historical curiosity among the highest-ranking executives.) Back in 1992, the SNCF only wanted to study the deportations, but the IHTP encouraged the organization to also investigate its broader activities during the war.[15] The resulting report became known as the "Bachelier report," named after the researcher Christian Bachelier, who spent years digging through 600 meters of documents in the SNCF archives.

When Bachelier presented a 150-page draft report that accused the SNCF of destroying or concealing archival materials, Rousso told me that he rejected it, saying he did not believe Bachelier could prove his claims. Showings holes in the records did not prove culpability, he said.[16] Rousso sent Bachelier back to work. Four and a half years after the project began, Bachelier produced a new nine-hundred-page report titled *La SNCF sous l'occupation allemande 1940–1944* (SNCF under German Occupation 1940–1944). Rousso discusses the tension between the pressure to produce a factual account that could help determine the SNCF's guilt in court and the goals of the report, which was to place the company's actions in the political and economic context of its time.[17] The company made the report publicly available in 1999. Note that the name of the report highlights the company's constraint—"*Sous l'occupation allemande*," under German occupation. The company presented the report's facts from the position of a victim acting under duress.

Many find this report extremely rough and poorly organized.[18] Historians still struggle to make sense of the patched-together materials. Those wishing to ask questions have no one to ask. Bachelier disappeared after the report's production, and to this day Rousso cannot find him.[19] In spite of the report's disorganization and even though the word "Jew" never appears and deportees are rarely mentioned, Bachelier's findings unearthed enough information to make the company even more vulnerable to legal attack than before. His findings revealed collaboration at the executive levels and in certain cases documented how French railway workers worsened the conditions of the deportees by not allowing water. Lawyers on both sides of the lawsuits often quote the report. Despite these ambiguous consequences, the SNCF impressively continued with its moves toward transparency.

In 1996, just before the report became available on the internet, SNCF president Fournier (not the same Fournier who led the SNCF during the war) opened the company archives, located in Le Mans, France, to the public. Jean-Jacques Fraenkel, who sued the SNCF, questioned putting the SNCF in charge of opening its own archives, given that their contents could incriminate the company. Few think that the contemporary SNCF continues to hide evidence of complicity in the Holocaust, although the Vichy historian Michael Marrus, SNCF's Bernard Emsellem, and others agree that many records were likely destroyed during the liberation or at some point shortly after the war.[20]

The SNCF's willingness to engage in historical self-examination inspired similar efforts in other Holocaust-complicit companies. Soon after the French National Railways study became public, the Deutsche Bahn (previously Deutsche Reichsbahn) commissioned a similar study of German railroad history.[21] Here the SNCF emerges as a leader, setting an example for other complicit corporations. The SNCF conflict will serve as a salient case study for years to come because not only did the SNCF face trials and participate in transparency efforts; it also held a historical commission, engaged (and continues to engage) in commemoration, *and* struggled with the politics around apologies.

THE SNCF's HISTORICAL COMMISSION

Truth commissions serve to construct collective memory as well as provide potential forums for renewed social solidarity. While some commissions also aim to serve as forums for communal grieving, the mandates generally construct these commissions to serve as temporary forums, distinct from formal prosecutions, designed to uncover the past and produce formal final reports.[22] These final reports aim to provide a detailed account of what occurred in the past.[23] They may also make recommendations about how the state ought to hold parties accountable.[24] Tunisia's Truth and Dignity Commission, established in

2013, issued a two-thousand-page report in March 2019 and went further by issuing 430 indictments throughout the course of its proceedings.[25] Commissions make the facts visible in order for them to be evaluated. In this way, truth commissions are not historical fact-finding missions for their own sake; they convene because the potential truths revealed will have some moral significance.

As of 2020, the Corporate Accountability and Transitional Justice database reports that half of the approximately forty truth and reconciliation commissions held in recent decades named complicit corporations.[26] Since 2000, for example, commissions in Sierra Leone, East Timor, Peru, the Philippines, and South Africa considered the role of business and industry, positioning these actors as possible perpetrators.[27] The UN Office of the High Commissioner for Human Rights (OHCHR) recommends including economic issues as part of any truth commission's mandate.[28] In most of these instances, the reports simply note corporate complicity without describing next steps. This may change.

The development of the related *historical* commission seeks to move beyond some of the limitations of truth commissions. Like truth commissions, historical commissions also increase transparency. Unlike truth and reconciliation commissions, in which victims and perpetrators ideally come together, historical commissions focus on producing a more accurate telling of the past as a way to address some ongoing sociopolitical disputes over collective memory.[29] Historical commissions also move away from the legal frameworks that dominate most truth commissions. In historical commissions, the role of corporations in the violence and the role of economics can be more fully explored.[30]

In 2000 the SNCF sponsored a historical commission under the auspices of the AHICF. This forum served as an official, collaborative review and revision of the company's history. The two-day, invitation-only conference, developed in conjunction with the Académie Française and hosted by the Assemblée Nationale, was titled *A Public Company during the War, the SNCF, 1939–1945*. This title positioned the SNCF as government controlled, whereas the Bachelier report had emphasized German control. The company again positioned itself as having its proverbial hands tied. This may have been a strategic move; the Lipietz lawsuit in France had not yet concluded, and debates about the SNCF were just heating up in the United States.

The colloquium, an effort at historical correction, conducted its work in a tightly controlled environment. This was a battle over meaning and positioning as much as an exploration of history. The rewriting of the SNCF's wartime history occurred after the commission carefully selected attendees and agreed to adhere to a strict discussion format. Invitees included more than fifty historians, SNCF employees (including then-chairman Louis Gallois), archivists, professors, and members of the Institut d'Histoire du Temps Présent. Fewer than five survivors received invitations.

Inviting so few survivors may reflect the historic distrust of testimony as a means for understanding history.[31] Limiting survivor involvement may also reflect a desire to keep emotion out of the room. Historical commissions typically rely on archives and official documents rather than testimony.[32] Child survivors Serge Klarsfeld and Kurt Schaechter had demonstrated their ability to engage in rigorous historical research and were likely invited because of this expertise as much as for their firsthand experiences. Survivors found themselves included in many commemorative efforts, but not this one.

René Redmond, then president of the Académie Française, opened the event by clarifying for those present that the meeting had *truth* as its primary goal: "La première est une exigence de vérité" (the first [goal] is a requirement of truth).[33] He reminded the participants that this was not a court of justice but a colloquium in which everyone would work together to understand what had happened and why. SNCF president Louis Gallois expressed the SNCF's increasing willingness to create a "new" company history, one more complex than that portrayed in *La Bataille du rail*. Effectively, the colloquium attempted to carefully "braid" the company's story of resistance with the story of the deportations.[34] However, with such different strands, even the most carefully secured braids could not hold very long. Survivors who had not been invited to the conference would eventually disrupt the neat, new, "improved" historical narrative designed by the colloquium.

In 2001 the Académie Française released the transcript of the colloquium. While the company's openness came in response to legal proceedings, not because of an eager engagement in postconflict healing, Marrus applauded the SNCF's efforts, saying, "The actions of the SNCF seem far less the machinations of an excuse-seeking wrongdoer than that of a company committed, however belatedly, to the full transparency and release of information about its wartime past—what the French refer to as their duty of memory, or *devoir de la mémoire*."[35]

The transparency efforts continued. In March 2004, the CNRS hosted a two-day colloquium on the SNCF archives at the company's archive center in Roubaix, France. Roughly fifty historians attended, as well as archivists from the SNCF, numerous SNCF employees, and even representatives from the French banks Credit Lyonnais and Société Générale. The event consisted of presentations of twenty-one papers. At the event, the renowned social historian of French railway workers Georges Ribeill communicated to the legal advocate Eric Freedman that the SNCF would never beg for forgiveness and that nothing could tarnish the SNCF's image as a hero in the Resistance.

He considered the Americans "méchant," or nasty, for continuing these legal battles.[36]

The absence of deportees in this chapter reflects their absence from these efforts. Including more survivors in the "serious" work of history could have eased some of the simmering resentment and healed some of the psychic pain. This was not the French way. To offer yet another example, in January 2007, when the University of Paris I held a panel discussion on the SNCF-related lawsuits, the panelists were professors and lawyers; no survivors, not even those behind the litigation, were invited to speak.[37] The "truer" story was crafted without them. Some survivors wrote memoirs, some spoke publicly about their experiences, but none of these were included in the construction of the official company history.

Within the SNCF, I witnessed both interest in and rejection of these omitted stories. In 2011, during the early days of my research, the head of SNCF's archives, Henri Zuber, reached out to me, eager to hear about my findings. When we met, I expressed concern about the lack of survivor participation in the construction of the SNCF's history and suggested that we add the stories survivors had shared with me. This would provide a counternarrative or at least another perspective to the bureaucratic story dominant in the archives. He agreed. SNCF America CEO Alain Leray, however, opposed this idea, saying that the narratives were not part of the SNCF's history. We see the various ways in which survivor voices are negotiated in and out of historical narratives.

Transparency and Corporations

In spite of the omission of survivor stories in the official history, it would be inaccurate to say that the SNCF denies its role in the Holocaust. In fact, one can learn far more about the SNCF's role during the occupation than about the role of almost any other corporate organization in France. The banks, for example, have closed archives, as do foreign companies such as J. P. Morgan that remained operational in France during the war. Many of the SNCF's wartime secrets are now visible because, as a publicly owned company, it maintained orderly archives.

For all the company's efforts toward transparency, the biblical promise in John 8:32 that "the truth will set you free" did not seem to apply to the SNCF. Marrus observed that, "ironically, the SNCF's own commitment to historical accuracy has played an important role in the successful litigation."[38] Rousso observed a similar phenomenon, reporting that the SNCF first commissioned the independent report to support its legal defense team, only to find it used by the prosecution.[39] The more the SNCF revealed about its past, the more this past was used against it in courts of law. Because of this, the SNCF's troubles could serve as a kind of warning to other corporations considering a movement toward greater transparency. Miranda rights were developed in the United States precisely because the truth may (and likely will) be used against the accused in court. Damned if they present the past openly, damned if they don't. Taking responsibility has its inconveniences. This is why many complicit corporations avoid openness, hoping instead to make amends through forms of commemoration. The SNCF tried this approach too.

The SNCF's Commemoration of the Holocaust

Today, the SNCF's logo can be found on most Holocaust-related exhibits in France. The company is an advocate for education and commemoration. The SNCF's largest contributions support the Mémorial de la Shoah, Musée et Centre de Documentation, opened in 2005 as the primary Holocaust museum and memorial located in the Marais, the historically Jewish neighborhood in Paris. The SNCF remains the organization's leading corporate partner.[40] The company co-funds the annual reading of the names at the Fondation pour la Mémoire de la Shoah, which Lou, Daniel, Pierre (Henry Blum's son), and Renée (Abram Zegman's daughter) regularly attend.

The company also sponsors various one-off events. Serge Klarsfeld, with SNCF's permission and financial support, developed a highly regarded exhibit titled "Deported Children," which traveled for several years throughout railway stations in France. People still talk about how the exhibit moved them. Just as the SNCF's independent report inspired a German study of a similar nature, the Klarsfelds' exhibit inspired the Deutsche Bahn (Germany's national railroad company) to create a similar installation that traveled throughout Germany.

More directly, the SNCF helped install memorial railcars in Drancy near the former internment camp and at the Compiègne, Les Milles, and Nanteuil rail stations; it also provided a railcar for an exhibit on the Champs-Élysées in 2003.[41] The SNCF continues to place commemorative plaques throughout railway stations in France. SNCF's Bernard Emsellem told me that in August 2014, for example, Serge Klarsfeld worked with the SNCF to mount a plaque in the Gare de Lyon, in Paris. The SNCF paid for the plaque, and Klarsfeld coordinated the production and mounting.[42]

The company was not always so eager to fund and participate in such commemorative events. Historian Henry Rousso recalled receiving a phone call in 2000 or 2001 from then-SNCF president Louis Gallois, who was concerned about mounting pressure from Serge Klarsfeld to add the plaques at train stations around France. Gallois asked Rousso if the company had a choice. Rousso told him "no." If Klarsfeld wanted those signs, the SNCF had better put them up, he said.[43]

Renée Fauguet-Zejgman points to the name of her father, Abram Zejgman, on the commemorative wall after the reading of the names for Convoy 77 at the Mémorial de la Shoah, July 31, 2014. (Author photo)

In 2010 SNCF president Guillaume Pepy took a trip to Auschwitz with Jacques Fredj, director of the Centre de Documentation Juive Contemporaine at the Mémorial de la Shoah. While some of the Jewish community fastened onto this trip as a cynical publicity stunt, the event, though receiving little media attention, showed at least an interest in symbolically honoring the events of the past. When Lou, whose mother, Estéra, had barely survived the death camps, heard about all of the SNCF's commemorative efforts and contributions, she said softly to her husband, whose mother was murdered along with many others, "It makes me feel good to hear they have done this."[44]

On the part of company loyalists, not everyone celebrated this revision of SNCF's lopsided wartime story. Some members of the CGT train union, for example, perceived some of these efforts as a defamation of the SNCF's heroic identity. This backlash emerged in some blogs in which cheminots defended the company. Others commented negatively online in response to articles about commemorative or transparency efforts.

CONTRIBUTIONS BEYOND FRANCE

The $60 million French–US settlement of 2014, which I discussed in the introduction, required the SNCF to donate an additional $5 million to Holocaust education and commemoration. The SNCF granted $200,000 to the Simon Wiesenthal Center, an international human rights organization that focuses on Holocaust research and on confronting modern antisemitism, terrorism, and hate crimes.[45] As recently as 2017, the SNCF made a donation to the Auschwitz Institute for Peace and Reconciliation from a discretionary fund unrelated to the French–US settlement.

The SNCF largely permits the organizations to conduct the work as they see fit, though sometimes their gifts target specific projects. Development professionals pay careful attention to what they call restricted versus unrestricted funds. As I discuss in the next chapter, some of the Jewish community in Florida interpreted the SNCF's local contribution as a way to control history. What distinguishes the SNCF's efforts from those of other corporate actors is the physical presence of company executives at many ceremonies. At the Bobigny Commemorative ceremony outside Paris, for example, the SNCF played a central role, speaking to both the victims and the larger French Jewish community. In total, the SNCF has contributed an estimated $12 million to support memory projects, transparency, research, and education. This total includes $4 million to be spent between 2015 and 2019.[46] And in 2017 the SNCF signed an agreement with the Mémorial de la Shoah to sponsor a *lieu de mémoire* to open in 2020 at the Pithiviers (Loiret) passenger rail station.[47] The new director of the Musée Mémorial des Enfants du Vel d'Hiv a Orléans (Loiret), Annaïg

Lefeuvre, anticipates that the project will be complete sometime in 2021.[48] This station, from which six convoys departed—including those carrying Marguerite, Simon, Sarah, and Jacqueline Federman—will have a commemorative plaque and an information center. These contributions, among others, point to the company's willingness to engage in ongoing commemoration efforts.

THE POLITICS OF CORPORATE APOLOGIES: BOBIGNY

Apologies have also become a familiar practice in the aftermath of atrocity. In 2005 the chief executive of the Dutch National Railways, Aad Veenman, apologized for the company's role in the deportation of more than 107,000 Jews as well as the deportations of homosexuals, disabled persons, and political prisoners. Six years later, on January 25, 2011, SNCF chairman Guillaume Pepy made the SNCF's first official apology at a commemorative event celebrating the SNCF's donation of a land title for the creation of a memorial at the largest deportation site in France, that in the town of Bobigny (as quoted in this chapter's epigraph).[49] To an audience of prominent members of French Jewish leadership (including Simone Veil and Serge Klarsfeld), Pepy said, "From where we are standing today, from here in Bobigny, nearly 25,000 people departed. They trod this ground, saw these buildings and asked questions of these rails. Today we know the answer. Their destination was Auschwitz-Birkenau. Here in these surroundings, which are henceforth engraved in the memory of each one of us, *I want to express the SNCF's deep sorrow and regret for the consequences of the acts of the SNCF of that era.* In its name, I am humbled before the victims, the survivors and the children of the deportees, and before the suffering, which lives on."[50] To these stirring words Pepy then added, "The SNCF, a state-owned business, had been constrained and requisitioned as a cog of the Nazi extermination machine. We will never forget this."[51]

Lou was not particularly impressed with Guillaume Pepy's apology on behalf of the SNCF. She told me it sounded more like making excuses than taking real responsibility.[52] Neither did the apology impress her lawyer Corinne Hershkovitch, who recalled a radio interview with Guillaume Pepy that she had heard just five years prior, in 2006. In response to the journalist's question about the SNCF's inhuman transport, Pepy responded, "La SNCF était là pour faire rouler les trains" (the SNCF was there to make the trains run). She did not believe his opinion had changed since that interview. Therefore, she felt the apology was insincere.[53] Henry Kerner, who worked on the SNCF conflict in the House of Representatives Fraud Department, similarly did not consider Pepy's words a sufficient apology. Kerner told me in no uncertain terms that the SNCF needed to issue a real apology and pay compensation directly to the victims.[54]

As is not uncommon in corporate apologies, many accused the SNCF of staging this event just to win favor with those attacking the company. In fact, the *New York Times* reported the apology as Pepy's response to years of litigation and pressure from survivors and their supporters.[55] Philippe Boukara, educational coordinator at the Mémorial de la Shoah in Paris, told me during our meeting that, while the lawsuits and legislation might have sped things up, the Bobigny project and the apology had been planned for years.[56]

At the Bobigny ceremony, each attendee received a DVD titled *The Former Bobigny Station: Between Drancy and Auschwitz*.[57] This fifteen-minute video, shot on the train tracks of Bobigny, includes interviews with several survivors and two sons of SNCF railway workers. All survivors highlighted in the film acquit the SNCF, including Yvette Levy Dreyfus, who was also deported on the last convoy from Paris to Auschwitz along with Daniel, Samuel, Henri, and Abram. "Could they do otherwise? I don't think they are responsible," Yvette said to the camera. The well-intentioned event and commemorative contribution still sit awkwardly in public memory.

As of 2020, the Bobigny memorial site and the visitors center were still unfinished and not yet open to the public. The site is short on funds, even though the SNCF remains officially involved in the project. The planning committee estimated a 2019 opening, since postponed. One thing is clear: by the time it does open, few survivors will be well enough to visit. Daniel, who had hoped to attend with me a couple of years ago, will likely be unable to visit because of his increasing age and frailty. This prompts two questions: who will the memorial serve, and what role will it play in a community largely composed of immigrants? With these questions still remaining, the donation of the land and the apology issued help us explore how corporations can engage with commemoration and forgiveness. Like justice generally, the wheels of accountability turn slowly. The site of the deportations will be turned—someday—into a memorial.

A REAL APOLOGY?

The SNCF's apology first given at the Bobigny event—like its historical materials and plaques—represents a cautious acknowledgment of harm without necessarily accepting total responsibility. This angered some survivors who, like Lou, believed that a half apology is worse than none at all. SNCF employees struggled to say "we did wrong" because they likely feared the financial consequences *and* because some have a hard time accepting themselves as symbolically responsible for events that occurred before their birth. "I wasn't even alive then," is a common refrain of those forced to account for predecessor behavior. Many heads of state, by contrast, accept this as part of the job: as a political leader, one inherits the past. Corporate leaders, in contrast, are less accustomed to this part of their role, though more are being asked to step up and carry the inherited decisions of the past.[58]

Some scholars advocate for official government apologies because of their macro-level benefits, allowing the new leaders to show the people their commitment to change future policy.[59] The apologizer, by demonstrating how predecessors failed, recalibrates the moral standard of society. Apologies offer the public an opportunity to examine norms, consider historical narratives, and acknowledge victims as moral agents.[60] An apology may legitimize the survivors and help them reconstitute their social identity. At the same time, apologies for complicity are rightly critiqued when they focus only on larger societal needs, while overlooking individuals.[61]

For apologies to perform this varied moral work, accepting responsibility proves essential. In *Moral Repair*, Margaret Urban Walker states that "nothing anyone does to relieve a harmed person's pain or suffering, stress, anger, resentment or indignation or outrage will count as 'making amends' without an acceptance of responsibility as the reason for the effort."[62] The SNCF's official apology sidestepped the notion of direct responsibility.

Some promote forgiveness by survivors after an official apology because the apology restores agency to the victim.[63] Griswold qualifies this, saying that such forgiveness is warranted only if the state comes through on its promises.[64] Even if the state does follow through, however, forgiveness restores agency only if survivors have the freedom to reject the apology. In the SNCF conflict, those challenging the company requested an apology that demonstrated sincerity and accepted responsibility. They rarely expounded on what such an apology would look like, although the success of former French president Jacques Chirac's 1995 apology for World War II might provide some clues. Much of France, both Jewish and non-Jewish, applauded Chirac's speech at an important anniversary of the Vel d'Hiv roundup, which occurred in Paris over two days, July 16 and 17, 1942.[65] In his speech, Chirac accepted total responsibility for France's actions. More than expressing regret, he accepted the burden of the harms of the past: "France, the homeland of the Enlightenment and of the rights of man, a land of welcome and asylum, on that day committed the irreparable . . . breaking its word, it handed those who were under its protection over to their executioners . . . we owe them an everlasting debt."[66]

Many French refer to Chirac's speech as a pivotal moment in the country's coming to terms with World War II. Isabelle, who survived the Vel d'Hiv roundup by hiding with her sister on her building's roof but who ultimately lost her parents, told me, "If Chirac had not spoken, there would still be silence."[67] Many survivors with whom I spoke in both the United States and France said that they appreciated Chirac's apology. This included Leon, whose parents, little brother (age six), and little sister (age eleven) all found themselves deported to

Auschwitz in November 1943 on Convoy 62. Speaking about the apology, Leon expressed to me its importance: "It was significant in that [Chirac] admitted that France was actively collaborating. . . . Charles de Gaulle said it was not France but the Germans who did everything. They had a choice and that's what Chirac recognized."[68] Good apologies matter to victims.

Churches are also capable of profound apologies when moved to do so. On September 30, 1997, in Drancy, the bishops of the French Catholic Church issued a declaration of repentance. Olivier de Berranger, who served as bishop of Saint-Denis between 1996 and 2009, read the declaration: "In the face of the enormity of the drama and the unheard-of nature of the crime too many pastors of the church offended the Church itself and its mission by their silence. Today, *we confess that this silence was a wrong.* We recognize also that the church of France thus failed at its mission as an educator of consciences and thus that it shares with the *Christian people the responsibility of not having helped at the first moments when protests and protection were possible and necessary,* even if countless acts of courage followed. This lack of action and the responsibility toward the Jewish people make up part of the Church's history. We confess this fault. We seek God's pardon and ask the Jewish people to listen to these words of repentance."[69] Apology, as an extension of confession, is part of the fabric of the Catholic Church.

Richard Prasquier, former president of CRIF, told me that the SNCF's lack of repentance made sense because apologies are a spiritual matter and the SNCF's mission is not a spiritual one.[70] Yet, in 2005, Aad Veenman, chief executive of the NS, apparently felt differently. He said, "On behalf of the company and from the bottom of my heart, I sincerely apologize for what happened during the war."[71] (The Dutch National Railways compensated survivors in 2019, fourteen years after its apology.) Moreover, train companies apologize often and over far lesser crimes. In 2018 the British railways offered more than 267,000 words of apology on Twitter for delayed trains.[72] Rail companies are less accustomed, however, to making apologies for trains that departed on time, as most of the convoys did. Of course, apologies for massive human rights violations require a different communication style.[73] I disagree with Prasquier, who believes that apologies only entangle the spiritually committed. Any one or any entity capable of causing harm carries the same moral capacity for apology.

As with many apologies, the question of the SNCF's sincerity emerged. Some believe that the act of apology proves more important than the sincerity with which it was given; others argue that without sincerity, apologies lack the moral impact needed to address the harm.[74] Sincerity becomes especially difficult for companies with a financial interest in being forgiven. Because the SNCF has business interests, it found its words scrutinized for indications of sincerity perhaps more than expressions of apology issued by churches or states.

The SNCF found itself in a double bind regarding apologies—damned if they apologize, damned if they don't.[75] Company apologies may always be critiqued as hollow. Even if executives do make heartfelt apologies, this in no way guarantees legal or social amnesty for the corporation.

Has the SNCF Made Amends?

For those working in postconflict contexts, complicit businesses cannot be overlooked as critical participants. Through the SNCF example, we can see how corporations can participate in historical commissions, transparency efforts, and education and can issue apologies. The problem of reaching the diaspora remains. Those in the United States do not see the plaques and cannot attend the commemorative ceremonies in France. Corporations can be chastised for participating solely to improve their reputations and to avoid being accused of shirking accountability. Untying these double binds requires focusing on the victims' needs. In other words, putting up a plaque improves brand image. Helping survivors afford adequate elder care may not emblazon the company name in a public space but does help those most harmed. Strewing the world with memorial plaques may remind pedestrians of past atrocities, and transparency helps books like this one get written. These efforts work toward prevention as well as cultural healing. However, somehow, in all this tumult, it is important to stay focused on the individual needs that such violations of public trust and mass crime create. As the remaining survivors reach their final days, many told me of a new phase of their trauma. Some find themselves haunted by resurgent memories; some—now watching loved ones die of old age—find themselves faced, again, with aloneness and the anamnesis that comes with proximity to death. Their needs are real but not impossible or even very costly to meet. The work of atonement is always unfinished. The lesson for company executives is that no amount of investing in research or commemoration makes up for victim services: all dimensions of coming to terms with the harms of the past are necessary.

Pardon Granted by French Leadership

> The past is past. It's not forgotten, but it has finally found its place.
>
> —Henry Rousso

Before shifting the scene of litigation to the United States, where the debates over the SNCF's responsibility reached new heights, I want to offer a brief note addressing some Vichy scholars' views about this conflict. Vichy historians have now largely exonerated the French state and—by extension—the SNCF. This may be surprising, as Vichy historians proved to be some of the first and harshest critics of wartime France and its institutions. In 1994 the French historians Henry Rousso and Eric Conan published *Vichy, un passé qui ne passe pas*, the title of which coined the famous phrase about the Vichy period in France—"the past that does not pass."[76] Today, more than thirty years after this book first appeared, Rousso believes a shift has occurred. He says, "The past is past. It's not forgotten, but it has finally found its place."[77] Other historians and Holocaust specialists called the attacks against the SNCF in the United States "uninformed and unfair." They feel that the SNCF is taking an unwarranted beating.[78] The Vichy historian Annette Wieviorka believes that the SNCF has largely taken responsibility for its role in the Holocaust.[79] She points to the opening of the archives and the train station exposition on the deportations as examples. She considers it scandalous that some say the company has done nothing; it is simply untrue. She is right. Michael Marrus is another among those who agrees that the SNCF has paid its dues. He told a reporter for the *Washington Post* that he is "a bit exasperated" by efforts to bar the railway from receiving US government contracts and thinks "these matters should be put to bed."[80] He goes on to say, "I don't diminish the tragedy or the pain and suffering, but I think at the end of the day, there will never be justice in the sense that most of the perpetrators have died by now and most of the people who suffered directly have died by now. I just don't see any merit in continuing this, especially when [there has been] open acknowledgment and contrition."[81] Jewish leaders have expressed themselves along similar lines. In a speech given in February 2011, Richard Prasquier, while president of CRIF, the leading French Jewish organization, stated that he believed the SNCF had done its work and now acts as a leader: "The SNCF, who is strongly engaged with the process of unveiling its own history, is an example of the shadows and lights intertwined. We support its approach."[82] Leaders in the French Jewish community have convinced many members, even some living in the United States, to let the matter rest. During our lunch in Washington, DC's Dupont Circle, Johanna, a child survivor who always reads the CRIF newsletter, said she knew of the organization's positions. If the SNCF had done enough to satisfy CRIF, she said, it had done enough for her.[83] When we met in his home in 2011, Serge Klarsfeld told me, "France a fait ce qu'il fallait faire!" (France has done what it needed to do), echoing the statement he would later make to a *Daily Motion* journalist.[84] He justified his position by referring to the $700 million allocated to surviving families and the $400 million given to set up the Fondation pour la Mémoire de la Shoah. He said that orphans from that time have received a pension for life. The SNCF helped support these projects through donations but never paid survivors directly.[85] Klarsfeld felt that these measures addressed the SNCF as well. Regarding the conflict in the United States, Klarsfeld believed that Americans had an overly simplistic view of what had happened in France. The SNCF conflict distracts from the *vrai coupable*—the truly guilty—meaning the Germans and the French Vichy state. So many individuals and organizations—past and present—were given de facto impunity because of the obsession with trains.[86] The SNCF conflict also distracts, he said, from those who gave their lives in support of France.

Klarsfeld's work in the aftermath of the Holocaust meant a tremendous deal to the thousands of people who learned more about themselves and their families through his tireless research. He initiated a government-sponsored compensation program for those orphaned by antisemitic persecution. This program brought material redress to many previously overlooked victims. He and his wife Beate's efforts to bring the collaborators to trial after the war continued even fifty years after the events. In 2014 Klarsfeld was awarded the Légion d'honneur, France's highest medal of honor, for his Holocaust activism. Although he has received some criticism for his defense of the SNCF, he continues to lead the French Jewish community when it comes to Holocaust issues. The Klarsfelds, however, have less influence over the US survivor community, whose members often express opinions and justifications different from those of their French counterparts.

Ultimately, the SNCF's efforts to make amends satisfied much of the French Jewish leadership and also seemed to satisfy Israel. During French president François Hollande's three-day visit to Israel in November 2014, the Israeli government contracted with the SNCF to improve the railway stations and the Israel Railways Ltd. (ISR) engineering training program. The ISR hoped this contract would help the Israeli company double its passengers in less than ten years.[87] To handle the sensitive subject of the SNCF's World War II participation, the parties agreed that the SNCF would invest in more research on the railroads through Yad Vashem, Israel's Holocaust museum and research center. SNCF's Bernard Emsellem detailed the company's wider efforts to make amends during an interview with *Israel National News*.[88] André Zdroui, a French-based survivor who escaped the Nazis several times and who lost his father in the Holocaust, says he followed Israel's lead on the SNCF matter: "One cannot be more royalist than the king."[89] If the SNCF's amends were good enough for Israel, they were good enough for him.

Aaron Greenfield, a lobbyist who would challenge the SNCF in Maryland, however, stated that a number of the Israel-based litigants fighting the SNCF were quite upset that Israel made the agreement with the SNCF.[90] US-based survivors did not feel compelled to follow Israel's or the French Jewish community's lead one way or another. Clearly, postconflict demands emerge differently in different localities and even vary within those localities. As I discuss in the next chapter, neither the French Jewish leadership, nor historians, nor Israel could persuade those who felt that the SNCF still had not made proper amends.

VOICES FROM THE LAST TRAINS

There are lingering disagreements about the SNCF that remain within families. Charlotte in Boca Raton, Florida, for example, joined the lawsuit against the SNCF to seek compensation for the loss of her father. She wanted to keep the company out of Florida forever. Charlotte tried to convince her cousin Renée to join the lawsuit, but she declined. Renée, based in Paris, wanted the lawsuits against the SNCF to stop.

During my first interview with Renée, I apologized in advance for having to cut the session a bit short. I explained that the Shoah Memorial was hosting a public reading of the names of deportees who had left on a convoy seventy years ago that day.

"Which convoy?" Renée asked.

"Convoy 77."

"My father was on that train!" she said.

Convoy 77 had carried Renée's father, Abram Zeigman, a shoe cutter who had been stopped by the Gestapo in Lyon while he was waiting for a tram on his way to work. He spent fifteen days in the Mon-Luc prison run by Klaus Barbie before being sent to the Drancy internment camp on July 27, 1944.[91]

We grabbed our things and moved as fast as we could from her home in Belleville to the Marais, where the event had already started. We found a space on some benches.

"Do you think they'll let me read my father's name?" Renée asked.

"Go ask them," I suggested.

Luckily, her father's name, Abram Zejgman, was at the end of the list so she had time to work her way to the podium and get registered as a speaker. Renée read her father's name, without visible emotion. After the ceremony, we went upstairs to meet the others from the convoy, including Daniel. It turned out that Renée, was actually quite shaken by reading her father's name and left early to recover. We met again later so she could tell me all she knew of her wartime experiences and the sorrow that had hung over her family for decades.

One of the things she told me, which had been passed on to her by her family, centered on Paris's Hôtel Lutetia. Like many institutions and individuals, the Hôtel Lutetia shifted between multiple identities during the war. In the 1930s, it was a posh Art Nouveau hotel frequented by famous guests. The hotel also hosted an antifascist committee. In 1939 it transformed into a refuge for those fleeing the invading German forces. During the occupation, the Abwehr (a German intelligence organization) used it as a headquarters. From the liberation of Paris (August 1944) until the end of World War II, the hotel served as a center of repatriation for POWs, camp survivors, and other displaced persons. With fewer than 5 percent of French deportees returning, however, most of those searching for their loved ones left the hotel with bad news.

Abram Zejgman's family—Renée was a babe in arms at the time—went to the hotel filled with hope of finding him.

"You don't need to keep waiting," said a man who had also been deported on Convoy 77 with Abram.

"He was gassed on arrival for trying to escape."

Crestfallen, Abram's wife, Mirla, went to Berlin to find Abram's brother and sister, who had survived Auschwitz. Their cultural tradition provided that she would marry her husband's brother, Israel. Israel had no wife and eight children, but Mirla refused to marry him. Soon after, her husband's siblings all moved to the United States, leaving her with little remaining family. Without her husband's salary from the grain factory, Mirla could not feed her children, so, at age seventeen, George, the eldest son, became the head of the family, a position that he held the rest of his life. His work as an accountant supported his mother, two sisters, and brother. Despite his best efforts in supporting the family, however, George could not get his mother out of her abyss of mourning.

"It felt like she wore black for an eternity," Renée recalled.

"No one helped my mother after the war," she explained. "I want to do better for these people," referring to today's refugees. To help, Renée volunteers with an organization whose members drive immigrants to doctor's appointments.[92] Even though her suffering lingers, she, like Daniel, tries to turn her attention to the needs of the living rather than focusing on the wrongdoings of the dead.

CHAPTER SIX

SNCF America

So, we continue to work in partnership with those most deeply affected to ensure such unspeakable horrors never occur again. That is why SNCF has made a long-term commitment to transparency, education of younger generations, and acts of remembrance. . . .

Much of what has been done is not known in the United States.

—GUILLAUME PEPY, SNCF chairman

That the SNCF may have made a contribution to a museum does not absolve it of responsibility.

—HARRIET TAMEN, lawyer

WITHOUT PLEASING EVERYONE, the SNCF's efforts in the 1990s helped it become an ally of the French Jewish community; in the United States, however, it still faced opposition significant enough to thwart lucrative overseas contracts. Achieving universal impunity in the wake of any atrocity is unlikely. What satisfies one group may be insufficient for another. Even if done with great care, efforts to atone for behavior can take decades and may yield mixed results. Simply said: irreparable harm does not easily lend itself to repair. Understanding this paradox of post-atrocity healing processes, Margaret Urban Walker encourages perpetrators to accept a certain amount of ongoing hostility and indignation.[1] In practice, this means that complicit parties must make conciliatory efforts, while accepting that some hostile feelings will always remain. Treating amends-making efforts as intrinsically rather than instrumentally valuable can help assuage frustration. Executives, postconflict practitioners, advocates, and others engage in this work knowing that it does not lend itself to completion. The memories and their legacy will always need tending. This often-uncomfortable emotional work without guaranteed outcomes can be especially challenging for corporations that rely heavily upon their reputations and earnings statements.

In the United States, as happened in France, acknowledging and addressing its role in the Holocaust became a Chinese finger trap for the company. The more SNCF America made Holocaust-related contributions, the more it became linked to its Holocaust history. Memorials, apologies, and educational funds reminded publics of the company's past.

The company's refusal to compensate survivors cast a shadow on these efforts. Henry Kerner, who worked for the House of Representatives Oversight Committee on the SNCF conflict, drafted letters to the SNCF urging it to take responsibility through financial redress. He offered this analogy: "if you hit someone's car to avoid hitting another car, you still have to pay."[2] Secretary of State John Kerry also pressured SNCF America CEO Alain Leray to pay the survivors.

Collette, a survivor, also wanted to see some financial compensation along with all the memorialization. As a girl, she had found herself crammed on a rail convoy that included her parents and roughly a thousand others. She survived, but her parents were murdered. Regarding the SNCF's commemorative efforts, she said, "I wish they could bring back my parents and all the members of my family who were lost. All that is done is nice, but it doesn't bring back my family. Nothing can bring them back and I can just imagine what happened to them."[3] She told me that she applauds the SNCF efforts but still thinks the company ought to pay survivors.[4]

Charles, who survived the war hidden in a Catholic orphanage, echoes this sentiment. He was involved in numerous Holocaust-related lawsuits, motivated by the murder of roughly three hundred of his family members. During our phone conversation, he said, "I don't care about those memorials—money should be paid to survivors that are left—period."[5]

Some survivors clearly felt atonement required compensation. However, had the company paid *only* survivors and not engaged in other efforts, many would likely see the company as trying to buy its way out of accountability. Many complicit German enterprises just paid into a national fund and wiped their hands of the past. When corporations just pay the bill, immoral actions become a cost of doing business. Issuing a check does not indicate remorse or a change in ethos any more than paying taxes demonstrates that you agree with government spending.

Morally empty payments remain a challenge for those wishing to increase the moral sensibilities of corporations more generally. The SNCF, while it failed to compensate survivors directly, has arguably engaged in far more soul-searching than other companies, even those German companies that paid into the Foundation Initiative of the German Industry.[6] While the German companies helped compensate survivors, few offered apologies or transparency about the past. In contrast, the SNCF's transparency efforts, historical dialogue commission, commemorative events, and apology each, in different ways, opened dialogues within the company; they led to debates, discussions, and memorialization in Jewish communities in both countries and provoked attention and action in US legislative offices. For the SNCF executives leading these efforts, simply paying a bill might have been easier.

THE US JEWISH COMMUNITY

While media coverage often polarized the conflict, the US Jewish community did not share a uniform opinion about the SNCF's worthiness to bid for contracts in the United States. Some demanded direct compensation (which, to them, represented recognition of the company's culpability) and found the SNCF's commemorative efforts insufficient. Many other French survivors residing in the United States perceived the events of the Holocaust as just too long ago to fuss about anymore. Many told me that they did not want to punish today's French taxpayers for the ill deeds of their parents and grandparents. Dr. Marc Gurwith, whose family escaped persecution in France, said to me that the Holocaust "seems like such a long time ago. The company has shareholders now who are so far removed from it. It seems implausible."[7] He is more concerned about the stolen paintings that some people's parents or grandparents acquired dishonestly and that have yet to be returned. Given the news coverage, I was startled by how many survivors shared his sentiments, a number having turned their attention to current suffering. Because journalists and others only quoted those who were challenging the company, these voices dropped out of the public debate.

In reality, the SNCF had a mix of friends and foes throughout the United States. SNCF America found itself struggling more with local Jewish organizations than with national organizations such as the American Jewish Committee (AJC) and the Anti-Defamation League (ADL). The ADL expressed concerns about legislative efforts to bar the SNCF from doing business in the United States or to allow Americans to sue the company in US courts.[8] The AJC also did not participate in the battles against the SNCF. In contrast, local Jewish organizations often supported their members in the quest for compensation.

Those who sought financial compensation hoped their legal action would push the SNCF to offer a settlement. More than once, US class action lawsuits successfully pushed French and Swiss banks as well as German companies toward settlements (see the appendix). These settlements all began as lawsuits launched in the 1990s. Stuart Eizenstat, who helped negotiate a number of settlements, describes class action lawsuits as "despised by most U.S. companies and feared by foreign corporations doing business in the United States."[9]

They are despised because if enough people join, even a relatively small wrong can result in extensive fines and a tarnished image.

Harriet Tamen, the New York–based lawyer knew about the power of class action. She had played a key role in the cases against the French banks and this prepared her to become the SNCF's champion opponent. Tamen would come to represent roughly 600 survivors against the SNCF; many lived in the United States, but others resided abroad. Stuart Eizenstat described Tamen, with whom he had worked on the French bank settlement, as "the most knowledgeable and the most unyielding, the most passionate and embittered [person] about the recent French efforts at restitution, which she deemed woefully inadequate. An intense person with a sharp mind, bristling with kinetic energy, and hair cropped so short it created an accurate impression of toughness."[10] In 2001, their team convinced the French banks to pay $50 million to survivors from whom they withheld ill-gotten gains. Tamen said that signing the agreement was one of the biggest mistakes of her life.[11] Richard Weisberg, who worked with Tamen on the lawsuit, agrees that the settlement fell short; the French banks owed far more than they had paid for the stolen Jewish assets they had housed and benefited from for half a century. He went on to say that as much as he respected Tamen's view, "It's never perfect when you settle a case. The perfect is the enemy of the good."[12] That said, he respected Tamen's ferocity, describing her as "tremendously devoted to her clients." A number of the survivors, like Lou, deeply appreciated the time Tamen dedicated to their cause, especially supporting those who had met dead ends in French courts.

Tamen launched her first lawsuit against the SNCF in 2000, with Holocaust survivor Raymonde Abrams as the lead plaintiff, joined by Jean-Jacques Fraenkel, who had earlier been lead plaintiff in the first lawsuit in France. *Abrams v. Société Nationale des Chemins de Fer* was heard in the Court for the Eastern District of New York.[13] These lawyers claimed that the SNCF had violated international customary law and the law of nations by participating in the deportations. In her public remarks surrounding the case, Tamen criticized the SNCF for trying to rewrite the history of the Holocaust and was unconvinced by documents that suggested the SNCF was not paid for the deportation trains. She believed the company had profited from the deportations. To further justify trying this case in US courts, she pointed out that SNCF trains also helped deport 168 US pilots. She wanted the contemporary company to say, "We are sorry for what we did, we accept responsibility, and we will pay."[14]

The New York court dismissed *Abrams v. Société Nationale des Chemins de Fer*, claiming that it lacked subject matter jurisdiction because the Foreign Sovereign Immunities Act (FSIA) of 1976 protects government-owned enterprises like the railway company.[15] In other words, the court could not hear a case against the nation of France via its state-owned railway company. The litigants appealed until the case was definitively dismissed in 2004.

Yet the lawsuits continued.

In 2008 Matilde Freund became the lead litigant on a similar case, which sought to circumvent the FSIA by focusing on property losses related to the SNCF's role in the transport of deportees.[16] The plaintiffs asked the District Court for the Southern District of New York for an exception to the FSIA. This lawsuit targeted the Republic of France, the SNCF, and Caisse des Dépôts et Consignations (CDC, Deposits and Consignments Fund), a French public financial institution. Litigants included Leo Bretholz and Freddie Knoller, both of whom became some of the best-known challengers of the SNCF. The court denied the request, saying it lacked jurisdiction, but it acknowledged the plaintiffs and their counsel for demonstrating their commitment to "bringing justice to victims of the Nazi era."[17]

In 2009 Representative Carolyn B. Maloney of New York introduced legislation to try to allow US courts to hear any lawsuits brought against the railroad.[18] The bill failed. Tamen was distraught by her inability to use courts or legislation. She told me that she just wanted her clients to see justice in their lifetimes and have some comfort in their final days.[19] She spoke specifically of Matilde Freund, the lead plaintiff in the case. Twenty-two of Freund's family members were murdered in the Holocaust. During the war, she tried to rescue her husband and was arrested and tortured, then escaped and spent time hiding in a forest. Today, Freund loves to go to the opera. Tamen recounted Freund's story to me and added that if the SNCF were to settle, Freund would be able to attend the opera whenever she likes.[20] In spite of the roadblocks, more survivors joined the effort: By 2011 Tamen and the New York–based law firm Akin Gump Strauss Hauer & Feld claimed to represent six hundred litigants worldwide.[21]

Ultimately legislative pressures did yield results, just perhaps not those Tamen expected. Her efforts helped pressure the French National Railways enough to strain U.S.-French relations; this catalyzed the involvement of the US Department of State. Diplomatic negotiations began, while the litigation continued. Four months after the French and US governments signed the $60 million settlement in December 2014 and before the French government had even ratified the agreement, another case was filed—*Scalin v. Société Nationale des Chemins de Fer Français*. This lawsuit similarly tried to circumvent the FSIA, this time by focusing on alleged theft by the SNCF workers.[22] On April 16, 2015—that is, on Yom Hashoah (Holocaust Remembrance Day)—a group filed a class action lawsuit in Chicago. The lead plaintiff, Karen Scalin, backed by other litigants, and Tamen alleged that the "SNCF confiscated the Holocaust victims' personal property (such as cash, jewelry, and artwork), either convert-ing the property to its own benefit or turning it over to the Nazis."[23]

Upon learning about this lawsuit, Lilly, a survivor who was deported with her family, said, "Stealing? Well, that was the least of it."[24] Survivors were some-times befuddled by the ways that legal lacunae pushed lawyers to focus on the case they could win rather than the one that addressed the moral wrongdoings at the heart of their suffering.

On March 26, 2018, the judge dismissed the case, again citing lack of sub-ject matter jurisdiction. To date, the SNCF maintains legal immunity in the United States, as it does in France. While the appendix provides a detailed outline of the lawsuits, the abridged table 6.1 presents a summary of the key SNCF-related lawsuits in the United States and France. The fact that the SNCF conflict was not decided in court is unsurprising. In the United States, litigation related to compensation for Nazi crimes is most often settled outside court. The lawsuits most often serve to increase pressure enough to create conditions for a settlement. The group fighting the French National Railways therefore turned to legislation designed to effectively boycott the company. They proved a powerful force even if they could not always stop the trains.

The multistate legislative battle threatened to make doing business in the United States challenging, miserable, and expensive for the SNCF. If lobbying expenses in the US are any indication of the SNCF's troubles, the company spent roughly $1 million a year between 2012 and the height of the conflict, in 2014. The majority of this lobbying money did not pertain to the Holocaust-related legislation, but much of it did. (Spending slowed to $200,000 in 2017 and to a mere trickle, $90,000, in 2018, reflecting an overall reduction in rail lobbying nationwide.)[31] But between 2010 and 2014, SNCF America found itself tethered to the Holocaust.

VIRGINIA

In 2010 Keolis, a subsidiary of SNCF America, bid for and won an $85 million contract from the Virginia Railway Express (VRE), which provides regional/commuter rail service for those in northern Virginia suburbs who travel back and forth to Washington, DC. More than 250 Holocaust survivors, with the help of attorney Dale Leibach (who offered pro bono services through the Washington-based firm Prism Public Affairs), objected to this contract. The group demanded an apology, transparency, and compensation before the com-pany could do business in the United States. Leo Bretholz joined the fight, saying, "The survivors are taxpayers. . . . Why should we subsidize a com-pany that has done us wrong? This adds insult to injury."[32] Peter Kelly, a Los Angeles lawyer representing the SNCF, tried to reassure the public about the

Table 6.1. Key legal cases related to the SNCF

Year	Name of Lawsuit	Location	Description
1998	*Jean-Jacques Fraenkel v. SNCF*	France	Jean-Jacques Fraenkel sues the SNCF for crimes against humanity on behalf of his parents, deported and murdered at Auschwitz. Court dismisses the case for insufficient evidence.
2001	*Abrams v. Société Nationale des Chemins de Fer Français*[25]	US	Class action lawsuit launched from the United States by New York lawyer Harriet Tamen. The District Court for the Eastern District of NY dismisses the complaint, saying the SNCF has immunity because of the Foreign Sovereign Immunities Act (FSIA). In 2003 the Court of Appeals reinstates the class action lawsuit, only to have it dismissed when the US Supreme Court rules in an unrelated case (see *Republic of Austria* in the appendix) that the FSIA is retroactive. Litigants appeal without success to the US Supreme Court in 2005.
2001	*Lipietz et al. v. Prefet de la Haute-Garonne and SNCF*[26]	France	Alain and Georges Lipietz (son and father, respectively) file against the French state and the SNCF for the injuries suffered by Alain's mother, father, and stepfather. The court dismisses the case. Litigants appeal, and in 2006 the Administrative Court of Toulouse rules against the SNCF and the French government. The SNCF appeals and wins in 2007.
2003	*Kurt Werner Schaechter v. SNCF*[27]	France	Kurt Schaechter sues for a symbolic euro on behalf of his murdered parents, transported on the SNCF. The Tribunal de grande instance rules in favor of the SNCF. Schaechter appeals. The Paris Court of Appeals rejects the case in 2004, saying the suit comes too long after the events.

Table 6.1. (*continued*)

Year	Name of Lawsuit	Location	Description
2008	*Freund et al. v. SNCF*[28]	US	Harriet Tamen, on behalf of her litigants (including Matilde Freund, Leo Bretholz, Freddie Knoller, Kurt Schaechter, and others), seeks restitution for property stolen by SNCF workers and asks the District Court for the Southern District of New York for an exception to the FSIA. They are denied. In February 2011, the lawyers petition the US Supreme Court, which denies the claim in October of that same year.
2008–9	Hoffmann-Glemane decision[29]	France	Conseil d'État (the high court for administrative matters) declares that France owes nothing more for the Holocaust.
2015	*Karen Scalin, Josiane Piquard, and Roland Cherrier v. SNCF*[30]	US	Claimants seek damages for international law violation, conversion, and unjust enrichment. Steven Blonder serves as the lead lawyer. This focus on theft attempts to circumvent the FSIA, which blocked the other class action suits. The judge dismisses the case in 2018.

company's World War II transparency, saying that the company was translating into English the independently researched 1,200-page report (known as the Bachelier report) on the company's wartime activities.[33] The report has yet to be translated.

Amtrak, as a corporate competitor, was equally distraught that the SNCF had won the contract, albeit for other reasons. Some suspected that this fierce SNCF competitor even encouraged the survivor outcry. For eighteen years, Amtrak had managed the commuter rail lines in Virginia. When the contract came up for renewal, Amtrak assumed it would win the bid. According to VRE CEO Dale Zehner, Amtrak executives were blindsided to learn that VRE wanted the more affordable SNCF subsidiary, Keolis. Amtrak responded to the defeat by punishing any of its own staff who chose to stay in the region and work for Keolis: "Former Amtrak staff now working for Keolis would be . . . permanently blacklisted. Crews who agreed to relocate to stay with Amtrak received a $5,000 bonus and were guaranteed a job. Amtrak, meanwhile, even tried to hire crews laid off from New Jersey Transit who had been approached by Keolis. The idea was to prevent Keolis from hiring enough crews to run the system by takeover day, June 28."[34]

Moreover, Amtrak refused to let Keolis engineers ride on its trains to learn the routes. Amtrak president Joe Boardman admitted he wanted Keolis to fail, allowing Amtrak to pitch again.[35] During our meeting in her office on the Quai d'Orsay in Paris, the French ambassador for human rights, Patrizianna Sparacino-Thiellay, who participated in the negotiations leading to the $60 million settlement reached in 2014, also wondered whether Amtrak might be fomenting the conflict in the United States against the SNCF.[36] Even though such accusations are difficult to prove, Amtrak's ability to benefit from a wounded SNCF should not be forgotten.

Airline companies serving cities that are deliberating about high-speed rail projects also benefit from crippled rail projects. In sum, there are more players pulling strings in this conflict than it might first appear. When considering corporate accountability in the aftermath of violence, it behooves us to consider who else stands to gain from the damaged company. Rage might be fomented by companies that would happily see a rival sidelined. This can help advance justice claims but also distract from the actions of the truly guilty (past and present).

MASSACHUSETTS

In Massachusetts, by contrast, the SNCF won an enormous contract without much contestation. In January 2014, Keolis won the bid for a Massachusetts commuter rail business from the Massachusetts Bay Transportation Authority (MBTA) rail line. The eight-year contract, worth more than $2 billion, was declared the largest contract in state history. It took effect in July 2014 and made Keolis responsible for the management of the rail system. At the same time, French president François Hollande gave the French government a mandate to negotiate with the US regarding a group of survivors currently not eligible for reparations. This was aimed at quelling the lobbying occurring in other states.

Curiously, local Jewish communities did not challenge the SNCF's business interests in Massachusetts.[37] Peter R. Gossels, a Massachusetts resident, had survived the war, but his mother, grandmother, and most of his family were deported and then murdered. When the SNCF (via Keolis) pitched for and won the MBTA contract, Gossels was ambivalent. He had never had an issue with France because on July 4, 1939, France admitted him and his brother Werner into the country after they fled Berlin. Once they were in France, the Oeuvre de Secours aux Enfants (OSE, Society for Assistance to Children), an organization that helped Jewish children in France, saved them.[38] In recent years, Gossels had become involved with the OSE-USA division that worked to bring an exhibit to the United States presenting the OSE's wartime heroism. He told me that when the costs became too high and the SNCF offered to help fund the exhibit, a lot of people in the group said, "No, no, no! It's a terrible thing . . . they have blood on their hands."[39] The group moved forward without requesting SNCF support. While the SNCF won the contract in Massachusetts without much fanfare, grumbling within a few local groups continued. Survivors in other states, however, made great strides toward passing legislation that blocked the company's ability to bid for contracts in Florida, California, and, eventually, Maryland, where, as I will discuss, the conflict eventually reached a climax.

FLORIDA

Whereas the SNCF's successful bids advanced largely uncontested in Massachusetts and Virginia, Florida presented the company with a more difficult situation. The company thought it was making progress in the state after executives attended a ribbon-cutting on October 30, 2014, during which the Simon Wiesenthal Center and the SNCF celebrated the launching of a Holocaust exhibit at Fort Lauderdale, Florida's, main library.[40] The company also helped sponsor a March of the Living, an annual program that brings students to Poland (and sometimes Israel) to study the Holocaust. But Florida nevertheless remained a challenge for the corporation.

Curiously, while a foe in Virginia, Amtrak became SNCF's ally in Florida in 2010 when the companies joined forces to bid for a high-speed rail project to connect Orlando and Tampa. In Florida, the tussle would be mostly with survivors who lived on the state's east coast. In contrast, a number of survivors whom I interviewed on Florida's west coast had no interest in participating in the legislative battles. This shows yet another difference between the diaspora subgroups.

Those on the east coast of Florida made the news when the group rejected the SNCF's $80,000 contribution to the state of Florida to fund additional Holocaust education. I called Rositta E. Kenigsberg, executive vice president of Florida's Holocaust Documentation and Education Center to ask how this came about. She said the SNCF offered a curriculum that no historian had reviewed and without the approval of a special task force. The group rejected the money.[41] Nina, a survivor living in Florida, became involved in this issue of the SNCF sponsoring Holocaust education. She expressed annoyance with the company for what she considered a circumvention of the task force: "We have been running programs for years and years and for them to try to buy into the program to get contracts for those French trains. . . . They wanted to teach their own curriculum. They wanted to give some money for some programs, really a piddly program. They wanted to get a big bargain. The money wasn't the issue. I would be against it no matter how much they offered. You cannot buy what has happened there. You cannot write your own history and teach it to the children, all in hopes of getting a contract."[42]

Nina survived the Warsaw ghetto and, although she did not spend any part of the war in France, more than 150 of her family members were murdered. "My feelings about the trains are very strong," she said. "They knew they were sending them to their death and there is no excuse for it." While there "is not enough money in the world to make up for what has been done to us," she wanted to make sure the remaining survivors do not die in poverty. She hoped that the SNCF would finally compensate survivors.[43]

In addition to the educational funds, some survivors in Florida also forcefully rejected an SNCF apology, which was first made in English. They believed the apology should have been first offered in France, and in French, and ought to have been coupled with financial compensation. When the SNCF did make an apology at the Bobigny ceremony (described in the preceding chapter), lawyer Harriet Tamen, capturing the sentiments of those who refused to accept it, said, "Too late, irrelevant, and an attempt to pull the wool over everyone's eyes. [SNCF chairman Guillaume Pepy] said he bows down before the survivors? Don't bow, write a check! Don't bow down, do something specific . . . dedicating a train station does nothing to help the victims . . . There are 170 or 180 Shoah memorials in the United States. We don't need more memorials; we need to help the victims."[44]

The relationship between the survivor group and the SNCF first improved before it worsened. Rositta Kenigsberg, who fought ardently against the SNCF in Florida, was upset when SNCF America CEO Dennis Douté died unexpectedly. She had wanted to continue conversations with him, feeling he was more open than his replacement, Alain Leray. When Leray became the new CEO, she said, she told him, "You can make the biggest difference in the world." She added, "All they have to do is the right thing. They can go build their rail cars for billions of dollars. What are they doing? What is being lost in this for them?" Finally, she asked him, "Why is there such resistance?"[45] When she discovered that the SNCF was lobbying all over the state to secure the lucrative contract, she was incensed. Rositta said, "Look what we do for our Vietnam vets. Look what we do with all different kinds of soldiers!" She did not understand why the company would prefer to spend $1 million on lobbying efforts instead of just paying the survivors. She said, "the company was spending the money in every other way." "If it was me," she said she had told the now-deceased Douté, "I would send a message to all the children of the future. We would say, we did this, we would make restitution—there is nothing wrong with that." As it is, she said, survivors living in France were calling her and her colleagues, crying and thanking them for their hard work because their own government was trying to shut them up.

Florida resident Rosette Goldstein also helped make survivor voices audible in Florida. Rosette responded to her losses by dedicating more than ten years to the battle in Florida as well as in other states. Goldstein had survived in hiding, but German authorities, with the help of the French, had deported her fourteen- and nineteen-year-old cousins, along with her aunt and uncle, on Convoy 8. Her father was deported on Convoy 64. Rosette learned that no one among them had survived Auschwitz. Rosette explained to me that she fought the SNCF because she believed the company had a choice and that the company collaborated willingly from the beginning of the war as an independent company under civilian control. She believes the company knew exactly what was happening and "never lifted a finger." Rosette was an active member of the Holocaust Rail Justice Group (2011–16), which lobbied against the SNCF in any state where it had leverage. She said the French newspaper (she did not disclose which one) with which the group wanted to speak had canceled an interview with them three times. She accused the contemporary SNCF of wining and dining people and giving them free trips to France as a means of currying favor in the United States. Instead of speaking to the angry survivors, she said, the company had hired a public relations company to promote its image.[46]

Seventy-two years old at the time of our interview, Rosette felt that time was running out for her to see justice done and for the SNCF to do the right thing. She felt that, as one of the youngest survivors, much of the burden of battling the company fell upon on her. Many other survivors were too old and frail to fight for themselves, she explained. Participating in the battle against the SNCF made her feel that she was doing something good for her dad, her cousins, and the six million others. She felt that the apologies made by the company were not done the right way and that the company still owed reparations for payments from the transports.[47] These symbolic rejections of SNCF amends-making efforts became part of a lobbying effort that succeeded in convincing Florida lawmakers to draft legislation that would effectively boycott the company until it met survivor demands.

When considering the intersection of transitional justice and corporations, the use of legislation might not be the first thing one assesses. First, few opportunities exist to create this form of leverage; seldom do people know which companies bidding for state contracts have committed human rights violations. Holocaust-implicated companies seldom bid for large state contracts. Even when they do, justice claimants are rarely as effectively mobilized as the Holocaust Rail Justice Group. That group's lobbying proved tremendously powerful in states where the SNCF bid for contracts, forcing the SNCF to listen to survivors who had been denied their day in court.

On September 29, 2010, Representative Ron Klein, a Democrat, introduced a bill requiring all companies pitching for high-speed rail business in Florida to provide materials explaining their role in transporting Jews to concentration camps.[48] In support of this legislation, Klein said, "No company whose trains carried innocent victims to death camps should have the right to lay the first inch of track in this country."[49]

Rosette went up to Orlando, Florida, to support this legislation, known as the Holocaust Accountability and Corporate Responsibility Act of 2010. She and her supporters succeeded in at least slowing down the railroad's bid. Unlike the prior bill aiming to open US courts to litigation, HR 6347 related directly to the *high-speed* train project. The bill would have required any company applying for high-speed rail projects to declare its involvement in deportations to death camps between January 1, 1942, and December 31, 1944.

Clearly the SNCF was the target.[50] This proposed legislation concerned only those companies that had any role in deportations to *death* camps. The German camp system for Jews was extremely complex, and choosing the term "death camp" could affect how debates unfolded.[51] The "death camp" designation could exempt, for example, the Japanese contender Shinkansen, which transported 700,000 Koreans to *work* camps during the war. The bill would also not cover US train companies that might have transported Japanese Americans to *detainment* camps. Most of those companies have since disbanded or been reorganized under Amtrak, which launched in 1971.[52] Had the bill targeted those companies that had a role in transporting people to *internment* camps as well as death camps, many other companies—including perhaps US competitors—might have had to comply with its terms. Internment camps were largely prison camps, which detained people without charges or due process. Harsh living conditions and immense psychological distress could lead to illness and death, even though these camps were not killing centers. The debates, however, focused mainly on the question of whether the SNCF had profited from transporting any prisoners. Douté, the former CEO of SNCF America, wrote a letter to Representative Klein, saying, "Despite claims to the contrary, no the SNCF did not 'profit' from the war or from the transport of deportees."[53] With the question still unresolved, the bill, which had a variety of supporters, did not pass.[54]

CALIFORNIA

In California, conflict also erupted around high-speed rail bids. In 2009, the same year that France issued the Hoffman-Glemane decision, which closed their administrative courts to World War II–related litigation, California issued its first legislative proposal to slow the SNCF in its quest for bids.[55] Existing

California law required state legislators to award state contracts to the best company offering the best price, but on February 25, 2009, Assemblyman Bob Blumenfield proposed legislation to allow legislators to consider a company's morality as well as its expertise and cost. Local Jewish groups lobbied for this legislation. This bill had the potential to make at least some measure of corporate social responsibility a qualification for all California state contracts. Had it done so, all companies would be under review for human rights violations. As written, however, California Assembly Bill 619 (2010) addressed only companies that had participated in World War II deportations, including companies involved in the transportation of people to work camps or POW camps.[56] I called Mark Rothman, executive director of the Los Angeles Museum of the Holocaust (the first Holocaust museum in the US) and a supporter of the bill, to hear more about his thoughts on how the conflict was unfolding in California. He said that he wished such legislation would extend to other sectors too and would apply to companies such as General Electric. He wanted to see greater corporate social responsibility more generally.[57] Even though he thought the bill fell short, his museum issued this official statement in support: "We believe that the residents of California have a direct interest in making sure that companies that are awarded the contracts publicly disclose their involvement in the deportations of California residents and families of California residents prior to being awarded any high-speed rail construction contract. Moreover, we believe it's important to require companies seeking the contracts to provide transparency and take responsibility for actions that have so tragically affected the lives of many Californians and thousands of others."[58]

Arguably, this proposed bill could have applied to US train companies that transported Japanese Americans to internment camps. Luckily for Amtrak, the company did not exist as a conglomerate until 1971, but others have a deeper history. Chessie Seaboard (CSX) Corporation and Union Pacific Corporation are made up of a number of railway companies that used slave labor in the United States.[59] The bill, if approved, would have applied to them and could also have applied to German train companies, which were worried about whether they should start lobbying in the United States to secure business opportunities. US Ambassador Douglas Davidson, who at the time directed the State Department's Office for the Special Envoy for Holocaust Issues, told them not to worry; curiously, the groups were after only the French National Railways.[60] Why not review all railroad companies operational during World War II?

The following local nonprofit Jewish organizations supported Assembly Bill 619 without requesting this addendum: 30 Years After, Bet Tzedek: The House of Justice, Jewish Family Services of Los Angeles, the Los Angeles Holocaust Museum, and Second Generation. California Jewish groups never directed their gaze beyond the French trains. Again, we see the problem of having one perpetrator remain in the spotlight: we miss opportunities to protect those currently suffering and hold other responsible actors accountable.

In February 2015, for example, no Jewish groups came to challenge an event planned at the state capitol sponsored by the Siemens Corporation, another train contender. Siemens had launched the event to rally support for its high-speed train initiative in California. During the war, Siemens sold electrical parts to the Nazis for use in concentration camps and used some eighty thousand forced laborers from extermination camps (including Jews, Sinti, Roma, prisoners of war, and other inmates). The company also had a number of factories operated by Nazi SS in the camps, where poor conditions and malnutrition often led to workers' deaths.

The curious exclusion of the Siemens Corporation from the protests is not unique to California. Oddly, the United States Holocaust Memorial Museum (USHMM) in Washington, DC, uses Siemens security systems. Today, all museum employees wear Siemens security badges around their necks. One day, when entering the museum with some survivors, I watched these elderly people taking off their coats and belts, walking through metal detectors, and being questioned by staff wearing dangling tags with the Siemens name prominently displayed. When I asked several senior staff members at the USHMM how Siemens came to be the security company of choice for the museum, many agreed the choice was odd. No one seems to know who had made this decision and whether the museum had at least received a discount.

Nationwide, the public gaze remained steadfastly fixed on the SNCF. California Assembly Bill 619 passed in the California Senate and House of Representatives. Then-governor Arnold Schwarzenegger vetoed the bill, writing,

> To the Members of the California State Assembly: I am returning Assembly Bill 619 without my signature.
>
> While I sympathize with the victims of the Holocaust and other individuals that were transported against their will during World War II, this bill needlessly places the state in a position of acknowledging the activities of companies during that time.
>
> For this reason, I am unable to sign this bill.
>
> Sincerely,
>
> Arnold Schwarzenegger[61]

Schwarzenegger argued that it was not the state's job to handle such cases. Even though the bill did not pass, Schwarzenegger's veto brought the question of the SNCF's wartime role into the national and international news. Articles

Table 6.2. Legal actions, boycotts, legislation, and apologies: Abridged, 2009–2014

Year	Location	Action
February 25, 2009	California	California legislators propose bill that would require railway companies to disclose whether they were involved in the deportation of individuals to concentration camps.[62]
September 29, 2010	US	Holocaust Accountability and Corporate Responsibility Act, introduced in US House of Representatives and Senate.[63] Bill requires entities bidding for US federal contracts to disclose whether they owned or operated trains on which deportees traveled to extermination camps, death camps, or any facility used to transit individuals to extermination or death camps, between January 1, 1942, and December 31, 1944. This bill is not passed.
November 23, 2010	US	SNCF chairman Guillaume Pépy presents his "regrets" in the US for the company's role in the Holocaust.
January 25, 2011	France	SNCF chairman Guillaume Pépy expresses regrets at a commemoration ceremony in France for "the consequences" of SNCF's role in the deportation, stating that the SNCF was "under constraint and requisitioned" and that it was "a cog in the Nazi war machine." The French press considers this to be the first public apology by the SNCF.
May 2011	Maryland	Governor Martin O'Malley signs a bill requiring the SNCF to digitize its archives before bidding for contracts. This is the only legislation signed into law.[64]
June 2014	Maryland	Maryland proposes new legislation to challenge the SNCF's bid for the Purple Metrorail Line.[65] This bill is introduced but not enacted.

ran in the *New York Times* and in *Le Figaro*, a leading French national newspaper. The press attention, along with much of the Jewish community's support for the legislation, convinced many across the nation that the California bill had merit. (See table 6.2 for an abridged list of legal actions against and apologies from the SNCF; for a full list, see the appendix).

Amid bad press, the SNCF ambled along in California. To demonstrate its commitment to transparency even without the bill passed, the SNCF sent the required documentation that the bill would have requested. According to Bernard Emsellem (who was serving at the time as the SNCF's head of corporate social responsibility), in spite of this conciliatory act, Assemblyman Blumenfield planned to resubmit the legislation as soon as Schwarzenegger left office. However, no new legislation has since been drafted. The company continues to bid for commuter, regional, and high-speed rail contracts in the United States. Survivors continue to live their lives.

Voices from the Last Trains

When the war ended, Pierre Blum confirmed that his parents, Henry Lippman Blum, born 1903, and Simone Fanny, born 1907, had been packed aboard Convoy 77 with Daniel and Samuel. His parents were gassed upon arrival at Auschwitz. He did not know what "Auschwitz" meant, but at eleven and a half years old, he had seen his parents' names on a deportation list and cried all night. He understood that the list meant death. For decades, he could not sleep without medication and rarely passed a night without nightmares. After the war, his sister lived with their aunt while their father's cousins in Paris cared for Pierre. The siblings visited during school vacations. Like Daniel, Pierre felt like a stranger in his new home. He endured a rigorous upbringing by those who provided food and shelter but little love. In 1957 he married Johanna, a woman who had also lost her entire family. After the war, she lived at a home for adolescent orphaned girls. Soon after they married, they had a daughter. Like most survivors, they found money scarce in the postwar years. The compensation that was to come later arrived, long after it made a difference in material terms.

He said that throughout her long life, his wife's depression never broke. She was shattered by the Holocaust. Neither of them wanted to speak to school groups about their experiences or participate in any justice battles. In fact, he says, they never even spoke to each other about the war. Pierre gave his testimony to the Shoah Foundation but says he has no interest in talking about misery. They raised their daughter telling her nothing about their wartime experiences; now, nearly eighty years after the events, she has started asking more and more questions.

As for compensation, his wife received €680 from Germany and was told she needed to go to Germany to collect more. She refused to go. He receives €500 a month from a French fund for orphans. Pierre is unimpressed with how France has handled the aftermath of the war. His father owned a hat store in the Marais, the Jewish neighborhood of Paris. But the bank claimed he had nothing in his accounts. The Commission pour l'Indemnisation des Victimes de Spoliations (CIVS), the organization responsible for returning ill-gotten gains to survivors, said it found very little with regard to the hat store. To compensate Pierre, CIVS required bills or documents showing that his father had insurance. The family had no records. "My father wasn't a squirrel," he said, meaning he did not store money or hang onto documents; he just ran his business.

Pierre made his own way. He became a watchmaker and saved up enough money to buy a little place in the country where he spends weekends in the mountains in a small cottage making mirabelle jam and nurturing his robust potato patch. When not at the cottage, he lives in Paris, alone. His wife died a number of years ago. In what had been her bedroom, he now tinkers with old watches. He is not interested in talking about justice or the symbolism of compensation payments. For him, money is practical. He attends the annual reading of the names, making sure not to miss the names of Convoy 77. What concerns him today is racism: "One cannot be racist," he told me. "My new neighbor in the country is Muslim and Moroccan. She is wonderful. I cannot make the distinction between Jew or Muslim, Christian or Protestant."[66]

CHAPTER SEVEN

Maryland Takes on the SNCF

We have no qualms with present-day French people. . . . We are only
looking for justice, and we want to see it in our time.

—LEO BRETHOLZ, survivor and Maryland resident

S THE PSYCHIATRIST David Hawkins aptly noted, "It is possible to
paralyze a giant locomotive if you know exactly where to put your
finger."[1] He meant it metaphorically of course, but his words proved
literally true for the SNCF. A few committed individuals grounded the SNCF
to a full halt, not in France but in the unlikely city of Annapolis, Maryland. In
May 2011, responding to powerful constituents, Maryland governor Martin
O'Malley signed into law the only piece of SNCF-related legislation to date.
Maryland House Bill 520 required the SNCF to digitize all its World War II
archives before contending for the Maryland Area Regional Commuter (MARC)
rail contract.[2] The Maryland legislation heartened class action plaintiffs, who
had recently learned that the US Supreme Court refused to hear their case,
thereby ending their lawsuit. The SNCF complied with the Maryland legislative
bill, however, and digitized its archives. The Vichy historian Michael Marrus
vetted the archives and confirmed that the SNCF had fulfilled its obligation.

Ultimately, the legislation proved more symbolic than groundbreaking.
At the time that Maryland signed the bill into law, in May 2011, the SNCF
archives in Le Mans, France, had already been open to the public since 1996.
The Bachelier report, discussing the most incriminating documents in the
archives, was also already available online. And Kurt Schaechter's collection
of documents that he found in the Toulouse archives was already housed at
Stanford University's Hoover Institution and open to the public. The requirement to digitize and place online the company archives made the SNCF's
broader wartime history more accessible and symbolically the act required the
SNCF to relinquish even more control over the events of the past and how
they are interpreted. That said, there is very little in the archives having to do
with the deportations, so having those documents online will do little to publicly reveal any unknown or revelatory Holocaust complicity.

Survivor Leo Bretholz shakes hands with Maryland governor Martin O'Malley after he signs into law the legislation requiring the SNCF to digitize its archives, May 2011. (Getty Images)

One might argue that such legislation serves as a warning to other companies that their archives could one day be forced open. Here again, however, we see a distinction between corporations and governmental organizations. The SNCF has archives to open only *because* the company served as an arm of the French state. Private companies hold onto archives for much shorter periods, largely determined by tax requirements. Once businesses pay their taxes and account for recent gains and losses, they can destroy documents detailing their pasts. J. P. Morgan, for example, which operated in France uninterrupted during the German occupation, has nearly completely eliminated the World War II archives in its Paris headquarters in the Place Vendôme. Philippe Rochefort, a historian and a former employee of J. P. Morgan, tried to gain access to the World War II archives of US corporations that operated in France during the war. They used, he said, "the most fallacious pretexts" to avoid providing him access, claiming "they had just been destroyed, or sent to the US headquarters, or lost when the company moved or anything else, like giving me a set of commercial pamphlets pretending it was all they had, etc."[3] He attributes their reticence to the fact that the company had operated like many French companies during the war, collaborating with the Germans.

Many US banks (except National City), and corporations also continued operations within Nazi Germany as did IBM-France, the Ford Corporation, General Electric, and others. Even if Germany classified them as enemy entities, the Nazi regime made use of them. Both benefited from the relationship. The SNCF can be held accountable more easily precisely because of its state ownership. For those working in corporate accountability, transparency will be a challenge: most corporations destroy documents and communications. Perhaps digital footprints will make more of that past easier to trace. Time will tell.

Even though the Maryland technical committee selected the SNCF as its top choice among the railway companies bidding for the contract, the SNCF's past affected its ability to move forward. Maryland ultimately awarded the MARC contract to Bombardier Transportation.[4] Some applauded the state's choice: Bombardier had no World War II history—or so they believed. Bombardier is considered a Canadian company, but over the years it has acquired a few companies with strong Nazi connections, including Waggonfabrik Talbot Gmbh & Co., which it acquired for $145 million in 1995. Under Nazi command, this company used slave labor and produced freight wagons.[5] No one contested Bombardier's win; and in spite of the SNCF's compliance with the state's requests, its situation in Maryland worsened.

Baltimore resident Leo Bretholz, who had fought the SNCF for years, was elated about the legislation that he had strongly encouraged Governor O'Malley to pass. By this time, Bretholz had become a kind of local star, at least in the Jewish community. His 1999 memoir *Leap into Darkness: Seven Years on the Run in Wartime Europe*, written and published with the help of Michael Olesker, a journalist at the *Baltimore Sun*, had reached thousands of readers.[6] His memoir details his seven harrowing escapes from German officials and French police, which makes his story stand out even among the thousands of other astonishing Holocaust memoirs. Bretholz continued to make media appearances and to speak out against the company, saying that he wanted the SNCF to admit it had done wrong *and* to compensate survivors. He would soon have another opportunity to pressure the company to pay for its misdeeds.

The Purple Line Bid

The conflict erupted forcefully in Maryland a second time when the SNCF returned to bid for a new project. In 2013 Washington, DC, in conjunction with Maryland, announced an extension of the DC Metrorail system. The Purple Line project would connect a greater portion of southern Maryland to Washington, DC. When the SNCF pitched for this combined state and federal project via its subsidiary Keolis, the debates resurfaced.[7]

The new proposed Maryland House bill introduced in January 2014 required Keolis North America (the SNCF subsidiary) to pay Maryland resident survivors or their families before becoming an approved contractor.[8] Asking for compensation, rather than transparency, changed the game. This proposed bill effectively had Maryland demanding compensation for activities during World War II from an arm of the French state. In support of the bill, Leo Bretholz wrote an impassioned statement in the *Baltimore Sun*, in an article titled "No Reparations, No Business," which I quote at length:

> While it was many years ago, the horrific injustices I experienced during the Holocaust are seared in my brain. I can still recall in explicit detail the atrocities I saw as I was placed in a cattle car bound for a Nazi death camp and as I watched families being separated and possessions taken away.
>
> And I cannot forget who was responsible. The train company that tried to send me to Auschwitz was owned and operated by SNCF, a French company that still exists today. SNCF collaborated willingly with the Nazis and was paid per head and per kilometer to transport 76,000 innocent victims—including American pilots shot down over France as well as 11,000 children—across France to death camps like Auschwitz and Buchenwald.
>
> It's been more than 70 years since the war, and only now is the French government negotiating with the U.S. to provide compensation for me and other victims of SNCF's deportation.
>
> SNCF's affiliate, Keolis America, is among the finalists bidding for a 35-year public-private partnership to operate the Purple Line, a planned mass rail project in Maryland, estimated at $6 billion. We cannot allow this to happen until reparations are made.
>
> SNCF carried out its transports with precision, cruelty and deception. On each convoy, we were packed into 20 cattle cars, 50 people each. For the entire multi-day trip, we were given only one piece of triangular cheese, one stale piece

of bread and no water. There was hardly room to stand or sit, and in the middle of the train was a single bucket to relieve ourselves.

Of the 1,000 people on my train, only five survived the war. I was one of the lucky ones. I jumped out of the moving train, managing to pry open the bars on the window just enough to slip through.

I even have a copy of an invoice SNCF sent the French government, seeking payment for the services it provided. They pursued payment on this after the liberation of Paris, after the Nazis were gone. They even charged interest for late payments. This was not coercion, this was business.

SNCF was not coerced into using cattle cars. It was not coerced into sending bills after the war. It was not coerced into serving no water on the trains. Had SNCF resisted, the number of those killed from France would have been greatly reduced. Had SNCF not imposed horrific conditions on its trains, many additional lives could have been saved.

Instead of taking responsibility for its actions during the past 70-plus years, the company has spent millions of dollars on a lobbying and public relations campaign to rewrite history and avoid accountability for its pivotal role in one of history's greatest atrocities.

While the recent talks are a step in the right direction, it is critical that any agreement must be reasonable and fair for the survivors and the families of those who have perished around the world.

Maryland State Sen. Joan Carter Conway and Del. Kirill Reznik, Democrats from Baltimore City and Montgomery County, respectively, have introduced legislation requiring that such companies with a relation to those responsible for Holocaust atrocities pay reparations before being eligible to participate in state public-private partnerships.

This would not be the first time that lawmakers in Maryland have taken a stand for what's just. A law was passed in 2011, with unanimous support, requiring companies to disclose their Holocaust-era ties before pursuing a contract to provide MARC train service. I hope the representatives of my home state will continue to ensure that only companies with clean hands receive our tax dollars.

I am overwhelmed by the support I have received. As of Friday, more than 128,000 people have signed a petition on Change.org urging SNCF to finally pay reparations. That is more than one signature for every man, woman and child sent on SNCF trains toward Nazi death camps.

I hope my fellow Maryland citizens will support these courageous legislators and also my petition at change.org/SNCF. All I am asking, all anyone is asking, is that SNCF finally take responsibility for its willing and deliberate participation in the Holocaust.

Until that happens, we will not forget and we will not be silent.[9]

On March 10, 2014, ten days after the publication of Bretholz's letter, the Maryland House of Representatives held a hearing to discuss the bill and the related federal threat to withhold funding. Representatives from Keolis (SNCF's subsidiary), lobbyists, lawyers, and other interested parties attended the public meeting. Leo Bretholz testified, as did SNCF America CEO Alain Leray. Leray denied that the SNCF had received payment for the transport of deportees to extermination camps. The legislator responded, "Why do you presume that numerous panelists that came before you are expressing that SNCF was paid, in fact, per head, per kilometer?"

Leray responded, "I would like to know."[10]

Distrust grew on both sides, and basic facts became distorted. The lawyer Harriet Tamen, for example, stated that the SNCF had hired Christian Bachelier *directly* to write the company's history when, in fact, the company had hired an independent organization (CNRS), under the direction of the historian Henry Rousso, who had selected Bachelier. Such details, trivial as they might seem, muddied the waters and set people against one another. On March 11, 2014, the Maryland Senate hearing would hear debates on the same issue.

A HEARING INTERRUPTED

On March 10, 2014, the day before the scheduled Senate hearing, Leo Bretholz died in his sleep. The hearing was postponed. That dreary March 11, many of us drove to the Sol Levinson & Brothers funeral home in Pikesville instead of to the Maryland State Senate in Annapolis. More than two hundred of his family members, friends, and students who had been touched by his visits to their schools to teach them about the Holocaust attended. After the service, ushers moved everyone toward the far doors, where they could find their cars for the drive to the cemetery for the burial. At the cemetery, the living kept a safe distance from his grave, both out of respect and likely to preserve whatever distance we could from our own deaths. He was buried next to his wife, Flo, who had died about five years earlier. The neighboring graves had Holocaust-related messages engraved on the tombstones. This was a graveyard of Holocaust survivors, a commemorative site unto itself. Funerals of survivors can become their own *lieux de mémoire* for the Holocaust because these funerals, often attended by other survivors and their descendants, help them continue processing of the trauma. Descendants and others make meaning of their loss and the world events they suffered.

People approached the open grave and placed small stones on the headstone, a Jewish tradition. The rabbi gathered the crowd and made a little speech about what it means to give to someone in death. He said when we give to the living, it is not truly altruism because we hope for reciprocity. When we give in death, it is true giving because we expect nothing. He described the Jewish tradition of having each attendee place a shovel of dirt on the casket—our final act of service in the moment of death. The pallbearers lowered Bretholz into the ground, and the rabbi passed a shovel to the first person.

I had never buried anyone before. Raphael Prober, a lawyer who had been working on the lawsuit with Leo Bretholz, handed me the shovel after he said his good-byes. I added my dirt to his. As the moistened earth fell from the shovel to the casket, I felt Leo say to me, "Okay, if you think this was the wrong way to handle the SNCF, *you* can figure out how to deal with the company. Now it's your turn." The dead take much of their pain with them but leave behind the worldly conundrums about how to handle the aftermath. The complicated questions of corporate accountability somehow seemed less clear with Leo gone. I had not recognized nor appreciated the enormous buffer he and the other survivors provide between the Holocaust and those of us born after. Being on the planet without them seemed frightening.

After the funeral, most of the mourners made their way to the nearby Doubletree Hotel to spend some time sitting shiva with the family.[11] In the rented ballroom at the hotel were several tables displaying some Bretholz memorabilia. The items included a special tribute from the State of Maryland honoring him for his ability to escape seven times in seven years and for his contribution to the country's first legislation designed to insist upon corporate transparency.

Tables at the other end of the room offered copious amounts of bagels, lox, and other typical Ashkenazi brunch food. Periodically, someone would rise and make a short speech. Many lamented that Bretholz could not live for another year, month, week, or even just one more day. One of his cousins stood up and said that toward the end of his life, Bretholz kept saying he was "Holocausted-out." Perhaps Bretholz did not *want* to live another day, I thought. Maybe his death the day before the Senate hearing was not a coincidence.

After his cousin finished speaking, a family member leaned over and said to me that at first Bretholz resisted participation in the fight against the SNCF. Initially, he did not want to be the spokesperson. He was, in fact, cast in the role of the SNCF's champion-opponent and later developed a passion for the part. The family also seemed conflicted about his participation—some were not sure the lawsuit and lobbying made sense. They speculated that SNCF competitors were behind this conflict, hoping to block the SNCF from the US market as long as possible. Moreover, some family members had received calls from cousins in France concerned that Bretholz's work would worsen the return of antisemitism abroad. The lawsuits would also be bad for the French economy, these cousins said.

The antisemitic backlash in France was not a trivial concern. According to Richard Weisberg, a lawyer who had worked on the French bank settlement signed in 2001, part of the agreement required that the French government speak to members of different Jewish communities and then monitor threats of antisemitism.[12] He thought that ideally the government ought to do the same with regard to the SNCF debates. Ambassador Douglas Davidson, who had worked on the early stages of the French–US negotiation, said the concerns about rising antisemitism in France often surfaced. Once, when his negotiation team dined with French Jewish leaders during an American Jewish Congress event, Davidson said, "It was like talking to the French government. It was interesting . . . their worries were far more about the rising levels of antisemitism—and to them [this is very dangerous]. . . . Cukierman [now president of CRIF] said, 'When I was a boy, 90 percent of Jews in France went to public school—now it's 30 percent. . . . And there are more people making Aliyah [moving to Israel] from France, I'm told, than from the United States.' They are very worried. That's what they wanted to tell us. There's not much that [the United States] can do. . . . So they made kind of a two-fold argument: 'It's really getting bad for us, but on the other hand . . . this [the SNCF conflict] makes it worse . . . this kind of stuff fuels antisemitism.'"[13]

Americans would more fully empathize with these fears in January 2015 after four Jews were murdered in a Paris kosher grocery store. Americans' fears of antisemitism would not fully surface until October 27, 2018, when a shooter killed eleven people at the Tree of Life synagogue in Pittsburgh, making it the largest attack on Jews in the United States in the country's history.

But back in 2014, fears of potential antisemitic backlash in France could not slow the conflict; the SNCF debates had acquired a momentum of their own. The conflict no longer needed any one individual to keep it going, although Bretholz's death deeply underscored both the urgency and the poignancy of the debates.

The Show Must Go On

Legislators rescheduled the Maryland Senate hearing for March 13, 2014, two days after Bretholz's funeral. Hosted by the Committee on Budget and Taxation, the hearing, titled Public-Private Partnerships—Disclosure of Involvement in Deportations, addressed Maryland House Bill 1326/Senate Bill 754.[14] The federal government threatened to withdraw $900 million in funding from the state project if the bill passed. Because of this, the event became largely performative. No delegate wanted to be responsible for the loss of this important and lucrative state project. So, while Bretholz's death accentuated the urgency of compensation, the bill was destined to die before any more of the survivors did. Rather than a legislative meeting for decision-making, the hearing became a forum to express pain. Survivors who had never seen their day in court had this legislative hearing to say their piece.

A legislative hearing allows council members to hear their constituents speak in support of or against a particular bill. This is not to be confused with a truth and reconciliation commission, which can include healing and mutual understanding as a goal. Both sides were present, but reconciliation was not the goal. The goal here was persuasion, the legislative equivalent of a verdict. By design, the forum amplifies the binaries already in circulation. At the event, I found myself, once again, pushed into a binary position: SNCF as perpetrator or SNCF as victim.

I arrived early and waited on the red velvet bench outside the hearing room. A man sat down and asked, "So, whose side are you on?"

The question took me by surprise. I explained that I was studying the conflict to better understand how we address postconflict accountability issues, to which he responded, "So, you're on the SNCF's side."

I said, "No, I'm *studying* the conflict."

He seemed unconvinced. The only recognizable positions were *for* or *against*.

The man turned out to be Martin Goldman, formerly the director of survivor services at the United States Holocaust Memorial Museum. He had been asked by the Jewish Community Relations Council to testify against the SNCF, although he admittedly knew very little about the SNCF's role in the war, its efforts to make amends, or the dialogues occurring in other states.

We were soon beckoned inside.

Twelve legislators sat in a U-shaped formation facing those testifying and an audience of about fifty people. The attendees replicated those who had attended the House hearing: SNCF executives, lawyers, lobbyists, survivors, and members of the Jewish community, with the press crammed behind a small table to the side. Senator Conway opened the hearing with the accusation that the SNCF had not complied with the prior bill, Maryland House Bill 520, which required the SNCF to digitize all its World War II archives before contending for the MARC rail contract.[15]

Aaron Greenfield, the lead lobbyist working against the SNCF in Maryland, offered the first testimony. He argued that the SNCF had not fulfilled the requirements because the archivist used to vet the records, the historian Michael Marrus, was on the SNCF payroll. Greenfield considered Marrus too biased to complete the task with integrity. Furthermore, he claimed, the SNCF had failed to make all the archives available. Greenfield later admitted that he had not confirmed the information for himself. He was not really sure what was available.[16] Greenfield's claim surprised delegate Sandy Rosenberg, a sponsor of the original bill. Rosenberg had heard that Marrus had been a real stickler on the archives, requiring heavy indexing even though the bill did not require it.[17]

Greenfield's opening statement both discredited the SNCF and demonstrated the performative nature of the hearing. After Greenfield's statement, the twelve state delegates listened to and sometimes asked questions of those testifying. Those speaking either for or against the company had five minutes each. Those choosing a neutral position would receive one minute instead of five. The binary framework of such a hearing encouraged people to take strong positions, even when they admitted to feeling uncertain about doing so. After the event, a number of those who spoke confided in me about their uncertainty about their adamant positions. Others, such as one child survivor who wore a sign around her neck displaying her father's name and his convoy number, expressed no such uncertainty.

Some who spoke knew a great deal about the SNCF's situation and made compelling statements. Survivor Rosette Goldstein, for example, flew in from Florida, replacing Leo Bretholz as the primary speaker against the SNCF. Rosette said, with tears flowing, "Leo and I had a special bond. *We* are Holocaust survivors, *we* are *mishpocha*—family. We can speak to each other—understand each other, feelings that cannot be understood by anyone who did not go through the Shoah. We have memories that will haunt us and haunt us to our dying day."[18] Rosette's testimony stressed the limited time survivors had left to see justice served as well as the inability of those who had not experienced the atrocities to understand.

Highlighting this generational gap becomes important because in the aftermath of mass atrocity, the second or third generation often joins the conversation and makes meaning of the past; this is a normal and healthy process through which new generations lay claim to understanding others' deepest personal experience. If some survivors believe more is owed, who are we, the nonvictims, to stop them from asking? The moderators granted victims this space, permitting them to speak beyond their allotted time. When the SNCF's turn came to represent itself, time contracted. The moderators repeatedly cut their answers short. During this portion of the session, lobbyists texted the senators questions that they might put to the company representatives.[19] The SNCF's answers were sometimes interrupted by additional new questions.

This event illustrates some of the narrative dynamics at play in postconflict contexts. Only a few roles were available in the room: the victim role (occupied by survivors), the hero role (occupied by lawyers, lobbyists, and legislators), and the villain or perpetrator role (SNCF). The more the CEO of SNCF America, Alain Leray, spoke, the more he appeared to embody the heartless corporate mogul and an extension of the Nazi regime. Leray's Jewish ancestry and Holocaust losses did little to protect him from his assigned role as perpetrator. When the SNCF tried to play the victim card with comments about the company's losses during the war, only their colleagues heard the comment with sympathetic ears. Elderly Holocaust survivors occupied the position of victim—and rarely can any victim group in the United States exceed the legitimacy of Holocaust survivors, especially not a train company being held partially responsible for their suffering.[20] The same courtesy was not extended to the SNCF, which was cast as the perpetrator. When the company failed to convince legislators of its victim status, it tried to claim a piece of the heroic role by reminding legislators of heroic acts of resistance by its employees, which I have described in chapter 3.

These claims fell on deaf ears for two reasons. First, US lawyers and legislators had already cast themselves in the role of hero. The static roles reinforced in legislative and legal spaces resist overlapping or competing positions. Additionally, the cheminots' acts of resistance had little to do with the deportations. Just as the heroic acts of one person do not make up for the failures of another, the bravery of a few railway workers does not wash away the sins of those who carried victims to their death. With the role of victim and hero already taken, the SNCF had no choice but to fill the role of perpetrator.

During the hearing, SNCF's head of corporate social responsibility, Bernard Emsellem, handed a piece of paper to Leray, on which he had scribbled "*Nazis?*" as a question.[21] The note expressed his confusion about why the legislators were treating the SNCF like a living Nazi organization.

When dealing with the long trail of atrocity, current corporate executives may benefit from understanding themselves as the inheritors of history. Just as heads of state inherit their country's legacy, so too Leray and Emsellem carried on their shoulders the SNCF's past, even though they are Jewish. The SNCF executives seemed frustrated because they expected that the legislative hearing would engage in a process of historical memory rather than the communion of collective memories.[22] They did not experience the controlled environment of the 2000 colloquium in France but witnessed heroic stories colliding with the tragic and individual stories designed to challenge institutional narratives. Most executives are unprepared for this genre of conflict, but corporate leadership increasingly requires these skills.[23] Transitional justice scholars and practitioners can help facilitate corporate participation in postconflict amends making by helping executives understand history as a shifting collection of individual stories rather than as an objective phenomenon that can be addressed and subdued. The SNCF executives, if they did not understand the futility of trying to "spin" their role in the Holocaust when these issues first became public, surely do now. In a free society, no one can close the door on the past forever.

While undoubtedly set up for a public flogging, the SNCF also made some poor decisions during the legislative hearing. As noted in the introduction, the French historically bestow the title of Holocaust "survivor" only upon individuals who returned from concentration or death camps, whereas in the United States, the definition that is used more often coincides with that espoused by the USHMM: a survivor is anyone who faced persecution during the Holocaust. Seemingly constrained by the French definition, the company brought a frail Auschwitz survivor to the hearing. The survivor, a former cantor, spoke at length and with a heavy accent on behalf of the SNCF, addressing topics seemingly unrelated to the SNCF. Few understood him. Out of respect, the legislators did not interrupt his mostly unintelligible testimony.

In contrast, those fighting the SNCF at this hearing had lost parents on the deportation trains and spoke clearly about their losses. As noted, many survivors interviewed for this book offered compelling arguments for now exculpating the SNCF. These arguments would have made good contributions to the collective memory deliberations in the Maryland House and Senate hearings. But understandably, perhaps, such survivors did not attend. Expressing such views in a contentious environment could ostracize them from local survivor communities. After the testimonies ended, an American-based survivor approached and chastised the old cantor for speaking on the SNCF's behalf. She told him that she found it disgusting that he had defended the company's actions. Survivors chastising one another contributes to the cycles of pain. With Jewish SNCF executives facing off with survivors, Jewish lobbyists, and lawyers, the room ultimately became a battle among Jews.

The Senate Hearing Outcome

If one were to score the event as a debate, those fighting the SNCF clearly won. The SNCF executives emerged from the hearing pummeled and discursively pinned. While there seemed clear winners and losers, the event had no effect on the bill. After the Senate hearing, legislators assigned the bill to four separate committees, requiring four separate approvals. With summer adjournment just weeks away, officials would be spared from even having to cast a vote.[24] No one would have to choose between Holocaust survivors and $900 million in federal funding.

On April 9, 2014, both the Obama administration and the US Department of State asked again that legislation pertaining to the SNCF be dropped, especially that in New York and Maryland. Jen Psaki, spokesperson for the US Department of State, said these state-level efforts "have begun to pose a serious obstacle" to negotiations between the countries on behalf of the Holocaust victims. She said the third round of negotiations would begin on April 10, 2014.[25] The US Department of State justified its threat by explaining that France and the United States had already commenced negotiations; this legislative bill was impeding their work. Maryland was obstructing international diplomacy. Away from the spotlight of the SNCF conflict, the Purple Line project advanced. Another company was chosen and the bill targeting the SNCF never surfaced again.

The US State Department now inherited this sticky conflict. Even though the US government had a two-hundred-year-old relationship with France, representatives befuddled and frustrated one another. The conflict picked at old wounds, including the 1990s negotiations regarding the French banks' obligation to return ill-gotten gains. The US Embassy in France so totally botched the whole affair that today's new foreign service officers study the embassy's actions pertaining to the SNCF conflict to learn "what not to do."[26] Their mistakes are a lesson to us all. Before the official negotiations began, the US Department of State issued a message to the embassy in Paris to pressure France to create a fund for survivors. The embassy officers asked the Department of State whether the priority was compensation or acknowledgment (i.e., apologies) and whether the Department of State wanted this from the government or the corporation. They received partial clarification and then approached the French government, demanding the creation of a fund. With little guidance and little understanding of the history of these issues, however, they approached the French in a most offensive way. US officials based in Paris knew nothing (or frightfully little) about either the existing French programs or France's other efforts to atone for actions during the German occupation. As a result, the US officials treated the French as if France still refused to address the past. While this fund would apply to groups that other programs missed, it would not be the first French fund for survivors. This new agreement would attend to a group that both countries overlooked. Part of the fault for this oversight lies with the US State Department staff, which in the 1950s, unlike the United Kingdom and several other countries, did not seek an agreement with France to protect survivors who would become citizens. US foreign service officers based in Paris knew nothing of this history. The resulting sloppy exchange soured relations. Even if the French government officials were angered by how the Americans approached the issue, they had no choice but to respond to the request for the fund. When it comes to the Holocaust and US relations, the French government has learned that ignoring the issue causes more problems than addressing it. François Hollande, the president of France at the time, moved forward with negotiations, ultimately creating the fund for which both countries took credit. Back in March 2014, however, no one knew whether or when the countries would reach an agreement. The survivors involved were frustrated.

A few days after the hearing, I met Lea Lieberman, a Maryland resident and survivor who had testified against the SNCF at the hearing. She had laid out dates and mandarin oranges on the coffee table while she told her story and showed me a bill used as currency in the Buchenwald concentration camp. Such a bill could have meant an extra piece of bread—something that could stave off death for another day. Lea expressed her appreciation of the opportunity to participate in the hearing, but as she spoke, it became clear that she had offered her testimony in Maryland believing that no current compensation programs existed for her.[27] She was incorrect. I became concerned that lawyers and lobbyists were not, at the very least, ensuring that everyone testifying had access to the existing monies for which they were eligible. I explained to her the availability of the compensation. After our meeting, Lea applied for, and received, compensation from an existing French fund. She later also applied for, and received, funding from the 2014 French–US settlement.

Harriet Tamen and other lawyers cared a great deal about the survivors they represented, but sometimes the focus on beating the SNCF distracted from ensuring survivor access to the funds and services available. The way law's momentum can pull attention from survivor voices became apparent again during a chat I had with a leading Holocaust litigator, Burt Neuborne, who said he had represented more than one million Holocaust survivors and who played a leading role in the Swiss bank and German corporation settlements. After attending a related conference at Tel Aviv University, we found ourselves heading to the same return flight from Ben Gurion airport. While waiting for our flight, I asked Neuborne what survivors said when he asked them what they wanted. Did they want money, apologies, commemoration, to find missing family, some combination of these, or something else? He paused, seemingly startled by the question, and then admitted, "I never thought to ask them. I thought of myself as a pit bull. I tried to get as much money as I could for them."[28] He greatly succeeded in that aim. Through my more meandering conversations and long visits with survivors, I discovered that many had other important unmet needs. One of those was simply to be listened to. They also appreciated being seen as experts on mass atrocity and qualified to guide justice pursuits in their name.

Justice pursuits do not necessarily lead to victim services, even for those victims spotlighted or revered. My time with Channah helped me see this. In 2014 the USHMM hosted its annual breakfast at the Mandarin Hotel in honor of the Day of Remembrance. I did not know Channah at the time.

I had simply found a seat next to her, at the farthest table from the stage, along with other Holocaust survivors. Because this frail-looking woman was confined to her wheelchair, I went to the buffet to get her something to eat. During an hour of awards and donor recognition, the survivors seated to the rear of the room—largely out of earshot—silently ate their breakfasts. Midway through the presentations, she reached over and squeezed my hand, looked at me intently with eyes milky with cataracts, and said, "My name is Channah. I survived Auschwitz."

Her husband turned around and shushed her: "Channah, not during the presentations!" She continued undeterred: "I don't think it matters if children study the Holocaust. My son doesn't and my daughter does."

Her hand now trembling as it held mine, she said, "What matters is that you are a good person, good to Jew and good to non-Jew."[29]

Channah released my hand, slumped back in her wheelchair, and returned to her croissant, struggling with unsteady hands to add the jam. I used her knife to add a little jam and removed her tea bag from her teacup. We sat together and ate in silence. She said nothing more. Those at the podium continued their speeches and proceeded with the awards ceremony. These events can become performances. For me, the most interesting part of these events is rarely the official proceedings but the comments whispered back and forth between those who lived through the horrors being commemorated.

SNCF: A Singular Villain in a Fixed Position

The public discursive landscape became increasingly contentious, and all the while survivors continued to chat quietly among themselves about the SNCF battle at potlucks, at commemorative events, or with friends over tea. Company executives increasingly spoke among themselves about how to handle the controversy. Unfortunately, these groups rarely came together with the intention to work restoratively. The polarized conflict now seemed to have a public life of its own. The Maryland legislation kept the SNCF conflict in the news, even though the state attorney general's office, the Federal Rail Administration, and the Maryland Department of Transportation objected to the legislation. They considered the bill a "red-headed Eskimo," a legislative term referring to bills that discriminate against one party or company.[30] Like California, Virginia, and Florida, the Maryland legislative propositions targeted the SNCF—rather than the German, American, Japanese, or other rail companies or other companies involved in contemporary crimes against humanity. When I asked why the bill did not extend to other companies, Maryland delegate Sandy Rosenberg, who had sponsored the original bill in 2011, said to me, "Well, that's what the people came to me about."[31]

Rosenberg's comment points to another salient lesson for advocates of transitional justice and human rights initiatives. While focusing on a singular actor can do much to galvanize support for a cause, it limits the reach of the campaign. In the SNCF conflict, there was a missed opportunity to advance corporate accountability more broadly. Had the state legislators and their supporters altered these bills to require *any* company bidding for state contracts to admit and/or make amends for *any* massive human rights violations, more companies might improve their standards and more people could be spared the consequences of those violations.

Retributive Justice as Discursive Chess

Retributive justice, as opposed to restorative justice, focuses on identifying and punishing the wrongdoer. Retributive frameworks isolate perpetrators rather than seeking ways that individuals or groups can help address the harms committed. Perpetrators cannot have a story beyond the incidents in question, and, as a result, onlookers sidestep deep reflection about the other factors that contribute to horrific acts and radicalization more generally. Forums for "justice" become spaces of accusation and exclusion rather than of responsibility and reflection.

The retributive justice project resembles a game of chess. First you trap and then you capture the king. The capture is initially discursive and then physical. The SNCF conflict and specifically the Maryland hearings demonstrate the discursive positioning that can occur. Once an entity is positioned as a perpetrator, transforming its spoiled identity can be challenging. When the crime is heinous, almost no amount of punishment will do. As Kieran McEvoy and Kirsten McConnachie observed, the more innocent the victim, the harsher the punishment.[32] As Klapp demonstrated, the villain must be destroyed, both "in status and person as illustrated by the ideal fate of the ogre in the folktale who is boiled in his own pot." The modern-day SNCF found itself in this situation, "boiled" by its own name.[33]

Just as in chess where each piece has prescribed moves, victims and perpetrators have different levels of discursive mobility. Greimas and Cortés's actant model of discourse analysis acknowledges this mobility, calling characters "actants" rather than heroes, villains, or victims.[34] Individuals and groups can shift among multiple roles, but the mobility afforded the roles is not the same. Victims have the fullest range of motion, moving with the freedom of the queen on a chessboard. Perpetrators, however, move discursively more like the king— they are limited in mobility (and speech). The SNCF could say little without its words being used against it.

Criminologists and transitional justice scholars speak to the fixed nature of identities once spoiled. Positions can become *forced* or *frozen*. A *forced* position still allows a person or group to negotiate on its own behalf, whereas a *frozen* position prevents the occupant from shifting its place in the shared moral order.[35] While positioning concepts are often applied to victim groups, the SNCF conflict demonstrates how the dynamics also apply to those classified as perpetrators. Erich Goode emphasizes the "stickiness" of the perpetrator label.[36] Orrin Klapp has found that the stigma, once assigned, can rarely be surpassed.[37] Marha Minow and John Braithwaite say these labels ignite blame and shaming cycles, keeping communities trapped in cycles of fear and revenge.[38] There seems to be no escape and no road to redemption. This is an increasing challenge as social media propel tarnishing statements faster than the facts that try to situate them. Without a path for reintegration and reflection, we leave societies fractured by trauma—and perhaps headed for more.

SNCF: The Ideal Perpetrator

These dynamics are not unique to the SNCF. Retributive systems always seek a guilty party. Blaming social systems, context, history, and family upbringing understandably fail to satisfy victims and postconflict societies. These factors are so much more difficult to change than simply incarcerating a person or invoicing a company for misdeeds. Yet these factors all matter, and understanding them helps us move toward prevention as well as restoration and resilience.

Before the physical isolation of perpetrators, Vivienne Jabri considers the discursive separation of the innocent from the guilty as violence.[39] Her work urges us to explore how we identify and articulate in-groups and out-groups. The binaries of good and evil, promoted by retributive models, reassure us of our innocence and tell us whom to fear. Eventually, however, these binary frameworks become like rusty hinges unable to provide the movement necessary for moral and social development. Rama Mani claims that postconflict work must focus on creating an *inclusive* political and civic community to "overcome the fragmentation of society that occurs or is exacerbated during war."[40] She advocates for a more "reparative" justice.

These dynamics help explain how the SNCF has found itself in the spotlight for a proportionally lopsided amount of time while many unaccountable companies, individuals, and groups continue along unimpeded. Marrus thought the SNCF's hypervisibility might be explained by the organization's "democratic" structure, its public ownership, the strong trade unions, and its efficiency, which "distinguish it from many other services in France."[41] While these may all be contributing factors, the SNCF largely fell into and remains in the spotlight because the company embodies certain attributes, what Goffman calls "ideal qualifications."[42] The SNCF is not just any perpetrator; it is an *ideal perpetrator* because it has the following attributes: it has strength and abstractibility; it represents the overall nature of the crime; and it has a champion opponent consistently focusing attention on it.[43] Having just two of these attributes can sustain a perpetrator label; the SNCF has all four. Let me elaborate on these attributes, giving somewhat more attention to the third and fourth points, which are less straightforward and require more explanation.

Ideal Perpetrator Attribute 1: The SNCF Is Strong and Growing

Just as weaker victims more easily achieve victim status, stronger perpetrators more easily maintain their perpetrator status.[44] After the war, the SNCF continued to grow, expanding well beyond France. As of 2018, French railroad engineering, from railcar production to transport management, remained world class, competing effectively against Japanese, German, and other train companies internationally. The company is perceived as wealthy; a connection with the French state makes it seem impenetrable. But if money were the only driving factor, other large Holocaust-implicated corporations like Siemens and the German train companies—which also bid for US contracts—would become targets.

Ideal Perpetrator Attribute 2: The SNCF Is an Inhuman Abstraction

Nils Christie discusses the public's preference for a distant and dehumanized offender.[45] The SNCF offers both. Abstractions prove more satisfying than individuals. Notions of *Nazis*, rather than actual Nazis, provided the needed distance and the needed numbers. *Nazis* are not actually people but uniformed, indistinguishable individuals who follow orders. As a concept, they seem anything but human. Inhuman, they can be despised and disposed of without remorse and punished in perpetuity. Similarly, the SNCF can serve as a blockbuster villain—a larger-than-life and inhuman entity. Already inhuman, trains could not be more perfect.

The SNCF—as a construct—proves a far more satisfying rogue than a deceased fearful employee or an opportunistic technocrat. With the individual perpetrators long dead, the company resembles a hermit crab shell, vacated by the previous SNCF cheminots and now inhabited by new residents. Corporate "monsters" may be on the rise because they lend themselves so easily to abstraction.

Ideal Perpetrator Attribute 3: The SNCF Represents the Atrocity

More than any other attribute, the SNCF's identity as a *train* company might be the most inescapable and important quality. Ideal perpetrators represent not just the ill deeds of one person or entity; they represent the atrocity itself. Players with a more marginal role rarely find themselves so aggressively targeted. The clothing company Hugo Boss, for example, designed and produced the SS uniform. Hugo Boss himself was a fervent Nazi throughout his life, and yet the company experiences little contemporary backlash, and when and where it does, the company makes no public statement.[46] As a train company, the SNCF represents what Hilberg identified as *the* symbol of the Holocaust.[47] Trains became the conveyor belt to hell upon which the majority of European Jews found themselves. Gerhard Drulacher, a former inmate, visiting the former Westerbork transit camp in the 1960s, commented: "Suddenly I realized that the essence of camp Westerbork, the *train*, the people-devouring *train*, has disappeared. My anguish fades away. The curse that dominated this place has been lifted."[48] Rail transport became the shared experience of almost all those taken to various death or work camps. And those who escaped or were hidden almost all eventually traveled on trains. Marrus observes how "railways have become a familiar trope in the cinematic representation of the Holocaust."[49] Holocaust museums rarely omit them. Formerly used cattle cars often sit out

Liliane-Lelaidier Marton (*right*), whose parents were murdered at Auschwitz, and her friend Monique Vatri visit the SNCF railcar on display in the middle of what was the Drancy internment camp, March 2016. (Author photo)

front or inside museums. Commemorative sites often include some symbol of the cars or rail tracks.[50]

Finally, because no one survived the gas chambers, those who survived the rail voyages can provide the closest access to these final moments. The convoys were not unlike the gas chambers: sealed boxes that dehumanized their contents. Those who survived the trains can tell us about that experience, the conversations, and the prayers uttered. These testimonials, once heard, are hard to forget. These railcars past and present come to be associated with murder as well as dehumanization. Marrus claims that because the SNCF lacked independence during the war, "the symbolic fit of the railways at issue with the Holocaust seems not quite right."[51] In the end, the trope trumps history.

Ideal Perpetrator Attribute 4: The SNCF's Champion Opponents

But what *kept* the SNCF in the public spotlight is what I call the *champion opponent.*[52] This outsider—when deeply committed and motivated by personal vendettas—can play a vital role. Serge and Beate Klarsfeld repeatedly shined the spotlight on individual perpetrators and, in doing so, brought to trial several major French collaborators, including Touvier, Barbie, Bousquet, Leguay, and Papon. Without the Klarsfelds as sponsors/dispatchers, these collaborators might have lived their final days free from public trial. Mark Osiel observed the enormous media attention Touvier's trial received, noting how it became a proxy for a trial of the whole Vichy government.[53] Touvier stood in as an ideal perpetrator: he came to represent all of French collaboration.

In the US portion of the SNCF conflict, both Leo Bretholz and Harriet Tamen played the role of champion opponent, dedicated to keeping the gaze fixedly upon, and upon only, the SNCF. Many observers believe that without Tamen's relentless commitment to making the company pay directly, the issue might have dissolved long ago. Tamen worked pro bono on the SNCF class action lawsuit for well over a decade.

Inspired by what was happening with the SNCF, survivor Salo Muller became a champion opponent of the Dutch National Railways. Like Bretholz, Muller never spoke of the Holocaust after the war, until an interested party coaxed the story out of him (in his case, a journalist working with Steven Spielberg's project to collect survivor testimonies). Once he allowed the past a place in the present, he found himself incensed, especially at the Dutch Railways, which even made those being deported buy their own tickets. Muller's minor celebrity status helped his advocacy. As team osteopath for the popular Dutch soccer team Ajax, he could easily reach the Dutch Railways CEO, Roger van Boxtel, who had been a commissioner of Ajax. Boxtel welcomed his call but then did little to address his justice concerns. Muller's wealthy friends helped him raise money for an international law expert, Liesbeth Zegveld, to take his case. Together they met with Boxtel and the company lawyer. Wishing to avoid a lawsuit, the company agreed to compensate survivors.[54] Unless someone commits himself or herself to the cause, most people (and companies) get away with murder.

The symbolism of the railway, the advocates, and the abstract nature of the company all contributed to keeping the SNCF (and, later, the Dutch Railways) in the spotlight. Marrus argues that the positioning of the SNCF front and center does society a disservice: "The difficulty in singling out an organization such as the SNCF, and particularly a judicial reckoning more than sixty years after the event, is precisely the diffusion of responsibility for the Holocaust, what Hannah Arendt referred to as the 'moral collapse' that the Nazis caused everywhere in European society."[55] Does the focus on the SNCF diffuse responsibility for the Holocaust and distract from the *vrais coupables*, as Serge Klarsfeld has also claimed? Does having one perpetrator stand in for all also distract from a deeper understanding of how such atrocities come to occur? The next chapter considers the fact that, while the US legislation targeted the French National Railways, the legislators effectively proposed memory laws to ensure that past complicity would not be forgotten. Of course, for many victims, forgetting would be a gift, but most find themselves forced to remember. A long life leaves much time to remember but also the chance to heal and reunite.

Voices from the Last Trains

Every February, I send Daniel a card on his birthday, and each year he reminds me that his birthday is the day his parents were deported—as if I could ever forget.

Daniel and I would meet many more times before I would meet his brother, Samuel. After a year or two of overtures and postponements during my visits to France, Samuel finally agreed to meet. I rode an SNCF train to Alsace, then a tram to a station near his home. He picked me up and drove me to a park near his apartment. We walked for about ten minutes, then sat on a bench. He launched straight into a reminiscence about the early days of the liberation when a man from the Red Cross carried Daniel away and Samuel thought him dead. He broke down into tears, berating himself for not running after Daniel. It became clear during our visit that the shame and misunderstandings that had developed over the years all came from that one fateful moment. I suggested that perhaps their differences could be addressed in a meeting.

The meeting took two years to plan. In their eighties, they found travel difficult, and with Samuel's tendency to cancel at the last minute, I was not sure it would ever happen.

"Samuel won't visit me. He didn't come when I had my heart surgery or when I won the award," Daniel said, referring to the Légion d'honneur he received for his work with the handicapped. The brothers had been distant ever since their rescue at the end of the war and had not seen each other for about five years before our scheduled reunion.

"We visited Mauthausen," Samuel told me. He had little to say about their visit to the former concentration camp from which they were liberated. They had not seen each other since.

The reunion took place on April 30, 2016, in Strasbourg, near Samuel and Elise's home. One of Daniel's sons, his wife, and their son came along to bring the brothers together. They had a short lunch at a restaurant near the train station. When I found them later, at 3 p.m., they seemed to have traded temperaments. Daniel had talked about Samuel as isolated and closed, but when I walked in, Samuel and Elise had big smiles and Daniel sat frozen on the other side of the table. He looked stunned and appeared to be barely breathing. They made room, and I slid in next to Daniel.

"Ça va?"—All okay?

They said they had spoken a bit about the past, largely about the questions I had raised with Samuel during our visit the day before. They fact-checked each other's memories.

Samuel told Daniel that to this day, he cannot explain why he let the medical team carry Daniel away without following. After Samuel found help for his brother, he just froze. Today, we have a term for this behavior among newly released prisoners—postincarceration syndrome (PICS). Samuel knew nothing about this and continues to chastise himself for his inability to follow Daniel. The medical aide knew of their relationship, but he was likely too occupied with the overwhelming medical needs before him to understand the importance of keeping the brothers together.

There is a lesson here for the contemporary handling of refugees: families must be kept together.

When I began this research, I never suspected these interviews could open up and shift relationships. As a scholar and practitioner of conflict resolution, I found this discovery as meaningful as any finding about the trains. Misunderstandings develop in the small spaces where we story ourselves and each other. Sometimes only through intimate engagement with these narratives can shifts occur.

Daniel assumed that Samuel had pulled away because he had been a burden to Samuel during the war. I told Daniel that Samuel had a different explanation. Samuel had to told me, "Once Daniel converted to Catholicism and had seven children, I figured he did not need me anymore."

"He really said that?" Daniel asked when I shared Samuel's version.

"Yes, he told me that he pulled away to give *you* space." Daniel was surprised by this.

Two days later, Daniel called to tell me he had spoken with Samuel over the phone. The tone of their conversation was no longer tight and fearful but friendly and open.

"I think we performed a *petit miracle*," he said.

CHAPTER EIGHT

Memory Laws and Atonement

States are skillful shapers of memory. . . . Those who hold political power
produce traditions and official histories bringing together key facts,
inventing legends, and ostracizing the vanquished.

—SARAH GENSBURGER AND SANDRINE LEFRANC,
À quoi servent les politiques de mémoire?

IN FEBRUARY 2018, Poland's president, Andrzej Duda, signed into law
an amendment to Article 55 of Poland's Act on the Institute of National
Remembrance. This law, which resulted in substantial controversy, prohibited any reference to "Polish death camps." It also declared that any accusation that Poland collaborated with the Nazis is a crime, punishable by fine or
up to three years in prison.[1] Poland's law is an example of a "memory law"
designed to control how the public talks about—and therefore remembers—
the past. Many were shocked by Poland's law. Memory laws currently exist in
Latvia, Estonia, Ukraine, Romania, and even France and Canada. More often
than not, these laws—created in response to demands from victim groups—
aim to prevent the *denial* of genocide. The Polish legislation shows how such
laws can be used to avert responsibility for participation in genocide and control
historical memory.

France also asserts control over memory. Rousso outlines how the notion of
memory law emerged and developed in France.[2] In July 1990, France passed the
Loi Gayssot, forbidding Holocaust denial.[3] This was followed by the *devoir de
mémoire*, the necessity of remembering the Holocaust, which achieved national
status in 1993. In 1999 France passed a law recognizing the Algerian War as an
actual war rather than simply a "conflict."[4] In January 2001, the government
recognized the Armenians as having suffered a genocide in 1915; and in May
2001, the Loi Taubira recognized the Atlantic slave trade and slavery as crimes
against humanity.[5] Because of these laws, *Le Monde* called former French president Jacques Chirac "*le président du devoir de mémoire*" (the president of the
duty of memory).[6] Chirac's 1995 apology for French complicity with the Nazis
during World War II further supports this title.

Perhaps the most shocking of the French memory laws is the most recent. In 2005 France passed a law prohibiting only negative representations of French colonialism.[7] This right-wing response to the earlier memory laws in France sought recognition of what the French nation offered to its former colonies and its "*Français repatriés.*"[8] In other words, some wanted to compel the view that benefits and good things came from the colonial period and that these must not be omitted from postcolonial critiques. To this list of memory laws, in March 2000 the French Parliament added July 16 as a day of commemoration for Jewish persons persecuted during the occupation and for the "Justes" who tried to save them. The decree added the recognition of the "Justes" to a Jewish commemoration day created in 1993. Sarah Gensburger observes how the institutionalization of this new political figure, the "Juste," revives the dated image of the resistant, while shifting French identity beyond a nation to a land of human rights.[9] Similarly, memory laws do political work, altering memory and shifting identities to better align with contemporary agendas.[10]

MEMORY LAWS IN THE UNITED STATES

American legislators can create holidays but cannot establish memory laws in the same way as their counterparts elsewhere because the First Amendment of the US Constitution protects freedom of expression. The government cannot prohibit someone from having an opinion about the past. The 2011 Maryland legislation, which required transparency about the SNCF's complicity in the Holocaust and was intended to make it impossible for the company to deny its Holocaust history, may be as close as America can get to a memory law. Maryland governor Martin O'Malley recognized Leo Bretholz for his help developing this first legislation to insist upon corporate transparency. Laws demanding transparency serve to record and preserve memory. While most of the memory laws in Europe address issues of state collusion or lack thereof, these legislative bills address corporate transparency—and this shift in focus to corporate memory is a significant turn.

By linking the SNCF in perpetuity to its past, the laws in some ways go further than requiring compensation. Compensation often buys silence: victims are paid, and the issue is considered "settled." By contrast, the legislation proposed in these states points a finger at the SNCF's past every time the company seeks a contract in the region in question. This form of memory law promotes *antagonistic memory*, a form of memory that reinforces binaries and nationalist narratives. Memory laws might work against a more cosmopolitan memory, which promotes inclusivity, dialogue, transnationality, and human rights memory.[11]

Memory-related legislation could be more effective if it moved beyond shaming to focus on advancing a more inclusive, larger human rights conversation through *agonistic memory*, which promotes reflection and dialogue. However, beyond the SNCF, companies that continue to commit or that have committed massive human rights violations retain impunity from such legislation. Consumers rarely boycott or challenge companies for their past actions. Corporate employees rarely consider the moral compromises that their employment might entail. All of which prompts the question with regard to these laws: *À quoi ça sert?* (What is the point?)

Today's SNCF Executives

Memory laws land a bit like a forced apology, giving the appearance of change where none may have occurred. Such external impositions are not the same as atonement, transformation, or true change. Poland can write almost any laws it wishes; Maryland can force the SNCF to digitize its archives; and survivor groups can pressure the SNCF to apologize. But is change really occurring if done under constraint and duress? What is the ethos of today's SNCF?

The SNCF now has roughly 250,000 employees, half the number it had during the war. The transition away from coal reduced the need for so many workers. The company's quarter million employees are still enough to make it challenging to forge a coherent identity. Because we often locate corporate accountability with the executives, I want to discuss the modern-day SNCF executives who are responsible for responding to attacks on their company's moral record. Access to these individuals offers a sense of the transformations that have occurred. I enter the story here together with portraits of these executives in order to humanize the SNCF. While the SNCF, like any corporate entity, exists as more than the sum of its agents (past and present), individual agents do matter, and I want to make them real by placing myself in interaction with them.

In the earliest days of my research, I met SNCF president Guillaume Pepy. A colleague's husband who worked in France for the Japanese train company Shinkansen helped me attend a train conference held at the Palais de Tokyo in Paris. I effectively snuck into the conference and approached Pepy. With my heart in my throat, I gave him my carefully prepared explanation of my intended research study. He replied enthusiastically, handed me his business card, and asked me to reach out after the conference. But not everyone was so enthusiastic. During the cocktail hour following the conference, I explained my research topic to a current employee. He turned bright red and said, "I'll tell you one thing. I'm Jewish and I work for the SNCF and I am very proud." Then he swiftly fled our conversation.

Other employees backed away when they learned of my research, but the SNCF chairman and other senior executives I met seemed less put off. After the conference, Pepy quickly connected me with Bernard Emsellem, the head of corporate social responsibility. In the following years, Emsellem and I would meet numerous times at the SNCF headquarters and at other places around Paris, including at SNCF events related to Holocaust commemoration. Emsellem made himself available to me during each visit and spoke openly about the company's history—at least what he knew of it—and shared his own story of losing family in the Holocaust. His interest seemed clearly personal as well as professional. As the executive in charge of matters relating to Holocaust claims and accountability, he said he wished that the SNCF had just changed its name, as the German national railways company had done in 1994.[12] Having the SNCF's name emblazoned on deportation convoys in Holocaust museums around the world created a difficult branding problem. Not creating a separate legal entity also created legal vulnerability. Changing the company's name was likely never discussed immediately after the war, because such a change would have been seen as an admission of guilt. In the early days after the war, however, the Holocaust was not even seen as a separate crime. The SNCF was deemed a hero, and why would a hero change its name?

I once offered to Emsellem the view that, perhaps as head of corporate responsibility, he might consider seeing this situation as an opportunity to *take* responsibility and be a leader in corporate accountability. He seemed unconvinced. This whole conflict seemed more of a burden than an opportunity. It put him in such an uncomfortable position: he was distraught by the SNCF's role in the Holocaust and simultaneously proud of its role in the Resistance. During one of our first visits, he proudly showed me the Légion d'honneur medal the SNCF had received in the 1950s for its role in the Resistance.[13]

Over the years, as my expertise and my network increased, Emsellem began to ask me about some of the survivors, about the US perspective, and other related questions. Because of the lawsuits and the contentious nature of the conflict, the differing sides had little access to each other. My position as a scholar and likely my US citizenship contributed to my role as occasional de facto mediator. This was sometimes evident at formal meetings to which I was invited and more often in small dialogues, which are as much a part of the transitional justice project as the larger, more demonstrative ceremonies. I paid careful attention to how I functioned as a connecting thread as I moved between different departments of the US government, survivor gatherings, and coffee meetings with SNCF executives as well as meetings with historians, archivists, Jewish leaders, and the ambassadors negotiating the French–US settlement. Scholarly research can allow tremendous mobility. I wanted to contribute without changing the story; I wanted to facilitate justice and, if possible, do so in a way that increased trust and at least improved the tone of the interactions between conflicting parties.

When I moved back to the Washington, DC, area to continue this research, I had the opportunity to visit multiple times with SNCF America CEO Alain Leray. Like Emsellem, he made himself available to me as often as I requested. We had numerous visits, phone calls, and emails over the years, at times disagreeing but always having lively conversations. These conversations can be, in and of themselves, a way to process conflict and grow. Having lived in France and a former corporate executive myself, I could relate to some of his conundrums. Emsellem, Leray, and I are all of Jewish ancestry. But in our professional lives, we experienced the conflict from different vantage points: Leray from that of a French CEO of SNCF America and I as an American conflict scholar who had spent hundreds of hours talking with Holocaust survivors and studying the debates. Our roles and experiences inevitably shaped our thinking.

Our different views became clear a few days after the Maryland hearing, when Leray and I met at Le Pain Quotidien for breakfast near his office in Bethesda, Maryland. Prior to the meeting, I reviewed his official statements about the legal and legislative battles, focusing in particular on Maryland. He had argued in these statements that these legal actions distracted from the *vrais coupables*, the truly guilty: "As a French railroader, I'm completely outraged at all the misrepresentation, mischaracterizations that are being spread around right now against the company. . . . What's being said right now is actually an insult. As a French Jew I am appalled because you're taking away responsibility from the Nazis, and that's the beginning of denial."[14]

Leray had said that the Conseil Représentatif des Institutions Juives de France (CRIF), France's largest Jewish organization, had come out in support of the SNCF, proclaiming the Maryland bill discriminatory and an insult to the SNCF workers who had died for their participation in the resistance. He reiterated the SNCF's position that the Nazis determined the horrific conditions and that the SNCF never profited from the transports. He resented the accusation that the SNCF collaborated willingly, stating: "Under the June 1940 armistice convention, France was defeated by the Nazis and it said all of the railroads would be under German command. . . . They took over and stole everything. They stole 2,000 locomotives and killed more than 2,100 of my colleagues— 820 were beheaded. How is this cooperating with the Nazis?"[15] As discussed in chapter 3, many of those SNCF workers who had been killed for acts of resistance during the war had been turned in at the encouragement of Robert Le Besnerais, the general director of the SNCF. And, of course, the loss of locomotives pales in comparison to the mass murder of children and their families. In conversation, Leray would not disagree.

Leray's comments underscore the challenge of locating what, for lack of a better term, might be called the "soul" of a corporation. Does it reside in the railwaymen who lost their lives? Or in the executives who condemned them? The material assets (in this case trains)? The *habitus* of the organization? And how much responsibility does context have for a corporations' behavior? Nelson Camillo Sánchez asks us to consider the degree of corporate complicity (high, medium, low).[16] Would this degree affect monies owed or actions required? As this conflict demonstrates, these questions become not just legal but social as well; the questions will outlive the legal debates.

When we met more recently, Leray looked quite different from the man I saw at the Maryland Senate hearing who was then dressed in a formal business suit prepared to represent his multibillion-dollar employer. Today, not cast in the role of public villain, he wore more casual business attire. His demeanor seemed lighter and less fierce.

We sat by the window. I ordered a café au lait.

"Aren't you going to eat?" he asked.

I had been out of the corporate life for a few years and had forgotten that people actually eat at breakfast meetings. Our difference in financial means was obvious; Leray arrived in his Maserati and I on foot from the Metro. I mention this to highlight the fact that, in spite of these financial differences, in *this* conversation we were on more or less equal terms. We each have a voice in how the Holocaust ought to be remembered and atoned for. And in these conversations, power is not always so obvious; while he held a leadership position in the SNCF, I would influence how the conflict would be storied.

Leray told me how he had come to his position at the SNCF. He had received a call one day announcing his transfer from SNCF France to the SNCF United States. The transfer would last only four months, he was told. This short stay would enable the SNCF to cover the gap created by the sudden death of Dennis Douté, the former CEO of SNCF America. Leray at first seemed an odd fit for the position, since he specialized in the rail transport of automobiles rather than the high-speed, commuter, and regional rail business. But Leray had already proved himself a trusted SNCF employee, was fluent in English, and was almost part American, at least via his education. He had attended Hamilton College in upstate New York as an undergraduate as well as Dartmouth's Tuck School of Business. Furthermore, as a Jewish man who had lost family in the Holocaust, he could perhaps handle Holocaust-related issues with the appropriate delicacy. So, what he lacked in commuter rail expertise he made up for through his US education and his Jewish heritage. The SNCF conflict continued far longer than the four months to which he had originally been assigned; Leray and his family found themselves facing these issues for several years.

In spite of the (at the time of our meeting) proposed legislation designed to thwart the company's business advances in Florida, Leray believed he had made progress because several Florida-based Jewish organizations had invited him to events. I asked how, then, he explained Florida's rejection of the company's 2011 apology, in which SNCF CEO Guillaume Pepy's statement (written by Bernard Emsellem) expressed only "his regrets" for what had happened without saying directly, "I'm sorry." Leray defended Pepy's words, saying that in French *je regrette* is stronger than *je m'excuse* (I'm sorry), which means, "I excuse myself and it's over."[17] The SNCF, he said, did not want to suggest finality or use a phrase so trivial as that which one might use when bumping into someone on the Metro. "I'm sorry" makes the company far more vulnerable to legal attacks because it acknowledges a different level of responsibility.

Rocky relations in Florida were still better than the venomous relations in Maryland, arguably made worse by the hearings we had just attended. Leray considered the Maryland bill dead because no legislator would risk the loss of federal funding, but this did not mean the SNCF would win the bid or that relations had improved. At this point, the SNCF had done all it could do, Leray said. The SNCF's archives, which had been digitized in accordance with the previous bill's requirements, and Israel's recent contract with the SNCF proved that the company had made amends. He said the negotiations between the federal governments would compensate survivors who were still owed.

Our meeting had landed during the heat of the negotiations between France and the US government, moving toward the $60 million settlement signed in December 2014. So, when I asked whether the SNCF could pay the survivors directly, he said the French state would not allow him to comment on that issue. Emsellem had told me the same thing. But a year after the settlement signing, in 2015, I again asked Leray whether it would have been better to just pay the survivors. He said he wished he had—and that the French government would have let him had he insisted.[18] This inconsistency is a good reminder for those negotiating with corporations: such declared limitations may either be perceived (rather than real) or a means of protection.

During this second meeting, Leray was hopeful that state-level negotiations would result in the coverage of twenty-five to thirty-five survivors who had not been included in the settlement as well as people in other programs who were very poor and who he believed deserved the money. He wanted them to receive the funds as quickly as possible. Back at the time of our meeting in 2014, Leray did not know whether the company would win the Purple Line contract in Maryland. He had mixed feelings about winning the contract anyway, he said. Exhausted by the battle, he said that of course the company wanted the business, and yet at this point he wanted to pull out and tell them to "go stick it." It bothered him that people in the United States held the company responsible for the deportations without giving the company credit for its transparency efforts and Holocaust commemoration donations, which totaled

$12 million by 2019. Because of the harm done, perpetrating entities cannot give back with the expectation of a warm welcome. The pain caused is just too deep and too irreparable.

At one point during our breakfast, Leray expressed exasperation at the US refusal to take responsibility for its own unwillingness to intercede in the Holocaust; he said, "You know the US ambassador to France had a role in setting up the Vichy government!" He pointed out that the United States did not declare war on Germany: Germany declared war on the United States. The United States got involved only after Pearl Harbor. Then he leaned back and said that, at the same time, for his parents after World War II, the United States meant *life*. He really appreciated what the United States eventually did do.

In these more intimate, off-stage conversations, complexity emerges. In many of the interviews I conducted, those fighting adamantly in public on one side or another admitted to having more fluid positions in private.

As with many involved, this conflict was not just a professional journey for Leray; it was also a personal one. When Leray moved to the United States and found himself in the middle of this conflict, he researched more about his own family history. He said CNN's Brianna Keilar had asked him very specific questions about his personal connection to the Holocaust, so he engaged in more research. This made the conflict increasingly personal. His parents, who met after the war, had both been deeply affected by the Holocaust. His Jewish father had barely survived. He suffered so much malnutrition during incarceration in Spain after escaping from France in 1943 that for the rest of his life, he could not drink any alcohol without becoming unconscious. To this day, Leray never drinks alcohol, which he notes is highly unusual for a French person. He attributes this to the fact that while he was growing up, his family never had any in the house—another example of the imprints left by persecution and how these imprints pass down between generations.

His grandmother on his mother's side was from Vienna, Austria. His mother's family, also Jewish, moved to Paris, but, realizing that France provided no safety either, they left for Algeria. When his mother's family returned to Paris after the German capitulation was signed, they found their apartment empty and all their beautiful furniture from Vienna gone.

"Not a pin was left," Leray said.

His grandmother cried when she saw the empty apartment.

"After what happened to our people, you are not allowed to cry for furniture!" his grandfather told his grandmother. His grandmother stopped crying immediately, and that became an important family story and lesson, especially for Leray's mother, who was sixteen when she witnessed this scene. Likely, Leray's grandmother's grief reflected the loss of a way of life rather than just the loss of material objects.

Leray said that, as a second-generation survivor, he has found being tasked to defend the company quite personally challenging. He often thought about how, once his daughter got older, he would explain his role in the SNCF conflict. At the time we spoke, he was not sure what he would say. He felt responsible for honoring the memory of the resistants in the company while also holding on to the memories of the survivors.

He wanted me to understand that the company could not advertise its participation in the Resistance, he said. It could not hang a sign outside and say, "We are in the Resistance." Chapter 3 showed that the network was much smaller, hidden, and operated by small individual acts without executive support. And the fact that every deportation train arrived at its destination and the Germans recorded no pushback from the company suggests that many acts were ineffective or at the very least not the norm. Those who survived those deportations largely did so on their own, as in the case of Leo Bretholz, who jumped off the train; through a combination of chance and strength of their youth, as in the case of Daniel and Samuel, who survived Auschwitz; or through sheer luck, as in the case of Estéra, who survived because the Nazis ran out of Zyklon B that day. Most SNCF employees had little to do with their survival, even if employees past and present would wish it to be so.

Had Leray insisted that the French government allow the SNCF to pay survivors directly, much of this conflict would have ended much sooner. Had the company just paid survivors directly, it also might not have participated as fully in commemorations, made so many transparency efforts, or issued apologies. It is precisely because of the SNCF's refusal to settle that the complicated issues of corporate accountability in the aftermath of atrocity became more visible.

In October 2017, I called Leray to check on the Chicago lawsuit. He said the judge had dismissed the case but had not released his ruling. He did not know if the litigants would appeal. To which I responded, "*Alors, c'est nulle part, mais ça continue quand même*" (So, the conflict is nowhere, but it continues anyway).

Leray agreed with the ironic turn of phrase. Postwar deliberations often take a great deal of time, and during this time many remain unsatisfied or simply die while waiting, but the unfolding continues anyway. Within these large justice projects that move forward and stall, sometimes in decade-long increments, there are chapters—and this one was coming to an end.

THE DENOUEMENT

The historian Michael Marrus has asked at various points during the SNCF conflict, "Is this the end of the line?"[19] Though many tried, no one seems to be able to predict when and where the conflict will end. Settlements, just like peace treaties, may serve as important symbolic markers and provide significant remuneration to victimized parties, but they can never guarantee the end of anything. The signing of the settlement in December 2014 between France and the US with which I opened this book did not actually end the SNCF conflict with the swiftness some had hoped. Another lawsuit was launched four months later, and in terms of its hoped-for rail contracts, the company was in irons for almost four years. Along the way, however, there seemed signs that this conflict might be wrapping up.

The $60 million settlement did not satisfy everyone, both because of its limited terms and because of its initial bureaucratically convoluted attempts at dispersing the funds. The pragmatics of acquiring and dispersing the restitution funds proved almost as complicated as negotiating the agreement. The agreement stated that, except for the countries that already had agreements, survivors could receive at least $100,000 each. Survivors with approved applications received $204,000. Spouses of the deportees received $51,000. Al Fogel, whose grandparents had their one-way trip on SNCF trains to Auschwitz, became a US- based lawyer and worked to help people obtain the settlement funds. When the announcement came, he said, "What is pretty clear, is that the $60 million fund that has been set up will probably go to nearly '*no one.*' The requirements of the fund are so impossible to meet, that it is doubtful that 100 persons or their families would qualify. It is doubtful that the US State Department would divide $60 million dollars between 100 persons."[20]

The US Department of State and Israel worked to disseminate the funds as quickly as possible but could do nothing until the French Parliament ratified the agreement.[21] During spring 2015, the French Parliament debated the agreement, especially taking issue with some of the wording. The French government wanted to ensure that the agreement sufficiently distinguished between the contemporary Fifth Republic government and the provisional, Nazi-allied government that ruled during the occupation and the Vichy regime.[22] By July 2015, six months after the signing, the government had still not finished ratifying the agreement. With survivors passing away every day, the six-month deliberation process was tragically slow.

When the claims process first began, a social services worker helping survivors with their applications reported that many applications were being rejected. The qualifications were too rigid, she said. Harriet Tamen and her colleague Steven Rodd, distraught at how difficult the claims process had been for their elderly and frail claimants, sent a letter to the US State Department on February 29, 2016. Tamen and Rodd had helped file fifty claims, but other claimants continued struggling with various issues. Some were told they needed to provide some official identification not mentioned in the instructions. Far more challenging, however, was the requirement that claimants provide difficult-to-obtain wills, death certificates, and/or marriage certificates. Additionally, the US State Department wanted all documents translated. Tamen urged the State Department to accept affidavits in which survivors attested on their honor to the truthfulness of their claims. Tamen and Rodd's letter also criticized the claimant website for being cold and official and for its use of legal language. They urged the State Department to create a more encouraging interface. The lawyers also took issue with the fact that orphans did not qualify and asked for clarification on this point. They sent a copy of the letter to a number of the legislators working on SNCF-related legislation, including Charles Schumer, Carolyn Maloney, Ileana Ros-Lehtinen, and Ted Deutch. By copying these legislators, Tamen let the US State Department know that the dreaded legislative stalling of SNCF contracts could be revived. In order to expedite the claims process, both governments agreed to waive the medical exam requirements that were part of earlier claims programs.

Concerned about the dispersal of funds, I also called the US State Department to see how the process was going. A young woman answered the hotline number and, in response to my question about how many claims had been received, said, "Not very many. You know how people leave things to the last minute." The survivors had left things to the last minute? Really? I bit my tongue. Some survivors had waited more than seventy years for this compensation. The suggestion that these elderly people were procrastinators did not sit well with me. Fearing many would not make the short deadline, I reached out to some contacts in the Jewish community that I had developed during this research and explained my understanding of the situation. The organization intervened and shortly thereafter, the deadline was extended.

Promising Silence

There is another aspect of the agreement, beyond payments, that is worthy of discussion. All survivors and descendants who accepted compensation through the French–US settlement had to waive the right—definitively—to demand anything else from France regarding the deportations. They also gave up the right (and the right of their descendants) to sue the French state or be involved in any US-based political actions that seek to hold France *or* the United States accountable for the Holocaust. This was not required, I believe, for those receiving funds from the French bank settlement or from the German compensation fund for forced labor, although similar terms may become more common in compensation agreements, as suggested by the conditions of the Canadian Indian Residential Schools Settlement Agreement of 2007.[23]

Transitional justice practitioners and scholars must remain vigilant regarding this shift. Is money offered in the hopes of also buying people's silence? The compensation is in response to irreparable harm, and now the state wants something in return. The victim must legally pardon the company. The apology and/or money will not be issued without ensuring future amnesty. If a similar release form had been issued immediately after the war expunging the French state, many might have forfeited their right to their money housed in French banks, art restitution, and insurance monies. The depth of French complicity in the war's mass atrocities might have remained buried. Trying to close the doors on the past is morally questionable work. What if archival documents are discovered in the future that show greater complicity than was previously known? New information and new political realities (like the end of the Cold War) create new opportunities. We need to leave room for new findings—and, perhaps, new justice claims.

VOICES FROM THE LAST TRAINS

The reunion of Daniel and Samuel *was* a small miracle as Daniel believed. Of course, one lunch could not heal the trauma in their past and their disconnected adult lives. I sent a picture of the brothers' reunion to their sister, who had up until this time refused to meet me. I thought evidence of reunion and our wish to include her might create a shift. It did. She responded immediately, saying she loved the photo and inviting me to visit. I flew to Nice, and we met for lunch. Sophie arrived wearing a silk scarf, looking stylish and urbane. She was clearly excited to be out on the town.

"I love the city," she said. "If Christine Lazard had not taken care of us, I would have been married to a cow farmer and had to live in the country. I hate the country. I hate grass. Too much grass."

She married a man who spent his career working for IBM (ironically another Holocaust-complicit company) and had lived a comfortable life and enjoyed the different cities where the company stationed him. But her feelings about her brothers remained unresolved. She told me about living with Daniel and his wife when she was a child and they were in their twenties. She thinks they wanted her to just serve as a free babysitter. She cannot forgive him for being such a terrible replacement for their parents. Daniel also expressed regret about the years that Sophie lived with them. So emotionally devastated himself and only six years her senior, he admitted he had no idea how to be a good surrogate parent.

Sophie tried to pass her resentment on to her own children. She told her son that he was not required to invite Daniel to his wedding, to which her son responded, "Mom, stop it." He invited Daniel, who gladly attended. Yet the bond with Sophie remained broken.

They all had such different ways of dealing with their pain. Samuel's more isolated life suggests his deep sense that visibility had made him vulnerable; Daniel chose to live as fully as possible. Both brothers think often about the past. Sophie's response reflects her age difference. She says she feels no emptiness regarding her birth family because she cannot remember the family she lost. She also has no memories before the sixth grade except for one vague memory of her mother saying she would be right back, before disappearing forever.

She said, "When I asked for my mother, someone said, 'She's taking care of something, come with me.' . . . But, I'm not even sure if that's true."

When she was old enough, someone explained to her that she had no parents. Her past remained obscured and somewhat mysterious to her. The name used on all her official documents was not a name she had ever heard. She seemed to feel slightly haunted by this mysterious name. Perhaps it was the name of the woman she would have become, had her life not been interrupted.

Part of what makes the visits among the siblings so curious and at times heartbreaking is that their pain and disappointment were often directed at one another and nowhere near the ultimate source of their pain—the Nazis, the French police, the Vichy government, collaborators, the SNCF.

When I asked Sophie about the SNCF, she said, "They didn't have a choice. Better to go after the police."

When I asked if the police had a choice, she paused a moment and said that the police could at least have done something to help people. After a few more moments of reflection, she asked me, "Does anyone care about this anymore?"

She is not sure she does. She knows for sure that she is not interested in going to any Shoah memorials. She's interested in more contemporary memorials like the one commemorating 9/11 in New York.

Perhaps less so in Nice, France, but in New York and Paris and in other places, many people still do care about the Holocaust. Teachers in the United States and Europe continue to invite the few remaining Holocaust survivors to attend their classes, hoping that students will learn something valuable. Daniel always accepts such invitations, even though he tells me that they are extremely difficult emotionally.

I attended one of these school visits with Daniel. A high school student asked him, "Have you been able to have a normal life?" Daniel replied, "I don't know if I have found a normal life. I'm not sure I know what that is. I am eighty-five and have never been liberated from this experience. I would have had an entirely different life."

Conclusion

Toward Corporate Accountability

Each man is questioned by life; he can only answer to life by answering
for his own life; to life, he can only respond by being responsible.

—VICTOR FRANKL, *Man's Search for Meaning*

O N DECEMBER 11, 2017, the SNCF conflict reached another moment
of symbolic conclusion. Whereas the treaty-signing ceremony that
I describe in the introduction represented a political end to the
debates, an invitation-only event held at the United States Holocaust Memorial Museum represented a symbolic peace between (at least part of) the American Jewish community and the SNCF. During this cocktail hour event, the
SNCF announced a donation to the museum to the fifty or so of us gathered
by the museum's donation wall. The SNCF executives spoke first, followed
by museum leaders, who expressed their gratitude. Then, SNCF's Bernard
Emsellem and Alain Leray unveiled the SNCF's name, embossed on the donor
wall. The event closed with wine and hors d'oeuvres spread out on artistically
decorated tables in the haunting museum foyer.

This was a momentous occasion: adding the SNCF's name to the museum
donor wall went against standard museum policy. In the early 2000s, the
museum's executive committee had decided to refuse to allow any permanent
recognition of Holocaust-complicit German-based or German-affiliated corporate donors.[1] Bestowing this honor upon the SNCF pointed to a remark-
able shift, perhaps toward greater corporate engagement more broadly. France's
Shoah Memorial and the SNCF have mutually benefited from such an alliance for more than a decade. In restorative justice terms, this acceptance of the
SNCF represents the reintegration that can occur after shaming.[2] The individual or group that has caused harm acknowledges the harm, helps repair the
harm, and then can be accepted back. Reentry serves as a critical component
of restoration, whereas continuing to shame those who demonstrate contrition
perpetuates the dynamics of exclusion, which often lead us back into various

forms of violence. Allowing the SNCF to transform its identity from perpetrator to ally has many advantages; the SNCF can become a model for other companies by demonstrating that amends-making efforts can improve relationships. Emergent programs can benefit the harmed and work to prevent future human rights abuses. The company can also seek ways to "earn" its heroic identity through present-day actions. In February 2020, the SNCF outlined its promise to release hybrid trains in 2020, hydrogen-powered trains by 2022, and discontinue diesel fuel by 2035.[3] The SNCF contributes to the public good in other ways. In March 2020, for example, the SNCF offered free transport to all medics during the COVID pandemic. Then, in July 2020, in the wake of George Floyd's murder and the resurgent Black Lives Matter movement, the company updated its diversity and gender equality policy to reflect new norms of fairness and inclusion.

These actions align the SNCF with the morality of our times, and I believe in reintegrating wrongdoers after they demonstrate consistent change, yet I felt uncomfortable seeing the SNCF's name embossed on the Holocaust Museum's donor wall. Renewable energy, COVID support, and inclusion are critically important. The SNCF seems to be on the right side of history during this era. But perhaps a plaque in one of the world's most preeminent Holocaust museums, however, offers the SNCF a perhaps too visible public relations payoff for an era in which its historical role was more questionable.

At this event, like so many others, no one spoke about the struggles of the few remaining survivors; in fact, consistent with their marginalization throughout the conflict, almost none even received invitations to the event. I also wondered whether the SNCF deserves such prominent recognition for making the amends and donations that survivors dragged them into. What about a space on the wall for survivors like Kurt Schaechter, Alain Lipietz, Lou Helwaser, and others who paid their own legal fees to bring the company to its knees? To this conundrum, I have no answer.

Perhaps one consolation is that no matter what kind of recognition the SNCF receives, trains will remain a *lieu de mémoire*—so long as anyone remembers the Holocaust. The Washington, DC, museum still displays the haunting convoy wagon that visitors can walk through or around, and on many deportation photos the SNCF's name remains visible. The past cannot be erased. Trains and train stations remain bound to both world wars. In November 2018, German chancellor Angela Merkel and French president Emmanuel Macron commemorated the one hundredth anniversary of the end of World War I at the replica railcar where the French and the Germans signed their treaty. This railcar also commemorates the site where the French surrendered to the Germans during World War II.

Today, in the Gare Montparnasse, a major Parisian rail station and the former headquarters of the SNCF, there is a freestanding monument at the base of some escalators commemorating another related armistice. On August 25, 1944, German troops signed a surrender to the French in this station, officially liberating Paris. Many rail stations throughout the country use plaques to commemorate the railway workers who died during the war. The role of trains will not soon be forgotten.

Trains as Sites of Contestation

In addition to active memory sites, trains also remain active sites of moral contestation. In the United States, several more recent incidents have raised questions regarding the moral obligation of train companies. In August 2018, the Amalgamated Transit Union, Washington DC's largest metro union, refused to transport "Unite the White" rally supporters in special trains to protect the white nationalists from protesters.[4] This act demonstrates how these employees understood themselves as moral agents, not order-obeying automatons. A West Coast train company found itself faced with a related moral debate just a month later. In September 2018, Bay Area Rapid Transit (BART) allowed ads from the Institute for Historical Review (IHR) to be posted in two of its stations. IHR has been classified as a Nazi-defending hate group that promotes Holocaust denial. A BART spokesperson, Alicia Trost, said the company cannot refuse the ads because of the First Amendment of the US Constitution, which protects free speech.[5] I wrote to the company expressing my understanding of this view as a citizen and as a former advertising executive. I understood that advertising divisions rarely involve themselves in the morality of an advertisement. I also expressed my appreciation of the protection of free speech. I then shared with the company the power of propaganda and, more specifically, the critical role that trains played in World War II and their role even today in undoing this legacy and helping us decrease hate propaganda. To their credit, the officials brought my letter to the board, which then voted to remove the ads. Sometimes companies simply need help seeing the ethical role they can and already do play in society.

Surprisingly to some, these morally charged debates can still involve issues of deportation. Airlines also now find themselves ensnared in related deportation debates. In 2018 a sticker graffiti campaign, "France Deports, Air France Transports," tried to shame the French airline for its part in transporting the Roma back to Eastern Europe as well as ferrying illegal immigrants (often refugees) back to Brazzaville and Kinshasa in the Congo, Khartoum in Sudan, and elsewhere. These stickers were placed throughout Paris and within many trains headed to and from the airport. American Airlines found itself in a similar

Sticker posted on a Parisian street sign accusing Air France of participating in the deportation of immigrants, June 2019. (Author photo)

position in 2018 when the US government asked it to transport children separated from their families at the southern border due to new immigration policies. The airline pushed back.[6] Soon after the airline made its public protest, President Trump signed an executive order allowing children and their parents to stay together. The airline company's protest provided critical support for that change in legislation. The contexts are different, of course, but questions of deportation and the moral choices that face transportation companies clearly remain. Those who remember cannot miss the connection to the Holocaust. Corporate resistance matters.

Life goes on, and new moral challenges arise. Though Harriet Tamen has expressed a desire to continue pursuing the SNCF, this train conflict seems be at the end of a cycle. The French-US settlement and the unveiling at the USHMM served as the symbolic end to the SNCF conflict (at least for now). In January 2018, SNCF America CEO Alain Leray packed up his belongings and returned with his family to France. SNCF's head of corporate social responsibility, Bernard Emsellem, moved up in the company and toward retirement. Patrizianna Sparacino-Thielly has stepped down as the French ambassador at large for human rights. Many of the lawyers who worked on this conflict, including former ambassador Stuart Eizenstat, have moved on to other projects.

Of course, survivors cannot wrap up the Holocaust with an international settlement, a check, or a museum event. But neither do they seem to have the energy for this specific fight anymore. Likely no one will speak out about SNCF chairman Guillaume Pepy's consideration of partnering with the Holocaust-complicit Siemens AG.[7] What about the continued evasion of accountability among other actors such as the French police force, which obediently served the Vichy regime, or the bus companies that carried rounded-up individuals to the internment camps?[8]

Outside France, however, one survivor seems to have the energy to carry on. Salo Muller, emboldened by his win in the Netherlands against the Dutch Railways, started talking about going after the Dutch trams that also played a role in the deportations.[9] Instead, he went bigger. In June 2020, Muller launched a complaint against Germany and the German railways, for their participation in the Holocaust. While eight thousand Germans sat in COVID quarantine with the rest of the country somewhere between partial opening and lockdown, Mueller's lawyer composed and sent a letter on Muller's behalf to German chancellor Angela Markel. Her spokesperson said it would be taken under consideration.[10]

The Deutsche Bahn (German National Railways) has engaged in a number of commemorative events and in 2017 agreed to name one of its newest high-speed trains "Anne Frank," but German train companies have other unresolved pasts. Some Herero rights advocates recently sued Orenstein & Koppel for its predecessor Arthur Koppel Company's use of slave labor to build its rail lines in Namibia (then German Southwest Africa) before and during the Herero-Nama genocide of 1904–8.[11] Bombardier, which beat the SNCF for the Maryland MARC contract in part because of its cleaner history, inherited the railway manufacturing unit of Koppel. Clean hands are hard to find.

Going further back in history than even the Herero-Nama genocide, we stumble upon other unaccounted-for railway companies. In 2002 Deadria Farmer-Paellmann launched a class action lawsuit against several US corporations, including CSX Transportation, which is composed of some predecessor railways with connections to slavery.[12]

These international and multigenerational justice claims encourage and inform one another, making them, in effect, transnational corporate accountability movements.[13] Though the SNCF's story can be told as an isolated example, it also exists within an intersecting web of associated campaigns and justice efforts. Described singularly, after the war, the company and the French government first storied the SNCF solely as a hero in the Resistance; decades passed before survivors could access the archives and prove the company's role in their suffering and/or that of their loved ones. Lawsuits, first launched in France, met a dead end when courts could not figure out how to try this public company under private law. When the Conseil d'État, France's highest administrative court, declared that it would hear no more cases related to World War II, the conflict became legally homeless. Yet, in response to public pressure, the SNCF opened its archives and partnered with Serge Klarsfeld and the Mémorial de la Shoah for commemoration, transparency, and education. Those seeking financial compensation tried lawsuits and lobbying efforts in various localities within the United States where the SNCF sought contracts. These efforts culminated in France's signing another restitution agreement.

To describe this conflict as part of a larger whole, however, we might start with the Nuremberg trials, which helped set the precedent for corporate accountability. The postwar creation of the term "genocide," the later fall of the Soviet Union, the resistance to corporate corruption more generally, along with documentaries, testimony collection, the efforts of second-generation Jews with law degrees, and other factors all contributed to the unfolding of this conflict. This conflict then influenced other movements. The SNCF conflict inspired Salo Muller to pursue the Dutch Railways. Lawsuits against the Hungarian National Railways sprang up too. While the Hungarian case was dismissed again in a US court in June 2018, it could resurface. Other industries continue to collide with their pasts as these movements gain traction. Unilever executives only recently came to see their company as having been complicit in the war.[14]

In recent years, contemporary executives of Degussa AG, complicit in the production of Zyklon B gas, were concerned about protests when bidding to provide antigraffiti paint for a Holocaust memorial.[15] Even if these sensitivities go dormant, new generations will continue to reopen old files and interpret the past in ways that help them seek answers to present-day conundrums.[16] Political shifts and new notions of justice develop and invite new conversations and contestations.

SNCF: A RELUCTANT LEADER IN CORPORATE ACCOUNTABILITY

The SNCF conflict inspired other related justice claims but also led to another surprising outcome: For all the SNCF's lobbying and legal defenses, the company now provides a model for corporate engagement with the past. There were problems, of course; the SNCF initially resisted accountability and French lawyer Corinne Hershkovitch makes a fair point when she argues that the lobbying money spent and time invested in fighting litigation could have been spent meeting with the five hundred or so survivors to whom this issue pertained.[17] I believe many survivors would have appreciated such a meeting, leading to a more restorative outcome for many.

This missed opportunity notwithstanding, the SNCF did participate in amends making through apologies, commemoration, research, historical commissions, transparency efforts, and dialogue. In November 2017, the SNCF became the first corporate sponsor of the Auschwitz Institute for Peace and Reconciliation, a nonprofit organization that educates, trains, and provides support for governments, officials, and institutions working toward genocide prevention. The institute conducts trainings at Auschwitz. Samantha Capicotto, a program director at the Auschwitz Institute for Peace and Reconciliation, said that no German corporation (except Bosch for some smaller related programs) has supported the organization.

"What really surprises me," says Capicotto, "is that even Bayer Aspirin has not helped. I mean, they *made* the gas for the gas chambers!"[18]

Of course, a donation does not equal atonement any more than donating money to a battered women's shelter makes up for beating your wife. For the SNCF, these donations became part of a larger amends-making effort. From this process, the SNCF emerged as a reluctant leader. When I asked SNCF's Bernard Emsellem whether other companies had contacted him for advice, he said only one had, and he would not share the name. This surprised me, as many companies could learn from the struggle of today's SNCF executives to address the actions (and inactions) of their predecessors. I suspect eventually others will call, perhaps after reading this book.

Ironically, the SNCF might have become a leader precisely because the company refused to pay survivors. True, the SNCF could have saved itself and many others significant grief by settling years ago, but if it had taken this route, the company's moral reckoning might have been stopped short. The extensive debates that arose out of the company's resistance to financial compensation allowed us to see what happens when a corporation engages in transparency, apology, commemoration, education, and research. Here we see the restorative potential of these transitional justice mechanisms; Holocaust-engaged groups in both countries now see the SNCF as an ally. The same certainly cannot be said for most Holocaust-complicit organizations.

There were some missed opportunities; the Maryland legislation requiring SNCF's transparency about its wartime role did little to set a standard for other corporations. Maryland legislators missed a chance to require *all* corporations applying for state contracts to speak to their human rights records. Shaming one perpetrator will do little to deter others. If the goal is truly to uphold human rights, future legislation must apply more generally. If not, others who inflicted harm will happily hide in the shadows while the SNCF takes a beating in the spotlight. Contemporary executives at Ford, IBM, Hugo Boss, Siemens, Bayer, Fanta (Coca-Cola), J. P. Morgan, and Barclays, among others, seemingly hope to bury their pasts with the dead. Some of these companies continue questionable practices. In 2019, for example, Hugo Boss received a very low rating from the Corporate Human Rights Benchmark.[19] Siemens remains implicated in China's notorious detention centers, providing security-related technology to help incarcerate up to a million Muslim Uyghurs.[20] Volkswagen, also a Nazi-complicit company, cannot seem to stay out of trouble in recent years, with its notorious emissions scandal, and is now using what looks like forced labor from the same Xinjiang detention centers for which Siemens provides security technology.[21] Human Rights Watch actively reports on these corporate activities, but unless people care about these report findings and act on their convictions, the corporations will continue on.

Lessons Regarding Corporate Complicity

Any debate about corporate accountability inevitably brings us back to Milton Friedman and his supporters who have long resisted the notion that corporations have moral obligations.[22] Under his influence, business and human rights have long operated in separate camps.[23] Whether or not you believe that companies have moral obligations, this book shows that their actions clearly have moral consequences. Corporate leaders play a crucial role in establishing the organization's role in society. They lead people toward or away from social responsibility. They welcome complex moral problems as part of the bottom line or they bury their heads in the sand, simply passing these questions down to their successors. Just as a nation's leader inherits a country's history, so too do corporate executives inherit the deeds of their predecessors. Corporate leadership means taking responsibility for a company's past as well as its present, even if national and international legal lacunae continue to protect corporations from liability.

Prosecuting corporations for mass atrocity will likely remain challenging for quite some time.[24] Michael Kelly points to Canadian law as a possible model for its ability to apply criminal jurisdiction in cases of corporate complicity in massive human rights violations.[25] Only recently have states been willing or able to hold corporations accountable for human rights violations on foreign soil.[26] The BRICS countries (Brazil, Russia, India, China, and South Africa) are especially reluctant to intervene in the affairs of other states and are less concerned with the actions of their companies abroad. To provide another pathway toward ethical action among corporations, John Ruggie, the UN special representative on business and human rights, proposed guidelines to evaluate and monitor corporate activity. The UN adopted the Guiding Principles on Business and Human Rights (UNGPs) in 2011. Since 2014, the UN Accountability and Remedy Project has tried to help victims of massive human rights violations access justice vis-à-vis corporate entities.[27] The next step will be finding ways to transform corporate cultures rather than simply having courts impose fines for participation in crimes against humanity. In corporate terms, court-imposed fines can be considered simply the "cost of doing business." If the profits of unethical corporate behavior still outweigh the costs (victims included), what guarantees that this behavior will not simply be replicated in other contexts or by the next generation of executives? Until ethical considerations become a natural expression of corporate culture, fines will do little to prevent future participation in rights violations, whether those victims are human, animal, or environmental.

Even when companies without human rights abuses in their histories come forth with goodwill campaigns, publics mistrust their motivations, and rightly so. Kentucky Fried Chicken (KFC) served chicken in pink buckets during Breast Cancer Awareness Month and made small donations to research, even though the FDA warned consumers to avoid fried foods because regular consumption of them leads to increased cancer risk.[28] How can publics trust these efforts? They are right to perceive them as insincere. The contradictions inherent in these actions suggest that the corporations want to improve their *images*, not support health or the environment.

For rights advocates (whether acting on behalf of humans, animals, or the environment), developing a long-term partnership with the corporation(s) will be crucial, whether this means challenging hypocritical campaigns or leveraging financial interests to support peacebuilding. Many corporations lose money during outbreaks of violence. Facing looting, traumatized workforces, and interrupted economies is rarely in corporations' best interest. In Sudan, for example, the oil industry has been both a cause of violence and a force to help quell violence through corporate involvement in peacemaking.[29] If corporate interests can be leveraged over the long term, human rights advocates gain powerful allies. Rights advocates would be well advised to partner with these giants, when possible.

Victim, Hero, or Perpetrator?

Partnering with corporations in peacebuilding and reconciliation requires one to assume that businesses can be more than potential adversaries. Reconciliation overall has a chance only if perpetrators can be more than their violations and engage in society in productive and restorative ways. The deeper dynamics of how we discursively frame perpetrators will affect what kind of healing can occur. How and where we locate perpetration facilitates certain responses and disregards others.[30] For example, if perpetrators are seen as psychologically ill, they may receive health services or rehabilitation. In contrast, if they are considered high functioning, then prisons may separate perpetrators from society. If mass radicalization is seen as the cause and the result of nationalism, then nationalism may be tempered. If nationalism is seen as a result of illiteracy, then education may be prioritized. How we frame problems affects the solutions we seek and the strategies we pursue.

The SNCF conflict demonstrates the public's discomfort with overlapping identities. This discomfort is shared by the retributive justice system and the media. Stigmatizing a perpetrator without offering a path to redemption hurts us all. We do a disservice to justice when we deny complexity. This book has shown how the SNCF can be storied as victim, hero, and/or perpetrator for its actions during World War II. To deny any of these identities is to deny an important dimension of history. If perpetrators cannot also be given their rightful complexity, then neither can heroes be challenged. Labels adhere in the public consciousness and can be hard to alter. Even after the public and private grappling with France's complicity in the war, in some places the country struggles to surrender the SNCF's singular heroic identity. The 2017 Cannes Film Festival, for example, screened the 1947 SNCF postwar film *La Bataille du rail*.[31] The audience erupted in applause. In spite of all the efforts to shift the national consciousness regarding this oversimplified story of the railway workers sabotaging trains carrying German armaments, the audience happily consumed the oversimplified account. Neither the event presenters nor the press acknowledged that while indeed some workers sabotaged German trains going west toward the Normandy beaches, other workers continued to drive deportees east to death camps in horrific conditions just as they had done throughout the occupation. The public, as well as the company, still seems uncomfortable with having the company occupy the position of hero and perpetrator simultaneously. Except for the survivors, I found that many involved in the conflict struggled to hold these multiple truths.

In fact, the company still emphasizes its position as wartime victim. In 2017 the SNCF published a two-thousand-page memorial report produced under the direction of the historian Thomas Fontaine that details the stories of all the SNCF workers who lost their lives during the war. The book offers an impressive collection of photos and stories in a moving acknowledgment of those who died, along with a reappraisal of corporate history. Its title, *Cheminots victims de la répression* (Railway workers victims of the repression), positions SNCF workers (and, by extension, the corporation) as *victims*.[32] Accounting for the more than two thousand victims produced an enormous book, but does this book correctly represent the company? The book covers 0.0075 percent of the 400,000 wartime workers. Is that enough to become the basis for a corporate identity? Furthermore, the SNCF itself handed over to the prefecture the names of 1,290 workers that Le Besnerais considered dangerous to the company. Many were arrested, some deported. The "repression" in the commemorative edition's title was the repression *by* the SNCF as well.

Serge Klarsfeld traced the destinies of every deportee sent from France who did not return. A page on each would create a book more than 70,000 pages. Here we see again the problems of corporate personhood. For an outsider, the SNCF's wartime identity remains ambiguous. During 2017 alone, the SNCF was vilified for its role in the Holocaust, celebrated for its role in the Resistance, and memorialized in a self-constructed depiction of its victimization. Rather than telling an integrated story each time, each story becomes a stand-alone identity. These identities do not rest comfortably alongside one another.

I have used this book to offer readers a chance to spend time with each of these overlapping identities of victim, hero, and perpetrator—to better understand the SNCF, yes, but, just as important, to understand the complex situations in which many workers found themselves. By no means does acknowledging complexity mean individual actions do not matter. It is interesting to speculate, for example, about how the SNCF might have operated differently during the war if Raoul Dautry had become its director general rather than Pierre Eugène Fournier. Recall Fournier's role as the head of SCAP, an organization tasked with Aryanizing Jewish businesses, a role that Fournier pursued with vigor. No documents show any efforts by him to push back against this process or the deportations. Dautry was a man of a different character, still celebrated today for his acts of resistance. From 1928 to 1937, Dautry served as director general of what was then the State Railways (Chemin de fer de l'État). In 1938, when the state created the SNCF, Dautry found himself relegated; he would not serve as just a member of the governing body. Before France fell to Germany, Dautry served as the French minister of armaments, working closely with the British to defeat the Germans. Ten days before France signed the armistice, which put the country in the hands of the Germans, Dautry wrote to the French Council of Ministers imploring France to fight for victory: "Everyone needs to join the fight [against the Germans] regardless of the consequences."[33] During the struggle against the German occupation, Dautry called upon his countrymen to evacuate French industrial sites and rebuild them abroad, in the United States, England, Canada, or Northern Africa, to build up the armaments necessary to fight the Germans. A man with so much resistance in his blood might not have so easily lent his railway company to the service of the Germans during the occupation. Or perhaps he would have been insubordinate and quickly executed. We will never know. Sidelined from central SNCF management during the war, Dautry spent the occupation working in the south near the Côte d'Azur. But his patriotism was not forgotten; after the war, he received the Légion d'honneur for his efforts to prevent the Germans from acquiring the ingredients needed to build an atomic bomb.[34] Today, near the former SNCF headquarters in Montparnasse, Paris commuters pass through Raoul Dautry Plaza. In contrast, Fournier's name is nowhere to be seen. In this exercise of the imagination, we see the importance of corporate leadership.

Lessons for Employees and Customers

Corporate leadership clearly has responsibility for immoral practices, but what about employees and customers; what role do (we) they play? Clearly the acts associated with these roles require mass participation. While the cheminots were certainly under constraint during the war, the eminent Holocaust historian Raul Hilberg reminds us that they were not "mindless robots."[35] They made choices, and those choices affected the lives of others. We also make choices. During the war, cheminots feared that resistance would cost them their lives. Do we not also look away even when we risk far less? We may find ourselves saying at work, "I just work here. It's what they told me to do" to justify our participation in harmful practices. Fearing only reprimand, we stay silent. To acknowledge our own complicity in various moral compromises does not exonerate the SNCF; holding the SNCF accountable helped support standards for corporate ethical responsibility. The SNCF's journey to accountability could well inspire and inform other movements trying to move corporations from culpability to redemption.

VOICES FROM THE LAST TRAINS

For the survivors still grappling with the murder of parents they hardly knew, such abstract conversations may seem superfluous or beside the point. I once asked Leo Bretholz, who as a boy escaped the Nazis seven times, including by jumping out of a train on its way toward Auschwitz, if there was some identity after "survivor." I framed my question with the explanation that survivor identities can link victims to their perpetrators in perpetuity. He scoffed and said, "You academics think too much." He may well be right.

Abstract notions of identity transformation can feel esoteric and distracting from justice pursuits, but words matter, even if they cannot heal all of the pain or stop the wheels of war. The connection of ideas to action seemed remote. That said, some survivors did acknowledge that words matter, even if they could not stop the wheels of war. Rosette Gerbosi, a Florida resident, recalled the first day that she had to wear the yellow star to school. The other children taunted her. Her teacher stood up before the whole class and said, "Enough! These children are our friends. Our world has gone mad, but we will not!"[36] Rosette's teacher could not save her from the violence and pain to come, but her words mattered. As do ours in today's world where hatred remains alive and well.

In their own ways, the people interviewed for this project continue on, trying to find out how to reconstitute missing pieces, promote healing, and prevent the next violent outbreak. The Convoy 77 commemorative meeting that I attended has resulted in a very robust website (www.convoi77.org) where visitors can see the list of all the deportees on this last train from Paris to Auschwitz and the biographies of roughly 150 of them. Georges Mayer, who, inspired by the loss of his own father, launched the website, engages high school students in the task of completing the biography database.[37] The next generation, now the fourth since the war, has become involved.

I keep in touch with many of the survivors, watch their Facebook activism, and visit them when I am in town. I sent wedding photos to Daniel, Samuel, Pierre, Renée, and Lou and checked on them during the COVID confinement. From time to time, I hear that a survivor friend who helped inform this book has died. Occasionally messages from their children or grandchildren appear in my inbox giving me this news, in one case leading me to inherit roughly one hundred books about the Holocaust. What to do with all these stories?

Even as survivors pass away, there are still discoveries to be had and connections to be made. Through the assistance of Betsy Anthony of the United

States Holocaust Memorial Museum, I discovered the existence of two of my great-uncles murdered at Auschwitz. She also helped me learn more about Sarah Federman, whose name on the Holocaust memorial in Paris was a key moment for this book and for my life. Together, we discovered that Sarah was the sister of the renowned author Raymond Federman, who survived because his mother pushed him into a hallway closet as the French police marched up the stairs. Sarah, his sister Jacqueline, and their parents were taken that day. Raymond's book *Shhh*, named for the last word his mother said to him, recounts his memories from that day and those that followed. While Raymond had already died when I discovered this information, his books told me a bit about Sarah. He wrote that throughout his life he expected to walk around a corner and run into his sisters. I feel that the day I saw Sarah's name in stone, I had done just that.

Luckily his daughter, Simone, is still alive and well. When I first reached out to her, she told me that she was accustomed to being asked by strangers if she was "Raymond's daughter"—her father having been so well known—but she had never been asked if she was "Sarah's niece." We set a date to meet. When the time came, I expressed my surprise at being picked up in a BMW. "It was my father's car," she explained. "He always bought German cars." We laughed at the

Raymond, Jacqueline, and Sarah Federman, circa 1938. Only Raymond survived. (Courtesy of Simone Federman)

irony. Then she drove us to her Harlem apartment. She showed me her father's memorabilia and allowed me to flip through his address book, filled with contact information for Michel Foucault, Samuel Beckett, Roland Barthes, Jacques Derrida, Robert Cover, and Kathy Acker, among others. All she had of Sarah was one photograph, a yellowed, frayed image that Raymond had found in his apartment when he returned home after months in hiding. No family and no furniture remained, only a small shoebox with memories of happier times.

Appendix

Legal and Legislative Tables

Year	Instrument	Description
1940	Convention d'armistice, Fr.-Ger., June 22, 1940, United States, Department of State, Publication No. 6312, Documents on German Foreign Policy 1918–1945	The French and Germans sign the Armistice of June 1940. The French surrender.
1946	Agreement Respecting Distribution of German Reparation, Establishment of Inter-Allied Reparation Agency and Restitution of Monetary Gold, January 14, 1946 61 Stat. 3157, 444 U.N.T.S. 69	One of the earliest agreements that requires Germany to repair the damage done in World War II.
1947	Treaty of Peace, US-Hung., art. 27, February 10, 1947, T.I.A.S. No. 1651	Hungary signs an agreement with the Allies in which Hungary agrees to provide compensation to Hungarian Holocaust victims. This agreement prevents US courts from hearing Hungarian cases related to he Holocaust.
1956	Bundesgesetz zur Entschädigung für Opfer der Nationalsozialistischen Verfolgung (Bundesentschädigungsgesetz), v. 29.6.1956, BGBI. I 1953, p. 559	West Germany starts taking responsibility for individuals harmed by the Nazis through this fund, known as the Federal Compensation Law of 1956.

Year	Instrument	Description
1998	UN Doc. A/CONF. 183/9; 37 ILM 1002 (1998); 2187 UNTS 90 (Rome Statute).	The United Nations General Assembly produces the Rome Statute of the International Criminal Court (ICC), which establishes the court.
1998	In re Holocaust Victim Assets Litigation, 105 F. Supp. 2d 139 (E.D.N.Y. 2000)	Known as the "Swiss bank cases," the suits are consolidated in a New York court under Judge Korman. In 1998 a $1.25 billion settlement is reached outside court.
2000	United States Germany Agreement Concerning the Foundation "Remembrance, Responsibility and the Future," July 17, 2000, US-Ger., 39I.L.M. 1298 (2000)	Germany creates the Foundation "Remembrance, Responsibility, and the Future" to compensate victims of slave and forced labor. The agreement is negotiated between a US government interagency team and German companies. The same team negotiates with Austrian companies to develop a similar agreement.
2000	The [German] Law on the Creation of a Foundation "Remembrance, Responsibility and Future." Federal Law Gazette I 1263. August 12, 2000 (amended September 1, 2008, becoming: Federal Law Gazette I 1797)	Law to compensate survivors of forced labor as well as others who have suffered under National Socialism. The fund, paid for with German industry and government funds, promises to support related research, education, and social justice projects.
2001	"French Banks Settlement" 37665, 2156 UNTS 281, 320	French banks create a $50 million fund to compensate victims for assets taken during the Vichy regime and withheld since. France's Mattéoli Commission facilitates the creation of the fund.
2014	Agreement between the Government of the United States of America and the Government of the French Republic on Compensation for Certain Victims of Holocaust-Related Deportation from France Who Are Not Covered by French Programs, US-Fr., Dec. 8, 2014, T.I.A.S. No. 15–1101	French–US settlement in which the French government allots $60 million to cover survivors not covered by other compensation programs.

NATIONAL AND STATE STATUTES AND BILLS

Memory Laws in France

Year	Memory Law	Description
1990	Loi 90-615 du 13 juillet 1990 tendant à réprimer tout acte raciste, antisémite ou xénophobe [Law 90-615 of July 13, 1990 for the Suppression of Racist, Antisemitic, or Xenophobic Acts], Journal Officiel de la République Française [J.O.] [Official Gazette of France], July 13, 1990, p. 8333	Known colloquially as the Loi Gayssot, the law forbids Holocaust denial in France.
1999	Loi 99-882 du 18 octobre 1999 relative à la substitution à l'expression "aux opérations effectuées en Afrique du Nord" de l'expression "à la guerre d'Algérie ou aux combats en Tunisie et au Maroc" [Law 99-882 of October 18, 1999 on the substitution for the expression "operations carried out in North Africa" by the expression "Algerian war and fighting in Tunisia and Morocco], Journal Officiel de la République Française [J.O.] [Official Gazette of France], October 20, 1999, p. 15647	This law acknowledges the Algerian conflict as a war.
2000	French Parliament declared July 16 a day of commemoration	The day honors Jewish persons persecuted during the occupation and the "Justes" who tried to save them.
2001	Loi 2001-434 du 21 mai 2001 tendant à la reconnaissance de la traite et de l'esclavage en tant que crime contre l'humanité [Law 2001-434 of May 21, 2001, for the recognition of trafficking and slavery as a crime against humanity], Journal Officiel de la République Française [J.O.] [Official Gazette of France], May 21, 2001, p. 8175	This act recognizes the Atlantic slave trade.

Year	Memory Law	Description
2001	Loi 2001-70 du 29 janvier 2001 relative à la reconnaissance du génocide arménien de 1915 [Law 2001-70 of January 29, 2001 concerning the recognition of the Armenian genocide of 1915], Journal Officiel de la République Française [J.O.] [Official Gazette of France], January 29, 2001, p. 1590	This law acknowledges the Armenian genocide.
2005	Loi n 2005-158 du 23 février 2005 portant reconnaissance de la Nation et contribution nationale en faveur des Français rapatriés [Law 2005-158 of February 23, 2005 for the recognition of the nation and national contribution in favor of repatriated French], Journal Officiel de la République Française [J.O.] [Official Gazette of France], February 23, 2005, p. 3128	This law requires that the contributions of colonization also be mentioned.

Legal Cases in Israel

Year	Legal Case	Description
1962	*Attorney General of Israel v. Eichmann*, 36 I.L.R. 277 (1962)	This lawsuit leads to the trial of Adolf Eichmann. Eichmann is condemned and executed on May 31, 1962.

Legal Cases in France

Year	Legal Case	Description
1946	CE [Conseil d'État] 14 juin 1946, Ganascia	The Conseil d'État (the high court) rules that individuals cannot request compensation from the French state for acts conducted by the Vichy government.

Year	Legal Case	Description
1988	Cour de cassation [Cass.] [supreme court for judicial matters] crim., June 3, 1988, Bull. crim., No. 87-84240	Klaus Barbie is convicted of crimes against humanity.
1993	Cour de cassation [Cass.] [supreme court for judicial matters] crim., January 6, 1993, Bull. Crim., No. 394 (Fr.)	Paul Touvier is convicted of crimes against humanity for torture, the deportation of members of the Resistance, and the murder of seven Jews in Rillieux, France, on June 28–29, 1944.
1998	*Fraenkel v. SNCF.* Claim submitted by Jean-Jacques Fraenkel to the Tribunal de grande instance Paris against the SNCF for crimes against humanity	Fraenkel's September 1998 complaint to the Tribunal de grande instance Paris accuses the SNCF of crimes against humanity. Judge Valat dismisses the claim for insufficient evidence.
2001	*Lipietz v. SNCF and France.* Claim submittted by Georges Lipietz against the SNCF and France for compensation for his arrest, transfer to, and internment at Drancy	Lipietz submits his claim on September 6, 2001. In October, both the French state and the SNCF reject the claim.
2001	Appeal by Lipietz to the Toulouse Administrative Court	Appeal is submitted on October 22, 2001.
2003	*Kurt Werner Schaechter v. SNCF.* Tribunal de grande instance [TGI] [ordinary court of original jurisdiction], Paris, May 14, 2003, 2001/07912	Schaechter sues for a symbolic euro on behalf of his parents, who were deported and murdered. His father was murdered at Sobibór and his mother at Auschwitz. Court rejects the case for time bar (statute of limitations).
2004	*Kurt Werner Schaechter v. SNCF* cont. Cour d'appel [CA] [regional court of appeal], Paris, 1e ch., June 8, 2004, 2003/12747	The case fails in the Paris Court of Appeals, which confirms the rejection by the Tribunal de grande instance (TGI). Court agrees that the suit comes too long after the events in question.

Year	Legal Case	Description
2006	*Lipietz v. SNCF and France* cont. Tribunal administratif [TA] [Administrative Court], Toulouse, June 6, 2006, 0101248	The Administrative Court of Toulouse finds the French state and the SNCF liable for their role in the deportations of Jews during World War II. Court fines the SNCF and French state €61,000.
2007	*Lipietz v. SNCF and France* cont. CAA (Cour administrative d'appel) de Bordeaux, form. plén., March 27, 2007, 06BX01570	After the Administrative Court rules in the favor of Lipietz, SNCF appeals the Toulouse decision in the Bordeaux administrative appeals court.
2007	*Lipietz v. SNCF and France* cont. CE [Conseil d'État], December 21, 2007, 305966, Rec Lebon	Lipietz appeals the Bordeaux decision. The SNCF wins the appeal.
2009	Hoffman-Glemane case CE [Conseil d'État], Ass., February 16, 2009, 315499, Rec Lebon	Hoffman-Glemane decision, in which the Conseil d'État (the high court) rules that no more cases related to compensation claims for World War II damages will be heard.

Legal Cases in the United States

Year	Legal Case	Description
1998	Related US class action lawsuit against German companies for slave and forced labor (circa 1998): In re *Nazi Era Cases Against German Defendants Litig.*, 198 F.R.D. 429 (D.N.J. 2000); *Frumkin v. JA Jones, Inc.* (In re *Nazi Era Cases Against German Defendants Litig.*), 129 F. Supp. 2d 370 (D.N.J. March 1, 2001)	Results in a settlement in July 2000 that creates a German foundation to compensate victims of slave and forced labor during the Nazi regime.
1999	*Iwanowa v. Ford Motor Co.*, 67 F. Supp. 2d 424 (D.N.Y. 1999)	Lawsuits against Ford Werke A.G. for forced labor performed between 1941 and 1945.

Year	Legal Case	Description
2000	*Bodner v. Banque Paribas*, 114 F. Supp. 2d 117 (E.D.N.Y. 2000)	Class action lawsuit against Banque Paribas (a French bank) for the unlawful seizure and withholding of assets for more than fifty years. Litigants try to use the Alien Tort Claims Act.
2000–2001	Austrian and German Bank Holocaust Litigation, 80 F. Supp. 2d 164, 180 (S.D.N.Y. 2000) Austrian and German Bank Holocaust Litigation, No. 98 CIV 3938 SWK, 2001 WL 228107 (S.D.N.Y. March 8, 2001)	US–based class action lawsuits against German and Austrian banks for ill-gotten gains. Results in a settlement.
2001	*Abrams v. Société Nationale des Chemins de Fer Français*, 175 F. Supp. 2d 423 (E.D.N.Y. 2001)	Twelve victims launch a class action lawsuit from the United States claiming that the SNCF violated international customary law and the law of nations when it participated in the deportations. The District Court for the Eastern District of New York dismisses the complaint, saying that the SNCF has immunity because of the Foreign Sovereign Immunities Act (FSIA) of 1976, which prevents suits against sovereign nations.
2002	In re African-American Slave Descendants Litigation, 231 F Supp 2d 1357 (E.D.N.Y. 2002)	Deadria Farmer-Paellmann, acting on behalf of herself and others, brings a class action lawsuit against Fleet Boston Financial Corporation, Aetna, and CSX for conspiring with slave traders and for profiting from slave labor in the United States. (CSX is a successor-in-interest to numerous predecessor railroad lines that were constructed or run, at least in part, by slave labor.)
2003	*Abrams v. Société Nationale des Chemins de Fer Français*, 332 F.3d 173 (2d Cir. 2003)	The court reopens the *Abrams* case and sends it back to a lower court for reconsideration.

Year	Legal Case	Description
2004	*Abrams v. Société Nationale des Chemins de Fer Français*, 389 F.3d 61 (2d Cir. 2004)	Court affirms the dismissal, again citing lack of subject matter jurisdiction. Litigants appeal to US Supreme Court, without success.
2004	*Republic of Austria v. Altmann*, 541 U.S. 677, 124 S. Ct. 2240, 159 L. Ed. 2d 1 (2004)	The US Supreme Court rules that the Foreign Sovereign Immunities Act (FSIA) applies retroactively. The SNCF uses this ruling to protect itself in the United States.
2008	*Freund v. Republic of France*, 592 F. Supp. 2d 540 (S.D.N.Y. 2008)	Survivors, heirs, and beneficiaries seek restitution for property stolen by SNCF workers and asks the District Court for the Southern District of New York for an exception to the FSIA. They are denied. The court rules that it is unable to hear confiscation claims against France, its rail service, and a certain French bank because it lacks subject matter jurisdiction due to provisions of the FSIA.
2010	*Freund v. Société Nationale des Chemins de Fer Français*, No. 09-0318-cv (2d Cir. September 7, 2010)	District court decision affirmed. Case could not be heard because of lack of subject matter jurisdiction. The plaintiffs fail to prove that the SNCF had possession of the stolen goods.
2011	*Freund v. Société Nationale des Chemins de Fer Français*, 132 S. Ct. 96. No. 10-1314 (October 3, 2011)	US Supreme Court denies petition for writ of certiorari to the United States Court of Appeals in the Second Circuit.
2013	*Kiobel v. Royal Dutch Petroleum Co.*, 133 S. Ct. 1659, 569 U.S. 108, 185 L. Ed. 2d 671 (2013)	US Supreme Court finds that the Alien Tort Claims Act presumptively does not apply extraterritorially.
2018	*Scalin v. Société Nationale des Chemins de Fer Français*, no. 15-cv-03362, March 26, 2018	Claimants seek damages for international law violation, conversion, and unjust enrichment. This focus on theft attempts to circumvent the FSIA, which blocked the other class action suits. The judge dismisses the case.

Hungarian Railways Cases in the United States

Year	Legislation	Description
2002	*Rosner v. US*, 231 F. Supp. 2d 1202 (S.D. Fla. 2002)	Hungarian Jews file a class action lawsuit against the US government to recover property seized by the US Army. Plaintiffs claim that in 1954, the US Army took possession of what became known as the "Hungarian Gold Train," filled with stolen Jewish possessions. The court determines that even though the statute of limitations under 28 U.S.C.S. § 2401(a) is only six years, equitable tolling is warranted and therefore the Hungarian Jews' action was timely filed. The case is settled out of court in 2005 for $2.5 million (see Tiefer et al. 2012).
2012	*Abelesz v. Magyar Nemzeti Bank*, 692 F.3d 661 (7th Cir. 2012)	In a suit first launched in 2010, survivors and their descendants sue the Hungarian National Railways and some Hungarian banks for their participation in the Holocaust (participation in genocide, unjust enrichment, and other offenses). The US Court of Appeals for the Seventh Circuit rules it can hear the case if the plaintiffs can prove they have exhausted possible remedies through Hungarian courts.
2015	*Fischer v. Magyar Allamvasutak Zrt.*, 777 F.3d 847 (7th Cir. 2015)	Lawsuit launched by Hungarian victims of the Holocaust and their descendants against the Hungarian National Railways, the National Bank, and several private banks for their participation in the Holocaust. They seek $1.25 billion from the railways. Plaintiffs are told to take their case back to Hungarian courts.

Year	Legislation	Description
2016	*Simon v. Republic of Hungary*, 812 F.3d 127 (D.C. Cir. 2016)	Court rules again that Hungarian litigants must exhaust remedies in Hungary before US courts can hear the case.
2018	*Fischer v. Magyar Allamvasutak Zrt.*, No. 17-3487 (7th Cir. June 13, 2018)	In a continuation of the Hungarian railways case, the court dismisses the appeal, saying that it lacks jurisdiction.

US LEGISLATION RELATED TO THE SNCF CONFLICT

Year	Legislation	Description
Ratified 1791	US Const. Amend. I	First Amendment to the US Constitution, which protects free speech and thereby prevents the construction of memory laws in the United States.
1789	Alien Tort Statute (28 U.S.C. § 1350; ATS)	Known also as the Alien Tort Claims Act (ATCA), which some human rights lawyers have used to try to hold corporations liable for crimes against humanity that occurred abroad. The US Supreme Court ruling in *Kiobel* makes this more difficult.
1976	Foreign Sovereign Immunities Act, Pub. L. No. 94-583, H.R. 11315, 94th Cong. (1976)	The FSIA prevents individuals from suing another country.
2009–10	A.B. 619, 2009–2010 Reg. Sess. (Cal. 2010)	Introduced February 25, 2009, this bill would require any entity applying for a contract related to high-speed train networks to certify whether it had any direct involvement in the deportation of any individuals to extermination camps, work camps, concentration camps, prisoner of war camps, or any similar camps during World War II. The bill is not passed.

Year	Legislation	Description
2010	Holocaust Accountability Corporate Responsibility Act of 2010, H.R. 6347, 111th Cong	Bill requires entities bidding for US federal contracts to disclose whether they owned or operated trains on which deportees traveled to extermination camps, death camps, or any facility used to transit individuals to extermination or death camps between January 1, 1942, and December 31, 1944. The bill is not passed.
2009–10	H.R. 4237, 111th Cong. (2009–2010)	New York Representative Carolyn Maloney introduces an act to allow US courts to hear any lawsuits brought against the railroad. The bill is not passed.
2011	H.B. 520, 428th Gen. Assem., Reg. Sess. (Md. 2011)	Maryland bill to prohibit entities that had direct involvement in the World War II deportations from being considered a responsible bidder or offeror for specified contracts to provide Maryland Area Regional Commuter (MARC) service unless the entities comply with specified requirements. The bill is approved.
2013–14	Holocaust Rail Justice Act, S.1393, 113th Cong. (2013–2014)	This bill proposed that US courts provide an impartial forum for claims brought by US citizens and noncitizens against any railroad organized as a separate legal entity concerning the deportation of individuals to Nazi concentration camps. The bill is not passed.
2014	New York City, New York. Proposed resolution pertaining to the Holocaust	New York City Councilmembers Kallos, Maloney, and Levine introduce a resolution asking the state legislature to support legislation to bar contracts with companies that profited from the Holocaust. No legislation is drafted.

Year	Legislation	Description
2014	Public-Private Partnerships—Disclosure of Involvement in Deportations, H.B. 1326, Maryland State House, Committee of Ways and Means and Environmental Matters (Annapolis, MD, March 10, 2014) (H.B. 1326, 431th Gen. Assem., reg. sess. (Md. 2014))	A bill is proposed in the Maryland House of Delegates to prohibit a private entity with direct involvement in the deportation of people to death or extermination camps from 1939 to 1945 from qualifying as a bidder on a public–private partnership with the state unless the entity makes specified certifications. The bill is not passed.

Notes

1. Richard Breitman, Norman J. W. Goda, Timothy Naftali, and Robert Wolfe, *U.S. Intelligence and the Nazis* (Cambridge: Cambridge University Press, 2005).

2. The United States Holocaust Memorial Museum eventually helped me identify Aaron Shlomo and his wife, Chawa, both gassed at Auschwitz in 1944.

3. In 2018 Poland's role in the war became of renewed international interest when the government approved a new memory law, passed a day before International Holocaust Remembrance Day, that permitted the country to imprison anyone who attributed the crimes committed at death camps like Treblinka to Poland, rather than Germany.

4. Serge Klarsfeld, *French Children of the Holocaust: A Memorial* (New York: New York University Press, 1996), 385. This boxcar, traveling first from Pithiviers to Drancy before heading to Auschwitz, carried many siblings as well as seven adults. The train carried roughly three hundred children. Yad Vashem lists about four hundred children. The exact numbers remain contested.

5. Maia de La Baume, "France: National Railway Apologizes for Its Role in Deporting Jews in War," *New York Times*, November 12, 2010.

6. M. Wolf, telephone conversation with author, May 27, 2014.

7. For a discussion of the narrative structures of testimony in a transitional justice setting, see Ronald Niezen, "Templates and Exclusions: Victim Centrism in Canada's Truth and Reconciliation Commission on Indian Residential Schools," *Journal of the Royal Anthropological Institute* 22, no. 4 (2016): 920–38.

8. Jean-Marc Dreyfus, *L'Impossible Réparation: Déportés, bien spoliés, or Nazi, comptes bloqués, criminels de guerre* (Paris: Flammarion, 2015), 244.

9. Raymond Federman, *Shhh: The Story of a Childhood* (Buffalo, NY: Starcherone Books, 2010).

10. Raymond, their brother, escaped persecution thanks to a last-minute decision by their mother to shove him into a small closet during the roundups. Raymond recounts some of his wartime experiences and writes of the forty-two parallel tracks in Federman, *Shhh: The Story of a Childhood*.

Introduction

1. Chris Isidore, "Krispy Kreme Owners Admit to Family History of Nazi Ties," *CNN*, March 25, 2019.

2. Kate Taylor, "The Secretive German Family behind the Company That Owns Panera Bread, Krispy Kreme, and Pret a Manger Is Donating More Than $11 Million after the Discovery of Its Nazi Past," *Business Insider*, March 25, 2019.

3. Jack Ewing, "German Automotive Giant Admits It Was a Nazi Accomplice," *New York Times*, August 27, 2020; Paul Erker, *Zulieferer für Hitlers Krieg: Der Continental-Konzern in der NS-Zeit* (Berlin: De Gruyter Oldenbourg, 2020).

4. Palko Karasz, "Dutch Railway Will Pay Millions to Holocaust Survivors," *New York Times*, June 27, 2019.

5. Choe Sang-Hun and Rick Gladstone, "How a World War II–Era Reparations Case Is Roiling Asia," *New York Times*, October 30, 2018.

6. Benjamin Haas, "Opinion: European Companies Get Rich in China's 'Open Air Prison,'" *New York Times*, August 21, 2019.

7. Simon Marks, "Belgian Exporters Found Guilty of Sending Chemicals to Syria," *Politico*, February 7, 2019, https://www.politico.eu/article/belgian-exporters-found -guilty-of-sending-chemicals-to-syria/.

8. Jan Hoffman, "Johnson & Johnson Ordered to Pay $572 Million in Landmark Opioid Trial," *New York Times*, August 26, 2019.

9. Raul Hilberg, "German Railroads/Jewish Souls," *Society* 14, no. 1 (1976): 62.

10. Serge Klarsfeld's *La Shoah en France, le calendrier des déportations (septembre 1942– août 1944), Tome 1, Tome 2, Tome 3, Tome 4* (2001) gives the number as 75,721. In recent years, that estimate has shifted.

11. Estimates of those returning have increased in recent years. For some time, 2,500 was the accepted estimate; at the time of the writing of this book, 3,500 is a number also used by some scholars.

12. Jean-Marc Dreyfus, *L'Impossible Réparation: Déportés, bien spoliés, or Nazi, comptes bloqués, criminels de guerre* (Paris: Flammarion, 2015), 9.

13. A full listing of the legislation and legal cases can be found in the appendix.

14. SNCF, *Profile and Key Figures*, pamphlet (Paris: SNCF, 2013).

15. *Abrams v. Société Nationale des Chemins de Fer Français*, 175 F. Supp. 2d 423 (E.D.N.Y. 2001).

16. Robert Gildea, *Marianne in Chains: Daily Life in the Heart of France during the German Occupation* (New York: Picador, 2002).

17. P. Blum, personal communication, Paris, August 12, 2014. All translations are mine unless otherwise noted.

18. Ruti G. Teitel, "Transitional Justice Genealogy," *Harvard Human Rights Journal* 16 (Spring 2003): 69–94.

19. Miriam J. Aukerman, "Extraordinary Evil, Ordinary Crime: A Framework for Understanding Transitional Justice," *Harvard Human Rights Journal* 15, no. 39 (2002): 39–97.

20. Susan Ariel Aaronson and Ian Higham, "'Re-Righting Business': John Ruggie and the Struggle to Develop International Human Rights Standards for Transnational Firms," *Human Rights Quarterly* 35, no. 2 (2013): 334.

21. Leora Bilsky, *The Holocaust, Corporations, and the Law: Unfinished Business* (Ann Arbor: University of Michigan Press, 2017).

22. US Department of State, "Agreement between the Government of the United States of America and the Government of the French Republic on Compensation for Certain Victims of Holocaust-Related Deportation from France Who Are not Covered by French Programs," December 8, 2014, *Treaties and Other International Acts Series,* no. 15-1101, https://www.state.gov/wp-content/uploads/2019/04/us_france_agreement .pdf.

23. For more on the Klaus Barbie extradition demand, expulsion, and trial, see Paul Gauthier, *Chronique du procès Barbie: Pour servir la mémoire* (Paris: Cerf, 1988); Christian Delage, "The Klaus Barbie Trial: Traces and Temporalities," in "Trials of Trauma," ed. Michael G. Levine and Bella Brodzki, special issue, *Comparative Literature Studies* 48, no. 3 (2011): 320–33; and Leon Boutbien, "Klaus Barbie," *Revue des Deux Mondes* (May 1983): 325–28. For more information on their Nazi pursuits, see Beate Klarsfeld and Serge Klarsfeld, *Mémoires* (Paris: Fayard/Flammarion, 2015).

24. Marie-Noëlle Polino, ed., *Une Entreprise publique dans la guerre, la SNCF 1939–1945* (Paris: Presses Universitaires de France, 2001).

25. S. Klarsfeld, personal communication, Paris, January 8, 2011; S. Klarsfeld, telephone conversation with author, April 27, 2011.

26. C. Hershkovitch, telephone conversation with author, July 28, 2020.

27. The agreement states that the US government "shall secure . . . the termination of any pending suits or future suits that may be filed in any court at any level of the United States legal system against France concerning any Holocaust deportation claim." US Department of State, "Agreement between the Government of the United States of America and the Government of the French Republic," art. 5 (2).

28. For debates surrounding the payments of lawyers for Nazi-era claims, see Libby Adler and Peer Zumbansen, "The Forgetfulness of Noblesse: A Critique of the German Foundation Law Compensating Slave and Forced Laborers of the Third Reich," *Harvard Journal on Legislation* 39, no. 1 (Winter 2002): 56–57.

29. See United Kingdom Secretary of State for Foreign Affairs to Parliament, "Agreement between the Government of the United Kingdom of Great Britain and Northern Ireland and the Government of the French Republic relating to Compensation for Disablement or Death due to War Injury Suffered by Civilians," January 23, 1950, *Treaty Series,* no. 2, Paris, France (1951).

30. D. Davidson, personal communication, Washington, DC, May 27, 2014.

31. US Department of State, "Agreement between the Government of the United States of America and the Government of the French Republic."

32. The French government agreed to this retroactive clause only after much debate; France rarely uses retroactivity in such claims.

33. A. Lipietz, personal communication, Paris, June 19, 2015.

34. S. Kalmanovitz, telephone conversation and email message to author, June 16, 2017.

35. United States Holocaust Memorial Museum, "Who Is a Survivor?," USHMM, accessed December 1, 2020, https://www.ushmm.org/remember/holocaust-survivors.

36. Shannon Fogg, *Stealing Home: Looting, Restitution, and Reconstructing Jewish Lives in France, 1942–1947* (Oxford: Oxford University Press, 2017); Claire Andrieu,

ed., *La Persécution des Juifs de France 1940–1944 et le rétablissement de la légalité républicaine: Recueil des textes officiels 1940–1999* (Paris: La Documentation française, 2000). Fogg observes the distinction in France between *restitution*, which provides compensation without the admission of moral wrongdoing, and *reparation*, which includes an admission of responsibility.

37. See Henry Rousso, "La Question du jour: Condamner la SNCF," *Le Monde*, June 3, 2006; Annette Wieviorka, "La SNCF, la Shoah et le juge," *L'Histoire* 316 (2007): 89–99; Alain Lipietz, *La SNCF et la Shoah: Le procès G. Lipietz contre État et SNCF* (Paris: Les Petits Matins, 2011); Georges Ribeill, "Dossier SNCF et déportations," *Historail* 4 (January 2008): 34–87; Jean-Pierre Richardot, *SNCF: Héros et salauds pendant l'occupation* (Paris: Broché, 2012); Arno Klarsfeld, "La SNCF et les trains de la mort, par Arno Klarsfeld," *Le Monde*, June 3, 2006; Arno Klarsfeld, "Facture de l'agence de voyage allemand au service des affaires juives de la Gestapo à Paris" (provided by Serge Klarsfeld, Paris, France, January 2011).

38. Michael J. Kelly and Luis Moreno-Ocampo, *Prosecuting Corporations for Genocide* (New York: Oxford University Press, 2016), address the legal lacunae. Sabine Michalowski produced the anthology *Corporate Accountability in the Context of Transitional Justice* (New York: Routledge, 2013) to address what she identities as the nearly "non-existent" literature addressing the link between transitional justice and corporate accountability.

39. See Mark Osiel, *Mass Atrocity, Collective Memory, and the Law* (New Brunswick, NJ: Transaction, 1999); Dustin Sharp, "Addressing Economic Violence in Times of Transition: Towards a Positive-Peace Paradigm for Transitional Justice," *Fordham International Law Journal* 35, no. 3 (2012): 780–814.

40. Dreyfus, *L'Impossible Réparation*, 244.

41. Annette Wieviorka, *The Era of the Witness* (Ithaca, NY: Cornell University Press, 1998).

42. See Paul Jaskot, "A Plan, a Testimony, and a Digital Map: Architecture and the Spaces of the Holocaust" (lecture, Grinnell College, Grinnell, IA, April 19, 2017). Jaskot's research on Auschwitz demonstrated that, while survivor testimony was far more disjointed and fragmented than the neatly laid Nazi architectural plans available in archives, digital maps showed that the testimonies proved *more* accurate about the actual layout of the camp.

43. Saul Friedlander, *Nazi Germany and the Jews: 1933–1945* (New York: Harper Perennial, 2009).

44. See Deborah Dwork and Robert Jan van Pelt, *Holocaust: A History* (New York: W. W. Norton, 2002); Fogg, *Stealing Home*; Renee Poznanski, *Jews in France during World War II*, trans. Nathan Bracher (Hanover, NH: Brandeis University Press and the University Press of New England, 2001).

45. Marc Howard Ross, *Cultural Contestation in Ethnic Conflict* (Cambridge: Cambridge University Press, 2007), 24.

46. Cited in Simone Gigliotti, *The Train Journey: Transit, Captivity, and Witnessing in the Holocaust* (New York: Berghahn Books, 2009).

47. Bilsky, *The Holocaust, Corporations, and the Law*.

48. I have conformed to the following guidelines of confidentiality: When quoting or referring to people in an official capacity, I use their names. Only when someone

requested anonymity did I change his or her name or remove it from mention in the book.

49. See Ronald Barthes, "An Introduction to the Structural Analysis of Narrative," *New Literary Theory* 6, no. 2 (1975): 237–72; Michael Bamberg, "Positioning with Dave Hogan: Stories, Tellings, and Identities," in *Narrative Analysis*, ed. Colette Daiute and Cynthia G. Lightfoot (London: SAGE, 2004), 135–57; Sara Cobb, "Narrative Braiding and the Role of Public Officials in Transforming the Publics Conflicts," *Narrative and Conflict: Explorations in Theory and Practice* 1, no. 1 (2013): 4–30.

50. Series AJ 419, 474, and 498 in the National Archives, Paris, France.

51. Convoy 77 departed July 31, 1944, and Convoy 78 departed August 11, 1944. An additional convoy departed August 17, 1944, from Drancy headed to Buchenwald concentration camp. At Buchenwald, next to Auschwitz, all prisoners engaged in forced labor. Though the camp did not have gas chambers, most prisoners died from the harsh conditions and many were executed.

52. Similarly, the Dutch train drivers did not conduct the trains all the way to Auschwitz. The Germans directed them to stop the trains a long way before reaching the camp. See David Barnouw, Dirk Mulder, and Guus Veenendaal, *De Nederlandse Spoorwegen in oorlogstijd 1939–1945* (Zwolle, Netherlands: W Books, 2019).

53. Jeffrey C. Alexander, *The Civil Sphere* (New York: Oxford University Press, 2006); Diane Enns, *The Violence of Victimhood* (University Park: Pennsylvania State University Press, 2012); Kieran McEvoy and Kirsten McConnachie, "Victimology in Transitional Justice: Victimhood, Innocence and Hierarchy," *European Journal of Criminology* 9, no. 5 (2012): 527–38.

54. Primo Levi, *The Drowned and the Saved* (New York: Simon and Schuster, 2017).

55. P. Feingold, personal communication, June 10, 2014.

56. A. Zdroui, personal communication, August 4, 2014.

57. Democracy Now!, "ExxonMobil's Dirty Secrets from Indonesia to Nigeria to D.C.: Steve Coll on 'Private Empire,'" YouTube, May 7, 2012, https://www.youtube.com/watch?v=TREblxdbJ1k.

58. Michalowski, *Corporate Accountability*; Ruben Carranza, "Plunder and Pain: Should Transitional Justice Engage with Corruption and Economic Crimes?," *International Journal of Transitional Justice* 2, no. 3 (2008): 310–30; Louise Arbour, "Economic and Social Justice for Societies in Transition," *New York University Journal of International Law and Politics* 40, no. 1 (2007): 1–27; Ismael Muvingi, "Sitting on Powder Kegs: Socioeconomic Rights in Transitional Societies," *International Journal of Transitional Justice* 3, no. 2 (2009): 163–82; Hugo Van der Merwe and Audrey R. Chapman, *Assessing the Impact of Transitional Justice: Challenges for Empirical Research* (Washington, DC: United States Institute of Peace, 2008); Sharp, "Addressing Economic Violence; Nelson Camillo Sanchéz, "Corporate Accountability, Reparations, and Distributive Justice," in *Corporate Accountability in the Context of Transitional Justice*, ed. Sabine Michalowski (New York: Routledge, 2013), 114–30. See also Zinaida Miller, "Effects of Invisibility: In Search of the 'Economic' in Transition Justice," *International Journal of Transitional Justice* 2, no. 3 (2008): 266–91; Rosemary L. Nagy, "The Scope and Bounds of Transitional Justice and the Canadian Truth and Reconciliation Commission," *International Journal of Transitional Justice* 7, no. 1 (2012): 52–73; Elizabeth F. Drexler, "Fatal Knowledge: The Social and Political Legacies of Collaboration and Betrayal in

Timor-Leste," *International Journal of Transitional Justice* 7, no. 1 (January 2013): 74–94; Lauren Marie Balasco, "The Transitions of Transitional Justice: Mapping the Waves from Promise to Practice," *Journal of Human Rights* 12, no. 2 (2013): 198–216; Kora Andrieu, "Dealing with a 'New' Grievance: Should Anticorruption Be Part of the Transitional Justice Agenda?," *Journal of Human Rights* 11, no. 4 (2012): 537–57; and Tricia D. Olsen, Andrew G. Reiter, and Eric Wiebelhaus-Brahm, "Taking Stock: Transitional Justice and Market Effects in Latin America," *Journal of Human Rights* 10, no. 4 (2011): 521–43.

59. Benjamin B. Ferencz and Telford Taylor, *Less than Slaves: Jewish Forced Labor and the Quest for Compensation* (Bloomington: Indiana University Press, 2002). These included the German bankers Walter Funk and Hjalmar Schacht; the antisemitic newspaper (*Der Stürmer*) founder and publisher Julius Streicher, and Alfried Krupp, whose father was too ill to stand trial. See Leigh A. Payne, Gabriel Pereira, and Laura Bernal-Bermudez, *Transitional Justice and Corporate Accountability from Below: Deploying Archimedes' Lever* (Cambridge: Cambridge University Press, 2020).

60. See Juan Pablo Bohoslavsky and Veerle Opgenhaffen, "The Past and Present of Corporate Complicity: Financing the Argentinean Dictatorship," *Harvard Human Rights Journal* 23, no. 1 (Spring 2010): 157–204. See also David Fraser, "(De)constructing the Nazi State: Criminal Organizations and the Constitutional Theory of the International Military Tribunal," *Loyola Los Angeles International and Comparative Law Journal* 39, no. 1 (Winter 2017): 117–86; and Doreen Lustig, "The Nature of the Nazi State and the Question of International Criminal Responsibility of Corporate Officials at Nuremberg: Revisiting Franz Neumann's Concept of Behemoth at the Industrialist Trials," *New York University Journal of International Law and Politics* 43 (2011): 965–1044. Fraser and Lustig debate the extent to which these trials truly held industrialists accountable.

61. Fraser, "(De)constructing the Nazi State."

62. See John Dewey, "The Historic Background of Corporate Legal Personality," *Yale Law Journal* 35, no. 6 (1926): 655–73; Sir John William Salmond and Patrick John Fitzgerald, *Salmond on Jurisprudence* (London: Sweet and Maxwell, 1966); and William S. Laufer, "Corporate Bodies and Guilty Minds." *Emory Law Journal* 43 (1994): 647–730. See also Payne et al., *Transitional Justice*. Payne also points to the lack of enforcement and lack of international pressure.

63. The International Commission of Jurists, launched in 1952, uses the rule of law to advance human rights matters globally.

64. In the absence of international law, they relied upon the norms of *jus cogens* to uphold these standards.

65. Bohoslavsky and Opgenhaffen, "The Past and Present of Corporate Complicity."

66. Payne et al., *Transitional Justice*.

67. See Payne et al., *Transitional Justice*; Bohoslavsky and Opgenhaffen, "The Past and Present of Corporate Complicity"; Michalowski, *Corporate Accountability*; and Michael J. Bazyler, *Holocaust Justice: The Battle for Restitution in America's Courts* (New York: New York University Press, 2005).

68. Wim Huisman and Elies van Sliedregt, "Rogue Traders: Dutch Businessmen, International Crimes and Corporate Complicity," *Journal of International Criminal Justice* 8, no. 3 (2010): 803–28.

69. Sarah Federman, "Genocide Studies and Corporate Social Responsibility: The Contemporary Case of the French National Railways (SNCF)," *Genocide Studies and Prevention: An International Journal* 11, no. 2 (2016): 13–35.

70. Bilsky, *The Holocaust, Corporations, and the Law*, 16. For more on legal challenges to holding corporations accountable for human rights violations, see Kelly and Moreno-Ocampo, *Prosecuting Corporations for Genocide*.

71. Payne et al., *Transitional Justice*.

72. Aaronson and Higham, "'Re-Righting Business,'" 333–64; Jacques Adler, *The Jews of Paris and the Final Solution: Communal Responses and Internal Conflicts, 1940–44* (New York: Oxford University Press, 1987).

73. Harvard Law Review Association, "Developments in the Law-Corporate Liability for Violations of International Human Rights Law," *Harvard Law Review* 114, no. 7 (2001): 2026.

74. Peter Hayes, *Industry and Ideology: I. G. Farben in the Nazi Era* (New York: Cambridge University Press, 2000); Ferencz and Taylor, *Less than Slaves*; Francis R. Nicosia and Jonathan Huener, eds., *Business and Industry in Nazi Germany* (New York: Berghahn Books, 2015); Edwin Black, *IBM and the Holocaust: The Strategic Alliance between Nazi Germany and America's Most Powerful Corporation* (New York: Crown, 2001).

75. Northrop Frye, *The Anatomy of Criticism* (London: Penguin Books, 1957).

76. Howard Zinn, *You Can't Be Neutral on a Moving Train: A Personal History of Our Times* (Boston: Beacon, 2002).

77. L. Vermont, personal communication, November 6, 2014.

78. See Richard J. Golsan, *The Vichy Past in France Today: Corruptions of Memory* (London: Lexington Books, 2016).

79. Michael R. Marrus, "The Case of the French Railways and the Deportation of Jews in 1944," in *Holocaust and Justice: Representation and Historiography of the Holocaust in Post-War Trials*, ed. David Bankier and Dan Michman (New York: Berghahn Books, 2010), 263.

80. Hannah Arendt, *Eichmann in Jerusalem: A Report on the Banality of Evil* (New York: Penguin Books, 2006). See *Attorney General of Israel v. Eichmann*, 36 I.L.R. 277 (1962).

81. Richard Wilson, *Writing History in International Criminal Trials* (New York: Cambridge University Press, 2011), 7.

82. Ronald Niezen, *Truth and Indignation: Canada's Truth and Reconciliation Commission on Indian Residential Schools*, 2nd ed. (Toronto: University of Toronto Press, 2017), 130.

83. C. Hershkovitch, telephone conversation with author, July 28, 2020.

84. Enns, *The Violence of Victimhood*, 15.

85. Klarsfeld, *La Shoah en France*. Klarsfeld estimated that there were 1,300 individuals on the convoy. Yad Vashem estimates that the maximum number of individuals was 1,321.

86. To see list of deportees on Convoy 77, the convoy's itinerary, and those responsible for organizing the convoy, see Yad Vashem, "Convoi 77 de Drancy, Camp, France à Auschwitz Birkenau, Camp d'extermination, Pologne le 31/07/1944," Yad Vashem: The World Holocaust Remembrance Center, http://db.yadvashem.org/deportation/

transportDetails.html?language=fr&itemId=5092649. To see biographies of the individuals deported on Convoy 77, see "The Convoi 77 Project: Teaching the History of the Shoah in a Different Way," Convoi 77, https://convoi77.org/en/.

87. He made this point on several occasions to me and to school groups, most recently in December 2016 at the Drancy memorial. I add this note because some may be in disbelief that survivors have such views. I heard many comments like this, especially in France, when I asked about the SNCF's needs to make amends. Many US-based survivors also absolved the company, but for different reasons.

88. The pass, issued by the Minister of Combatants, was given not long after the war and provided him with a 75 percent reduction on SNCF regional tickets and free use of the metro. The pass has an expiration date of 2022.

Chapter 1. The German Occupation

1. Nils Christie, "The Ideal Victim," in *From Crime Policy to Victim Policy*, ed. Ezzat A. Fattah (London: Macmillan, 1986), 17–30.

2. Kieran McEvoy and Kirsten McConnachie, "Victimology in Transitional Justice: Victimhood, Innocence and Hierarchy," *European Journal of Criminology* 9, no. 5 (2012): 527–38.

3. Diane Enns, *The Violence of Victimhood* (University Park: Pennsylvania State University Press, 2012). See also Hannah Arendt, *Eichmann in Jerusalem: A Report on the Banality of Evil* (New York: Penguin Books, 2006); and Laurel E. Fletcher, "Refracted Justice: The Imagined Victim and the International Criminal Court," in *Contested Justice: The Politics and Practice of International Criminal Court Interventions*, ed. Christian De Vos, Sara Kendell, and Carsten Stahn (Cambridge: Cambridge University Press, 2015). Arendt expressed concern about the pure innocence appropriated to victims and sought to create hierarchies of purity within this group. McEvoy and Fletcher echo Arendt's concern.

4. Nicolas Sohr, "SNCF Execs Pressed for Answers," *Daily Record*, March 3, 2011.

5. See Erica Bouris, *Complex Political Victims* (Bloomfield, CT: Kumarian, 2007); Enns, *The Violence of Victimhood*; Alyson Manda Cole, *The Cult of True Victimhood: From the War on Welfare to the War on Terror* (Stanford: Stanford University Press, 2007); Mark A. Drumbl, *Atrocity, Punishment, and International Law* (New York: Cambridge University Press, 2007); and Kieran McEvoy, "Beyond Legalism: Towards a Thicker Understanding of Transitional Justice," *Journal of Law and Society* 34, no. 4 (2007): 411–40.

6. Vichy France would arrest Blum in 1940, convicting him just over a year later. He was sent to the Buchenwald concentration camp in 1943. He survived and played a major role in postwar France governance.

7. Michel Margairaz, "Companies under Public Control in France 1900–50," in *Governance and Labour Markets in Britain and France*, ed. Noel Whiteside and Robert Salais (London: Routledge, 1998), 25–51.

8. B. Emsellem, email message to author, March 9, 2015.

9. Peter Muchlinski, *Multinational Enterprises and the Law* (Oxford: Oxford University Press, 2007).

10. Ludivine Broch, *Ordinary Workers, Vichy and the Holocaust: French Railwaymen and the Second World War* (Cambridge: Cambridge University Press, 2016).

11. Two days after Germany's invasion of Poland, on September 1, 1939, France and Britain declared war on Germany. The term "the Phony War" became attached to the period immediately after the declaration of war, beginning in September 1939 and running through May 1940. No fighting broke out between France and Germany during this time. The actual fighting between France and Germany occurred in May and June of 1940—resulting in France's very embarrassing six-week defeat.

12. Joseph Jones, *Politics of Transport in Twentieth-Century France* (Montreal: McGill-Queen's University Press, 1984).

13. Raymond Federman, *Shhh: The Story of a Childhood* (New York: Starcherone Books. 2010), 149.

14. Federman, *Shhh: The Story of a Childhood*, 149.

15. Federman, *Shhh: The Story of a Childhood*, 149.

16. Broch, *Ordinary Workers*, 41–49.

17. Compiègne was already symbolic as the site of Joan of Arc's capture and handover to the British. After the war, the town would also be remembered as a significant deportation site.

18. Convention d'armistice, Fr.-Ger., June 22, 1940, Documents on Germany Foreign Policy 1918–1945, Publication No. 6312, US Department of State. Translation provided by the Yale Law School Lillian Goldman Law Library's Avalon Project: Documents in Law, History and Diplomacy, http://avalon.law.yale.edu/wwii/frgearm.asp#art13. The full text of Article 13 reads: "The French Government obligates itself to turn over to German troops in the occupied region all facilities and properties of the French armed forces in undamaged condition. It [the French Government] also will see to it that harbors, industrial facilities, and docks are preserved in their present condition and damaged in no way. The same stipulations apply to transportation routes and equipment, especially railways, roads, and canals, and to the whole communications network and equipment, waterways and coastal transportation services. Additionally, the French Government is required on demand of the German High Command to perform all necessary restoration labor on these facilities. The French Government will see to it that in the occupied region necessary technical personnel and rolling stock of the railways and other transportation equipment, to a degree normal in peacetime, be retained in service." Note that the Germans outlined similar obligations in the Netherlands involving the Dutch Railway. See David Barnouw, Dirk Mulder, and Guus Veenendaal, *De Nederlandse Spoorwegen in oorlogstijd 1939–1945: Rijden voor Vaderland en Vijand* (Zwolle, Netherlands: W Books, 2019).

19. Paul Durand, *La SNCF pendant la guerre* (Paris: Presses Universitaires de France, 1968), 117.

20. SNCF archives at the Mémorial de la Shoah in File XLVIII.3.8: section 0375 LM0009/001, letter dated July 3, 1940, provided by Eric Freedman.

21. Jones, *Politics of Transport*.

22. Jones, *Politics of Transport*.

23. Marie-Noëlle Polino, ed., *Une Entreprise publique dans la guerre, la SNCF 1939–1945* (Paris: Presses Universitaires de France, 2001), 79.

24. Jones, *Politics of Transport*.

25. Margairaz, "Companies under Public Control in France 1900–50."

26. Broch, *Ordinary Workers*.

27. Christian Bachelier, *La SNCF sous l'occupation allemand 1940–1944* (Paris: AHICF, 1996).

28. Broch, *Ordinary Workers*.

29. "Monsieur de Directeur Général with M. le Président Münzer à la HVD, le 29-12-42," January 3, 1943, Box 72, AJ 474, National Archives, Paris, France. Some of the French archival sources from the wartime period do not contain names and/or legible signatures. Titles with no corresponding names in the text mean that only titles were used or visible.

30. See Roman Köster and Julia Schnaus, "Sewing for Hitler? The Clothing Industry during the 'Third Reich,'" *Business History* 62, no. 3 (2018): 1–13.

31. Broch, *Ordinary Workers*, 143.

32. In December 1942, the SNCF calculated that the cumulative amount owed for the transport of German soldiers totaled 19.6 million francs but that it had received only 10 million francs. "Prestations Fournies Par la SNCF Seulement au titre des transports militaires allemands en zone occupée," April 1, 1943, SNCF archives, Le Mans, France.

33. For example, an SNCF document discusses a July 11, 1942, demand from the German HVD for 150 new SNCF locomotives. Even though a German railway chief named Arend had pushed back in an earlier document, the SNCF insists that it receive the sums listed in the document. (While this demand came five days prior to the Vel d'Hiv roundup, one cannot be sure the locomotives would have been used for the deportation.) "Note: sur la demande de 150 locomotives faite par la H.V.D. à la SNCF le 11 Juillet 1942," SNCF archives, Le Mans, France; author can provide other related documents upon request.

34. "Facturation des transports de l'Armée allemande—PARIS le—Adressée à Le Director Général," SNCF Service Commercial, written by three SNCF officials (Boyaux, Fournier, Besnerais), November 8, 1940, National Archives, Paris, France.

35. Wendt, "Délègue du Ministre Des Communications du Reich to Monsieur Ministre et Secretaire d'Etat à la Production Industrielle & aux Communications," March 15, 1943, Box 72, AJ 419, National Archives, Paris, France.

36. Catherine Bernstein, director, *La SNCF sous l'occupation* (Paris: Zadig Productions, 2019).

37. See Wendt, "Délègue du Ministre Des Communications du Reich to Monsieur Ministre et Secretaire d'Etat à la Production Industrielle & aux Communications"; Patrice Arnaud, *Les STO: Histoire des Français requis en Allemagne nazie, 1942–1945* (Paris: CNRS Èditions, 2010). Wendt estimated eighteen thousand, and Arnaud estimated closer to twenty-four thousand.

38. A different letter attributed this "explosion" to an act of sabotage.

39. Ambassador of France in the occupied zone to German General Feldmarschall von Rundstedt, April 4, 1944, Box 72, AJ 419, National Archives, Paris, France.

40. Ambassador of France in the occupied zone to German General Feldmarschall von Rundstedt.

41. Commission consultative des dommages et reparations, 1947, Monographie TC 1, chemins de fer d'intérêt général, data compiled by Georges Ribeill (courtesy Georges Ribeill). And of SNCF's 130 large locomotive depots established before the war, 74 had been destroyed by the war's end.

42. France's Jewish population at the beginning of the war was estimated at 330,000, two-thirds of whom lived in Paris. See Shannon Fogg, *Stealing Home: Looting, Restitution, and Reconstructing Jewish Lives in France, 1942–1947* (Oxford: Oxford University Press, 2017), 33.

43. Even before the Germans arrived, France had operated internment camps for refugees from the Spanish Civil War and also for "political enemies" from Germany, Austria, and Italy. The Jews would eventually be placed in many of these camps. As Germany expanded into Eastern Europe, thousands fled to France, including approximately thirty-five thousand refugees from Czechoslovakia and other "enemies of the Reich." See Doris Bensimon, *Les Grandes Rafles: Juifs en France 1940–1944* (Toulouse: Privat, 1987).

44. Michael R. Marrus and Robert O. Paxton, *Vichy France and the Jews* (New York: Basic Books, 1981).

45. See Bensimon, *Les Grandes Rafles*, 56; and Claire Zalc, *Dénaturalisés: Les retraits de nationalité sous Vichy* (Paris: Éditions du Seuil, 2016).

46. Only when Germany took control of the entire country did those in the former unoccupied zone have to wear the star. See Serge Klarsfeld, *L'Etoile des Juifs: Témoignages et documents* (Paris: L'Archipel, 1992).

47. Eric Freedman found these documents in the SNCF archives at the Mémorial de la Shoah in Paris in File XLVIII.3.8: section 0375LM0009/001.

48. Eric Freedman, email message to Harriet Tamen and Richard Weisberg, April 25, 2012, provided to author by Freedman on August 10, 2014.

49. Bernstein, *La SNCF sous l'occupation*.

50. This figure varies. See Georges Ribeill, "Dossier SNCF et déportations," *Historail* 4 (January 2008): 34–87. After the war, Ribeill found evidence of 141 Jewish personnel.

51. Broch, *Ordinary Workers*, 171.

52. Lemme was eventually released and recommenced work on August 29, 1944.

53. Broch, *Ordinary Workers*.

54. Broch, *Ordinary Workers*.

55. Nathalie Bibas, *Henri Lang 1895–1942: Un dirigeant de la SNCF mort à Auschwitz* (Paris: Editions LBM, 2012).

56. Broch, *Ordinary Workers*; Bernstein, *La SNCF sous l'occupation*.

57. Bibas, *Henri Lang*.

58. Polino, *Une Entreprise publique dans la guerre*, 141.

59. In France, Roma (known as *tsiganes* or *nomades*) were held in internment camps during the war, though some cases of deportation to other camps existed. For example, on January 13, 1943, seventy Roma were taken from the Poitiers internment camp and sent to a work camp, known as Oraniengurg-Sachsenhausen, located thirty kilometers from Berlin. Almost all seventy died in the camp. A convoy that left Compiègne for Buchenwald in June 1943 is also believed to have carried a number of Roma. Emmanuel Filhol and Marie-Christine Hubert, *Les tsiganes en France: Un sort à part (1939–1946)* (Paris: Perrin, 2009), 268–74.

60. Ludivine Broch, "Professionalism in the Final Solution: French Railway Workers and the Jewish Deportations, 1942–4," *Contemporary European History* 23, no. 3 (2014): 371.

61. Of these, 50,000 would come from the occupied zone and 50,000 from the unoccupied zone; 22,000 of those in the occupied zone would come from Paris. As of October 1940, an estimated 150,000 Jews lived in Paris, 86,000 of whom were French nationals and 64,000 were recent foreign immigrants. France had a total population of roughly thirty-eight million between 1939 and 1945. For more on the number of Jews in France during the war, see Renee Poznanski, *Jews in France during World War II*, translated by Nathan Bracher (Hanover, NH: Brandeis University Press and the University Press of New England, 2001), 1.

62. Heinz Röthke, German lawyer and SS member, also worked with Dannecker to secure the destruction of Jews in France.

63. Marrus and Paxton, *Vichy France and the Jews*.

64. While the foreign-born Jews most often found themselves on the deportation trains ordered by the Germans, the first transports included dozens of prominent French Jews, known as *de vieille souche*, referring to the old roots of France.

65. While some French-born Jews were deported, the vast majority were foreign-born Jews.

66. Raul Hilberg, *The Destruction of the European Jews* (Chicago: Quadrangle Books, 1961).

67. Marrus and Paxton, *Vichy France and the Jews*, 246.

68. Ribeill, "Dossier SNCF et déportations."

69. Claude Lévy and Paul Tillard, *La Grande Rafle du Vel d'Hiv: 16 juillet 1942* (Paris: R. Laffont, 1992), 103–5.

70. Marrus and Paxton, *Vichy France and the Jews*, 267–68.

71. Hilberg, *The Destruction of the European Jews* (1961); Poznanski, *Jews in France during World War II*, 256.

72. See Serge Klarsfeld's estimate cited by Marrus and Paxton, *Vichy France and the Jews*, 263.

73. Marrus and Paxton claimed there were 11,000 children. The most current figure is 11,400. See Marrus and Paxton, *Vichy France and the Jews*; Serge Klarsfeld and Beate Klarsfeld, *Le Mémorial de la déportation des Juifs d France* (Paris: Association des fils et filles des déportés juifs de France (FFDJF), 2012).

74. I have also seen estimates, based on the work of Serge Klarsfeld, that there were 430 individuals on this train.

CHAPTER 2. THE DEPORTATIONS

1. Holocaust Rail Justice Act, S. 1393, 113th Cong., 1st sess. (July 30, 2013), https:// www.govinfo.gov/content/pkg/BILLS-113s1393is/pdf/BILLS-113s1393is.pdf. New York Representative Carolyn B. Maloney (D-NY) proposed the same act to the US House of Representatives on April 11, 2013. The bill "grants U.S. district courts jurisdiction over any civil action for damages for personal injury or death that: (1) arose from the deportation of persons to Nazi concentration camps between January 1, 1942, and December 31, 1944, and (2) is brought by or on behalf of such person against a railroad that owned or operated the trains on which the persons were deported and that was organized as a separate legal entity. Declares that: (1) no law limiting the jurisdiction of the U.S. courts shall preclude any such action, and (2) no such action shall be barred because a statute of limitations has expired. Makes this Act applicable to any action

pending on or commenced after January 1, 2002. Directs the Secretary of State to report to Congress on the status of access to wartime records and archives concerning the wartime activities of any such railroad that engaged in the deportation of such persons to Nazi concentration camps." Holocaust Rail Justice Act, H.R. 1505, 113th Cong., 1st sess. (April 11, 2013), https://www.congress.gov/bill/113th-congress/house-bill/1505/text?r=5&s=1.

2. Foreign Sovereign Immunities Act, Pub. L. No. 94-583, H.R. 11315, 94th Cong. (October 21, 1976), https://www.govinfo.gov/content/pkg/STATUTE-90/pdf/STATUTE-90-Pg2891.pdf.

3. Holocaust Rail Justice Act, S. 1393.

4. Georges Ribeill, "Dossier SNCF et déportations," *Historail* 4 (January 2008): 34–87; Michel Margairaz, "Companies under Public Control in France 1900–50," in *Governance and Labour Markets in Britain and France*, ed. Noel Whiteside and Robert Salais (London: Routledge, 1998), 25–51.

5. Annette Wieviorka, "La SNCF, la Shoah et le juge," *L'Histoire* 316 (2007): 89–99.

6. See Jacqueline Duhem, "Compe-rendu de lecture: 'Dossier SNCF et Déportations,'" *Historail* 4 (January 2008): 2–5; Ribeill, "Dossier SNCF et déportations"; Wieviorka, "La SNCF, la Shoah et le juge."

7. M. N. Polino, email message to author, November 7, 2017.

8. Ludivine Broch, *Ordinary Workers, Vichy and the Holocaust: French Railwaymen and the Second World War* (Cambridge: Cambridge University Press, 2016), 49.

9. Broch, *Ordinary Workers*, 72.

10. Broch, *Ordinary Workers*, 38. Broch states that there were six thousand soldiers overseeing the SNCF workers. Bernstein's documentary estimated that there were ten thousand. Catherine Bernstein, director, *La SNCF sous l'occupation* (Paris: Zadig Productions, 2019).

11. See Alfred Gottwaldt, "Les Cheminots allemands pendant l'occupation en France de 1940 à 1944," in *Une Entreprise publique dans la guerre, la SNCF, 1939–1945*, ed. Marie Noëlle Polino (Paris: Presses Universitaires de France, 2001), 175–94. Gottwaldt also estimated that Germany initially sent 6,500 monitors to oversee the SNCF.

12. Michael R. Marrus and Robert O. Paxton, *Vichy France and the Jews* (New York: Basic Books, 1981), xvi.

13. "Voix cheminotes: Une Histoire orale des années 1930 à 1950 [Voices of French Railway Workers: An Oral History, 1930–1950]," produced by Rails et histoire (French Railway History Association) Exposition, Archives nationales, site de Pierrefitte, April 8–July 4, 2015.

14. Broch, *Ordinary Workers*, 78.

15. Ribeill, "Dossier SNCF et déportations," 45. Note that while today Novéant is about 100 kilometers from the German border, at this time Alsace and Moselle had been annexed by the Reich. Ribeill found the evidence for action in the Bachelier report.

16. Broch, *Ordinary Workers*, 189.

17. Marrus and Paxton, *Vichy France and the Jews*; Raul Hilberg, *The Destruction of the European Jews*, 3rd ed., 3 vols. (New Haven, CT: Yale University Press, 2003).

18. Marrus and Paxton, *Vichy France and the Jews*; Hilberg, *The Destruction of the European Jews* (2003); Broch, *Ordinary Workers*. The historians Marrus and Paxton, Hilberg, and Broch agree that the number marked for deportation by Berlin dropped by about half; Hilberg states that a June 23, 1942, order confirmed that forty thousand would be taken from France, with thirty-five thousand coming from Paris, one thousand from Rouen, one thousand from Nancy, one thousand from Dijon, and two thousand from Bordeaux.

19. SS Franz Novak directly supported Eichmann as his timetable expert coordinating with the seventy-six SNCF deportation trains from France. See Christopher Browning, *The Origins of the Final Solution: The Evolution of Nazi Jewish Policy, September 1939–March 1942*, with contributions by Jürgen Matthäus (Lincoln: University of Nebraska Press, 2004); and Raul Hilberg, "German Railroads / Jewish Souls," *Society* 14, no. 1 (1976): 60–74.

20. Some of the trains were referred to in correspondence as "*transports de l'espèce*" (species transports), reflecting, perhaps, the dehumanization process. See Kurt Werner Schaechter, "Letter sent to the Procurer of the French Republic in Paris," September 9, 1999, Kurt Werner Schaechter Collection: 1933–2006, Hoover Institution Archives, Stanford, CA.

21. Schaechter, "Letter sent to the Procurer of the French Republic in Paris."

22. Christian Bachelier, *La SNCF sous l'occupation allemand 1940–1944* (Paris: AHICF, 1996).

23. Bernstein, *La SNCF sous l'occupation*.

24. Yad Vashem, "Convoi 77 de Drancy, Camp, France à Auschwitz Birkenau, Camp d'extermination, Pologne le 31/07/1944," Yad Vashem: The World Holocaust Remembrance Center, http://db.yadvashem.org/deportation/transportDetails.html?language=fr&itemId=5092649.

25. R. Esrail, email message to author, March 21, 2014. A few deportation trains from other locations may also have been third-class passenger cars.

26. Wieviorka, "La SNCF, la Shoah et le juge."

27. Herscu's description was on display at the temporary commemorative site at Bobigny (still under construction as of 2020).

28. Simone Veil, *Une Vie* (Paris: Éditions Stock, 2007), 50: "Des autobus nous ont conduits à la gare de Bobigny, ou l'on nous a fait monter dans des wagons à bestiaux formant un convoi aussitôt parti vers l'Est."

29. Wieviorka, "La SNCF, la Shoah et le juge," *L'Histoire* 316 (2007): 89–99.

30. Kurt Werner Schaechter Collection: 1933–2006, Hoover Institution Archives, Stanford, CA.

31. Wieviorka, "La SNCF, la Shoah et le juge."

32. Schaechter Collection: 1933–2006.

33. Schaechter Collection: 1933–2006.

34. Broch, *Ordinary Workers*, 190.

35. Schaechter Collection: 1933–2006.

36. Marie-Noëlle Polino, ed., *Une Entreprise publique dans la guerre, la SNCF 1939–1945* (Paris: Presses Universitaires de France, 2001), 200.

37. Ribeill, "Dossier SNCF et déportations."

38. Raphaël Delpard, *Les Convois de la honte: Enquête sur la SNCF et la déportation (1941–1945)* (Neuilly-sur-Seine: Lafon, 2005).

39. Quoted in Richard Lerchbaum and Olivier Nahum, "La SNCF ne souciait pas de ce qu'elle transportait," *Actualité juive,* July 1, 1999.

40. Leo Bretholz and Michael Olesker, *Leap into Darkness: Seven Years on the Run in Wartime Europe* (New York: Anchor, 1999), 163.

41. S. Kalmanovitz, telephone conversation with author, June 17, 2017.

42. E. Freedman, personal communication, Paris, August 10, 2014.

43. Broch, *Ordinary Workers,* 18.

44. Broch, *Ordinary Workers.*

45. The organization started again as a union after the war. For more information about the current organization, see Confédération Générale du Travail (CGT), "Construisons ensemble le Jour d'après! Signer la petition," https://www.cgt.fr/actualites/europe/mobilisation/plus-jamais-ca-construisons-ensemble-le-jour-dapres.

46. Broch, *Ordinary Workers.*

47. Bernstein, *La SNCF sous l'occupation.*

48. Survivor, telephone conversation with author, 2014.

49. Sometimes these drivers were German, Polish, or from other nations but not, as far as we know, French.

50. Theodor Dannecker, "Directive to the Commander of the Security and Secret Police in the Militarbahahlahaber's sector in France," June 26, 1942, Document RF 1221, SNCF archives, Le Mans, France; Bernstein, *La SNCF sous l'occupation.* In a directive sent to the secret police in France in June 1942, Theodor Dannecker demands that "special freight cars" be used for the transports but does not specify whether they should be French or German. Bernstein claims that the minister of the interior demanded that merchandise cars be used because they were easier to guard.

51. Arno Klarsfeld, "La SNCF et les trains de la mort, par Arno Klarsfeld," *Le Monde,* June 3, 2006 (emphasis mine).

52. Ribeill, "Dossier SNCF et déportations."

53. Merlin served as the sous-chef de gare de 1e classe à Compiègne.

54. Raoul Merlin, "Chef de Gare Principal Honoraire COMPIEGNE to Monsieur L'Ingénieur en Chef. Compiègne," March 28, 1966, Box 72, AJ 498, National Archives, Paris, France.

55. Marrus and Paxton, *Vichy France and the Jews,* 259.

56. Quoted in Ribeill, "Dossier SNCF et déportations," 37.

57. Holocaust Rail Justice Act, S. 1393.

58. Ribeill, "Dossier SNCF et déportations," 39. Of the 2,521 who made the voyage, 984, or nearly 40 percent, died during the trip. Germans seem to have removed these bodies.

59. Dannecker, "Directive to the Commander of the Security and Secret Police in the Militarbahahlahaber's sector in France."

60. Ludivine Broch, "Professionalism in the Final Solution: French Railway Workers and the Jewish Deportations, 1942–4," *Contemporary European History* 23, no. 3 (2014): 372.

61. Bernstein, *La SNCF sous l'occupation.*

62. Bretholz and Olesker, *Leap into Darkness,* 152.

63. Broch, *Ordinary Workers*, 193.

64. Robert Paxton, Stanley Hoffman, and Claude Bertrand, *La France de Vichy* (Paris: Points Histoire, 1999), 180.

65. Holocaust Rail Justice Act, S. 1393.

66. Jonathan A. Bush, "The Prehistory of Corporations and Conspiracy in International Criminal Law: What Nuremberg Really Said," *Columbia Law Review* 109, no. 5 (2009): 1094–1262.

67. Roman Köster and Julia Schnaus, "Sewing for Hitler? The Clothing Industry during the 'Third Reich,'" *Business History* 62, no. 3 (2018): 1–13.

68. Harm Ede Botje and Mischa Cohen, "Hoe Salo Muller de NS alsnog de rekening van de oorlog presenteerde," *Vrij Nederland*, May 4, 2019.

69. See David Barnouw, Dirk Mulder, and Guus Veenendaal, *De Nederlandse Spoorwegen in oorlogstijd 1939–1945: Rijden voor Vaderland en Vijand* (Zwolle, Netherlands: W Books, 2019); and Daniel Boffey, "Dutch Rail to Pay Compensation for Transporting Jews to Nazi Death Camps," *Guardian*, November 28, 2018.

70. Hilberg, "German Railroads / Jewish Souls," 66.

71. Raul Hilberg, *The Destruction of the European Jews* (Chicago: Quadrangle Books, 1961), 298. Hilberg writes, "The Reich Security Main Office [RSHA] paid for costs of the deportations. . . . However, the RSHA did not actually furnish the funds from its own money, either. Instead the Gestapo used its very close association with the Jewish community machinery to confiscate the money which the Reichsvereinigung had collected from the Jews in the forms of special taxes."

72. Hilberg, *The Destruction of the European Jews* (1961).

73. Ribeill, "Dossier SNCF et déportations," 37.

74. Hilberg, "German Railroads / Jewish Souls," 66; Hilberg, *The Destruction of the European Jews* (1961).

75. Bachelier, *La SNCF sous l'occupation allemand*.

76. Schaechter Collection: 1933–2006.

77. Schaechter Collection: 1933–2006. This likely referred to transports to and from the internment camp at Recebedou, located near Toulouse. A number of deportees housed here eventually went on to Drancy and then Auschwitz.

78. Schaechter Collection: 1933–2006.

79. The document can be found in the departmental archives of the Loiret.

80. This invoice is dated February 10, 1944. Whether invoices were issued during the German defeat (after D-Day) is not known.

81. Today, even in the United States, railroads calculate the cost per seat, per mile. In Europe, they use per seat, per kilometer. In the past, railway companies would determine ticket prices on the basis of the cost per passenger, per mile. Around 2000, Amtrak and the SNCF started to use yield management systems similar to what is used to determine airline prices. They now set prices in accordance with availability (demand) and other factors such as proximity to date of travel. The per-head-per-kilometer metric is no longer used.

82. Bachelier, *La SNCF sous l'occupation allemand*.

83. M. N. Polino, personal communication, Paris, May 3, 2011.

84. B. Emsellem, personal communication, Paris, March 24, 2011.

85. Thomas J. Laub, *After the Fall: German Policy in Occupied France, 1940–1944* (New York: Oxford University Press, 2010).

86. Laurent Joly, *L'Antisémitisme de bureau* (Paris: Grasset, 2011). SCAP, created in December 1940, existed through June 1941, when it was reunited with the Commissariat Général aux Questions Juives (CGQJ, Commissariat-General for Jewish Affairs). In June 1942, the organization shifted again and was called La Direction de l'Aryanisation Économique.

87. It was not unusual for technocrats to serve in various capacities for the government in addition to holding their primary positions.

88. Joly, *L'Antisémitisme de bureau*; Philippe Verheyde, *Les Mauvais Comptes de Vichy: L'aryanisation des entreprises juives* (Paris: Perrin, 1999).

89. M. N. Polino, personal communication, Paris, May 3, 2011.

90. Joly, *L'Antisémitisme de bureau*.

91. See Jean-Pierre Richardot, *SNCF: Héros et salauds pendant l'occupation* (Paris: Broché, 2012) 76.

92. See Joly, *L'Antisémitisme de bureau*, 39, 169. Joly cites J. Billig, *Le Commissariat général aux questions juives*.

93. Joly, *L'Antisémitisme de bureau*.

94. Laub, *After the Fall*.

95. Verheyde, *Les Mauvais Comptes de Vichy*.

96. Jacques Adler, *The Jews of Paris and the Final Solution: Communal Responses and Internal Conflicts, 1940–44* (New York: Oxford University Press, 1987).

97. Eric Freedman, personal communication, Paris, August 10, 2014. Eric Federman, who works on French restitution issues in Paris, said most Aryanization went unreported. This means some of those collecting the money likely held it, yet there is no evidence to suggest that Fournier stole assets.

98. Richardot, *SNCF: Héros et salauds*.

99. Fournier's tenure as France's chief railway executive ended in 1946, possibly for political reasons (he faced charges relating to the storage of gold in 1939 and 1940, during his term as governor of the Bank of France).

100. Alfred C. Mierzejewski, *The Most Valuable Asset of the Reich: A History of the German National Railway, 1933–1945*, 2nd vol. (Chapel Hill: University of North Carolina Press, 2000), xiv.

101. See Broch, *Ordinary Worker*; Mierzejewski, *The Most Valuable Asset of the Reich*.

102. L. Helwaser, personal communication, Paris, July 25, 2014.

103. For more information on this transport, see Yad Vashem, "Convoi 42 de Drancy, Camp, France à Auschwitz Birkenau, Camp d'extermination, Pologne le 06/11/1942," Yad Vashem: The World Holocaust Remembrance Center, https://deportation.yadvashem.org/index.html?language=en&itemId=5092615.

104. Frederick N. Rasmussen, "Leo Bretholz Dies at 93; Holocaust Survivor Fought for Reparations," *Los Angeles Times*, March 12, 2014.

Chapter 3. The Resistance

1. Thomas Fontaine, *Cheminots victims de la répression: 1940–1945 Mémorial* (Paris: Perrin, 2017).

2. Raul Hilberg, "German Railroads/Jewish Souls," *Society* 14, no. 1 (1976): 72.

3. Leo Bretholz and Michael Olesker, *Leap into Darkness: Seven Years on the Run in Wartime Europe* (New York: Anchor, 1999).

4. S. Levi, personal communication, Paris, July 24, 2014.

5. Shannon Fogg, *Stealing Home: Looting, Restitution, and Reconstructing Jewish Lives in France, 1942–1947* (Oxford: Oxford University Press, 2017).

6. Jim Vulpes, *La Guerre du rail* (Paris: Éditions Rouff, 1948), 16.

7. Vulpes, *La Guerre du rail*, 24.

8. Michael R. Marrus and Robert O. Paxton, *Vichy France and the Jews* (New York: Basic Books, 1981).

9. Catherine Bernstein, director, *La SNCF sous l'occupation* (Paris: Zadig Productions, 2019). The battle for the liberation of Paris lasted from August 19 to August 25, 1944.

10. Marrus and Paxton, *Vichy France and the Jews*.

11. A. Leray, personal communication, Maryland, March 18, 2014.

12. Christian Bachelier, *La SNCF sous l'occupation allemand 1940–1944* (Paris: AHICF, 1996). The SNCF archives reveal an important distinction between acts of resistance that took place before the Battle of Stalingrad and those that took place after it. While some Resistance scholars refer to either the invasion of the Soviet Union or the implementation of the Service du Travail Obligatoire (STO, forced labor service), as the turning point, SNCF executives experienced their own turning point during the Battle of Stalingrad.

13. Bernstein, *La SNCF sous l'occupation*.

14. Bernstein, *La SNCF sous l'occupation*.

15. Bachelier, *La SNCF sous l'occupation allemand*.

16. Bernstein, *La SNCF sous l'occupation*.

17. Jean-Pierre Richardot, *SNCF: Héros et salauds pendant l'occupation* (Paris: Broché, 2012), 40; "Ordre du Jour n 38," December 4, 1940, Box 72, AJ 477, National Archives, Paris, France; Bachelier, *La SNCF sous l'occupation allemand*.

18. Richardot, *SNCF: Héros et salauds*, 85.

19. Richardot, *SNCF: Héros et salauds*.

20. Bachelier, *La SNCF sous l'occupation allemand*.

21. Ludivine Broch, *Ordinary Workers, Vichy and the Holocaust: French Railwaymen and the Second World War* (Cambridge: Cambridge University Press, 2016).

22. Broch, *Ordinary Workers*, 143.

23. Broch, *Ordinary Workers*.

24. Bernstein, *La SNCF sous l'occupation*.

25. Broch, *Ordinary Workers*.

26. Ludivine Broch, "Professionalism in the Final Solution: French Railway Workers and the Jewish Deportations, 1942–4," *Contemporary European History* 23, no. 3 (2014).

27. Bernstein, producer, *La SNCF sous l'occupation*.

28. Broch, *Ordinary Workers*, 22.

29. Richardot, *SNCF: Héros et salauds*, 96.

30. Richardot, *SNCF: Héros et salauds*.

31. SNCF Heritage, www.SNCFhighspeedrail.com/heritage/world-war-ii (website removed by company).

32. Bachelier, *La SNCF sous l'occupation allemand*.

33. "Minister de la Production Industrielle et des Communications Cabinet du Minister (P. Cosmi) to Monsieur le Conseiller Hoffmann Ambassade d'Allemagne," December 1, 1943, Box 72, AJ 419, National Archives, Paris, France.

34. Richardot, *SNCF: Héros et salauds*, 178.

35. See Ludivine Broch, "French Railway Workers and the Question of Rescue during the Holocaust," *Diasporas* 25 (2015): 147–67. Historians disagree as to whether he refused to drive one train of German soldiers or two including the political prisoners. Even though in 1994 Yad Vashem awarded Bronchart the title of Righteous Among Nations for assisting Jews in various capacities, he never refused to drive a train of Jewish deportees as fabled.

36. Bronchart was arrested on January 8, 1943, for other acts of resistance not associated with his refusal to drive the train.

37. SNCF Heritage website.

38. The train, moving at 90 km/hour, comprised ten railcars, eight of which were metallic. The derailment threw the locomotive, causing it to roll 60 meters and pulverize two nonmetallic cars.

39. Bachelier, *La SNCF sous l'occupation allemand*. An official report on this incident can be found in the SNCF Archives at Le Mans, France: "Note pour le ministre," April 16, 1942, DGT AN, F14 13643.

40. For other detailed descriptions of acts of sabotage and resistance within the SNCF, see Richardot, *SNCF: Héros et salauds*.

41. Some of the Polish railwaymen coordinated significant sabotage of their rails. The Polish railway company claims that some of their employees "poured sand into wagon grease tanks, falsified transport documents, replaced address stickers on wagons." See Polish Railways, "Occupation 1939–1945," http://www.polish-railways.com/default_235.html.

42. Unfortunately, the Diamond Match Company cannot trace who commissioned these matchbooks. Their creator and funder remain a mystery.

43. Marie-Noëlle Polino, ed., *Une entreprise publique dans la guerre, la SNCF 1939–1945* (Paris: Presses Universitaires de France, 2001), 352.

44. Marrus and Paxton, *Vichy France and the Jews*, 331.

45. Broch, "French Railway Workers."

46. See Fondation pour la Mémoire de la Déportation (FMD), *Livre-Mémorial des déportés de France arêtes par mesure de répression et dans certains cas par measure de pérsecution 1940–1945*, 4 vols. (Paris: Tirésias, 2004).

47. Bachelier, *La SNCF sous l'occupation allemand*; Serge Klarsfeld, "Analyse des excuses présentées par le président de la SNCF à propos des convois de déportés," *Daily Motion*, January 27, 2011.

48. Broch, "French Railway Workers."

49. Broch, *Ordinary Workers*, 173.

50. Broch, *Ordinary Workers*, 180; Broch, "Professionalism in the Final Solution," 377. The train ultimately arrived. Only 5 of the 1,008 deportees crammed aboard survived the war.

51. Marrus and Paxton, *Vichy France and the Jews*, 331.

52. David Barnouw, Dirk Mulder, and Guus Veenendaal, *De Nederlandse Spoorwegen in oorlogstijd 1939–1945: Rijden voor Vaderland en Vijand* (Zwolle, Netherlands:

W Books, 2019). The Dutch Railway workers similarly thought sabotage was futile, arguing that repairs would be immediate or that buses would immediately replace the rails. See also Michael J. Neufeld and Michael Berenbaum, *The Bombing of Auschwitz: Should the Allies Have Attempted It?* (New York: St. Martin's, 2000); Yisrael Gutman, Michael Berenbaum, and United States Holocaust Memorial Museum, *Anatomy of the Auschwitz Death Camp* (Bloomington: Indiana University Press, 1998).

53. Broch, "Professionalism in the Final Solution."

54. Bachelier, *La SNCF sous l'occupation allemand*. While the SNCF Heritage website also claimed that some SNCF drivers slowed trains to allow deportees to jump off, substantiating this claim proved challenging. If it did occur, this account from Belgium provides an example of what might have occurred in France. Simon Gronowski, an eleven-year-old Jewish boy in 1943, escaped from his train headed for Auschwitz on April 19, 1943, as three young members of the Belgian Resistance slowed down Gronowski's train, enabling some deportees to force the doors open and escape. See Nick Tabor, "Compromises Fail on Several High-Profile Md. Bills," *The Republic*, April 9, 2014.

55. Georges Ribeill, "Dossier SNCF et déportations," *Historail* 4 (2008): 39.

56. Raoul Merlin, "Chef de Gare Principal Honoraire COMPIEGNE to Monsieur L'Ingénieur en Chef. Compiègne," March 28, 1966, Box 72, AJ 498, National Archives, Paris, France.

57. Bachelier, *La SNCF sous l'occupation allemand*. This help would not have been available at the major departure sites, Drancy (Bobingy) and Compiègne stations. Overall, the Red Cross had very little access to or information about Drancy and Compiègne, from which most trains departed. See Jean-Claude Favez, *The Red Cross and the Holocaust* (Cambridge: Cambridge University Press, 1999).

58. Merlin, "Chef de Gare Principal Honoraire COMPIEGNE to Monsieur L'Ingénieur en Chef. Compiègne." Merlin, an SNCF employee, says his colleagues sent a number of the letters: "Certain SNCF workers told me they took a good number of the letters the deportees had managed to drop onto the tracks a little before the departure or during the departure to the post office after having put them in envelopes. The letters were written on whatever paper the deportees had been able to find (notably MM Paques, ex CMVP and Lecocq, ex-IN2 at the time)."

59. Charlotte Delbo, *Le Convoi du 24 janvier* (Paris: Les Editions de minuit, 1965), 10.

60. The text of the letters by Herscu and Golgevit was on display at the Bobigny deportation site during a construction phase of the memorial in 2014.

61. P. Blum, personal communication, Paris, August 12, 2014.

62. For more examples of assisted escapes, see Broch, "French Railway Workers." She also points to some German reports that highlight some cheminots who tried to help Jews escape. These documents can be found at the Centre de Documentation Juive Contemporaine (CDJC): XXVc-208, Series of documents dated February 10–18, 1943.

63. Maurice Lemaire, "Le Président Régional NORD de RESISTANCE-FER, to Monsieur Legrand, Director de la Région du NORD, at the request of the Historic Committee of the 2nd World War," April 4, 1966, Box 72, AJ 498, National Archives, Paris, France.

64. Delbo, *Le Convoi du 24 janvier*, 10.

65. Merlin, "Chef de Gare Principal Honoraire COMPIEGNE to Monsieur L'Ingénieur en Chef. Compiègne."

66. Freddie Knoller and John Landaw, *Living with the Enemy: My Secret Life on the Run from the Nazis* (London: John Blake, 2005).

67. Robert Paxton, *Vichy France: Old Guard and New Order* (New York: Columbia University Press, 2001).

68. R. Zaks, personal communication, Paris, July 29, 2014.

69. R. Zaks, personal communication, Paris, October 7, 2014.

70. J. Birn, personal communication, Maryland, February 23, 2014. See also Jacqueline Mendels Birn, *À Dimanche prochain: A Memoir of Survival in World War II France* (United States: Jacqueline Mendels Birn, 2013).

71. Marrus and Paxton, *Vichy France and the Jews*, 331.

72. Grégory Célerse, *Sauvons les enfants!* (Lille: Les Lumieres de Lille, 2016).

73. G. Célerse, personal communication, July 13, 2018; G. Célerse, email message to author, November 1, 2018. Célerse found testimonies that claimed that up to sixty people were rescued.

74. Célerse, *Sauvons les enfants!*

75. Arno Klarsfeld, "No, French Railways Are Not Guilty," provided by Serge Klarsfeld, Paris, France, January 8, 2011.

76. The Maquis were French resistants who lived in lightly populated regions, including forests, during the war. These guerrilla bands, beginning mostly as small groups of men hiding from conscription, became active in the Resistance.

77. "Rapport concernant la liberation du wagon de déportés en gare d'Annonay (Ardèche)," Resistance de la SNCF, 1945, Box 72, AJ 498, National Archives, Paris, France.

78. Bernstein, *La SNCF sous l'occupation.*

79. Broch, *Ordinary Workers.*

80. S. Kalmanovitz, phone conversation with author, June 16, 2017.

81. This would not have been unusual. The 71st American Infantry, which found the Gunskirchen camp, saw at least two hundred people die within two days of the troops' arrival. Some literally collapsed as they ran to meet the Americans at the gate or within hours of their arrival. Others died from eating too quickly or from eating the wrong types of food, which shocked their system. The Allies quickly adjusted the food provided to survivors.

82. He thinks he was probably in Linz, Austria, at one of Mauthausen's annex camps, roughly 100 kilometers from the central camp.

83. They rode on wooden benches, suggesting that these patients received only fourth-class tickets.

Chapter 4. Holding the SNCF Accountable

1. Quoted in Jon Elster, *Explaining Social Behavior: More Nuts and Bolts for the Social Sciences* (Cambridge: Cambridge University Press, 2015), 154. Rolland worked with a professional Resistance group; some members of the group also worked for the SNCF.

2. Doreen Lustig, "The Nature of the Nazi State and the Question of International Criminal Responsibility of Corporate Officials at Nuremberg: Revisiting Franz

Neumann's Concept of Behemoth at the Industrialist Trials," *New York University Journal of International Law & Politics* 43 (2011): 965–1044; David Fraser, "(De)Constructing the Nazi State: Criminal Organizations and the Constitutional Theory of the International Military Tribunal," *Loyola Los Angeles International and Comparative Law Journal* 39, no. 1 (Winter 2017): 117–86. Lustig and Fraser argue that the focus on individual responsibility distorted the central role of corporate capitalism in carrying out the Nazi agenda. Lustig says by positioning industrialists as political leaders of a totalitarian state, the tribunals constrained their ability to hold corporate entities and their leaders truly accountable.

3. Michael J. Bazyler, *Holocaust, Genocide, and the Law: A Quest for Justice in a Post-Holocaust World* (New York: Oxford University Press, 2017).

4. Sally Falk Moore, "A Life of Learning Sally Falk Moore" (ACLS Occasional Paper No. 75, Charles Homer Haskins Prize Lecture for 2018, Philadelphia, PA, April 27, 2018), 8–9.

5. Jean-Marc Dreyfus, *L'Impossible Réparation: Déportés, bien spoliés, or Nazi, comptes bloqués, criminels de guerre* (Paris: Flammarion, 2015).

6. Shannon Fogg, *Stealing Home: Looting, Restitution, and Reconstructing Jewish Lives in France, 1942–1947* (Oxford: Oxford University Press, 2017), 61. Fogg cites CDJC CCXVI-118, "Situation économique et perspectives pour la France" (December 1944), 3.

7. Herrick Chapman, *France's Long Reconstruction: In Search of the Modern Republic* (Cambridge, MA: Harvard University Press, 2018).

8. Chapman, *France's Long Reconstruction*.

9. Chapman, *France's Long Reconstruction*.

10. J. Friedman, personal communication, France, July 28, 2014.

11. The number of Jewish deportees who survived their deportation ranges between 2,500 and 3,500. Serge Klarsfeld says the number may be impossible to establish because so many survivors were misclassified after the war.

12. Henry Rousso and Arthur Goldhammer, *The Vichy Syndrome: History and Memory in France since 1944* (Cambridge, MA: Harvard University Press, 1994). Rousso and Goldhammer referred to this as the transition from a "mourning" period to an era of repression that would last until the 1980s.

13. Fogg, *Stealing Home*.

14. Pascale Froment, *René Bousquet* (Paris: Fayard, 2001).

15. See Fogg, *Stealing Home*; Renee Poznanski, *Jews in France during World War II*, translated by Nathan Bracher (Hanover, NH: Brandeis University Press and the University Press of New England, 2001).

16. Julian Jackson, *France: The Dark Years 1940–44* (New York: Oxford University Press, 2001); Roy C. Macridis, "France, from Vichy to the Fourth Republic" in *From Dictatorship to Democracy: Coping with the Legacies of Authoritarianism and Totalitarianism*, ed. John H. Herz (Westport, CT: Greenwood Press, 1982), 161–17. Jackson estimates that there were ten thousand such executions; Macridis's estimate is between twenty thousand and fifty thousand.

17. Conseil d'État, "Conseil d'État, Assemblée," June 14, 1946, Ganascia.

18. Fournier's tenure as France's chief railway executive ended in 1946, possibly for political reasons growing out of charges he faced relating to the storage of gold between 1939 and 1940 during his term as governor of the Bank of France.

19. Catherine Bernstein, director, *La SNCF sous l'occupation* (Paris: Zadig Productions, 2019). This reflects Lustig and Fraser's findings that executives were treated in postwar trials as extensions of the state rather than as independent corporate executives. See Lustig, "The Nature of the Nazi State"; and Fraser, "(De)Constructing the Nazi State."

20. Note that during this period of purges, the deportations were not yet considered a particular or separate war crime.

21. Ludivine Broch, "French Railway Workers under German Occupation, 1940–1944," Order No. U566539, University of Oxford, 2011, http://search.proquest.com.proxy-ub.researchport.umd.edu/docview/1314571868?accountid=28969.

22. Dreyfus, *L'Impossible Réparation*, 103.

23. See Pierre Nora, "Between Memory and History: Les Lieux de Mémoire," *Representations*, no. 26 (Spring 1989): 7–24.

24. Coralie Immelé, "La Résistance des cheminots entre 1940 et 1944, une histoire à la croisée des engagements individuels et collectifs," *Gazette des archives* 198, no. 2 (2005): 142.

25. Today, the French use the word *shoah*, meaning "catastrophe," because the word *holocaust* comes from old French and means "to offer up in ash as a religious offering."

26. Sylvie Lindeperg, "L'Opération cinématographique: Équivoques idéologiques et ambivalences narratives dans La Bataille du rail," *Annales: Histoire, Sciences Sociales* 51, no. 4 (1996): 759–79. Other groups overseeing and approving the final screenplay included the Commission Militaire Nationale, the Resistance Fer, and Coopérative: Committee de Liberation du Cinema Français.

27. Ludivine Broch, *Ordinary Workers, Vichy and the Holocaust: French Railwaymen and the Second World War* (Cambridge: Cambridge University Press, 2016).

28. Lindeperg, "L'Opération cinématographique."

29. Certain SNCF workers received the Médaille de la Résistance, but, as the photo confirms, the company itself received the Légion d'honneur. The medal remains on display.

30. Broch, *Ordinary Workers.*

31. Chapman, *France's Long Reconstruction.*

32. Robert Gildea, *Fighters in the Shadows: A New History of the French Resistance* (London: Faber & Faber, 2015).

33. Hilde Lindemann Nelson, *Damaged Identities, Narrative Repair* (Ithaca, NY: Cornell University Press, 2001).

34. Rousso and Goldhammer, *The Vichy Syndrome.*

35. François Azouvi, *Le mythe du grand silence: Auschwitz, les Français, la mémoire* (Paris: Fayard, 2012); Annette Wieviorka, *The Era of the Witness* (Ithaca, NY: Cornell University Press, 1998); Beate Klarsfeld and Serge Klarsfeld, *Mémoires* (Paris: Fayard/Flammarion, 2015); Rousso and Goldhammer, *The Vichy Syndrome.*

36. Leslie Dwyer, "A Politics of Silences: Violence, Memory and Treacherous Speech in Post-1965 Bali," in *Genocide: Truth, Memory, and Representation*, ed. Alexander Hinton and Kevin Lewis O'Neill (Durham, NC: Duke University Press, 2009), 113–46.

37. Maurice Halbwachs, *On Collective Memory* (Chicago: University of Chicago Press, 1992).

38. Sarah Gensburger and Marie-Claire Lavabre, "Entre 'devoir de mémoire' et 'abus de mémoire': La sociologie de la mémoire comme tierce position," in *Histoire, mémoire et épistémologie: A propos de Paul Ricoeur*, ed. Bertrand Müller (Lausanne: Payot, 2005), 76–95; Sarah Gensburger, "Les figures du Juste et du Résistant et l'évolution de la mémoire historique française de l'occupation," *Revue française de science politique* 52, no. 2 (2002): 291–322.

39. Azouvi, *Le mythe du grand silence.*

40. See Fogg, *Stealing Home*, 175.

41. E. Caspi, personal communication, New York, October 2, 2015.

42. M. Wolf, phone conversation with author, May 26, 2014.

43. M. Kern, personal communication, Paris, August 12, 2014.

44. A. Zdroui and I. Zdroui, personal communication, France, August 4, 2014.

45. See Hubert J. M. Hermans, "The Coherence of Incoherent Narratives," *Narrative Inquiry* 10, no. 1 (1999): 223–27; Marc Howard Ross, *Cultural Contestation in Ethnic Conflict* (Cambridge: Cambridge University Press, 2007).

46. Richard J. Golsan, *The Vichy Past in France Today: Corruptions of Memory* (London: Lexington Books, 2016).

47. This decision overturned the amnesty awarded by the Conseil d'État (the French high court) in the 1946 Ganascia decision. This decision proclaimed that individuals could not request compensation from the French state for acts conducted by the Vichy government.

48. Raul Hilberg, *The Destruction of the European Jews* (Chicago: Quadrangle Books, 1961).

49. Olga Wormser-Migot, *Le Système concentrationnaire Nazi (1933–1945)* (Paris: Presses Universitaires de France, 1968).

50. Robert Paxton, *Parades and Politics at Vichy: The French Officer Corps under Marshal Pétain* (Princeton, NJ: Princeton University Press, 1966).

51. Marcel Ophuls, director, *The Sorrow and the Pity* (1969; Harrington Park, NJ: Milestone Film & Video, 2011), DVD.

52. Simone Veil, *Une Vie* (Paris: Éditions Stock, 2007).

53. Peter Novick, *The Holocaust in American Life* (Boston: Houghton Mifflin, 1999).

54. Novick, *The Holocaust in American Life.*

55. Rousso and Goldhammer, *The Vichy Syndrome.*

56. Michael R. Marrus and Robert O. Paxton, *Vichy France and the Jews* (New York: Basic Books, 1981).

57. Claude Lanzmann and Simone de Beauvoir, *Shoah: The Complete Text of The Acclaimed Holocaust Film* (New York: Da Capo Press, 1995).

58. Cour de cassation [Cass., supreme court for judicial matters], crim., 3 juin 1988, Bull crim., no. 87-84240.

59. Vamik Volkan, "Large-Group Identity, International Relations and Psychoanalysis," *International Forum of Psychoanalysis* 18, no. 4 (2009): 206–13.

60. Cour d'assises du Rhône, 4 juillet 1987. For the appeal related to this case, see Cour de cassation [Cass., supreme court for judicial matters], crim., 3 juin 1988, Bull crim., no. 87-84240.

61. Joan Beth Wolf, *Harnessing the Holocaust: The Politics of Memory in France* (Palo Alto, CA: Stanford University Press, 2004).

62. S. Klarsfeld, personal communication, Paris, January 8, 2011.

63. Michael R. Marrus, *Some Measure of Justice: The Holocaust Era Restitution Campaign of the 1990s* (Madison: University of Wisconsin Press, 2009).

64. Annette Wieviorka, *The Era of the Witness* (Ithaca, NY: Cornell University Press, 1998).

65. Dreyfus, *L'Impossible Réparation*, 256.

66. Leora Bilsky, *The Holocaust, Corporations, and the Law: Unfinished Business* (Ann Arbor: University of Michigan Press, 2017), 35; B. Neuborne, email message to author, October 17, 2017.

67. Some corporations paid small amounts in the late 1950s. These companies included Siemens, Krupp, and I. G. Farben, which paid small amounts to individuals who had suffered under slave labor. See Ben Ferencz, *Less than Slaves* (Bloomington: Indiana University Press, 2002); Detlev Vagts and Peter Murray, "Litigating Labor Claims: The Path Not Taken," *Harvard International Law Journal* 43, no. 2 (Summer 2002): 503–30.

68. Vagts and Murray, "Litigating the Nazi Labor Claims."

69. Ken Silverstein, "Ford and the Fuhrer," *Nation* 270, no. 3 (2000): 11–16. Participating companies included Bayer, BMW, Volkswagen, and Daimler-Chrysler. The next major landmark endeavor involved UBS, Credit Suisse, and other banks housing the monies of World War II deportees and slave laborers. Ford Motor Company, accused of force, slave labor, and "unjust enrichment" at its German subsidiary during the war, became an outlier. In 1999 a New Jersey judge threw out a lawsuit against the company, citing the expiration of the statute of limitations; in other words, too much time had passed. Ironically, Ford itself had applied for restitution in 1965 for wartime losses, ultimately receiving $1.1 million from the Foreign Claims Settlement Commission in 1965.

70. Bilsky, *The Holocaust, Corporations, and the Law.*

71. D. Ruzié, personal communication, France, August 8, 2014. The Commission did not report a final sum, but the press estimated that the accounts held 1.5 billion euros in modern currency; the Commission did not challenge the estimate. The Mattéoli Commission report also points to the rail transport of stolen furniture and other personal items to Germany. SNCF trains likely transported these items, and the company was likely paid for this work.

72. Société Generale, Paribas and BNP (now BNP Paribas), Caisse Nationale de Credit Agricole, the CNCA unit of Credit Agricole Indosuez, Credit Lyonnais, Natexis, and CCF (part of the HSBC).

73. Stuart Eizenstat, *Imperfect Justice: Looted Assets, Slave Labor, and the Unfinished Business of World War II* (New York: Public Affairs, 2009), 337.

74. Klarsfeld and Klarsfeld, *Mémoires*; Froment, *René Bousquet*. After the war, Bousquet went on to become a deputy general director of the Bank of Indochina. Bousquet briefly lost his honors and access to public service positions, only to be reinstated and receive amnesty in 1958. In 1993 Christian Didier shot Bousquet in the head less than a month before his trial. The Klarsfelds also spotlighted Pierre Laval, Jean Leguay, Jacques Schweblin, F. François, and Louis Draquier.

75. Cour de cassation [Cass., supreme court for judicial matters], crim., 6 janvier 1993, Bull. crim., no. 394.

76. Michael R. Marrus, "The End of the Line: The French Courts and Liability for the Holocaust in France: The Glemane Avis 2009" (presentation at the Minerva Institute at Tel Aviv University Conference on Corporate Accountability for Mass Atrocity, Tel Aviv, Israel, December 16, 2012).

77. R. Weisberg, phone conversation with author, June 27, 2014.

78. His father had been deported on convoy 50 from the Gurs French internment camp to the Sobibór extermination camp. His mother had been interned at the Noé camp in France and was transported to Auschwitz on May 30, 1944 (Convoy 75), about one week before D-Day.

79. The public prosecutor closed this letter with the suggestion that Schaechter read an article written by Hochen Gluckes on the role of the railways in deporting Jews from France. In his follow-up letter, Schaechter wrote that yes, thank you very much, he knew the article but was seeking justice for the death of his parents, not historical renditions of the railway's role in the Holocaust.

80. Kurt Werner Schaechter, "Letter sent to the Procurer of the French Republic in Paris," September 9, 1999, Hoover Institution Archives, Stanford, CA.

81. UN General Assembly, "Rome Statute of the International Criminal Court," *United Nations Treaty Series* 2187, no. 1-38544 (1998).

82. Jonathan A. Bush, "The Prehistory of Corporations and Conspiracy in International Criminal Law: What Nuremberg Really Said," *Columbia Law Review* 109, no. 5 (2009): 1094–1262.

83. Michael J. Kelly and Luis Moreno-Ocampo, *Prosecuting Corporations for Genocide* (New York: Oxford University Press, 2016).

84. Cristina Chiomenti, "Corporations and the International Criminal Court," in *Transnational Corporations and Human Rights*, ed. Olivier De Schutter (Oxford: Hart, 2006), 287–312.

85. In May 2020, after he spent more than twenty years fleeing ICC indictments, authorities arrested Félicien Kabuga, the man behind the radio station.

86. Kurt Werner Schaechter Collection: 1933–2006. No one has yet found the names of these witnesses or their testimonies.

87. Tribunal de grande instance [TGI, ordinary court of original jurisdiction], Paris, May 14, 2003, 2001/07912. Some say incorrectly that Schaechter's first case was in the 1990s, but the case he launched in 1991 was not about the SNCF but on behalf of his wife, Collette Gisselmann. The case was against a cheese factory (E.R.U. Kaasfabriek) for a commission promised on a sale of cheese to the Middle East.

88. Cour d'appel [CA, regional court of appeal] Paris, 1e ch., June 8, 2004, 2003/12747.

89. Eric Freedman, email message to Harriet Tamen, Richard Weisberg, Ken McCallion, Shimon Samuels, March 8, 2004 (provided to author by Freedman, August 10, 2014). These numbers were offered by SNCF assistant archivists to Eric Freedman at the 2004 archives colloquium in Roubaix, France.

90. The last deportation train from this station left on July 30, 1944, just fifteen days before the town's liberation. Schaechter claimed by this late date the town had no more German troops or Milice (Vichy police regime) and only a small group of mostly powerless Gestapo. Yet deportation trains still departed. These trains arrived at Auschwitz-Birkenau, where most of the deportees were murdered. In translation, the

plaque reads, "In this Longages-Noé station, a number of deportation trains left France between 1942 and 1944, during the period of the Vichy government. The little station of Longages-Noé was chosen as the principal deportation station in the southwest region in order to avoid the major stations of the Midi-Pyrenees and of Toulouse. PASSERS-BY, REMEMBER!"

91. Kurt Schaechter is still listed as a plaintiff in the 2008 class action lawsuit *Freund v. Republic of France*, though he had died the year prior. His battle continued posthumously.

92. Richard Lerchbaum and Olivier Nahum, "La SNCF ne souciait pas de ce qu'elle transportait," *Actualité Juive*, July 1, 1999.

93. Vivian Grosswald Curran, "Gobalization, Legal Transnationalization and Crimes against Humanity: The Lipietz Case," *American Journal of Comparative Law* 56, no. 2 (2008): 363–402.

94. Julie Remy, "Frenchman Suing France over Holocaust Deportation," Reuters, December 30, 1998.

95. Specifically, they filed for compensation for their arrest by the Gestapo on May 8, 1944, their transfer via the SNCF on May 10 and 11 from Toulouse to Paris-Austerlitz, and their internment at Drancy from May 11 through August 17, 1944.

96. Alain Lipietz, *La SNCF et la Shoah: Le procès G. Lipietz contre État et SNCF* (Paris: Les Petits Matins, 2011).

97. "Case No. 0101248 Mr. A. and the similarly situated LIPIETZ plaintiffs, versus the Prefect of Haute-Garonne and the Société nationale des chemins de fer [French National Railway Company, hereinafter 'SNCF']," Administrative Court of Toulouse, France (Toulouse, France, June 6, 2006), http://lipietz.net/spip.php?article 1891.

98. Arno Klarsfeld, "La SNCF et les trains de la mort, par Arno Klarsfeld," *Le Monde*, June 3, 2006.

99. The lawyer for the French state did not attend, even though the case was against the government as well as the SNCF.

100. Lipietz, *La SNCF et la Shoah*.

101. Michael R. Marrus, "The Case of the French Railways and the Deportation of Jews in 1944," in *Holocaust and Justice: Representation and Historiography of the Holocaust in Post-War Trials*, ed. David Bankier and Dan Michman (New York: Berghahn Books, 2010), 251.

102. A. Lipietz, personal communication, Paris, June 19, 2015.

103. A commissioner is an independent magistrate specializing in administrative law. A commissioner is not a judge but confers with the judge throughout the case. Their comments are influential and often reflect those of the judge at the time they are read.

104. Curran, "Gobalization, Legal Transnationalization and Crimes against Humanity."

105. CAA Bordeaux, form. plén., March 27, 2007, 06BX01570.

106. Conseil d'État, December 21, 2007, 305966, Rec Lebon.

107. Lipietz, *La SNCF et la Shoah*.

108. A. Lipetz, personal communication, Paris, January 28, 2016.

109. Marrus, "The Case of the French Railways," 255.

110. Marrus, "The Case of the French Railways," 254.

111. Georges Ribeill, "Dossier SNCF et déportations," *Historail* 4 (2008): 34–87.

112. Ribeill, "Dossier SNCF et déportations."

113. Marrus, "The Case of the French Railways."

114. "Case No. 0101248 Mr. A. and the similarly situated LIPIETZ plaintiffs, versus the Prefect of Haute-Garonne and the Société nationale des chemins de fer [French National Railway Company, hereinafter 'SNCF'']," Administrative Court of Toulouse, France (Toulouse, France, June 6, 2006), http://lipietz.net/spip.php?arti cle1891. Received written permission for citations.

115. Emphasis mine.

116. C. and J. Friedman, personal communication, Deauville, France, March 28, 2014.

117. The compensation fund for orphans whose parents perished in an antisemitic persecution was created on the recommendation of the French Holocaust activist Serge Klarsfeld and the Mattéoli Commission. See Mémorial de la Shoah, "Compensation and Reinstitution for Holocaust Victims in France," Mémorial de la Shoah, http://holocaust-compensation-france.memorialdelashoah.org/en/holocaust-orphans .html.

118. Marrus, "The End of the Line." In February 2009, the Conseil d'État announced that beyond existing reparations programs the state owed nothing more with regard to World War II. The decision came as a result of the case *Hoffman-Glemane v. France and SNCF*. The court decided that while the crimes themselves were incommensurable, pragmatically speaking there would have to be a financial cap. The court ruled specifically on claims sought by Madeline Hoffman-Glemane against the French state and the SNCF totaling €280,000 for the deportation and murder of her father and for her own suffering. The administrative court in Paris passed the question to the Conseil d'État. The state dismissed the claims against the SNCF, referring to the decision issued on the Lipietz case. With regard to the French state, the court held the state responsible for the atrocities, reiterating the Papon decision (addressing the accusations against former Vichy police secretary general Maurice Papon) that the state's actions completely violated the rights of man and citizen. The decision also declared, however, that the Papon trial had led to a variety of reparations programs, paying roughly €800 million for compensation programs and commemorative projects. The court issued its decision on February 16, 2009, after all SNCF-related suits had already been dismissed by French courts. The court determined that these efforts were satisfactory and declared that these measures "must be seen as having permitted, to the extent that has been possible, the indemnification of victims and their families . . . for the wrongs of every sort caused by the actions of the state that contributed to deportations." France had paid enough, the court said. The court decision claimed there had to be limits on the sums paid and found that the French sums proved commensurate with those paid by the rest of Europe. The original text of the *avis* (opinion), translated by Marrus, is that the claims "doivent être regardées comme ayant permis, autant qu'il a été possible, l'indemnisation . . . des préjudices de route nature causés par les actions de l'Etat qui ont concouru à la déportation." See Conseil d'État, Ass., February 16, 2009, 315499, Rec Lebon.

119. C. Hershkovitch, telephone communication, July 28, 2020.

120. Hélene Lipietz, "Circulez, il n'y a rien à juger . . . Le Conseil d'État a rendu son avis: il n'y a plus rien à indemniser," *Madame Hélene Lipietz Ancienne Sénatrice*, February 16, 2009, http://helene.lipietz.net/spip.php?article183.

121. France in the United States: Consulate General of France in Miami, "Holocaust Education and Compensation of Victims of Spoliation," http://www.consulfrance-miami.org/spip.php?article1969.

122. *La Rafle*, directed by Roselyne Bosch (Paris: Legende Films, 2010); *Elle s'appelait Sarah*, directed by Gilles Pacquet-Brenner (Neuilly-sur-Seine: UGC Distribution, 2010); Tatiana de Rosnay, *Sarah's Key* (London: John Murray, 2008); and Françoise Laborde, *Une Histoire qui fait du bruit* (Paris: Fayard, 2011). The films *La Rafle* and *Elle s'appelait Sarah* both address the French deportations. Françoise Laborde's *Une Histoire qui fait du bruit* (*A History That Makes Noise*) tells the fictional story of a star reporter, Diane Allard, who produces a television program on the role of the SNCF in the deportations. The book recounts the negative reactions, first of her boss who sanctions her work and then those of her children and her second husband, Henri, a high-level functionary. Her family and her husband's colleagues accuse her of presenting a biased presentation, playing politics, and seeking incendiary topics she knows will enrage the country. Henri's colleagues berate him for not being aware of his wife's activities and not being able to control her. They all distance themselves from her as a result; the marriage comes under threat. No one defends her investigation. Her husband further chastises her for contributing to the SNCF's troubles in the United States. She flees Paris to escape the tension and has her children meet her over the weekend. She buys them tickets to take the train to Bordeaux but accidently hands them the wrong documents; her son and daughter are accosted by the SNCF ticket controller, who recognizes the family name. He accuses their mother of producing a television program against the cheminots. Diane abandons the network and hires a young historian to help her turn her research into a book. This contemporary book shows the continued highly vitriolic nature of these debates in France.

123. When she reached her eighties, in 1980, her mother, Estéra, received some financial compensation for her separation from her children and her deportation. She would receive €500 a month until she died, ten years later, on April 23, 1990. Her compensation totaled roughly €60,000. Estéra died before Schaechter went public with his archival findings, and so she never knew about the lawsuits against the SNCF.

124. L. Helwaser, personal communication, Paris, July 25, 2014.

Chapter 5. The SNCF Struggles to Clear Its Name

1. Priscilla B. Hayner, *Unspeakable Truths: Transitional Justice and the Challenge of Truth Commissions* (New York: Routledge, 2010).

2. Elaine Scarry, *The Body in Pain: The Making and Unmaking of the World* (New York: Oxford University Press, 1987).

3. Leslie Dwyer, "A Politics of Silences: Violence, Memory and Treacherous Speech in Post-1965 Bali," in *Genocide: Truth, Memory, and Representation*, ed. Alexander Hinton and Kevin Lewis O'Neill (Durham, NC: Duke University Press, 2009), 113–46.

4. Sigfried Giedion, *Mechanization Takes Command: A Contribution to Anonymous History* (Minneapolis: University of Minnesota Press, 2014).

5. Marie Amélie Lombard-Latune, "La SNCF rattrapée par son passé," *Le Figaro*, November 25, 2010.

6. R. Prasquier, personal communication, Paris, May 9, 2011.

7. A. Leray, email message to author, November 2, 2017.

8. André du Toit, "The Moral Foundations of the South African TRC: Truth as Acknowledgment and Justice as Recognition," in *Truth v. Justice: The Morality of Truth Commissions*, ed. Robert I. Rotberg and Dennis F. Thompson (Princeton, NJ: Princeton University Press, 2000), 122–40.

9. Priscilla B. Hayner, *Unspeakable Truths: Transitional Justice and the Challenge of Truth Commissions* (New York: Routledge, 2010).

10. Robert I. Rotberg and Dennis F. Thompson, *Truth v. Justice: The Morality of Truth Commissions* (Princeton, NJ: Princeton University Press, 2000).

11. Hugo Van der Merwe and Audrey R. Chapman, *Assessing the Impact of Transitional Justice: Challenges for Empirical Research* (Washington, DC: United States Institute of Peace, 2008).

12. Stanley Cohen, *States of Denial: Knowing about Atrocities and Suffering* (Malden, MA: Blackwell, 2001).

13. This research was conducted under the provision of the AHICF.

14. H. Rousso, email message to author, March 17, 2016.

15. Henry Rousso, *The Latest Catastrophe: History, the Present, the Contemporary* (Chicago: University of Chicago Press, 2016).

16. H. Rousso, personal communication, Paris, January 22, 2016.

17. Rousso, *The Latest Catastrophe*.

18. B. Emsellem, personal communication, Paris, March 24, 2011.

19. H. Rousso, personal communication, Paris, January 22, 2016.

20. Jon Elster, *Closing the Books: Transitional Justice in Historical Perspective* (Cambridge: Cambridge University Press, 2004); Marie-Noëlle Polino, ed., *Une Entreprise publique dans la guerre, la SNCF 1939–1945* (Paris: Presse Universitaires de France, 2001); Eric Freedman, personal communication, Paris, August 10, 2014. I found holes in the SNCF archives. The file named "Le Train a L'Affiche 1937–1977," for example, has no images available for the years 1938–48. This was strange, as there are many images available for other years. The staff had no explanation. Elster claims the SS destroyed the records from Drancy before fleeing in 1944, and moreover many other archives were shredded because they revealed a France acting in opposition to its own espoused republican values. Serge Klarsfeld noted specific omissions, such as the archives housing the liaison between the SNCF and the Germans who managed the civil and military transport in occupied France. The SNCF's communications with the ninth bureau of the Vichy national police, which organized the special convoys of Jews, are also missing. Klarsfeld says these vital documents would help us understand any reluctance the SNCF might have expressed about their actions. Some believe that such documents may exist but cannot be found because the archives are disorganized. Eric Freedman, who works with Harriet Tamen on the lawsuits against the SNCF, notes that even though the SNCF claims all the materials are at the Le Mans archives, many interesting and relevant documents appear to be available at archives in Lyon, Toulouse, and Compiègne. Some new evidence may emerge as the years roll on. I say this because SNCF archives staff literally pulled one of the file boxes with war documents

from my hands because it contained documents from more recent years. Some archivist had housed various war documents with recent documents. This means that the box cannot be opened until a few more years have passed.

21. This resulted in the book *The Railroad in Germany: From the Beginnings to Today* (*Die Eisenbahn in Deutschland: Von den Anfängen bis zur Gegenwart*), by Lothar Gall and Manfred Pohl, published in 1999.

22. Kevin Avruch, "Truth and Reconciliation Commissions: Problems in Transitional Justice and the Reconstruction of Identity," *Transcultural Psychiatry* 47, no. 1 (2010): 33–49.

23. Avruch, "Truth and Reconciliation Commissions"; Priscilla B. Hayner and Lydiah Bosire, *Should Truth Commissions Address Economic Crimes? Considering the Case of Kenya* (New York: International Center for Transitional Justice, 2003).

24. Leora Bilsky, *The Holocaust, Corporations, and the Law: Unfinished Business* (Ann Arbor: University of Michigan Press, 2017).

25. "Justice to Come? Tunisia's Truth and Dignity Commission," Brookings Institution, February 20, 2020, https://www.brookings.edu/events/justice-to-come-tunisias-truth-and-dignity-commission/.

26. See "Corporate Accountability in Transitional Justice," University of Oxford, May 26, 2020, https://ahra.web.ox.ac.uk/catj#collapse281876. See also Louise Arbour, "Economic and Social Justice for Societies in Transition," *New York University Journal of International Law and Politics* 40, no. 1 (2007): 1–27; Ruben Carranza, "Plunder and Pain: Should Transitional Justice Engage with Corruption and Economic Crimes?," *International Journal of Transitional Justice* 2, no. 3 (2008): 310–30; James Cavallaro and Sebastián Albuja, "The Lost Agenda: Economic Crimes and Truth Commissions in Latin America and Beyond," in *Transitional Justice from Below: Grassroots Activism and the Struggle for Change*, ed. Kieran McEvoy and Lorna McGregor (Portland, OR: Hart, 2008), 121–88; and Rama Mani, "Editorial: Dilemmas of Expanding Transitional Justice, or Forging the Nexus between Transitional Justice and Development," *International Journal of Transitional Justice* 2 (2008): 253–65.

27. Sierra Leone Truth and Reconciliation Commission, *Witness to Truth: Final Report of the Sierra Leone Truth and Reconciliation Commission* (2004), https://www.sierraleonetrc.org/index.php/view-the-final-report/download-table-of-contents.

28. See Office of the High Commissioner for Human Rights (OHCHR), *Rule-of-Law Tools for Post-Conflict States: Truth Commissions* (New York and Geneva: United Nations, 2006), 9, https://www.ohchr.org/Documents/Publications/RuleoflawTruthCommissionsen.pdf.

29. Alexander Karn, *Amending the Past: Europe's Holocaust Commissions and the Right to History* (Madison: University of Wisconsin Press, 2015).

30. Bilsky, *The Holocaust, Corporations, and the Law.*

31. A. Lipietz, personal communication, Paris, January 28, 2016.

32. Karn, *Amending the Past.*

33. Polino, *Une Entreprise publique dans la guerre.*

34. Sara Cobb, "Narrative Braiding and the Role of Public Officials in Transforming the Publics Conflicts," *Narrative and Conflict: Explorations in Theory and Practice* 1, no. 1 (2013): 4–30. See also Sarah Federman, "Altering Institutional Narratives and

Rewriting History to Make Amends: The French National Railroads (SNCF)," *Narrative and Conflict: Explorations in Theory and Practice* 3, no. 1 (2016): 45–63.

35. Michael R. Marrus, "The Case of the French Railways and the Deportation of Jews in 1944," in *Holocaust and Justice: Representation and Historiography of the Holocaust in Post-War Trials*, ed. David Bankier and Dan Michman (New York: Berghahn Books, 2010), 259.

36. Eric Freedman, email message to Harriet Tamen, Richard Weisberg, Ken McCallion, and Shimon Samuels, March 8, 2004 (provided to author by Freedman, August 10, 2014).

37. Contemporary Jewish and Shoah historian professor Anne Grynberg chaired the panel event, held on January 12, 2007. Panelists included the Vichy historian Henry Rousso; Michel Zaoui, a lawyer who participated in the trials of Klaus Barbie, Paul Touvier, and Maurice Papon; and Corrine Hershkovitch, who represented some survivors in lawsuits against the SNCF.

38. Marrus, "The Case of the French Railways," 249.

39. Rousso, *The Latest Catastrophe*.

40. The Shoah Memorial, *Annual Report: Mémorial de la Shoah*, booklet (Paris: The Shoah Memorial, 2013).

41. SNCF, *History and Memory: SNCF & World War II*, booklet (Paris: SNCF, 2012). From May 17 through June 15, 2003, France hosted an exhibit on the Champs-Élysées that focused on 150 years of train history. The SNCF included a deportation car and a plaque in both French and English: "SNCF was keen to show the wagon used during the Second World War for transporting deported people to the German frontier, and then from there to the Nazi concentration and death camps, in the name of duty and remembrance."

42. B. Emsellem, email message to author, July 30, 2014.

43. H. Rousso, personal communication, Paris, January 22, 2016.

44. L. Helwaser, personal communication, Paris, July 25, 2014.

45. Public-Private Partnerships—Disclosure of Involvement in Deportations, H.B. 1326, Maryland State House, Committee of Ways and Means and Environmental Matters (Annapolis, MD, March 10, 2014).

46. A. Leray, email message to author, May 11, 2016.

47. Mémorial de la Shoah, "Lancement des travaux pour la création d'un nouveau lieu de mémoire au sein de l'ancienne gare de Pithiviers (Loiret)," Mémorial de la Shoah, www.memorialdelashoah.org/le-memorial-de-la-shoah-et-la-sncf-lancent-les-travaux-pour-la-creation-dun-nouveau-lieu-de-memoire-au-sein-de-lancienne-gare-de-voyageurs-de-pithiviers-loiret.

48. François-Xavier Rivaud, "Orléans : à la tête du Cercil, Annaïg Lefeuvre prépare une année 2021 riche en événements," *leparisien.fr*, June 9, 2020, https://www.leparisien.fr/societe/orleans-a-la-tete-du-cercil-annaig-lefeuvre-prepare-une-annee-2021-riche-en-evenements-09-06-2020-8332224.php.

49. On March 16, 2005, the SNCF donated the site for a symbolic euro. Of an estimated seventy-nine convoys that left France for the death camps, sixty-seven left from the Bobigny station. An estimated twenty thousand deportees departed from this SNCF-managed station. This is Klarsfeld's estimate, cited by Michael R. Marrus and Robert O. Paxton, *Vichy France and the Jews* (New York: Basic Books, 1981), 252.

50. SNCF, *La SNCF et la Seconde Guerre Mondiale*, SNCF press kit distributed at the Bobigny Commémoration, January 25, 2011 (emphasis mine).

51. Quoted in Thomas Fontaine, *Cheminots victims de la répression: 1940–1945 Mémorial* (Paris: Perrin, 2017).

52. L. Helwaser, personal communication, Paris, July 25, 2014.

53. C. Hershkovitch, personal communication, phone, July 28, 2020.

54. H. Kerner, personal communication, February 28, 2014.

55. Maia de La Baume, "French Railway Formally Apologizes to Holocaust Victims," *New York Times*, January 25, 2011.

56. P. Boukara, personal communication, Paris, February 8, 2011.

57. *L'ancienne gare de Bobigny, entre Drancy et Auschwitz* (Ville de Bobigny, France, 2011).

58. See Raymond Federman, *Shhh: The Story of a Childhood* (Buffalo, NY: Starcherone Books. 2010).

59. Michael R. Marrus, "Official Apologies and the Quest for Historical Justice," *Journal of Human Rights* 6, no. 6 (2007): 75–105.

60. Ernesto Verdeja, "Official Apologies in the Aftermath of Political Violence," *Metaphilosophy* 41, no. 4 (2010): 563–81.

61. Verdeja, "Official Apologies in the Aftermath of Political Violence"; Erving Goffman, *Relations in Public* (London: Allen Lane, 1971). The close Christian links with the notion of apology as a source of cleansing lead to critiques of apology as part of a neoliberal imperialism rooted in Christian doctrine. Verdeja, for example, refers to the theologian Martin Marty, who sees apologies as changing the rapport between the victim and the perpetrator as well as between the perpetrator and God. Verdeja outlines the three components formal apologies require: (1) a verbal act expressing sorrow or regret to victims and society at large, (2) restitution of some form, and (3) a promise that such acts will never reoccur. Erving Goffman offered a model of apology that focused less on responsibility and more on the expression of humiliation or remorse, the offering of compensation, and a demonstration that the guilty party knows now what a proper response would be. Scholars debate whether victims must forgive the apologizer after such an apology is made.

62. Margaret Urban Walker, *Moral Repair: Reconstructing Moral Relations after Wrongdoing* (New York: Cambridge University Press, 2006), 191.

63. See Joanna North, "The 'Ideal' of Forgiveness: A Philosopher's Exploration," in *Exploring Forgiveness*, ed. Robert D. Enright and Joanna North (Madison: University of Wisconsin Press, 1998), 15–34; and Margaret Holmgren, "Forgiveness and the Intrinsic Value of Persons," *American Philosophical Quarterly* 30, no. 4 (1993): 340–52.

64. Charles Griswold, *Forgiveness: A Philosophical Exploration* (New York: Cambridge University Press, 2008).

65. Note that the date was originally set for July 13–15, but the French anticipated resistance during the Bastille Day celebrations, which take place on July 14, and thus delayed the roundup by two days. See United States Holocaust Memorial Museum (USHMM), "The Vélodrome d'Hiver (Vel d'Hiv) Roundup," USHMM, https://encyclopedia.ushmm.org/content/en/article/the-velodrome-dhiver-vel-dhiv-roundup.

66. Marlise Simons, "Chirac Affirms France's Guilt in Fate of Jews," *New York Times*, July 17, 1995.

67. I. Zdroui, personal communication, France, August 4, 2014.

68. L. Vermont, telephone conversation with author, July 7, 2014.

69. Olivier de Berranger, Bishop of Seine-Saint-Denis, "La Déclaration de repentance des évêques de France," Declaration of Repentance, Drancy, France, September 30, 1997, http://www.dialogue-jca.org/Repentance_des_eveques_de_France (emphasis mine, my translation).

70. R. Prasquier, personal communication, Paris, May 9, 2011.

71. "Dutch Railway Firm Apologizes for Deporting Jews during WWII," *Haaretz*, September 28, 2005.

72. Sam Haysom, "Genius Site Tracks the Twitter Apologies Issues by UK Transport Companies," *Mashable*, December 15, 2016.

73. Claudia I. Janssen, "Addressing Corporate Ties to Slavery: Corporate Apologia in a Discourse of Reconciliation," *Communication Studies* 63, no. 1 (2012): 18–35.

74. See Leigh A. Payne, *Unsettling Accounts: Neither Truth nor Reconciliation in Confessions of State Violence* (Durham, NC: Duke University Press, 2008).

75. Carlos E. Sluzki, Donald C. Ransom, and Gregory Bateson, *Double Bind: The Foundation of Communicational Approach to the Family* (New York: Psychological Corporation, 1976).

76. Eric Conan and Henry Rousso, *Vichy, un passé qui ne passe pas* (Paris: Hachette Pluriel Editions, 2013).

77. Quoted in Johannes Wetzel, "'The Past Doesn't Pass'—A German Look at France's Nazi Collaboration," *World Crunch*, October 15, 2012, http://www.world crunch.com/culture-society/-quot-the-past-doesn-039-t-pass-quot-a-german-look-at -france-039-s-nazi-collaboration/france-nazis-occupation-holocaust-vichy/c3s9843/# .UobobMfTaOg.

78. La Baume, "French Railway Formally Apologizes to Holocaust Victims," *New York Times*, January 25, 2011.

79. Annette Wieviorka, "La SNCF, la Shoah et le juge," *L'Histoire* 316 (2007): 89–99.

80. Katherine Shaver, "Maryland Lawmaker Says He Won't Jeopardize Purple Line Funding with Holocaust Bill," *Washington Post*, March 11, 2014.

81. Shaver, "Maryland Lawmaker Says He Won't Jeopardize Purple Line Funding."

82. Richard Prasquier, "Discours de Richard Prasquier au diner du CRIF," Conseil Représentatif des Institutions Juives de France, February 9, 2011, http://www.crif.org/ fr/lecrifenaction/Discours-de-Richard-Prasquier-au-diner-du-CRIF-du-mercredi-9 -fevrier-201123633.

83. J. Rotblut, personal communication, Washington, DC, May 24, 2014.

84. Serge Klarsfeld, "Analyse des excuses présentées par le président de la SNCF à propos des convois de déportés," *Daily Motion*, January 27, 2011.

85. S. Klarsfeld, personal communication, Paris, January 8, 2011.

86. S. Klarsfeld, personal communication, Paris, January 8, 2011.

87. Manfred Gerstenfeld, "The French Railway and the Jews 1943–44—Op-Eds," *Israel National News*, March 6, 2014.

88. Gerstenfeld, "The French Railway and the Jews 1943–44—Op-Eds."

89. A. Zdroui, personal communication, France, August 4, 2014.

90. H.B. 1326, 431th Gen. Assem., reg. sess. (Md. 2014).

91. L. Helawaser, personal communication, Paris, July 25, 2014, December 5, 2014, December 15, 2016.

92. R. Fauguet-Zejgman, personal communication, Paris, August 13, 2014.

Chapter 6. SNCF America

Chapter epigraphs are from Guillaume Pepy, "Statement By: Guillaume Pepy, Chairman of SNCF, Regarding SNCF's Role in World War II (WWII)," *PRNewswire*, November 4, 2010, https://www.prnewswire.com/news-releases/statement-by-guillaume-pepy-chairman-of-sncf-regarding-sncfs-role-in-world-war-ii-wwii-106716278.html; and H.B. 1326, 431th Gen. Assem., reg. sess. (Md. 2014).

1. Margaret Urban Walker, *Moral Repair: Reconstructing Moral Relations after Wrongdoing* (New York: Cambridge University Press, 2006).

2. H. Kerner, personal communication, February 28, 2014.

3. Name changed, personal communication, May 7, 2014.

4. Name changed, personal communication, May 7, 2014.

5. C. Srebnik, telephone conversation with author, June 14, 2017.

6. Foundation Initiative of the German Industry, a group of companies with ties to slave labor during the war, and the German federal government joined together to compensate forced laborers and others who suffered under the National Socialist period. The Law on the Creation of a Foundation "Remembrance, Responsibility and Future" came into effect on August 12, 2000 (officially known as Federal Law Gazette I 1263). The fund also supported other related social interest, research, and educational projects.

7. M. Gurwith, telephone conversation with author, June 10, 2014.

8. M. Reinstein, email message to author, October 2, 2017.

9. Stuart Eizenstat, *Imperfect Justice: Looted Assets, Slave Labor, and the Unfinished Business of World War II* (New York: Public Affairs, 2009), 76.

10. Eizenstat, *Imperfect Justice*, 325.

11. Eizenstat, *Imperfect Justice*. Known as the "French Bank Settlement" (legal references: 37665, 2156 UNTS 281, 320).

12. R. Weisberg, telephone conversation with author, June 27, 2014.

13. *Abrams v. Société Nationale des Chemins de Fer Français*, 175 F. Supp. 2d 423 (E.D.N.Y. 2001).

14. That same year, France (via the Matteoli Commission) produced its final report regarding theft of Jewish assets during the Vichy regime. The orphans' pension campaign also began distributing funds to children of murdered deportees.

15. For the district court decision, see *Abrams v. Société Nationale des Chemins de Fer Français*. The plaintiffs were represented by Stephen T. Rodd, Harriet Tamen, Clifford James, Richard H. Weisberg, and Lucille A. Roussin. Mitchell A. Karlan represented the SNCF. The litigants tried, unsuccessfully, to bring their case to the Supreme Court in 2005. The Court of Appeals reinstated the case on the basis of the claim by the litigants that the FSIA did not exist during the time of the crime. The Supreme Court had ruled in a prior case that the FSIA applied retroactively, forcing the Court of Appeals to eventually dismiss the case.

16. *Freund v. Republic of France*, 592 F. Supp. 2d 540 (S.D.N.Y. 2008). The decision was upheld in 2010.

17. The group appealed. For the rejection of the appeal, see *Freund v. De Fer Français*, no. 09-0318-cv, 2d Cir. (September 7, 2010), https://www.leagle.com/decision/infco20100907061.

18. "To ensure that the courts of the United States may provide an impartial forum for claims brought by United States citizens and others against any railroad organized as a separate legal entity, arising from the deportation of United States citizens and others to Nazi concentration camps on trains owned or operated by such railroad, and by the heirs and survivors of such persons." H.R. 4237. 111th Cong., 1st sess. (December 8, 2009), https://www.congress.gov/bill/111th-congress/house-bill/4237?s=1&r=90.

19. H. Tamen, telephone conversation with author, May 30, 2011.

20. H. Tamen, telephone conversation with author, May 30, 2011.

21. Of these six hundred, roughly two hundred lived in France, two hundred lived in the United States, and two hundred lived elsewhere. Tamen and her team demanded roughly €60,000 per deportee, which would total €36 million, the corporation's 2013 revenue.

22. *Scalin v. Société Nationale des Chemins de Fer Français*, no. 15-cv-03362 (March 26, 2018), https://www.leagle.com/decision/infdco20180326d86.

23. *Scalin v. Société Nationale des Chemins de Fer Français*.

24. Name changed. Note that, in the early postwar years in France, victims also found it easier to seek restitution of looted goods and stolen dwellings than to focus on the deportations. See Shannon Fogg, *Stealing Home: Looting, Restitution, and Reconstructing Jewish Lives in France, 1942–1947* (Oxford: Oxford University Press, 2017), 143.

25. *Abrams v. Société Nationale des Chemins de Fer Français*.

26. "Case No. 0101248 Mr. A. and the similarly situated LIPIETZ plaintiffs, versus the Prefect of Haute-Garonne and the Société nationale des chemins de fer [French National Railway Company, hereinafter 'SNCF']," Administrative Court of Toulouse, France (Toulouse, France, June 6, 2006), http://lipietz.net/spip.php?article1891.

27. Tribunal de grande instance [TGI, ordinary court of original jusridiction], Paris, May 14, 2003, 2001/07912.

28. *Freund v. Republic of France*; *Freund v. Société Nationale des Chemins de Fer Français*, 132 S. Ct. 96, 181 L. Ed. 2d 25 (U.S. 2011).

29. Conseil d'État, February 16, 2009, 315499, Rec Lebon.

30. *Scalin v. Société Nationale des Chemins de Fer Français*.

31. Center for Responsive Politics, "Client Profile: SNCF," Open Secrets, 2018, https://www.opensecrets.org/lobby/clientsum.php?id=D000065089&year=2018.

32. Katherine Shaver, "Holocaust Group Faults VRE Contract," *Washington Post*, July 7, 2010.

33. Shaver, "Holocaust Group Faults VRE Contract."

34. Don Phillips, "An Old-Fashioned Rail Battle Erupts in the Nation's Capital: Boardman Admits He Was Asleep at the Switch," *Trains Magazine*, September 2010.

35. Phillips, "An Old-Fashioned Rail Battle."

36. P. Sparacino-Thiellay, personal communication, Paris, January 21, 2016.

37. The SNCF received some accusations regarding discrimination within the company; these accusations related to allegations of racial discrimination rather than to its World War II history.

38. The OSE supported Jewish children during the war in various and often creative ways. The organization hid children with non-Jewish families, placed them in residences that it could control, and even—at times—freed them from camps. Andrée Salomon, chief of the social services of OSE, saved more than 1,500 children, sneaking many from the French internment camps. The organization then worked to get them out of the country. See Anny Latour, *La Resistance juive en France (1940–1944)/Anny Latour* (Paris: Stock, 1970).

39. P. Gossels, telephone conversation with author, April 28, 2014.

40. "Broward County Libraries Division: Addressing Social Issues and Providing Community Support," Broward County, Florida, September 19, 2014, https://web apps6.broward.org/newsrelease/View.aspx?intMessageID=5522.

41. R. Kenigsberg, telephone conversation with author, March 12, 2014.

42. Name changed, telephone conversation with author, November 18, 2012.

43. Name changed, telephone conversation with author, November 18, 2012.

44. H. Tamen, telephone conversation with author, May 30, 2011 (emphasis mine).

45. R. Kenigsberg, telephone conversation with author, March 12, 2014.

46. R. Goldstein, email message to author, May 27, 2011.

47. R. Goldstein, email message to author, May 27, 2011.

48. Holocaust Accountability and Corporate Responsibility Act of 2010, H.R. 6347, 111th Cong., 2nd sess. (September 29, 2010), https://www.congress.gov/bill/111th-con gress/house-bill/6347?q=%7B%22search%22%3A%5B%22gun+control%22%5D%7D &s=1&r=2.

49. Anthony Man, "US Rep. Ron Klein Goes after Company with Holocaust Ties," *Sun Sentinel*, September 28, 2010.

50. The December 31 cutoff date was peculiar since the convoys from Drancy continued into January.

51. Deborah Dwork and Robert Jan van Pelt, *Holocaust: A History* (New York: W. W. Norton, 2002). Historians are still working out the classification of camps. Dwork and van Pelt noted that the Nazis developed three central types of camps: concentration, forced labor, and Operation Reinhard killing centers. The authors note that, in actuality, many more types of camps existed. One survivor could have, they observed, moved through more than twenty kinds of camps, including transit camps, ghettos, punishment camps, and others (358, 426). See also Aharon Weiss, "Categories of Camps," in *The Nazi Concentration Camps: Structure and Aims; The Image of the Prisoner, The Jews in the Camps Proceedings of the Fourth Yad Vashem International Historical Conference—January 1980*, ed. Israel Gutman and Avital Saf (Israel: Yad Vashem, 1984), 115–32; Raul Hilberg, *The Destruction of the European Jews*, 3rd ed., 3 vols (New Haven, CT: Yale University Press, 2003) (the first chapter of volume 3 also speaks to the designation and division of camps).

52. Amtrak's creation was catalyzed by the Rail Passenger Service Act of 1970.

53. Dennis Douté, "SNCF Letter to Representative Robert Klein of Florida," letter, September 28, 2010.

54. Other supporters of the bill included Carolyn Maloney, Jerrold Nadler, Ileana Ros-Lehtinen, and Charles Schumer. Cosponsors included Representatives Gary Ackerman, Theodore Deutsch, Maurice Hinchey, Ron Klein, and Senators Evan Bayh, Russ Feingold, Al Franken, and Joseph Lieberman. Congresswoman Corrine Brown supports

the SNCF and the state's effort to seek federal funding for rail projects. See History, Art & Archives, "Brown, Corrine," United States House of Representatives, https://history.house.gov/People/Detail/7695.

55. Conseil d'État, February 16, 2009, 315499, Rec Lebon.

56. Transportation Projects: High-Speed Rail, AB 619, California State Senate, Transportation and Housing Committee (June 25, 2010); Bob Blumenfield, Assembly Bill 619 (California, February 25, 2009), http://leginfo.ca.gov/pub/09-10/bill/asm/ab _0601-0650/ab_619_bill_20100831_enrolled.html. "This bill would require any entity applying for a contract with the authority for goods or services related to the high-speed train network, as specified, to affirmatively certify whether it had any direct involvement in the deportation of any individuals to extermination camps, work camps, concentration camps, prisoner of war camps, or any similar camps between specified dates during World War II. The bill would also require the authority to acknowledge and note the importance of complying with this certification, as provided."

57. M. Rothman, telephone conversation with author, March 24, 2011.

58. Transportation Projects: High-Speed Rail, AB 619.

59. Theodore Kornweibel, *Railroads in the African American Experience: A Photographic Journey* (Baltimore, MD: Johns Hopkins University Press, 2010).

60. D. Davidson, personal communication, Washington, DC, May 27, 2014.

61. Arnold Schwarzenegger, veto of Assembly Bill 619 (Sacramento, CA, September 30, 2010).

62. Transportation Projects: High-Speed Rail, AB 619.

63. Holocaust Accountability and Corporate Responsibility Act of 2010, H.R. 6347, 111th Cong. (September 29, 2010), https://www.govtrack.us/congress/bills/111/hr6347. Florida legislators introduced the Holocaust Accountability and Corporate Accountability Act (S. 28/H.R. 4237).

64. H.B. 520, 428th Gen. Assem., reg. sess. (Md. 2011).

65. H.B. 1326, 431st Gen. Assem., reg. sess. (Md. 2014).

66. P. Blum, personal communication, Paris, August 12, 2014.

CHAPTER 7. MARYLAND TAKES ON THE SNCF

1. David Hawkins, *Power vs. Force* (Carlsbad, CA: Hay House, 2014), 8.

2. H.B. 520, 428th Gen. Assem., reg. sess. (Md. 2011).

3. P. Rochefort, email message to author, December 14, 2017.

4. Bombardier won the maintenance portion of the contract. The SNCF (Keolis) won no part of the bid.

5. See *Mergent International Manual*, vol. 1. (New York: Mergent Business Press, 2016). In 1998 the Deutsche Waggonbau AG was sold to Bombardier for $517.8 million (CAD). During the war, the Nazis used the Waggonbeau factories to support the war effort, relying increasingly on forced labor. The factories provided turbines and steam generators for Nazi V-2 rocket facilities.

6. Leo Bretholz and Michael Olesker, *Leap into Darkness: Seven Years on the Run in Wartime Europe* (New York: Anchor, 1999).

7. On January 8, 2014, the following were finalists for the Purple Line project:

- Maryland Purple Line Partners, composed of Vinci Concessions, Walsh Investors, InfraRed Capital Partners, Alstom Transport, and Keolis

- Maryland Transit Connectors, composed of John Laing, Kiewit Development Co., and Edgemoor Infrastructure
- Purple Line Transit Partners, composed of Meridiam Infrastructure, Fluor Enterprises, and Star America Fund
- Purple Plus Alliance, composed of Macquarie Capital and Skanska Infrastructure Development.

8. H.B. 1326, 431th Gen. Assem., reg. sess. (Md. 2014).

9. Leo Bretholz, "No Reparations, No Business [Commentary]," *Baltimore Sun*, March 1, 2014.

10. H.B. 1326, 431th Gen. Assem., reg. sess. (Md. 2014).

11. Sitting shiva is the Jewish act of mourning. Friends and family visit the mourners, often bringing food and sharing stories.

12. R. Weisberg, telephone conversation with author, June 27, 2014.

13. D. Davidson, personal communication, Washington, DC, May 27, 2014.

14. H.B. 1326, 431th Gen. Assem., reg. sess. (Md. 2014); Public-Private Partnerships—Disclosure of Involvement in Deportations, S. 754, Maryland State Senate, Committee on Budget and Taxation (Annapolis, MD, March 13, 2014).

15. H.B. 520, 428th Gen. Assem., reg. sess. (Md. 2011).

16. A. Greenfield, personal communication, Annapolis, MD, March 24, 2014.

17. S. Rosenberg, personal communication, Annapolis, MD, March 19, 2014. Prior to the hearing, with the help of library staff at the USHMM, I had checked the status of the archives. The whole archive appeared indexed and digitized, although some specific documents were not yet available online and could be obtained only by request. But those requests could be made.

18. H.B. 1326, 431th Gen. Assem., reg. sess. (Md. 2014).

19. A. Greenfield, personal communication, Annapolis, MD, March 24, 2014.

20. Wendy Kaminer, *I Am Dysfunctional, You Are Dysfunctional* (Reading, MA: Soapbox Books, 2004).

21. A. Leray, personal communication, Bethesda, MD, November 4, 2014.

22. Maurice Halbwachs, *On Collective Memory* (Chicago: University of Chicago Press, 1992).

23. Sarah Federman, "Corporate Leadership and Mass Atrocity," *Journal of Business Ethics*, April 15, 2020, https://link.springer.com/article/10.1007/s10551-020-04506-4.

24. K. Reznik, personal communication, Annapolis, MD, March 19, 2014.

25. Associated Press, "U.S. in Talks with France on Holocaust Compensation," *USA Today*, April 7, 2014.

26. Source within the Foreign Service Institute, personal communication, February 13, 2020.

27. L. Liberman, personal communication, March 24, 2014.

28. B. Neuborne, personal communication, January 14, 2012.

29. Channah (last name unknown), personal communication, Washington, DC, April 30, 2014.

30. Barry Rascover, "Legislators Refight the Holocaust and Endanger Purple Line," *Maryland Reporter*, March 16, 2014.

31. S. Rosenberg, personal communication, Maryland, March 19, 2014.

32. Kieran McEvoy and Kirsten McConnachie, "Victimology in Transitional Justice: Victimhood, Innocence and Hierarchy," *European Journal of Criminology* 9, no. 5 (2012): 527–38.

33. Orrin Klapp, "Heroes, Villains and Fools, as Agents of Social Control," *American Sociological Review* 19, no. 1 (1954): 60.

34. Algirdas Julien Greimas and Joseph Cortés, *Semiotics and Language: An Analytical Dictionary* (Bloomington: Indiana University Press, 1982).

35. Tobias Greiff, Violent Places: Everyday Politics and Public Lives in Post-Dayton Bosnia and Herzegovina (Berlin: Tectum, 2018).

36. Erich Goode, "Labeling Theory," in *Encyclopedia of Criminology and Criminal Justice*, ed. Gerben Bruinsma and David Weisburd (New York: Springer, 2014), 2807–14.

37. Klapp, "Heroes, Villains and Fools."

38. Martha Minow, *Between Vengeance and Forgiveness: Facing History after Genocide and Mass Violence* (Boston: Beacon, 1999); John Braithwaite, "Restorative Justice: Theories and Worries," in Annual Report for 2003 and Resource Material Series No. 63, Asia and Far East Institute for the Prevention of Crime and the Treatment of Offenders (UNAFEI) (Fuchu, Tokyo: UNAFEI, 2004), 47–56.

39. Vivienne Jabri, *Discourses on Violence: Conflict Analysis Reconsidered* (New York: Manchester University Press, 1996).

40. Rama Mani, "Rebuilding an Inclusive Political Community After War," *Security Dialogue* 36, no. 4 (2005): 511.

41. Michael R. Marrus, "The Case of the French Railways and the Deportation of Jews in 1944," in *Holocaust and Justice: Representation and Historiography of the Holocaust in Post-War Trials*, ed. David Bankier and Dan Michman (New York: Berghahn Books, 2010), 254.

42. Erving Goffman, *The Presentation of Self in Everyday Life* (New York: Doubleday, 1959).

43. Sarah Federman, "The 'Ideal Perpetrator': The French National Railways and the Social Construction of Accountability," *Security Dialogue* 49, no. 5 (2018): 327–44.

44. Nils Christie, "The Ideal Victim," in *From Crime Policy to Victim Policy*, ed. Ezzat A. Fattah (London: Macmillan, 1986), 17–30.

45. Christie, "The Ideal Victim."

46. Michael J. Bazyler, *Holocaust Justice: The Battle for Restitution in America's Courts* (New York: New York University Press, 2005). For an example of contemporary backlash against Hugo Boss, see Guy Walters, "Shameful Truth about Hugo Boss's Links to the Nazis Revealed: As Russell Brand Is Thrown Out of a Party for Accusing Fashion Designer of Helping Hitler," *Daily Mail*, September 5, 2013.

47. Raul Hilberg, *The Destruction of European Jews*, vol. 1, rev. ed. (New York: Holmes & Meier, 1985).

48. David Barnouw, Dirk Mulder, and Guus Veenendaal, *De Nederlandse Spoorwegen in oorlogstijd 1939–1945: Rijden voor Vaderland en Vijand* (Zwolle, Netherlands: W Books, 2019), 114.

49. Marrus, "The Case of the French Railways," 256.

50. For examples, see the National Monument for Westerbork, the memorial at Prague's Bubny train station, the Drancy internment camp, or the Baltimore Holocaust Memorial Park.

51. Marrus, "The Case of the French Railways," 256.

52. Vladimir Propp, *Morphology of the Folktale*, 2nd ed. (Austin: University of Texas Press, 2010), uses the term "dispatcher," building his typology of characters from Russian folktales. He found that one character first makes the perpetrator visible and then dispatches the hero to slay this villain. Greimas and Cortés, *Semiotics and Language*, use the term "sponsor" to describe a similar role.

53. Mark Osiel, *Mass Atrocity, Collective Memory, and the Law* (New Brunswick, NJ: Transaction, 1999).

54. Harm Ede Botje and Mischa Cohen, "Hoe Salo Muller de NS alsnog de rekening van de oorlog presenteerde," *Vrij Nederland*, May 4, 2019.

55. Marrus, "The Case of the French Railways," 259.

Chapter 8. Memory Laws and Atonement

1. Barbara Bodalska, "Polish President Signs Anti-Defamation Bill, Causing International Protests," EURACTIV, February 7, 2018, https://www.euractiv.com/section/central-europe/news/polish-president-signs-anti-defamation-bill-causing-international-protests/.

2. Henry Rousso, "French Memory Laws and the Crisis of the Republican Model" (presented at the Memory Laws: Criminalizing Historical Narrative Conference, Columbia University, New York, October 28, 2017).

3. As of 2017, ten individuals had been arrested under this law. See Loi no. 90-615 du 13 juillet 1990 tendant à réprimer tout acte raciste, antisémite ou xénophobe [Law 90-615 of July 13, 1990, for the Suppression of Racist, Antisemitic, or Xenophobic Acts], Journal officiel de la République française [J.O., Official Gazette of France], July 13, 1990, 8333.

4. Loi no. 99-882 du 18 octobre 1999 relative à la substitution, à l'expression "aux opérations effectuées en Afrique du Nord," de l'expression "à la guerre d'Algérie ou aux combats en Tunisie et au Maroc" [Law 99-882 of October 18, 1999, on the Substitution of the Expression "Operations Carried out in North Africa" with the expression "Algerian War and Fighting in Tunisia and Morocco], Journal officiel de la République française [J.O., Official Gazette of France], Oct. 20, 1999, 15647.

5. For the law pertaining to the Armenian genocide, see Loi no. 2001-70 du 29 janvier 2001 relative à la reconnaissance du génocide arménien de 1915 [Law 2001-70 of January 29, 2001, concerning the Recognition of the Armenian Genocide of 1915], Journal officiel de la République française [J.O., Official Gazette of France], January 29, 2001, 1590. For the law pertaining to the Atlantic slave trade, see Loi no. 2001-434 du 21 mai 2001 tendant à la reconnaissance de la traite et de l'esclavage en tant que crime contre l'humanité [Law 2001-434 of May 21, 2001, for the Recognition of Trafficking and Slavery as a Crime against Humanity], Journal officiel de la République française [J.O., Official Gazette of France], May 21, 2001, 8175.

6. Béatrice Gurrey, "Le président du devoir de mémoire," *Le Monde*, March 12, 2007.

7. Loi no. 2005-158 du 23 février 2005 portant reconnaissance de la Nation et contribution nationale en faveur des Français rapatriés [Law 2005-158 of February 23, 2005, for the recognition of the nation and national contribution in favor of the French repatriated], *Journal officiel de la République française [J.O.,* Official Gazette of France], February 23, 2005, 3128.

8. Rousso, "French Memory Laws."

9. Sarah Gensburger, "Les Figures du Juste et du Résistant et l'évolution de la mémoire historique française de l'occupation," *Revue française de science politique* 52, no. 2 (2002): 291–322.

10. See Sarah Gensburger and Marie-Claire Lavabre, "Entre 'devoir de mémoire' et 'abus de mémoire': La sociologie de la mémoire comme tierce position," in *Histoire, mémoire et épistémologie: À propos de Paul Ricoeur*, ed. Bertrand Müller (Lausanne: Payot, 2005), 76–95. Gensburger and Lavabre consider the complex line between the necessity and the abuse of memory, offering memory studies as a different vantage point for the discussion.

11. Lars Waldorf, "Victors' Memory: Criminalizing Remembrance in Rwanda and Sri Lanka" (presented at the Memory Laws: Criminalizing Historical Narrative Conference, Columbia University, New York, October 28, 2017).

12. Not long after the fall of the Berlin Wall, in 1994 the modern Deutsche Bahn was created from the Deutsche Bundesbahn (German Federal Railway), which had operated in West Germany during the Cold War, and the Deutsche Reichsbahn (German Reich Railway), which had operated in East Germany. The new company was a separate legal entity as well; this provided the company some protection from the transnational Holocaust litigation that occurred throughout the 1990s.

13. B. Emsellem, personal communication, Paris, April 16, 2011.

14. Jack Lepiarz, "MassDOT Selects New Commuter Rail Operator," *WBUR*, January 9, 2014, http://www.wbur.org/2014/01/09/keolis-commuter-rail-contract.

15. Stewart Ain, "Maryland Mulls Reparation Push from French Rail Firm," *Jewish Week*, February 25, 2014.

16. Nelson Camillo Sánchez, "Corporate Accountability, Reparations, and Distributive Justice," in *Corporate Accountability in the Context of Transitional Justice*, ed. Sabine Michalowski (New York: Routledge, 2013), 114–30.

17. "Guillaume Pepy reconnait le rôle de la SNCF dans la Shoah," *Le Monde*, January 25, 2011.

18. A. Leray, telephone conversation with author, November 2, 2015.

19. Michael R. Marrus, "The End of the Line: The French Courts and Liability for the Holocaust in France: The Glemane Avis 2009" (presentation at the Minerva Institute at Tel Aviv University Conference on Corporate Accountability for Mass Atrocity, Tel Aviv, Israel, December 16, 2012).

20. A. Fogel, email message to author, March 13, 2016.

21. For the United States, this was a sole executive agreement, meaning it did not require congressional ratification.

22. Initially the agreement referred to the "Vichy Government." Staff at the US Department of State said that their French counterparts took issue with Vichy being referred to as an actual, legitimate French government. They wanted the agreement to clarify that Vichy was a ruling body under the Nazis.

23. 37665, 2156 UNTS 281, 320. United States Germany Agreement Concerning the Foundation "Remembrance, Responsibility and the Future," July 17, 2000, U.S.–Ger., 39 I.L.M. 1298 (2000); Ronald Niezen, *Truth and Indignation: Canada's Truth and Reconciliation Commission on Indian Residential Schools*, 2nd ed. (Toronto: University of Toronto Press, 2017).

CONCLUSION

1. C. Sodos, personal communication, December 11, 2017, and April 18, 2018. These companies could receive other recognition but not an inscription on the donor wall or their name embossed or etched anywhere else. Siemens's name had somehow snuck in, but I was told this was an oversight.

2. See John Braithwaite, "Restorative Justice: Theories and Worries," in *Annual Report for 2003 and Resource Material Series No. 63*, Asia and Far East Institute for the Prevention of Crime and the Treatment of Offenders (UNAFEI) (Fuchu, Tokyo: UNAFEI, 2004), 47–56.

3. SNCF, "Promoting Sustainability," February 11, 2020, https://www.sncf.com/en/commitments/sustainble-development/leading-the-charge-for-the-planet.

4. Erin Corbett, "DC Metro's Largest Union Refuses to Transport White Nationalists," *Fortune*, August 4, 2018.

5. Sam Levin, "California Transit Agency Allows Ad from Holocaust Denial Group," *Guardian*, September 12, 2018.

6. Richard Fausset, "Airlines Ask Government Not to Use Their Flights to Carry Children Separated at Border," *New York Times*, June 20, 2018.

7. Christopher Jasper, "French Rail Giant SNCF Braced for German Threat to Iconic TGV," *Bloomberg*, September 20, 2018.

8. See Jean-Marie Dubois and Malka Marcovich, *Les Bus de la honte* (Paris: Tallandier, 2016).

9. See Harm Ede Botje and Mischa Cohen, "Hoe Salo Muller de NS alsnog de rekening van de oorlog presenteerde," *Vrij Nederland*, May 4, 2019.

10. See Lianne Kolirin and Laura Smith-Spark, "Holocaust Survivor Wants Compensation for Rail Journeys to Death Camps," *CNN*, July 31, 2020; and Daniel Boffey, "Holocaust Survivor Launches Legal Claim against German Railway," *The Guardian*, July 30, 2020.

11. Jeremy Sarkin-Hughes, *Germany's Genocide of the Herero: Kaiser Wilhelm II, His General, His Settlers, His Soldiers* (New York: Boydell & Brewer, 2011), 235.

12. In re *African-American Slave Descendants Litigation*, 231 F. Supp. 2d 1357 (E.D.N.Y. 2002).

13. See John G. Dale, *Free Burma: Transnational Legal Action and Corporate Accountability* (Minneapolis: University of Minnesota Press, 2011).

14. See Neil Forbes, "Multinational Enterprise, 'Corporate Responsibility' and the Nazi Dictatorship: The Case of Unilever and Germany in the 1930s," *Contemporary European History* 16, no. 2 (2007): 149–67.

15. Al Rosenbloom and RuthAnn Althaus, "Degussa AG and Its Holocaust Legacy," *Journal of Business Ethics* 92, no. 2 (2010): 183–94.

16. Marc Howard Ross, *Cultural Contestation in Ethnic Conflict* (Cambridge: Cambridge University Press, 2007).

17. C. Hershkovitch, personal communication, July 28, 2020.

18. S. Capicotto, telephone conversation with author, November 21, 2017. The SNCF donation to the Auschwitz Institute was not part of the company's normally allocated funds (which had been dispensed already for year) and also not part of the $5 million it was required to provide as part of the $60 million French–US settlement.

The donation came about, Capicotto says, because SNCF America CEO Alain Leray knew a board member of the Institute, met with the board, and was moved by the program's intention and strategy.

19. See Corporate Human Rights Benchmark (CHRB), *Corporate Human Rights Benchmark: 2019 Key Findings* (CHRB Ltd., 2019), https://www.corporatebenchmark .org/sites/default/files/2019-11/CHRB2019KeyFindingsReport.pdf.

20. Austin Davis, "China Cables: Germany under Pressure to Respond to Beijing's Uighur Internment," *DW*, November 25, 2019, https://www.dw.com/en/china-uighurs -siemens-germany-partnership/a-51405883.

21. Lily Kuo, "China Transferred Detained Uighurs to Factories Used by Global Brands—Report," *Guardian*, March 1, 2020.

22. Milton Friedman, *Capitalism and Freedom* (Chicago: University of Chicago Press, 1962).

23. Florian Wettstein, "CSR and the Debate on Business and Human Rights: Bridging the Great Divide," *Business Ethics Quarterly* 22, no. 4 (2012): 739–70.

24. Michael J. Kelly and Luis Moreno-Ocampo, *Prosecuting Corporations for Genocide* (New York: Oxford University Press, 2016).

25. Kelly and Moreno-Ocampo, *Prosecuting Corporations for Genocide*. This could be useful in domestic courts and could also be an amendment to the Rome Statute, which frames the mandate of the International Criminal Court.

26. Susan Ariel Aaronson and Ian Higham, "'Re-Righting Business': John Ruggie and the Struggle to Develop International Human Rights Standards for Transnational Firms," *Human Rights Quarterly* 35, no. 2 (2013): 333–64.

27. See Office of the United Nations High Commissioner for Human Rights (OHCHR), "OHCHR Accountability and Remedy Project: Improving Accountability and Access to Remedy in Cases of Business Involvement in High Rights Abuses," OHCHR, https://www.ohchr.org/EN/Issues/Business/Pages/OHCHRaccountability andremedyproject.aspx.

28. Shamaria Randolph, "Breast Cancer Awareness: The Controversy behind the Cause" (presented at the University of Baltimore, Ethnic and Cultural Factors of Conflict course, Baltimore, MD, November 14, 2018).

29. Øystein H. Rolandsen, "Small and Far Between: Peacekeeping Economies in South Sudan," *Journal of Intervention and State Building* 9, no. 3 (2015): 1–19.

30. Sara Cobb, Sarah Federman, and Alison Castel, *Introduction to Conflict Resolution: Discourses and Dynamics* (London: Rowman & Littlefield, 2019).

31. Anne McCarthy, "La Bataille du Rail: Paris under German Occupation Revisited at Cannes Film Festival," *France Today*, May 30, 2017.

32. The book seems to be a complement or response to the well-known book compiled by Serge and Beate Klarsfeld that traced the destinies of all the deportees. Serge Klarsfeld and Beate Klarsfeld, *Le Mémorial de la déportation des Juifs d France* (Paris: Association des fils et filles des déportés juifs de France, 2012).

33. See R. Dautry, "Note Remise Par M. Dautry Ministre de L'Armement à M. Paul Reynaud Président du Conseil: Destinée au Conseil des Ministres Dur Mercredi 12 Juin 1940, 14 Heures Mais Remise Seulement le Lendemain au Président du Conseil," *Revue d'histoire de la Deuxième Guerre Mondiale* 1, no. 3 (1951): 56–58.

34. Specifically, Dautry worked with the British to purchase from Norway all of the "heavy water" needed for the bomb. Heavy water, deuterium oxide, is a type of water used to cool nuclear reactors. See Lynne Olson, *Last Hope Island: Britain, Occupied Europe, and the Brotherhood That Helped Turn the Tide of War* (New York: Random House, 2017).

35. Raul Hilberg, "German Railroads/Jewish Souls," *Society* 14, no. 1 (1976): 73.

36. R. Gerbosi, personal communication, Florida, January 10, 2013.

37. See "The Convoi 77 Project: Teaching the History of the Shoah in a Different Way," Convoi 77, https://convoi77.org/en/.

Bibliography

BOOKS, JOURNALS, ARTICLES

Aaronson, Susan Ariel, and Ian Higham. "'Re-Righting Business': John Ruggie and the Struggle to Develop International Human Rights Standards for Transnational Firms." *Human Rights Quarterly* 35, no. 2 (2013): 333–64.

Adler, Jacques. *The Jews of Paris and the Final Solution: Communal Responses and Internal Conflicts, 1940–44.* New York: Oxford University Press, 1987.

Adler, Libby, and Peer Zumbansen. "The Forgetfulness of Noblesse: A Critique of the German Foundation Law Compensating Slave and Forced Laborers of the Third Reich." *Harvard Journal on Legislation* 39, no. 1 (Winter 2002): 1–61.

Ain, Stewart. "Maryland Mulls Reparation Push from French Rail Firm." *Jewish Week*, February 25, 2014.

Alexander, Jeffrey C. *The Civil Sphere.* New York: Oxford University Press, 2006.

L'ancienne gare de Bobigny, entre Drancy et Auschwitz. Ville de Bobigny, France, 2011.

Andrieu, Claire, ed. *La Persécution des Juifs de France 1940–1944 et le rétablissement de la légalité républicaine: Recueil des textes officiels 1940–1999.* Paris: La Documentation française, 2000.

Andrieu, Kora. "Dealing with a 'New' Grievance: Should Anticorruption Be Part of the Transitional Justice Agenda?" *Journal of Human Rights* 11, no. 4 (2012): 537–57.

Arbour, Louise. "Economic and Social Justice for Societies in Transition." *New York University Journal of International Law and Politics* 40, no. 1 (2007): 1–27.

Arendt, Hannah. *Eichmann in Jerusalem: A Report on the Banality of Evil.* New York: Penguin Books, 2006.

Arnaud, Patrice. *Les STO, histoire des Français requis en Allemagne nazie, 1942–1945.* Paris: CNRS Éditions, 2010.

Associated Press. "U.S. in Talks with France on Holocaust Compensation." *USA Today*, April 7, 2014.

Aukerman, Miriam J. "Extraordinary Evil, Ordinary Crime: A Framework for Understanding Transitional Justice." *Harvard Human Rights Journal* 15, no. 39 (2002): 39–97.

Avruch, Kevin. "Truth and Reconciliation Commissions: Problems in Transitional Justice and the Reconstruction of Identity." *Transcultural Psychiatry* 47, no. 1 (2010): 33–49.

Azouvi, François. *Le Mythe du grand silence: Auschwitz, les Français, la mémoire*. Paris: Fayard, 2012.

Bachelier, Christian. *La SNCF sous l'occupation allemande, 1940–1944*. Paris: AHICF, 1996.

Balasco, Lauren Marie. "The Transitions of Transitional Justice: Mapping the Waves from Promise to Practice." *Journal of Human Rights* 12, no. 2 (2013): 198–216.

Bamberg, Michael. "Positioning with Dave Hogan: Stories, Tellings, and Identities." In *Narrative Analysis*, edited by Colette Daiute and Cynthia G. Lightfoot, 135–57. London: SAGE, 2004.

Barnouw, David, Dirk Mulder, and Guus Veenendaal. *De Nederlandse Spoorwegen in oorlogstijd 1939–1945: Rijden voor Vaderland en Vijand*. Zwolle, Netherlands: W Books, 2019.

Barthes, Ronald. "An Introduction to the Structural Analysis of Narrative." *New Literary Theory* 6, no. 2 (1975): 237–72.

Bazyler, Michael J. *Holocaust, Genocide, and the Law: A Quest for Justice in a Post-Holocaust World*. New York: Oxford University Press, 2017.

Bazyler, Michael J. *Holocaust Justice: The Battle for Restitution in America's Courts*. New York: New York University Press, 2005.

Bensimon, Doris, *Les Grandes Rafles: Juifs en France 1940–1944*. Toulouse: Privat, 1987.

Bernstein, Catherine, director. *La SNCF sous l'occupation*. Paris: Zadig Productions, 2019.

Bibas, Nathalie. *Henri Lang 1895–1942: Un dirigeant de la SNCF mort à Auschwitz*. Paris: Éditions LBM, 2012.

Bilsky, Leora. *The Holocaust, Corporations, and the Law: Unfinished Business*. Ann Arbor: University of Michigan Press, 2017.

Birn, Jacqueline Mendels. *A Dimanche Prochain: A Memoir of Survival in World War II France*. 2013. Self-published and available at http://jacquelinemendelsbirn.com.

Black, Edwin. *IBM and the Holocaust: The Strategic Alliance between Nazi Germany and America's Most Powerful Corporation*. New York: Crown, 2001.

Blumenfield, Bob. Assembly Bill 619. California. February 25, 2009. http://leginfo.ca .gov/pub/09-10/bill/asm/ab_0601-0650/ab_619_bill_20100831_enrolled.html.

Bodalska, Barbara. "Polish President Signs Anti-Defamation Bill, Causing International Protests." EURACTIV, February 7, 2018. https://www.euractiv.com/section/ central-europe/news/polish-president-signs-anti-defamation-bill-causing-interna tional-protests/.

Boffey, Daniel. "Dutch Rail to Pay Compensation for Transporting Jews to Nazi Death Camps." *The Guardian*, November 28, 2018.

Boffey, Daniel. "Holocaust Survivor Launches Legal Claim against German Railway." *The Guardian*, July 30, 2020.

Bohoslavsky, Juan Pablo, and Veerle Opgenhaffen. "The Past and Present of Corporate Complicity: Financing the Argentinean Dictatorship." *Harvard Human Rights Journal* 23, no. 1 (Spring 2010): 157–204.

Bosch, Roselyne, director. *La Rafle*. Paris: Legende Films, 2010.

Bouris, Erica. *Complex Political Victims*. Bloomfield, CT: Kumarian, 2007.

Boutbien, Leon. "Klaus Barbie." *Revue des deux mondes* (May 1983): 325–28.

Braithwaite, John. "Restorative Justice: Theories and Worries." In *Annual Report for 2003 and Resource Material Series No. 63*, Asia and Far East Institute for the Prevention of Crime and the Treatment of Offenders (UNAFEI), 47–56. Fuchu, Tokyo: UNAFEI, 2004.

Breitman, Richard, Norman J. W. Goda, Timothy Naftali, and Robert Wolfe. *U.S. Intelligence and the Nazis*. New York: Cambridge University Press, 2005.

Bretholz, Leo. "No Reparations, No Business [Commentary]." *Baltimore Sun*, March 1, 2014.

Bretholz, Leo, and Michael Olesker. *Leap into Darkness: Seven Years on the Run in Wartime Europe*. New York: Anchor, 1999.

Broch, L. M. E. "French Railway Workers under German Occupation, 1940–1944." Order No. U566539. PhD diss., University of Oxford, 2011.

Broch, Ludivine. "French Railway Workers and the Question of Rescue during the Holocaust." *Diasporas* 25 (2015): 147–67.

Broch, Ludivine. *Ordinary Workers, Vichy and the Holocaust: French Railwaymen and the Second World War*. Cambridge: Cambridge University Press, 2016.

Broch, Ludivine. "Professionalism in the Final Solution: French Railway Workers and the Jewish Deportations, 1942–4." *Contemporary European History* 23, no. 3 (2014): 359–80.

"Broward County Libraries Division: Addressing Social Issues and Providing Community Support." Broward County, Florida, September 19, 2014. https://webapps6.broward.org/newsrelease/View.aspx?intMessageID=5522.

Browning, Christopher. *The Origins of the Final Solution: The Evolution of Nazi Jewish Policy, September 1939–March 1942*. With contributions by Jürgen Matthäus. Lincoln: University of Nebraska Press, 2004.

Bush, Jonathan A. "The Prehistory of Corporations and Conspiracy in International Criminal Law: What Nuremberg Really Said." *Columbia Law Review* 109, no. 5 (2009): 1094–1262.

Carranza, Ruben. "Plunder and Pain: Should Transitional Justice Engage with Corruption and Economic Crimes?" *International Journal of Transitional Justice* 2, no. 3 (2008): 310–30.

Cavallaro, James, and Sebastián Albuja. "The Lost Agenda: Economic Crimes and Truth Commissions in Latin America and Beyond." In *Transitional Justice from Below: Grassroots Activism and the Struggle for Change*, edited by Kieran McEvoy and Lorna McGregor, 121–88. Portland, OR: Hart, 2008.

Célerse, Grégory. *Sauvons les enfants!* Lille: Les Lumieres de Lille, 2016.

Center for Responsive Politics. "Client Profile: SNCF America, 2018." Open Secrets. https://www.opensecrets.org/lobby/clientsum.php?id=D000065089&year=2018.

Chapman, Herrick. *France's Long Reconstruction: In Search of the Modern Republic*. Cambridge, MA: Harvard University Press, 2018.

Chiomenti, Cristina. "Corporations and the International Criminal Court." In *Transnational Corporations and Human Rights*, edited by Olivier De Schutter, 287–312. Oxford: Hart, 2006.

Chirac, Jacques. "Discours du 16 juillet 1995 au Vélodrome d'Hiver." Speech, Commemorative Ceremony of the "Great Roundup," Paris, France, July 16–17, 1995.

Chirac, Jacques. "Speech by M. Jacques Chirac, President of the Republic, at the Inauguration of the Shoah Memorial, Paris 25.01.2005." France in the United Kingdom—Embassy of France in London, January 25, 2005. http://www.ambafrance-uk.org/spip.php?page=recherche&id_rubrique=2&id_sous_secteur=2&lang=en&recherche=Jacques+Chirac.

Christie, Nils. "The Ideal Victim." In *From Crime Policy to Victim Policy*, edited by Ezzat A. Fattah, 17–30. London: Macmillan, 1986.

Clément, René, director. *La Bataille du rail.* Paris: Coopérative Générale du Cinéma Français, 1946.

Cobb, Sara. "Narrative Braiding and the Role of Public Officials in Transforming the Publics Conflicts." *Narrative and Conflict: Explorations in Theory and Practice* 1, no 1 (2013): 4–30.

Cobb, Sara, Sarah Federman, and Alison Castel. *Introduction to Conflict Resolution: Discourses and Dynamics.* London: Rowman & Littlefield, 2019.

Cohen, Stanley. *States of Denial: Knowing about Atrocities and Suffering.* Malden, MA: Blackwell, 2001.

Cole, Alyson Manda. *The Cult of True Victimhood: From the War on Welfare to the War on Terror.* Stanford: Stanford University Press, 2007.

Commission consultative des dommages et reparations. 1947, Monographie TC 1, chemins de fer d'intérêt général. Data compiled by Georges Ribeill (courtesy Georges Ribeill).

Conan, Éric, and Henry Rousso. *Vichy, un passé qui ne passe pas.* Paris: Hachette Pluriel Editions, 2013.

Confédération Générale du Travail (CGT). "Construisons ensemble le Jour d'après! Signer la petition." https://www.cgt.fr/actualites/europe/mobilisation/plus-jamais-ca-construisons-ensemble-le-jour-dapres.

Convention d'armistice. Fr.-Ger., June 22, 1940. Documents on Germany Foreign Policy 1918–1945. Publication No. 6312. US Department of State.

"The Convoi 77 Project: Teaching the History of the Shoah in a Different Way." Convoi 77. https://convoi77.org/en/.

Corbett, Erin. "DC Metro's Largest Union Refuses to Transport White Nationalists." *Fortune*, August 4, 2018.

"Corporate Accountability in Transitional Justice." University of Oxford, 2020. https://ahra.web.ox.ac.uk/catj#collapse281876.

Corporate Human Rights Benchmark (CHRB). *Corporate Human Rights Benchmark: 2019 Key Findings.* CHRB Ltd., 2019.

Curran, Vivian Grosswald. "Gobalization, Legal Transnationalization and Crimes against Humanity: The Lipietz Case." *American Journal of Comparative Law* 56, no. 2 (2008): 363–402.

Dale, John G. *Free Burma: Transnational Legal Action and Corporate Accountability.* Minneapolis: University of Minnesota Press, 2011.

Dautry, R. "Note Remise Par M. Dautry Ministre de L'Armement à M. Paul Reynaud Président du Conseil: Destinée au Conseil des Ministres Dur Mercredi 12 Juin 1940, 14 Heures Mais Remise Seulement le Lendemain au Président du Conseil." *Revue d'histoire de la Deuxième Guerre Mondiale* 1, no. 3 (1951): 56–58.

Davis, Austin. "China Cables: Germany under Pressure to Respond to Beijing's Uighur Internment." *DW*, November 25, 2019. https://www.dw.com/en/china-uighurs-sie mens-germany-partnership/a-51405883.

de Berranger, Olivier. Bishop of Seine-Saint-Denis. "La Déclaration de Repentance Des Évêques de France." Declaration of Repentaence, Drancy, France, September 30, 1997. http://www.dialogue-jca.org/Repentance_des_eveques_de_France.

Delage, Christian. "The Klaus Barbie Trial: Traces and Temporalities." In "Trials of Trauma," edited by Michael G. Levine and Bella Brodzki. Special issue, *Comparative Literature Studies* 48, no. 3 (2011): 320–33.

Delbo, Charlotte. *Le Convoi du 24 janvier.* Paris: Les Editions de minuit, 1965.

Delpard, Raphaël, director. *Les Convois de la honte.* Paris: Panoceanic Films, 2010. DVD.

Democracy Now! "ExxonMobil's Dirty Secrets from Indonesia to Nigeria to D.C.: Steve Coll on 'Private Empire.'" YouTube, May 7, 2012. https://www.youtube.com/watch?v=TREblxdbJ1k.

de Rosnay, Tatiana. *Sarah's Key.* London: John Murray, 2008.

Dewey, John. "The Historic Background of Corporate Legal Personality." *Yale Law Journal* 35, no. 6 (1926): 655–73.

Douté, Dennis. "SNCF Letter to Representative Robert Klein of Florida." Letter, September 28, 2010. In author's possession.

Drexler, Elizabeth F. "Fatal Knowledge: The Social and Political Legacies of Collaboration and Betrayal in Timor-Leste." *International Journal of Transitional Justice* 7, no. 1 (January 2013): 74–94.

Dreyfus, Jean-Marc. *L'Impossible Réparation: Déportés, bien spoliés, or Nazi, comptes bloqués, criminels de guerre.* Paris: Flammarion, 2015.

Drumbl, Mark A. *Atrocity, Punishment, and International Law.* New York: Cambridge University Press, 2007.

Dubois, Jean-Marie, and Malka Marcovich. *Les bus de la honte.* Paris: Tallandier, 2016.

Duhem, Jacqueline. "Compe-rendu de lecture: 'Dossier SNCF et Déportations'" *Historail* 4 (January 2008): 2–5.

Durand, Paul. *La SNCF pendant la guerre.* Paris: Presses Universitaires de France, 1968.

"Dutch Railway Firm Apologizes for Deporting Jews during WWII." *Haaretz*, September 28, 2005.

du Toit, Andre. "The Moral Foundations of the South African TRC: Truth as Acknowledgment and Justice as Recognition." In *Truth v. Justice: The Morality of Truth Commissions*, edited by Robert I. Rotberg and Dennis F. Thompson, 122–40. Princeton, NJ: Princeton University Press, 2000.

Dwork, Deborah, and Robert Jan van Pelt. *Holocaust: A History.* New York: W. W. Norton, 2002.

Dwyer, Leslie. "A Politics of Silences: Violence, Memory and Treacherous Speech in Post-1965 Bali." In *Genocide: Truth, Memory, and Representation*, edited by Alexander Hinton and Kevin Lewis O'Neill, 113–46. Durham, NC: Duke University Press, 2009.

Ede Botje, Harm, and Mischa Cohen. "Hoe Salo Muller de NS alsnog de rekening van de oorlog presenteerde." *Vrij Nederland*, May 4, 2019. https://www.vn.nl/salo-muller -ns-rekening-oorlog/.

Eizenstat, Stuart. *Imperfect Justice: Looted Assets, Slave Labor, and the Unfinished Business of World War II*. New York: Public Affairs, 2009.

Elster, Jon. *Closing the Books: Transitional Justice in Historical Perspective*. Cambridge: Cambridge University Press, 2004.

Elster, Jon. *Explaining Social Behavior: More Nuts and Bolts for the Social Sciences*. Cambridge: Cambridge University Press, 2015.

Enns, Diane. *The Violence of Victimhood*. University Park: Pennsylvania State University Press, 2012.

Erker, Paul. *Zulieferer für Hitlers Krieg: Der Continental-Konzern in der NS-Zeit*. Berlin: De Gruyter Oldenbourg, 2020.

Ewing, Jack. "German Automotive Giant Admits It Was a Nazi Accomplice." *New York Times*, August 27, 2020.

"Facture de l'agence de voyage allemand au service des affaires juives de la Gestapo à Paris." Provided by Serge Klarsfeld, Paris, January 2011.

Fausset, Richard. "Airlines Ask Government Not to Use Their Flights to Carry Children Separated at Border." *New York Times*, June 20, 2018.

Favez, Jean-Claude. *The Red Cross and the Holocaust*. Cambridge: Cambridge University Press, 1999.

Federman, Raymond. *Shhh: The Story of a Childhood*. Buffalo, NY: Starcherone Books. 2010.

Federman, Sarah. "Altering Institutional Narratives and Rewriting History to Make Amends: The French National Railroads (SNCF)." *Narrative and Conflict: Explorations in Theory and Practice* 3, no. 1 (2016): 45–63.

Federman, Sarah. "Corporate Leadership and Mass Atrocity." *Journal of Business Ethics*, April 15, 2020. https://link.springer.com/article/10.1007/s10551-020-04506-4.

Federman, Sarah. "Genocide Studies and Corporate Social Responsibility: The Contemporary Case of the French National Railways (SNCF)." *Genocide Studies and Prevention: An International Journal* 11, no. 2 (2016): 13–35.

Federman, Sarah. "The 'Ideal Perpetrator': The French National Railways and the Social Construction of Accountability." *Security Dialogue* 49, no. 5 (2018): 327–44.

Ferencz, Benjamin B., and Telford Taylor. *Less Than Slaves: Jewish Forced Labor and the Quest for Compensation*. Bloomington: Indiana University Press, 2002.

Filhol, Emmanuel, and Marie-Christine Hubert. *Les Tsiganes en France: Un sort à part (1939–1946)*. Paris: Perrin, 2009.

Fletcher, Laurel E. "Refracted Justice: The Imagined Victim and the International Criminal Court." In *Contested Justice: The Politics and Practice of International Criminal Court Interventions*, edited by Christian De Vos, Sara Kendell, and Carsten Stahn, 302–25. Cambridge: Cambridge University Press, 2015.

Fogg, Shannon. *Stealing Home: Looting, Restitution, and Reconstructing Jewish Lives in France, 1942–1947*. Oxford: Oxford University Press, 2017.

Fondation pour la Mémoire de la Déportation (FMD). *Livre-Mémorial des déportés de France arêtes par mesure de répression et dans certains cas par measure de pérsecution 1940–1945*. Vols. 1–4. Paris: Tirésias, 2004.

Fontaine, Thomas. *Cheminots victimes de la répression: 1940–1945 Mémorial*. Paris: Perrin, 2017.

Forbes, Neil. "Multinational Enterprise, 'Corporate Responsibility' and the Nazi Dictatorship: The Case of Unilever and Germany in the 1930s." *Contemporary European History* 16, no. 2 (2007): 149–67.

France in the United States: Consulate General of France in Miami. "Holocaust Education and Compensation of Victims of Spoliation." http://www.consulfrance-miami .org/spip.php?article1969.

Frankenheimer, John, and Arthur Penn, directors. *The Train*. Los Angeles: United Artists, 1964.

Frankl, Viktor Emil. *Man's Search for Meaning: An Introduction to Logotherapy*. Boston: Beacon, 1992.

Fraser, David. "(De)Constructing the Nazi State: Criminal Organizations and the Constitutional Theory of the International Military Tribunal." *Loyola Los Angeles International and Comparative Law Journal* 39, no. 1 (Winter 2017): 117–86.

Friedlander, Saul. *Nazi Germany and the Jews: 1933–1945*. New York: Harper Perennial, 2009.

Friedman, Milton. *Capitalism and Freedom*. Chicago: University of Chicago Press, 1962.

Froment, Pascale. *René Bousquet*. Paris: Fayard, 2001.

Frye, Northrop. *The Anatomy of Criticism*. London: Penguin Books, 1957.

Gall, Lothar, and Manfred Pohl, eds. *Die Eisenbahn in Deutschland: Von den Anfängen bis zur Gegenwart* [The railroad in Germany: From the beginnings to today]. Munich: Verlag C. H. Beck, 1999.

Gauthier, Paul. *Chronique du procès Barbie: Pour servir la mémoire*. Paris: Cerf, 1988.

Gensburger, Sarah. "Les Figures du Juste et du Résistant et l'évolution de la mémoire historique française de l'occupation." *Revue française de science politique* 52, no. 2 (2002): 291–322.

Gensburger, Sarah, and Marie-Claire Lavabre. "Entre 'devoir de mémoire' et 'abus de mémoire': La sociologie de la mémoire comme tierce position." In *Histoire, mémoire et épistémologie: A propos de Paul Ricoeur*, edited by Bertrand Müller, 76–95. Lausanne: Payot, 2005.

Gensburger, Sarah, and Sandrine Lefranc. *À quoi servent les politiques de mémoire*. Paris: Presses de Sciences Po, 2017.

Gerstenfeld, Manfred. "The French Railway and the Jews 1943–44—Op-Eds." *Israel National News*, March 6, 2014.

Giedion, Sigfried. *Mechanization Takes Command: A Contribution to Anonymous History*. Minneapolis: University of Minnesota Press, 2014.

Gigliotti, Simone. *The Train Journey: Transit, Captivity, and Witnessing in the Holocaust*. New York: Berghahn Books, 2009.

Gildea, Robert. *Fighters in the Shadows: A New History of the French Resistance*. London: Faber & Faber, 2015.

Gildea, Robert. *Marianne in Chains: Daily Life in the Heart of France during the German Occupation*. New York: Picador, 2002.

Goffman, Erving. *The Presentation of Self in Everyday Life*. New York: Doubleday, 1959.

Goffman, Erving. *Relations in Public*. London: Allen Lane, 1971.

Golsan, Richard J. *The Vichy Past in France Today: Corruptions of Memory*. London: Lexington Books, 2016.

Goode, Erich. "Labeling Theory." In *Encyclopedia of Criminology and Criminal Justice*, edited by Gerben Bruinsma and David Weisburd, 2807–14. New York: Springer, 2014.

Gottwaldt, Alfred. "Les Cheminots allemands pendant l'occupation en France de 1940 à 1944." In *Une Entreprise publique dans la guerre: La SNCF, 1939–1945*, edited by Marie Noëlle Polino, 175–94. Paris: Presses Universitaires de France, 2001.

Greiff, Tobias. *Violent Places: Everyday Politics and Public Lives in Post-Dayton Bosnia and Herzegovina*. Berlin: Tectum, 2018.

Greimas, Algirdas Julien, and Joseph Cortés. *Semiotics and Language: An Analytical Dictionary*. Bloomington: Indiana University Press, 1982.

Griswold, Charles. *Forgiveness: A Philosophical Exploration*. New York: Cambridge University Press, 2008.

"Guillaume Pepy reconnait le role de al SNCF dans la Shoah." *Le Monde*, January 25, 2011.

Gurrey, Béatrice. "Le président du devoir de mémoire." *Le Monde*, March 12, 2007.

Gutman, Yisrael, Michael Berenbaum, and United States Holocaust Memorial Museum. *Anatomy of the Auschwitz Death Camp*. Bloomington: Indiana University Press, 1998.

Haas, Benjamin. "Opinion: European Companies Get Rich in China's 'Open Air Prison.'" *New York Times*, August 21, 2019.

Halbwachs, Maurice. *On Collective Memory*. Chicago: University of Chicago Press, 1992.

Harvard Law Review Association. "Developments in the Law-Corporate Liability for Violations of International Human Rights Law." *Harvard Law Review* 114, no. 7 (2001): 1943–2073.

Hawkins, David. *Power vs. Force*. Carlsbad, CA: Hay House, 2014.

Hayes, Peter. *Industry and Ideology: I. G. Farben in the Nazi Era*. New York: Cambridge University Press, 2000.

Hayner, Priscilla B. *Unspeakable Truths: Transitional Justice and the Challenge of Truth Commissions*. New York: Routledge, 2010.

Hayner, Priscilla B., and Lydiah Bosire. *Should Truth Commissions Address Economic Crimes? Considering the Case of Kenya*. New York: International Center for Transitional Justice, 2003.

Haysom, Sam. "Genius Site Tracks the Twitter Apologies Issues by UK Transport Companies." Mashable, December 15, 2016. https://mashable.com/2016/12/15/uk-transport-twitter-apologies-site/.

Hermans, Hubert J. M. "The Coherence of Incoherent Narratives." *Narrative Inquiry* 10, no. 1 (1999): 223–27.

Hilberg, Raul. *The Destruction of the European Jews*. Chicago: Quadrangle Books, 1961.

Hilberg, Raul. *The Destruction of the European Jews*. Vol. 1. Rev. ed. New York: Holmes & Meier, 1985.

Hilberg, Raul. *The Destruction of the European Jews*. 3rd ed. 3 vols. New Haven, CT: Yale University Press, 2003.

Hilberg, Raul. "German Railroads/Jewish Souls." *Society* 14, no. 1 (1976): 60–74.

History, Art & Archives. "Brown, Corrine." United States House of Representatives. https://history.house.gov/People/Detail/7695.

Hoffman, Jan. "Johnson & Johnson Ordered to Pay $572 Million in Landmark Opioid Trial." *New York Times*, August 26, 2019.

Holmgren, Margaret. "Forgiveness and the Intrinsic Value of Persons." *American Philosophical Quarterly* 30, no. 4 (1993): 340–52.

Huisman, Wim, and Elies van Sliedregt. "Rogue Traders: Dutch Businessmen, International Crimes and Corporate Complicity." *Journal of International Criminal Justice* 8, no. 3, (2010): 803–28.

Immelé, Coralie. "La Résistance des cheminots entre 1940 et 1944: Une histoire à la croisée des engagements individuels et collectifs." *Gazette des archives* 198, no. 2 (2005): 139–49.

Isidore, Chris. "Krispy Kreme Owners Admit to Family History of Nazi Ties." *CNN*, March 25, 2019.

Jabri, Vivienne. *Discourses on Violence: Conflict Analysis Reconsidered*. New York: Manchester University Press, 1996.

Jackson, Julian. *France: The Dark Years, 1940–1944*. New York: Oxford University Press, 2001.

Janssen, Claudia I. "Addressing Corporate Ties to Slavery: Corporate Apologia in a Discourse of Reconciliation." *Communication Studies* 63, no. 1 (2012): 18–35.

Jaskot, Paul. "A Plan, a Testimony, and a Digital Map: Architecture and the Spaces of the Holocaust." Lecture, Grinnell College, Grinnell, Iowa, April 19, 2017.

Jasper, Christopher. "French Rail Giant SNCF Braced for German Threat to Iconic TGV." *Bloomberg*, September 20, 2018. https://www.bloomberg.com/news/articles/2018-09-20/french-rail-giant-sncf-braced-for-german-threat-to-iconic-tgv.

Joly, Laurent. *L'Antisémitisme de bureau*. Paris: Grasset, 2011.

Jones, Joseph. *Politics of Transport in Twentieth-Century France*. Montreal: McGill-Queen's University Press, 1984.

"Justice to Come? Tunisia's Truth and Dignity Commission." Brookings Institution, February 20, 2020. https://www.brookings.edu/events/justice-to-come-tunisias-truth-and-dignity-commission/.

Kaminer, Wendy. *I Am Dysfunctional, You Are Dysfunctional*. Reading, MA: Soapbox Books, 2004.

Karasz, Palko. "Dutch Railway Will Pay Millions to Holocaust Survivors." *New York Times*, June 27, 2019.

Karn, Alexander. *Amending the Past: Europe's Holocaust Commissions and the Right to History*. Madison: University of Wisconsin Press, 2015.

Kelly, Michael J., and Luis Moreno-Ocampo. *Prosecuting Corporations for Genocide*. New York: Oxford University Press, 2016.

Klapp, Orrin. "Heroes, Villains and Fools, as Agents of Social Control." *American Sociological Review* 19, no. 1 (1954): 56–62.

Klarsfeld, Arno. "No, French Railways Are Not Guilty." Provided by Serge Klarsfeld, Paris, January 8, 2011.

Klarsfeld, Arno. "La SNCF et les trains de la mort, par Arno Klarsfeld." *Le Monde*, June 3, 2006.

Klarsfeld, Beate, and Serge Klarsfeld. *Mémoires*. Paris: Fayard/Flammarion, 2015.

Klarsfeld, Serge. "Analyse des excuses présentées par le président de la SNCF à propos des convois de déportés." *Daily Motion*, January 27, 2011.

Klarsfeld, Serge. *L'Etoile des juifs: Témoignages et documents.* France: l'Archipel, 1992.

Klarsfeld, Serge. *French Children of the Holocaust: A Memorial.* New York: New York University Press, 1996.

Klarsfeld, Serge. *Le Mémorial de la déportation des Juifs de France.* Paris: Klarsfeld, 1978.

Klarsfeld, Serge. *La Shoah en France, le calendrier des déportations (septembre 1942–août 1944), Tome 1, Tome 2, Tome 3, Tome 4.* Paris, France: Fayard, 2001.

Klarsfeld, Serge, and Beate Klarsfeld. *Le Mémorial de la déportation des Juifs de France.* Paris: Association des fils et filles des déportés juifs de France, 2012.

Knoller, Freddie, and John Landaw. *Living with the Enemy: My Secret Life on the Run from the Nazis.* London: John Blake, 2005.

Kolirin, Lianne, and Laura Smith-Spark. "Holocaust Survivor Wants Compensation for Rail Journeys to Death Camps." *CNN,* July 31, 2020.

Kornweibel, Theodore. *Railroads in the African American Experience: A Photographic Journey.* Baltimore: Johns Hopkins University Press, 2010.

Köster, Roman, and Julia Schnaus. "Sewing for Hitler? The Clothing Industry during the 'Third Reich.'" *Business History* 62, no. 3 (2018): 1–13.

Kuo, Lily. "China Transferred Detained Uighurs to Factories Used by Global Brands—Report." *The Guardian,* March 1, 2020.

La Baume, Maia de. "France: National Railway Apologizes for Its Role in Deporting Jews in War." *New York Times,* November 12, 2010.

La Baume, Maia de. "French Railway Formally Apologizes to Holocaust Victims." *New York Times,* January 25, 2011.

Laborde, Françoise. *Une Histoire qui fait du bruit.* Paris: Fayard. 2011.

Lanzmann, Claude, and Simone de Beauvoir. *Shoah: The Complete Text of the Acclaimed Holocaust Film.* New York: Da Capo Press, 1995.

Latour, Anny. *La Resistance juive en France (1940–1944)/Anny Latour.* Paris: Stock, 1970.

Laub, Thomas J. *After the Fall: German Policy in Occupied France, 1940–1944.* New York: Oxford University Press, 2010.

Laufer, William S. "Corporate Bodies and Guilty Minds." *Emory Law Journal* 43 (1994): 647–730.

Lepiarz, Jack. "MassDOT Selects New Commuter Rail Operator." *WBUR,* January 9, 2014. http://www.wbur.org/2014/01/09/keolis-commuter-rail-contract.

Lerchbaum, Richard, and Olivier Nahum. "La SNCF ne souciait pas de ce qu'elle transportait." *Actualité juive,* July 1, 1999.

Levi, Primo. *The Drowned and the Saved.* New York: Simon and Schuster, 2017.

Levin, Sam. "California Transit Agency Allows Ad from Holocaust Denial Group." *The Guardian,* September 12, 2018.

Lévy, Claude, and Paul Tillard. *La Grande Rafle du Vel d'Hiv: 16 juillet 1942.* Paris: R. Laffont, 1992.

Lindeperg, Sylvie. "L'opération cinématographique: Équivoques idéologiques et ambivalences narratives dans La Bataille du Rail." *Annales. Histoire, Sciences Sociales* 51, no. 4 (1996): 759–79.

Lipietz, Alain. *La SNCF et la Shoah: Le procès G. Lipietz contre État et SNCF.* Paris: Les Petits Matins, 2011.

Lipietz, Hélène, "Circulez, il n'y a rien à juger . . . Le Conseil d'État a rendu son avis: il n'y a plus rien à indemniser." *Madame Hélène Lipietz Ancienne Sénatrice*, February 16, 2009. http://helene.lipietz.net/spip.php?article183.

Lombard-Latune, Marie Amélie. "La SNCF rattrapée par son passé." *Le Figaro*, November 25, 2010.

Lustig, Doreen. "The Nature of the Nazi State and the Question of International Criminal Responsibility of Corporate Officials at Nuremberg: Revisiting Franz Neumann's Concept of Behemoth at the Industrialist Trials." *New York University Journal of International Law & Politics* 43 (2011): 965–1044.

Macridis, Roy C. "France, from Vichy to the Fourth Republic." In *From Dictatorship to Democracy: Coping with the Legacies of Authoritarianism and Totalitarianism*, edited by John H. Herz, 161–17. Westport, CT: Greenwood Press, 1982.

Man, Anthony. "US Rep. Ron Klein Goes after Company with Holocaust Ties." *Sun Sentinel*, September 28, 2010.

Mani, Rama. "Editorial: Dilemmas of Expanding Transitional Justice, or Forging the Nexus between Transitional Justice and Development." *International Journal of Transitional Justice* 2 (2008): 253–65.

Mani, Rama. "Rebuilding an Inclusive Political Community after War." *Security Dialogue* 36, no. 4 (2005): 511–26.

Margairaz, Michel. "Companies under Public Control in France 1900–50." In *Governance and Labour Markets in Britain and France*, edited by Noel Whiteside and Robert Salais, 25–51. London: Routledge, 1998.

Marks, Simon. "Belgian Exporters Found Guilty of Sending Chemicals to Syria." *Politico*, February 7, 2019. https://www.politico.eu/article/belgian-exporters-found-guilty-of-sending-chemicals-to-syria/.

Marrus, Michael R. "The Case of the French Railways and the deportation of Jews in 1944." In *Holocaust and Justice: Representation and Historiography of the Holocaust in Post-War Trials*, edited by David Bankier and Dan Michman, 245–64. New York: Berghahn Books, 2010.

Marrus, Michael R. "The End of the Line: The French Courts and Liability for the Holocaust in France: The Glemane Avis 2009." Presentation at the Minerva Institute at Tel Aviv University Conference on Corporate Accountability for Mass Atrocity, Tel Aviv, Israel, December 16, 2012.

Marrus, Michael R. "Official Apologies and the Quest for Historical Justice." *Journal of Human Rights* 6, no. 6 (2007): 75–105.

Marrus, Michael R. *Some Measure of Justice: The Holocaust-Era Restitution Campaign of the 1990s*. Madison: University of Wisconsin Press, 2009.

Marrus, Michael R., and Robert O. Paxton. *Vichy France and the Jews*. New York: Basic Books, 1981.

McCarthy, Anne. "La Bataille du Rail: Paris under German Occupation Revisited at Cannes Film Festival." *France Today*, May 30, 2017. https://www.francetoday.com/culture/cinema-film/cannes-film-festival-la-bataille-du-rail/.

McEvoy, Kieran. "Beyond Legalism: Towards a Thicker Understanding of Transitional Justice." *Journal of Law and Society* 34, no. 4 (2007): 411–40.

McEvoy, Kieran, and Kirsten McConnachie. "Victimology in Transitional Justice: Victimhood, Innocence and Hierarchy." *European Journal of Criminology* 9, no. 5 (2012): 527–38.

Mémorial de la Shoah. "Compensation and Reinstitution for Holocaust Victims in France." Mémorial de la Shoah. http://holocaust-compensation-france.memorial delashoah.org/en/holocaust-orphans.html.

Mémorial de la Shoah. "Lancement des travaux pour la création d'un nouveau lieu de mémoire au sein de l'ancienne gare de Pithiviers (Loiret)." Mémorial de la Shoah. www.memorialdelashoah.org/le-memorial-de-la-shoah-et-la-sncf-lancent-les-tra vaux-pour-la-creation-dun-nouveau-lieu-de-memoire-au-sein-de-lancienne-gare -de-voyageurs-de-pithiviers-loiret.

Mergent International Manual. Vol. 1. New York: Mergent Business Press, 2006.

Michalowski, Sabine. *Corporate Accountability in the Context of Transitional Justice.* New York: Routledge, 2013.

Mierzejewski, Alfred C. *The Most Valuable Asset of the Reich: A History of the German National Railway, 1933–1945.* Vol. 2. Chapel Hill: University of North Carolina Press, 2000.

Miller, Zinaida. "Effects of Invisibility: In Search of the 'Economic' in Transition Justice." *International Journal of Transitional Justice* 2, no. 3 (2008): 266–91.

Minow, Martha. *Between Vengeance and Forgiveness: Facing History after Genocide and Mass Violence.* Boston: Beacon Press, 1999.

Moore, Sally Falk. "A Life of Learning Sally Falk Moore." ACLS Occasional Paper No. 75. Charles Homer Haskins Prize Lecture for 2018, Philadelphia, PA, April 27, 2018.

Muchlinski, Peter. *Multinational Enterprises and the Law.* Oxford: Oxford University Press, 2007.

Muvingi, Ismael. "Sitting on Powder Kegs: Socioeconomic Rights in Transitional Societies." *International Journal of Transitional Justice* 3, no. 2 (2009): 163–82.

Nagy, Rosemary L. "The Scope and Bounds of Transitional Justice and the Canadian Truth and Reconciliation Commission." *International Journal of Transitional Justice* 7, no. 1 (2012): 52–73.

Nelson, Hilde Lindemann. *Damaged Identities, Narrative Repair.* Ithaca, NY: Cornell University Press, 2001.

Neufeld, Michael J., and Michael Berenbaum. *The Bombing of Auschwitz: Should the Allies Have Attempted It?* New York: St. Martin's, 2000.

Nicosia, Francis R., and Jonathan Huener, eds. *Business and Industry in Nazi Germany.* New York: Berghahn Books, 2015.

Niezen, Ronald. "Templates and Exclusions: Victim Centrism in Canada's Truth and Reconciliation Commission on Indian Residential Schools." *Journal of the Royal Anthropological Institute* 22, no. 4 (2016): 920–38.

Niezen, Ronald. *Truth and Indignation: Canada's Truth and Reconciliation Commission on Indian Residential Schools.* 2nd ed. Toronto: University of Toronto Press, 2017.

Nora, Pierre. "Between Memory and History: Les Lieux de Mémoire." *Representations,* no. 26 (Spring 1989): 7–24.

North, Joanna. "The 'Ideal' of Forgiveness: A Philosopher's Exploration." In *Exploring Forgiveness,* edited by Robert D. Enright and Joanna North, 15–34. Madison: University of Wisconsin Press, 1998.

Novick, Peter. *The Holocaust in American Life.* Boston: Houghton Mifflin, 1999.

Office of the United Nations High Commissioner for Human Rights (OHCHR). "OHCHR Accountability and Remedy Project: Improving Accountability and Access to Remedy in Cases of Business Involvement in High Rights Abuses." OHCHR. https://www.ohchr.org/EN/Issues/Business/Pages/OHCHRaccountabilityandrem edyproject.aspx.

Office of the United Nations High Commissioner for Human Rights (OHCHR). *Rule-of-Law Tools for Post-Conflict States: Truth Commissions.* New York and Geneva: United Nations, 2006. https://www.ohchr.org/Documents/Publications/Ruleoflaw TruthCommissionsen.pdf.

Olsen, Tricia D., Andrew G. Reiter, and Eric Wiebelhaus-Brahm. "Taking Stock: Transitional Justice and Market Effects in Latin America." *Journal of Human Rights* 10, no. 4 (2011): 521–43.

Olson, Lynne. *Last Hope Island: Britain, Occupied Europe, and the Brotherhood That Helped Turn the Tide of War.* New York: Random House, 2017.

Ophuls, Marcel, director. *The Sorrow and the Pity.* [1969.] Harrington Park, NJ: Milestone Film & Video, 2011. DVD.

Osiel, Mark. *Mass Atrocity, Collective Memory, and the Law.* New Brunswick, NJ: Transaction, 1999.

Pacquet-Brenner, Gilles, director. *Elle s'appelait Sarah.* Neuilly-sur-Seine: UGC Distribution, 2010.

Paxton, Robert. *Parades and Politics at Vichy: The French Officer Corps under Marshal Pétain.* Princeton, NJ: Princeton University Press, 1966.

Paxton, Robert. *Vichy France: Old Guard and New Order.* New York: Columbia University Press, 2001.

Paxton, Robert, Stanley Hoffman, and Claude Bertrand. *La France de Vichy.* Paris: Points Histoire, 1999.

Payne, Leigh A. *Unsettling Accounts: Neither Truth nor Reconciliation in Confessions of State Violence.* Durham, NC: Duke University Press, 2008.

Payne, Leigh A., Gabriel Pereira, and Laura Bernal-Bermudez. *Transitional Justice and Corporate Accountability from Below: Deploying Archimedes' Lever.* Cambridge: Cambridge University Press, 2020.

Pepy, Guillaume. "Statement By: Guillaume Pepy, Chairman of SNCF, Regarding SNCF's Role in World War II (WWII)." *PRNewswire*, November 4, 2010. https:// www.prnewswire.com/news-releases/statement-by-guillaume-pepy-chairman-of-sncf -regarding-sncfs-role-in-world-war-ii-wwii-106716278.html.

Phillips, Don. "An Old-Fashioned Rail Battle Erupts in the Nation's Capital: Boardman Admits He Was Asleep at the Switch." *Trains Magazine*, September 2010.

Polino, Marie-Noëlle, ed. *Une Entreprise publique dans la guerre, la SNCF 1939–1945.* Paris: Presses Universitaires de France, 2001.

Polish Railways. "Occupation 1939–1945." http://www.polish-railways.com/default_ 235.html.

Poznanski, Renée. *Jews in France during World War II.* Translated by Nathan Bracher. Hanover, NH: Brandeis University Press and the University Press of New England, 2001.

Prasquier, Richard. "Discours de Richard Prasquier au diner du CRIF." Conseil Représentatif des Institutions Juives de France, February 9, 2011. http://www.crif.org/fr/

lecrifenaction/Discours-de-Richard-Prasquier-au-diner-du-CRIF-du-mercredi-9
-fevrier-201123633.

Propp, Vladimir. *Morphology of the Folktale.* 2nd ed. Austin: University of Texas Press, 2010.

Randolph, Shamaria. "Breast Cancer Awareness: The Controversy behind the Cause." Presented at the University of Baltimore, Ethnic and Cultural Factors of Conflict course, Baltimore, MD, November 14, 2018.

Rascover, Barry. "Legislators Refight the Holocaust and Endanger Purple Line." *Maryland Reporter,* March 16, 2014.

Rasmussen, Frederick N. "Leo Bretholz Dies at 93; Holocaust Survivor Fought for Reparations." *Los Angeles Times,* March 12, 2014.

Remy, Julie. "Frenchman Suing France over Holocaust Deportation." Reuters, December 30, 1998.

Ribeill, Georges. "Dossier SNCF et Déportations." *Historail* 4 (January 2008): 34–87.

Richardot, Jean-Pierre. *SNCF: Héros et salauds pendant l'occupation.* Paris: Broché, 2012.

Rivaud, François-Xavier. "Orléans : à la tête du Cercil, Annaïg Lefeuvre prépare une année 2021 riche en événements." *leparisien.fr,* June 9, 2020. https://www.leparisien
.fr/societe/orleans-a-la-tete-du-cercil-annaig-lefeuvre-prepare-une-annee-2021-riche
-en-evenements-09-06-2020-8332224.php.

Rolandsen, Øystein H. "Small and Far Between: Peacekeeping Economies in South Sudan." *Journal of Intervention and State Building* 9, no. 3 (2015): 1–19.

Rosenbloom, Al, and RuthAnn Althaus. "Degussa AG and Its Holocaust Legacy." *Journal of Business Ethics* 92, no. 2 (2010): 183–94.

Ross, Marc Howard. *Cultural Contestation in Ethnic Conflict.* Cambridge: Cambridge University Press, 2007.

Rotberg, Robert I., and Dennis F. Thompson. *Truth v. Justice: The Morality of Truth Commissions.* Princeton, NJ: Princeton University Press, 2000.

Rousso, Henry. "French Memory Laws and the Crisis of the Republican model." Presented at the Memory Laws: Criminalizing Historical Narrative Conference, Columbia University, New York, October 28, 2017.

Rousso, Henry. *The Latest Catastrophe: History, the Present, the Contemporary.* Chicago: University of Chicago Press, 2016.

Rousso, Henry. "La Question du jour: Condamner la SNCF." *Le Monde,* June 3, 2006.

Rousso, Henry, and Arthur Goldhammer. *The Vichy Syndrome: History and Memory in France since 1944.* Cambridge, MA: Harvard University Press, 1994.

Salmond, Sir John William, and Patrick John Fitzgerald. *Salmond on Jurisprudence.* London: Sweet & Maxwell, 1966.

Sanchéz, Nelson Camillo. "Corporate Accountability, Reparations, and Distributive Justice." In *Corporate Accountability in the Context of Transitional Justice,* edited by Sabine Michalowski, 114–30. New York: Routledge, 2013.

Sang-Hun, Choe, and Rick Gladstone. "How a World War II–Era Reparations Case Is Roiling Asia." *New York Times,* October 30, 2018.

Sarkin-Hughes, Jeremy. *Germany's Genocide of the Herero: Kaiser Wilhelm II, His General, His Settlers, His Soldiers.* New York: Boydell & Brewer, 2011.

Scarry, Elaine. *The Body in Pain: The Making and Unmaking of the World.* New York: Oxford University Press, 1987.

Schwarzenegger, Arnold. Veto of Assembly Bill 619. Sacramento, CA, September 30, 2010.

Sharp, Dustin. "Addressing Economic Violence in Times of Transition: Towards a Positive-Peace Paradigm for Transitional Justice." *Fordham International Law Journal* 35, no. 3 (2012): 780–814.

Shaver, Katherine. "Holocaust Group Faults VRE Contract." *Washington Post*, July 7, 2010.

Shaver, Katherine. "Maryland Lawmaker Says He Won't Jeopardize Purple Line Funding with Holocaust Bill." *Washington Post*, March 11, 2014.

Shoah Memorial. *Annual Report: Mémorial de la Shoah.* Booklet. Paris: Shoah Memorial, 2013.

Sierra Leone Truth and Reconciliation Commission. *Witness to Truth: Final Report of the Sierra Leone Truth and Reconciliation Commission.* 2004.

Silverstein, Ken. "Ford and the Fuhrer." *Nation* 270, no. 3 (2000): 11–16.

Simons, Marlise. "Chirac Affirms France's Guilt in Fate of Jews." *New York Times*, July 17, 1995.

Sluzki, Carlos E., Donald C. Ransom, and Gregory Bateson. *Double Bind: The Foundation of Communicational Approach to the Family.* New York: Psychological Corp., 1976.

SNCF. *History and Memory: SNCF & World War II.* Booklet. Paris: SNCF, 2012.

SNCF. *Profile and Key Figures.* Pamphlet. Paris: SNCF, 2013.

SNCF. *La SNCF et la Seconde Guerre Mondiale.* SNCF Press Kit. Distributed at the Bobigny Commémoration, January 25, 2011.

SNCF Heritage. www.SNCFhighspeedrail.com/heritage/world-war-ii. Website removed by company.

Sohr, Nicolas. "SNCF Execs Pressed for Answers." *Daily Record*, March 3, 2011.

Tabor, Nick. "Compromises Fail on Several High-Profile Md. Bills." *The Republic*, April 9, 2014.

Taylor, Kate. "The Secretive German Family behind the Company That Owns Panera Bread, Krispy Kreme, and Pret a Manger Is Donating More than $11 Million after the Discovery of Its Nazi Past." *Business Insider*, March 25, 2019. https://www.businessinsider.com/jab-holding-reimann-family-nazi-past-donates-millions-2019-3.

Teitel, Ruti G. "Transitional Justice Genealogy." *Harvard Human Rights Journal* 16 (Spring 2003): 69–94.

Tiefer, Charles, Jonathan W. Cuneo, and Annie Reiner. "Could This Train Make It Through: The Law and Strategy of the Gold Train Case." *Yale Human Rights and Development Law Journal* 15 (2012): 129–54.

United States Holocaust Memorial Museum (USHMM). "The Vélodrome d'Hiver (Vel d'Hiv) Roundup." https://encyclopedia.ushmm.org/content/en/article/the-velodrome-dhiver-vel-dhiv-roundup.

United States Holocaust Memorial Museum (USHMM). "Who Is a Survivor?" https://www.ushmm.org/remember/holocaust-survivors.

US Department of State. "Agreement between the Government of the United States of America and the Government of the French Republic on Compensation for Certain

Victims of Holocaust-Related Deportation from France Who Are not Covered by French Programs." December 8, 2014. *Treaties and Other International Acts Series*, no. 15-1101. https://www.state.gov/wp-content/uploads/2019/04/us_france_agreement.pdf.

US Department of State. "Holocaust Issues." http://www.state.gov/p/eur/rt/hlcst/.

Vagts, Detlev, and Peter Murray. "Litigating the Nazi Labor Claims: The Path Not Taken." *Harvard International Law Journal* 43, no. 2 (Summer 2002): 503–30.

Van der Merwe, Hugo, and Audrey R. Chapman. *Assessing the Impact of Transitional Justice: Challenges for Empirical Research.* Washington, DC: United States Institute of Peace, 2008.

Veil, Simone. *Une Vie.* Paris: Éditions Stock, 2007.

Verdeja, Ernesto. "Official Apologies in the Aftermath of Political Violence." *Metaphilosophy* 41, no. 4 (2010): 563–81.

Verheyde, Philippe. *Les Mauvais Comptes de Vichy: L'Aryanisation des entreprises juives.* Paris: Perrin, 1999.

"Voix cheminotes: Une histoire orale des années 1930 à 1950 [Voices of French Railway Workers: An Oral History, 1930–1950]." Produced by Rails et histoire. Exposition, Archives nationales, site de Pierrefitte, April 8–July 4, 2015.

Volkan, Vamik. "Large-Group Identity, International Relations and Psychoanalysis." *International Forum of Psychoanalysis* 18, no. 4 (2009): 206–13.

Vulpes, Jim. *La Guerre du rail.* Paris: Éditions Rouff, 1948.

Waldorf, Lars. "Victors' Memory: Criminalizing Remembrance in Rwanda and Sri Lanka." Presented at the Memory Laws: Criminalizing Historical Narrative Conference, Columbia University, New York, October 28, 2017.

Walker, Margaret Urban. *Moral Repair: Reconstructing Moral Relations after Wrongdoing.* New York: Cambridge University Press, 2006.

Walters, Guy. "Shameful Truth about Hugo Boss's Links to the Nazis Revealed: As Russell Brand Is Thrown out of a Party for Accusing Fashion Designer of Helping Hitler." *Daily Mail*, September 5, 2013.

Weiss, Aharon. "Categories of Camps." In *The Nazi Concentration Camps: Structure and Aims; The Image of the Prisoner, The Jews in the Camps Proceedings of the Fourth Yad Vashem International Historical Conference—January 1980*, edited by Israel Gutman and Avital Saf, 115–32. Jerusalem: Yad Vashem, 1984.

Wettstein, Florian. "CSR and the Debate on Business and Human Rights: Bridging the Great Divide." *Business Ethics Quarterly* 22, no. 4 (2012): 739–770.

Wetzel, Johannes. "'The Past Doesn't Pass'—A German Look at France's Nazi Collaboration." *World Crunch*, October 15, 2012. http://www.worldcrunch.com/culture-society/-quot-the-past-doesn-039-t-pass-quot-a-german-look-at-france-039-s-nazi-collaboration/france-nazis-occupation-holocaust-vichy/c3s9843/#.UobobMfTaOg.

Wieviorka, Annette. *The Era of the Witness.* Ithaca, NY: Cornell University Press, 1998.

Wieviorka, Annette. "La SNCF, la Shoah et le juge." *L'Histoire* 316 (2007): 89–99.

Wilson, Richard. *Writing History in International Criminal Trials.* New York: Cambridge University Press, 2011.

Wolf, Joan Beth. *Harnessing the Holocaust: The Politics of Memory in France.* Palo Alto: Stanford University Press, 2004.

Wormser-Migot, Olga. *Le Système concentrationnaire Nazi (1933–1945)*. Paris: Presses Universitaires de France, 1968.

Yad Vashem. "Convoi 42 de Drancy, Camp, France à Auschwitz Birkenau, Camp d'extermination, Pologne le 06/11/1942." Yad Vashem: World Holocaust Remembrance Center. https://deportation.yadvashem.org/index.html?language=en&itemId=5092615.

Yad Vashem. "Convoi 77 de Drancy, Camp, France à Auschwitz Birkenau, Camp d'extermination, Pologne le 31/07/1944." Yad Vashem: World Holocaust Remembrance Center. http://db.yadvashem.org/deportation/transportDetails.html?language=fr&itemId=5092649.

Zalc, Claire. *Dénaturalisés: Les retraits de nationalité sous Vichy*. Paris: Éditions du Seuil, 2016.

Zinn, Howard. *You Can't Be Neutral on a Moving Train: A Personal History of Our Times*. Boston: Beacon Press, 2002.

ARCHIVES

French National Archives—BOX 72

"Ambassador of France in the occupied zone to German General Feldmarschall von Rundstedt." April 4, 1944. Box 72, AJ 419. National Archives, Paris, France.

Lemaire, Maurice. "Le Président Régional NORD de RESISTANCE-FER, to Monsieur Legrand, Director de la Région du NORD, at the request of the Historic Committee of the 2nd World War." April 4, 1966. Box 72, AJ 498. National Archives, Paris, France.

"Les Difficultés Recontrées par la S.N.C.F postérieurement à la Armistice." Circa 1942. Box 72, AJ 419. National Archives, Paris, France.

Merlin, Raoul. "Chef de Gare Principal Honoraire COMPIEGNE to Monsieur L'Ingénieur en Chef. Compiègne." March 28, 1966. Box 72, AJ 498. National Archives, Paris, France.

"Minister de la Production Industrielle et des Communications Cabinet du Minister (P. Cosmi) to Monsieur le Conseiller Hoffmann Ambassade d'Allemagne." December 1, 1943. Box 72, AJ 419. National Archives, Paris, France.

"Monsieur de Directeur Général with M. le Président Münzer à la HVD, le 29–12–42." January 3, 1943. Box 72, AJ 474. National Archives, Paris, France.

"Ordre du Jour n 38." December 4, 1940. Box 72, AJ 477. National Archives, Paris, France.

"Rapport concernant la liberation du wagon de déportés en gare d'Annonay (Ardèche)." Resistance de la SNCF. 1945. Box 72, AJ 498. National Archives, Paris, France.

Schaechter, Kurt Werner. Collection: 1933–2006. Hoover Institution Archives, Stanford, CA.

Wendt. "Délègue du Ministre Des Communications du Reich to Monsieur Ministre et Secretaire d'Etat à la Production Industrielle & aux Communications." March 15, 1943. Box 72, AJ 419. National Archives, Paris, France.

French National Archives—BOX 498

Paris, M., Lead Engineer of the SNCF. "La Resistance Ferroviaire Juin 1940–Juin 1944." Circa 1945. Box 498. National Archives, Paris, France.

French National Archives—Box not listed

"Facturation des transports de l'Armée allemande- PARIS le—Addressed to Le Director Général." SNCF Service Commercial, from 3 SNCF officials, Boyaux, Fournier, Besnerais. November 8, 1940. National Archives, Paris, France.

SNCF Archives

Dannecker, Theodor. "Directive to the Commander of the Security and Secret Police in the Militarbahahlahaber's sector in France." June 26, 1942. Document RF 1221. SNCF Archives, Le Mans, France.

"Decompte de Sums Due a la SNCF au titre de transports et des presentations y afferentes de l'armee." October 1942. SNCF Archives, Le Mans, France.

"Monsieur Le Besnerais, Le Director Général [Report]." Circa 1943. Box 26, LM 36 #5. SNCF Archives, Le Mans, France.

"Monsieur Le Besnerais with Monsieur Berthlot [Conversation with the Germans about materials delivered]." October 22, 1941. Box 26, LM 36 #5. SNCF Archives, Le Mans, France.

"Note pour le ministre." April 16, 1942, DGT AN, F14 13643. SNCF Archives, Le Mans, France.

"Note: sur la demande de 150 locomotives faite par la H.V.D. à la SNCF le 11 Juillet 1942." SNCF Archives, Le Mans, France.

"Prestations Fournies Par la SNCF Seulement au titre des transports militaires allemands en zone occupée." April 1, 1943. SNCF Archives, Le Mans, France.

Index

CPSIA information can be obtained
at www.ICGtesting.com
Printed in the USA
LVHW080921251121
704424LV00002B/181